D1218361

In a Moment of **Enthusiasm**

HN
786
Z9
E43

In a Moment of **Enthusiasm**

Political Power
and the Second Stratum
in Egypt

Leonard Binder

University of Chicago Press
Chicago and London

LEONARD BINDER, a past president of the Middle East
Studies Association, is professor of political science at
the University of Chicago and the author of numerous
books on Middle Eastern affairs, including *Religion and
Politics in Pakistan*; *Iran: Political Development in a
Changing Society*; and *The Ideological Revolution in the
Middle East*. He is coauthor of *Crises and Sequences in
Political Development* and has edited and contributed to
Politics in Lebanon and *The Study of the Middle East*.

The University of Chicago Press, Chicago 60637
The University of Chicago Press, Ltd., London

© 1978 by The University of Chicago
All rights reserved. Published 1978
Printed in the United States of America
82 81 80 79 78   5 4 3 2 1

Library of Congress Cataloging in Publication Data

Binder, Leonard.
    In a moment of enthusiasm.

    Bibliography: p.
    Includes index.
    1. Elite (Social sciences)—Egypt. 2. Egypt—Rural
conditions. 3. Middle classes—Egypt. 4. Egypt—
Politics and government—1970–   I. Title.
HN786.Z9E43   301.44′92′0962   77–15480
ISBN: 0–226–05144–7

For Guyora

One

Contents

Illustrations

Figures

ix

Maps

Tables

Note on transliteration.—A consistent, but not standard, system of transliteration has been followed. No diacriticals have been used. For the 'ayin a single opening quote and for the hamza a single closing quote have been used. Names are transliterated according to the way they are found in the western press if widely known. Authors' names and titles are retained as printed. Some place names and words which are found in English dictionaries have not been transliterated. The only variance from the system used in the text occurs in the maps, in the assimilation of the definite article in the names of some provinces; it is hoped that, since this is not a work for orientalists, this minor inconsistency will not disturb the reader.

Preface

I have no doubt that, in this study, my reach has exceeded my grasp; and though this thought may please commencement speakers, it cannot but make seekers after truth somewhat uneasy. It is, however, not surprising that this should be the case, if only that so much has happened to Egypt and to myself since I first resolved to break the epistemological barrier between area studies and behavioral science. A good deal has happened in area studies and behavioral science as well. When I first arrived in Egypt in 1961, I had a simple plan. I was going to observe more or less as I had in Iran in 1958 and 1959. I would then synthesize and interpret. Then I would go further and try to sustain that interpretation with statistical measures—even while necessarily rendering that interpretation partitive and probabilistic—rather than employ illustrative, but episodic, salient cases. If possible, I intended to integrate the ideological, the structural, and processual even more systematically, though that might not have been apparent from my earlier articles in the Princeton Political Development Series and in *The Ideological Revolution in the Middle East*. While developing my original interpretive ideas under the somewhat contrary influences of the Comparative Politics Committee and the New Nations Committee, I was able to begin the exploration of the analytical potential of the register of National Union committee members. In 1965 and 1966 I gradually became con-

vinced that the National Union data had some real possibility of providing empirical measures of political structure in Egypt's agricultural
provinces. Furthermore, even the most preliminary quantifications suggested that there might be a significant systematic geographical dimension of the social structural configuration that was partially uncovered.
The scope of the task of preparing the data, compiling, analyzing, and
testing was gradually revealed to be of sobering magnitude, especially
for one who was more adept at using Arabic dictionaries than statistical packages, but even then it was substantially underestimated. But
the very long time taken in preparing the data and the maps was neither
simply a matter of "numbers crunching" nor of deferring the writing
of what was already intuited until suitable supporting statistics were
produced. Each partial analysis raised questions of interpretation and,
in turn, required new statistical analyses. In the end, I learned that it is
not so much the application of standard analytical techniques that is so
important as it is to tease meaningful political indicators out of an
ordered and extensive data base.

While all this was going on with much assistance from others, the far
more lonely task of critically reevaluating development theory, elite
theory, and the tension between the concept "political culture" and the
notion of area studies commanded my attention. I have gone into these
matters only to the extent deemed necessary to carry out the work of
analyzing the Egyptian case, but even then it will be apparent that I
have become mildly heretical. My revisionist views are expressed in a
greater emphasis on social structure and a lesser emphasis on cultural
influences, in a greater emphasis on relationship to the political process
and a lesser emphasis on the descriptive characteristics of elites, and
in the employment of multiple interpretive alternatives rather than the
standard concepts of tradition and modernity. But if I thought the juxtaposition of ideologically laden alternatives to be a form of critique via
relativization in my essay on the crises of political development, I have
here attempted to overcome the nihilistic risks of relativism by means
of the careful use of empirical data of a unique and culturally relevant
sort. I must, therefore, acknowledge that I intend this work as a contri-
bution to the study of modernization, of the politics of the developing
areas, and of elites. That this intention is expressed in a work that never
strays very far from an Egyptian immediacy is not even paradoxical.
That is precisely the point. A comparable study of another country
would probably have to be based on the measurement of entirely different phenomena related to very different social processes if it were to
be concerned with both the central features of that society and with its
mode of change. The point is not that abstract theory is irrelevant but

that the purpose of theory is to elucidate the particular and in that sense
theory can only receive its fullest expression in the form of application.
Some might go so far as to say that theory is otherwise unintelligible,
but I would not take so extreme a position.

I do think it is possible to learn from the Egyptian experience even
if one is not an Egyptian and even if one wishes to apply that knowledge in another historical context. Of course, one does not really learn
from the Egyptian experience unless that experience can itself be
summed up, correctly interpreted, and then conveyed in a meaningful
manner. All the empirical data one might wish to have, and more, cannot guarantee that one has chosen to study the right thing. But if at
least a few Egyptians recognize the image of their own society in this
study, then the incompleteness of the data available and the logical
limitations of statistical explanation may impose quite tolerable burdens
on the reader's credulity.

I have been at work on Egyptian politics off and on, since the fall of
1960. I did not start to write this book until the summer of 1970, although I did write some shorter pieces and, in the interim, I directed
the analysis of the data. The data analysis continued right up to the
completion of the manuscript in February 1976. Throughout this lengthy
period I received an enormous amount of assistance from a great number of colleagues, students, research assistants, and above all from many
Egyptian officials and friends.

Too much cannot be said about the degree of cooperation I have had
both at the official and unofficial levels in Egypt. There is no doubt that
Egypt stands out as one of the few countries in which it is possible to
carry out objective political research without gratuitous administrative
interference. Egypt is also among the very few Middle Eastern countries which have a strong and sympathetic scholarly establishment of
their own. During many months of residence in Egypt, my family and I
have acquired a strong affection for the people, the culture, the life
style, and the language. Put simply, the traveler who has never lived in
Cairo has missed one of the greatest cities and most exciting experiences that this world has to offer.

In naming only a few of those many Egyptians who have kindly
helped me over the years I intend nothing invidious. I regret that I have
forgotten the names of many and some names, I admit, I never knew.
Of those I remember here some gave crucial support at the right time
while others have become old friends who have grown accustomed to
my endless inquiries. None of those whom I now thank is in any way
responsible for the interpretations I have made and a few have long
been of the opinion that I have been going in the wrong direction. I am

particularly grateful to President Anwar al-Sadat in his old capacity
as Speaker of the National Assembly, to Dr. 'Abd al-Salam al-Zayyat,
Salah al-Dessouqi, Dr. Sarwat Badawi, Tahsin Bashir, Muhammad
Hasanain Haykal, Lutfi al-Kholi, Ahmad Baha al-Din, Sayyid Mare'i,
Louis 'Awad, Muhammad 'Anis, Muhammad Sayyid Ahmad, Abu Sayf
Yusuf, Dr. 'Asim al-Dessouqi, Dr. 'Abd al-Qadir Hatim, and last but
not least my good friend 'Isam al-Khudhari.

A number of my students have helped me in various ways, usually
by their criticism, but some have taught me things I did not know,
some have served as research assistants, some have done work of their
own using my data and thus have answered some difficult questions,
and some have offered warm hospitality when I suddenly arrived in
Cairo. I would like to acknowledge, with no little pride, the help of
Professor Louis J. Cantori, Professor Ilya Harik, Professor Eric Davis,
Judith Gran and Professor Peter Gran, Sidney Chesnin, John Anderson, Hamid Ansari, and Khalil Jahshan. Sidney Chesnin wrote a remarkably good M.A. paper using an innovative analytical technique
in relating the ownership of 'izab to political influence. I have quoted
relevant aspects of his work in this book, but that hardly does justice
to the comprehensive character of his study. I hope he will agree to
submit it for separate publication. A similarly excellent M.A. paper
was written by John Anderson on the question of whether the descendants of Wafdists or non-Wafdists were more influential after the 1952
revolution. Parts of his work are also quoted in what follows and I
look forward to the inclusion of most of it in his doctoral dissertation.
Hamid Ansari is now researching his own doctoral dissertation, but
before he left for Cairo we discussed much of the new literature on the
Nasser period and he was very helpful in offering criticisms of chapter
14. Khalil Jahshan collected most of the information on which the
analysis of the May 15 "corrective operation" was based, and we discussed the purport of that information at length. Several of these students and others participated in a seminar based on an earlier draft of
this book in which relevant issues were discussed in Arabic. Many
useful criticisms came out of that seminar. Academic structures being
what they are, students are perforce drawn into the work of their professors and even into their intellectual frameworks. In acknowledging
their assistance, I do not wish to imply that these present and former
students either agree with my conclusions or are in any way responsible
for them. Anyone who has read the work of those who have published
studies of their own knows that each of these scholars is of a decidedly
independent intellectual bent.

Many research assistants worked on parts of this study over the years. Bernard McFall, Wallett Rogers, Eweidah Eweidah, Wahbah Sayegh, Mme Muhammad Sharif, and one or two others worked on the list of names of the members of the National Union and Socialist Union committees. There were tens of thousands of names and the task required devotion, patience, and concentration on the subtleties of Egyptian naming patterns in order to determine who might be related to whom. Throughout this very time-consuming operation we were constantly reviewing our procedures and selection criteria. These research assistants contributed considerably to the determination of the methods employed. The original maps were sketched by Bob Murdie. The computerized maps were handled from card punching through end product by Phil Lankford. The final rendering of the camera-ready cartography was done by Doug Cargo, and the diagrams were drawn by Chris Müller-Wille. These four scholars were all at one time students in the Department of Geography at the University of Chicago and they have become or will certainly become well known in their own academic field. I am especially grateful to Muram Shammas who, as an undergraduate at Stanford, took all our unwieldy name and occupation data and set it up efficiently and logically on the computer. His intelligence, skill, and patience are matched only by his congeniality and courtesy. Sue Hull and Jae Kim both helped considerably with the statistical analysis of this data. I am very much indebted to Hani Khaireddine, who, in addition to assisting me in my own studies, did an outstanding job of finding assistants and organizing their work while I was at the Center for Advanced Study in the Behavioral Sciences. Mr. Khaireddine became a trusted friend, a source of much good advice and encouragement.

Every scholar knows how lonely a task research and analysis can be and how important it is to have colleagues with whom one can share one's ideas and from whom one can receive honest and forthright criticism. I was fortunate through most of the years during which this study was in preparation to have been a member of the Comparative Politics Committee of the Social Science Research Council, the New Nations Committee at the University of Chicago, and the Center for the Comparative Study of Political Development in the Department of Political Science at the University of Chicago. My colleagues in those organizations will readily recognize the impact of our long association in the treatment of many questions in this book. Obviously, the influence of our frequent, prolonged and multilateral exchanges has manifested itself dialectically rather than directly, so it would be wrong indeed to assume that anything that I have written reflects the views of my colleagues. Since some of us have been reviewed and referred to as though we were a single person (with half a mind), this is not an idle disclaimer so much as a desperate assertion of identity.

I am particularly grateful to have been able to spend a year at the Center for Advanced Study in the Behavioral Sciences. Most of that year was spent on this book, even though I found myself, in the fall of 1968, further from completing it than I thought I had been in the summer of 1967. The time was spent in ordering the data, assessing the impact of the 1967 war, and in responding to the panoply of opportunities for new kinds of intellectual distraction. It is probably the experience of that year which fixed the intellectual orientation expressed in the argument of this book. I thoroughly enjoyed both the opportunities for distraction and for concentration, and I am invidiously sorry for all those who have never spent a year on the hill.

The Middle East Center at the University of Chicago has generously sponsored the weekly seminar of al-Nadwah al-'Arabiyyah for the last four years, and during that time I have had several opportunities to present various parts of my work to colleagues and students. I have benefitted greatly from these discussions, and I cannot help but feel that the fact the discussions were in Arabic made them more apposite. I think it an unparalleled opportunity that I was able to discuss my work with a group of Arab and Arabic-speaking intellectuals, although once again it must be stressed that I alone am responsible for the outcome.

My family has lived with this effort for so long that they are likely to think of me as a figurative amputee when it is finally published. I owe them a great debt of gratitude for their support and concern through all these years. My wife, Yona, has shared a great deal of the work and the special interest in Egyptian affairs. She was also able to offer expert advice in a number of areas of methodology and computer science in which she is skilled. This study, and I personally, have benefitted from their love and forebearance.

One

The Argument

Forced to admit a necessary internal
social struggle, Nasser has seen it
only as an unpleasant inevitability
that unleashes bad instincts. The
good is national cohesion, the evil,
division. This is exactly the opposite
of the Marxist conception. For the
Marxists, it is the internal struggle
that is healthy, that brings out the
noblest qualities.

M. Rodinson, "The Political
System," in P. J. Vatikiotis, ed.,
Egypt since the Revolution

Egypt is one of a restricted group of developing countries whose politics have assumed a special significance as test cases of opposing models of development. Egypt shares with India, China, Algeria, Yugoslavia, and Cuba the analytical interest of partisan and academic observers for the light its experience may shed upon the competing theories of development and for the possibility that its history may reveal a unique and unanticipated model. Even among this special group of countries, considering its size and its population, Egypt appears to be particularly favored by political and scholarly attention. The reasons for this interest are related to the keen rivalry between the United States and the Soviet Union for influence in that country, to Nasser's relatively successful policy of alternating accommodative arrangements with the great powers, to Egypt's leading position in the Arab world, and to Egypt's strategic location. The great powers are more than ordinarily interested in the success of their own preferred developmental strategy in Egypt because, as in no other such situation, they are both heavily and competitively engaged in Egypt at the same time.

As might be expected, the result of all this attention has been controversy. Observers disagree about the nature of the Egyptian regime, about where it is going, and about how it got where it is. It is not surprising that journalists and academics, reflecting and representing the

prevailing modes of thought in their own countries or among those who
share the same political ideology, should appear to praise Egypt—
according to their own values—when it befriends their own country or
political movement and to blame Egypt when it becomes hostile. The
political literature on Egypt has been influenced by these orientations
and, therefore, may be divided into four segments. The two major tendencies reflect the American and the Soviet theories of development,
emphasizing, respectively, the goal of liberal representative government
and that of the nationalization of the means of production. These two
tendencies are further subdivided into studies which are inclined toward
a favorable or an unfavorable assessment of Egypt's progress toward
one or the other goal. Egyptian observers are themselves divided between the liberal and Marxist persuasions, except, of course, for the
official and almost official spokesmen and apologists for the regime.

The Egyptian situation is ambiguous. Throughout the Nasser period
the public sector was increasingly expanded through nationalization, to
the detriment of the private capital sector. Yet, in the crucial area of
land reform, politically significant limits were set on the redistribution
of private holdings. The multiparty system was abolished but a sem-
blance of parliament has been maintained, and a sequence of mass
single parties (the Liberation Rally, the National Union, the Socialist
Union) has, until the fall of 1976, taken the place of the prerevolutionary party system. Still, the mass party lacked a clear ideological commitment and it was so loosely organized that it seemed unsuited to play
any weighty political role. Egypt claims to be at once socialist, nationalist, democratic, constitutionalist, and parliamentary. For the most
part, those who are not paid to say so, disagree, but some of these
disagreements are not entirely negative. Soviet authors have used the
explanatory device of the "noncapitalist path" to mitigate their criticism
and to dispense faint praise.[1] Western authors have pointed to the occasions when political competition and independent judicial decisions have
surfaced to justify optimism about future trends. Both sets of observers
appear to alternate between declaring the glass half full and, again,
half empty.

An important group of American writers have taken a surprisingly
benign view of the Egyptian revolution despite the primacy of the role
of the military and despite the authoritarian character of the government produced by that revolution. Of this group, which includes such
influential scholars as P. J. Vatikiotis, Nadav Safran, Manfred Halpern,
and Richard Dekmejian, none would assert that Egypt was an established liberal democracy, but neither has any excluded the possibility
that Nasserist Egypt might evolve along liberal lines.

Vatikiotis presented the Egyptian case as paradoxical. The power elite was drawn from the military, and the military, in turn, created a one-party system to mobilize both ideological and organizational support. He pointed out, however, that many officers were of rural middle class origins, that the military was generally related to the "new" middle class, and that they seemed to aspire quite genuinely toward democracy. Poverty and an authoritarian political culture constituted formidable obstacles, so that Vatikiotis cautiously accepted the need for a "tutelary dictatorship" in Egypt, and he speculated about the possibility that political liberalization might be achieved.[2] Safran, though he wrote about the prerevolutionary period, was relieved that the Free Officers had staved off the possibility that the Muslim Brethren might have seized power. From his point of view, under the circumstances prevailing in Egypt in 1952, Nasser represented a triumph for the liberal and rational ethos which had been badly battered in Egypt during the thirties and forties.[3] Manfred Halpern was also optimistic about the direction of Egyptian development. He identified the military rulers with the "new" middle class, and he believed that the military regime was only a prelude to the eventual establishment of a more liberal regime based on broader segments of this modernizing, educated, essentially urban class.[4]

Richard Dekmejian is, perhaps, the most sanguine about the liberal and democratic tendencies of the Nasser regime. Dekmejian was especially impressed by the emergence of controversy in the press, by occasional recalcitrance in parliament, and by an occasional display of apparent independence by a judge. He correctly discerned that there are many individuals in Egypt who would like to see liberal political practices strengthened and that these were more outspoken after the disastrous defeat of 1967 and especially after the student demonstrations of February 1968.[5] Dekmejian was inclined to see the strengthening of liberal tendencies as part of a larger development which included a shift away from military predominance in the cabinet and an increased preference for technically trained civilian administrators. Hence, Dekmejian would link instrumental rationality with liberal government and he appears to believe, as does Halpern, that social origins are far less significant than occupation, education, or administrative or political office in determining political ideology and political strategy.

The counterpart to Vatikiotis is the Egyptian leftist Anwar 'Abd al-Malik, who similarly stressed the military-oligarchical aspects of the regime. As Vatikiotis used this theme in order to sharpen the relief in which the limitations of liberal parliamentary institutions might be seen, so did 'Abd al-Malik stress the role of the military in explaining the nonrevolutionary class basis of the regime. Both Vatikiotis and 'Abd al-Malik agree on the importance of the class origins or links between the military officers and the rural middle class, even though Vatikiotis writes of the early postrevolutionary period and 'Abd al-Malik writes after the passage of the July Socialist Laws of 1961. On the whole, however, 'Abd al-Malik is as optimistic about the possible development of socialism in Egypt as Vatikiotis is about the development of liberal institutions.[6]

Soviet critics and the Egyptian leftists who were resident in Egypt were more circumspect in their assessment of the socialist claims of the Nasser regime. While there were many ups and downs in Egyptian-Soviet relations, the period from late 1963, after the death of President Kennedy, until early 1974 was one of continuously strained cooperation. The ideological differences between the two countries were most diminished in mid-1964, at the time of Khruschev's visit to Egypt. Nasser's Egypt was declared to be on the "noncapitalist" road of development toward socialism.[7] Later, Soviet authors and Khruschev's successors expressed greater doubts about the nature of the Nasser regime and about the direction and speed of its progress—but usually within a framework of speculation which assumed that Egypt was generally on the right path though not necessarily far advanced on that path.

The official Egyptian left, or at least that part of it which was established in the editorial offices of *al-Tali'ah* from 1965 onward, were consistently critical of the failure of the regime to produce a militant vanguard party even while reaffirming their loyalty to the transitional organizational and ideological formulae of the 1962 charter. Articles in *al-Tali'ah* were critical of the achievements of the Arab Socialist Union in the areas of labor unions, youth organizations, and the political participation of the poorest peasants. Nevertheless, the former Communists declared their adherence to the interim formula of the coalition of five groups: workers, peasants, intellectuals, army, and national capital.

Other Egyptian Marxists, especially those who remained in exile, were more critical of the regime. Hasan Riad, writing at about the same time as 'Abd al-Malik, in the mid-1960s, sees the military as little more than the instrument of the haute bourgeoisie. His analysis stresses the persistence of a rich peasantry and the increase of "agro-capitalism" in the countryside, but he is even more concerned to point out how little was done to weaken the influence and the economic base of the urban capitalist class.[8] Two leftist critics, writing under the pseudonym Mahmoud Hussein, admit the socialist orientation of the regime but fault it for its organizational rigidity and its fear of mass political participation. Mahmoud Hussein held the view that in Egypt the normal transition to socialism had been blocked by the persistence of feudal values and economic structures among the prerevolutionary rulers. The "proletarianized masses" (i.e., not the industrial proletariat) has therefore emerged as an explosive revolutionary class. It expressed itself in the "burning of Cairo" on the eve of the revolution of 1952, and again on June 9 and 10 of 1967, when Nasser announced his intention of resigning. These mass risings failed because the Communists failed to supply the necessary leadership and allowed the "petty-bourgeois forces from the army" to take the initiative. But now, concludes Mahmoud Hussein, the masses have seized the banner of revolution and, guided by "the lessons of the great Chinese Revolution and the example of the peoples of Indochina . . . as well as the precedent of the Palestinian revolution . . . ," they will struggle on autonomously.[9]

After Nasser's death, and especially after the 1973 war, when Sadat inaugurated the new policy of an economic and political opening to the right, some liberal and some Marxist observers changed their assessment of the Nasserist regime. Even before October 1973 there had been some de-Nasserization, but by mid-1974 a number of opponents of the Nasser regime, liberals, Muslim Brethren, and some ex-Communists became outspoken in their criticism of the previous administration as repressive and authoritarian.[10] In some cases revelations were made regarding the high degree of military involvement in decision making, suggesting that Nasser was not as much in control (nor as responsible for the failures) as had appeared to be the case.[11] In response to these criticisms a new group of Nasserists emerged, including both intellectuals of the left and bureaucratic and even bourgeois beneficiaries of the previous administration, who now criticized the critics and emphasized how much progress had been made toward socialism and real equality.[12]

The very term "Nasserist" had been deplored and avoided in Egypt during Nasser's lifetime, but it was freely employed after his death as a means of identifying the newer leftist Muslim elements in Lebanon which had entered the political arena under Egyptian patronage. At times Ghaddafi of Libya also claimed to be Nasserist, or to be following a nationalist and independent policy identified with Nasser's policies. Nevertheless, the application of this term to Egyptian political factions in the aftermath of the May 1971 attempted coup was a new ideological departure.

The Nasserist position is, in brief, that Nasser had made genuine achievements in the partial attainment of national, revolutionary, anti-imperialistic, anti-Zionist, and democratic goals, but that he had not completed the task. The reasons he had not completed the task were

that he was not a committed socialist, that Egyptian economic development had not proceeded far enough, that there were external pressures
from both the imperialist powers and the conservative Arab regimes,
and that there were powerful domestic opponents on the right that had
secretly sabotaged Nasser's program. For the Nasserists, the task for
the future is, naturally, to complete the work begun by Nasser, but to
do so with greater ideological and historical awareness of the nature
and tenacity of the opposition and a more thorough commitment to
revolution.

It is mildly ironic, when such celebrated authors as Tawfiq al-Hakim
and Najib Mahfuz have finally come out openly in criticism of the
repressive character of the Nasser regime, that among the major de-
fenders of Nasser's achievements should be the editors of *al-Tali'ah*—
the leftist writers who were constantly criticizing the failure of that
regime to live up to its socialist pretensions. Perhaps of even greater
interest is the reversion of Soviet observers to their earlier view that
Nasser was on the noncapitalist road to development, that the revolutionary efforts of the "courageous" members of the Free Officers organization in 1952 were laudable and that the progress made under
Nasser was considerable, given such adverse social conditions as the
lack of a strong and politically conscious working class and the alliance
of the indigenous Egyptian bourgeoisie with the imperialist powers.[13]
For the contemporary Nasserists of the left and for Soviet observers,
the failures of the Nasser regime are explained in terms of the imma-
turity of the Egyptian class system.

There is a curious kind of convergence between the most severe
liberal critics of the Nasser regime and its most generous leftist apologists. Both groups assert that Egypt's problems stem from the absence
of a modernized social structure, but the liberals deplore the absence of
a viable middle class while the leftists, deploring the power, the resil-
ience, and the versatility of the bourgeoisie, are concerned with the
absence of a strong proletariat. Both types of analysis are, however,
inclined to agree with the majority of observers of all types that, in one
way or another, the rural middle class was favored by the policies of
the Nasser period. Examples of these two interpretive tendencies may
be found in the diffusely liberal critique of S. Akhavi and the misleadingly precise theses of the newly reestablished Communist Party of
Egypt.

In an effort to establish the applicability of the term "neopatri-
monial" to Egypt and to the role of the military elite under Nasser,
Akhavi argues that there has been no "class stratification in Egyptian
society."[14] Akhavi states that there was no bourgeois *class* in Egypt,
though he is willing to admit that there were important "strata" both

in the city and in the country. Among such strata we find the rural middle class, the importance of which is by no means minimized. Akhavi writes, "True enough, many of the officers hail from peasant households with medium size landholdings."[15] And more strongly, "Although hard data would be invaluable to help demonstrate the point, it does seem that the regime has always identified with the rural middle sectors at least implicitly."[16]

The June 1975 manifesto of the Egyptian Communist Party declared that the ruling authority in Egypt is pursuing a path which is counter to the historical trend in which the progressive forces in Viet Nam, in Angola, and elsewhere have been winning victory after victory. That ruling group has been in power since 15 May 1971, when it first struck at the Nasserist left. The Nasserist left, identified with 'Ali Sabri, Sha'rawi Goma'a, and their alleged co-conspirators, is described as "basically the bureaucratic bourgeoisie, functionally organized and benefitting from and holding fast onto the nationalization operations and the leadership role within the public sector." When the Nasserist left was disposed of, a coalition of classes and groups took over, arrogating power to itself. This coalition included: "(a) The rural bourgeoisie (the rich peasants) whose cadres took control of most of the leadership posts in the Arab Socialist Union and most of the seats in the Popular Assembly. (b) The highest strata among the bureaucratic leadership, the technocracy and the political organization . . . . (c) The commercial capitalist elements, the rentiers, and large scale parasitic elements that made their profits . . . from the black market and from smuggled goods . . . . And after the October War of 1973 . . . new social forces were joined to the ruling coalition: (d) big capital in the contracting sector . . . and (e) the largest of the old [i.e. pre-1952] capitalists and landowners . . . ."[17]

The ideological perspectives and the social analyses may be very different, but the rural middle class, like lucky Pierre, always seems to turn up as a beneficiary of the system. Despite their agreement, none of these analyses offer much of an explanation of why this should be the case. The sociological significance of the rural middle class is generally played down, and its political role is never worked out in such a way that it might be incompatible with any given analysis. Furthermore, very little empirical data has been brought to bear on the question so that interpretations of the political significance or insignificance of this stratum are both unconstrained by any factual limitations and unconstraining of any explanatory context.

The question of class origins is, of course, a difficult one, whether approached from the perspective of western elite theory or Marxist class theory. In western social science the emphasis on previous social origins in a mobile society is bound to lead to some emphasis on cultural or ideological preferences of a noninstrumental sort (e.g., primordial sentiments).[18] Contrarily, the most acceptable definition of materially related, instrumentally rational, values is generally based on the present occupation, profession, or office of the individual concerned.[19] In Marxist theory, occupation, profession, or office are all set in a class context rather than in the framework of a system of functional prerequisites which are supposed to lend meaning to the notion of instrumental rationality.[20] Usually, the postulate of a material nexus linking traditional social origin and modern occupation is ignored or left unexplored.[21] The frequent assumption is that the expression of primordial sentiments masks class interests, is an expression of false consciousness, or represents minority interests.[22] Hence, especially in a homogeneous society, modernization overcomes parochial attachments and residual sentiments become transformed into modern (or bourgeois) nationalism, and, depending upon class position, some form of socialism or of political liberalism.[23]

Thus in the popular controversy between Manfred Halpern and Amos Perlmutter, traditional social origins are largely neglected, and the issue is whether the Egyptian military is the vanguard of the new middle class as Halpern would have it, or whether it represents itself alone and is therefore a merely authoritarian oligarchy.[24] Halpern's class analysis is based upon functionalist assumptions regarding modernization processes, and it follows from such assumptions that the set of new occupations based on education, urbanization, mobility, and centralization of authority should be considered as contributing to a common historical outcome, and, consequently as forming a single class. Perlmutter's assumptions remain within the framework of liberal democracy, and he gives Egypt low marks and no benefit of any doubt about the direction of future development. Halpern, of course, is hopeful of future democratic developments because of the relationship between the military and other new middle class groups; but those relationships are essentially functional or, if ideological, they grow out of a common socialization and modernization experience and not so much out of common traditional social origins.

Like Perlmutter, Clement Moore is critical of the lack of liberalism in Egypt. He, too, minimizes the importance of the bourgeoisie, but he attributes more significance to the government and party bureaucracy than to the army. In a somewhat paradoxical analysis, Moore rejects the thesis that urbanization has created a mass, anomic, atomistic society, but he also omits any suggestion that urban society is shaped by traditional rural structures and sentiments.[25] Urban society is structured by associations. For Moore, the society is "unincorporated" because the bureaucratic elite prevents urban associations from becoming autonomous and vigorous. The members of these associations acquiesce in bureaucratic control because they adhere to an authoritarian political culture. Authority and venality alone hold the system together, for even the ruling elite do not know one another and cannot be said to form a group.

Moore does not resolve the apparent contradiction between a political culture favoring the frequent formation of associations and a political culture which accepts authoritarianism with equanimity. This problem becomes even more interesting when we note that rural voluntary associations are increasing more rapidly than urban voluntary associations and that the impact of urbanization is often softened by the buffering activities of informal associations of people who come from the same village.

It is evident that critics and supporters alike, whether liberal or Marxist, are uneasy about the concentration of political power in the military and the bureaucracy. The liberal critics would brush aside all attempts to "interpret" and justify the composition of the Egyptian power elite in terms of some pragmatic theory of political transition. Indeed, for the liberal critics it often seems that all that counts is that the military has got the power and will not share it.

Liberal apologists and all leftists tend to agree that there are significant links between the members of the power elite and the middle classes, whether urban or rural. They agree that the least important sociological characteristic of the military elite is that it consists of military professionals. They view the military oligarchy, alternatively, as the vanguard of the liberal-modernizing middle class, or as the instrumentality of a skillful, manipulative, and tenacious bourgeoisie, or as a well-intentioned segment of the petite bourgeoisie which has but a transitional role to play in the intensifying class struggle.

The theories of development are, consequently, closely tied to political-sociological interpretations of the Egyptian regime. The liberals deplore the slow and inadequate development of the urban middle classes, and the leftists deplore the slow and inadequate development of the proletariat. Each explains the persistence of authoritarianism by the absence of something, as though the military and bureaucratic elite itself was created ex nihilo, as though its regime had no cultural and social substructure, and as though Egypt had no history before July 1952.

The scientific importance of rival theories of development is not necessarily vitiated by their ideological aspects. They may be taken as hypotheses to be used to inform our observation of historical cases. In this sense one of their most important methodological contributions is to call our attention to what we might otherwise miss. In the case of Egypt, however, our attention is usually diverted from further inquiry into the social, cultural, and political significance of the rural middle class because it does not fit in with prevailing interpretive schemas. As a result, I think, some errors have been made regarding the nature of the present regime, and there is probably even greater confusion regarding the range of possible developments in the foreseeable future.

The twin goals of this study are, first, to provide as thorough an empirical description of the political size and power of the rural middle class as may be allowed by available data and, second, to offer an interpretation of the Egyptian political system—under Nasser and thereafter —that takes account of these empirical constraints as well as the course of Egyptian political history as seen from various ideological perspectives.

In attempting to understand the importance of the rural middle class, this analysis will not rely on statistical data alone. The selection and interpretation of the data will be related to a number of middle range theoretical contributions and to my own earlier work on Egypt. Theoretical insight will be sought in the work of Mosca on the "second stratum," in the work of Marx on the nature of a "partial revolution," in the work of Barrington Moore on the agrarian prerequisites of modernization, and in the work of various liberal scholars on the concepts "mobilization" and "participation." It may not be expected that such theoretical eclecticism will resolve the ideological problem of which major developmental paradigm is correct. Nevertheless, when coupled with a more rigorously empirical description of the size, the historical development, the political origins, the geographical distribution, the economic role, and the social mobility of the rural middle class some critical limits may be set to the employment of ideological polemic, and areas of convergence intelligible to both perspectives may be discerned. Such areas are most likely to be found in particular, situational applications rather than when we use case histories to "prove" the validity of an ideological paradigm. The grander the theory, the more difficult and meaningless is the task of proving its truth. What is more relevant for scholarship is to render the "facts," past, present, and probable, intelligible and coherent within both major ideological paradigms. Such a task is impossible, of course, if the "facts" are simply determined by those or other paradigms. If, on the other hand, we find particular phenomena, particular historical events, and particular statistics commonly referred to by analysts of both persuasions, it may just be possible that some piece of social knowledge may be partly freed of its relativistic and polemical character by the deliberate method of collating middle range theory which deals with the phenomena in question regardless of the major paradigm from which it may be taken. This method recommends starting from something that is said to be known by both groups of analysts and developing our broader interpretation in the light of the constraints of the empirical data. The key phenomenon, the factual nature of which is determined by the relevance of these middle range theoretical contributions, is the rural notability's consistent domination of office in the National Union and its successor, the Socialist Union and the failure of this mass party to develop into an instrument for ruling, an organizational weapon, a mobilizational device, or a vanguard party.

Elite political roles and the relationship between culture and ideology have been the subject of my own earlier research on Pakistan and Iran.[26] For Egypt these two topics were treated in separate works dealing with the ideology of Nasserism, the integrative uses of the political culture of the rural notables of Egypt, and the role of the National Union and the Arab Socialist Union in restricting participation while yet maintaining and even enhancing the intermediary elite position of the rural notability.[27] In working out my views on Egyptian political development, I have been influenced by those scholars who were more concerned with the contemporary political roles of traditional elites, with the adaptive strategies of traditional elites, and with the intergenerational transformation of elite roles. These concerns were made more explicit in a theoretical exposition in which I argued that the pattern of political development within a given society may depend upon the ideological formulations most favorable to the interests of strategically situated traditional elites or the sons of such elites.[28]

The axiomatic foundation of elite theory is that the number of rulers is always smaller than the number of the ruled, and even though there may be some societies where this is untrue, and even though this axiom cannot be valid a priori, to all intents and purposes this is a sound starting point. The important question is why a majority acquiesces in minority rule and in attempts to justify the authority of a particular minority. Most elite theorists deny that elites rule by coercion alone, and so these two issues are, for all practical purposes, one. There is only one issue insofar as a minority may be deemed to be—logically, or ab initio—incapable of coercing a majority and hence must necessarily rely on legitimating arguments. The most important explanations of minority government and their related legitimating arguments are functionalist, in the sense that legitimacy is based on the function performed

by the rulers for some collectivity. There is broad agreement that an
elite which rules in the interest of the community is legitimate. Marxists
claim that the rulers of bourgeois states rule in the interest of the bourgeois class regardless of whence the rulers are recruited. Liberal theorists argue that the rulers must be representative of the ruled in order
to be expected to rule in the interest of the ruled. Neither liberals nor
Marxists will justify an elite that rules in its own interest. The Communist party elite, whose task is theoretically transitional, also enjoys only
functional legitimacy.

In this simplified statement of elite theory, there are at least two
highly problematic concepts, "representation" and "interest." These
two are given to sufficiently diverse and polemical interpretations to
keep an army of scholars and propagandists busy for a long while.
Suffice it for our present purposes that representation may refer to
similarity of social status or class (etc.) or to the expression of the
policy preferences of those represented. Interest may refer to the partitive interest of a collectivity, the interest of the entire community,
self-consciously recognized interests, or rationally attributed interests
of which the subject is unaware. These ambiguities demonstrate that
the two are not independent concepts and that their referential uncertainties will frequently produce a gap between the comfortably logical
alternatives of coercion and consensus. Insofar as consensus cannot be
explained in terms of shared interests and insofar as coercive force is
not constantly employed, stable government is anomalous and requires
additional explanation. Mosca provided an interesting and probably
relevant explanation which emphasized the expressive aspect of representation and which elaborated a specialized and secondary function
for "closing" the gap, or rather for coping with the inevitable problems
arising out of the existence of the gap. Mosca dealt with the expressive
aspects of representation in his discussion of the concept "social type"
—a concept broad enough to include social class as well as nationality.
The function of coping with the gaps between social types, between
modernity and tradition, and between interest and representation is
dealt with in Mosca's theory of the "second stratum."

Mosca may not have been altogether clear about the composition of
the "ruling class," but he seems to have been much more certain about
the composition and character of the "political class" or what we shall
call the second stratum of the ruling class. For Mosca, the second
stratum is the necessary mediating instrument without which the ruling
class or the ruling oligarchy cannot rule. The political function of the
second stratum extends from representation through expressive identification to the exercise of authority. The second stratum shares with

the holders of power membership in what Mosca calls the political class, and though the function of the second stratum is often ancillary, the social origins of the members of the second stratum are far more significant than those of the actual rulers. Do the rulers rule in the interest of the second stratum, or does the second stratum merely perform a necessary function on behalf of the rulers, for which they are modestly rewarded? As we shall see, the relationship is complicated and less determinative than dialectical. It is clear to me that Mosca was himself from this second stratum, and much of his work was devoted to determining and justifying the political role of the second stratum. Mosca was antidemocratic and antiparliamentarian, but he also strongly opposed all intervening organization or association between the government and the people. The second stratum was to be the only structure mediating between government and people. Mosca's ruling class, or the actual incumbents in authority, could be a caste, class, or profession. He saw them as Marx saw prebourgeois rulers.[29] The second stratum was related to what he called social forces. The term "social forces" was used rather than "social classes," I suspect, to emphasize regional and cultural differences and to permit the differentiation of economic segments among groups that fall within the same class in terms of their relationship to the means of production. Most particularly, it permits a subtle differentiation of groups of peasant small holders and of the newly emergent nineteenth-century intelligentsia.

Now Mosca did not elaborate a comprehensive theory of the second stratum any more than he did of the ruling class, but he has given us many leads toward a theory of the second stratum. I have assembled some of his widely dispersed statements from Meisel's study, but because Meisel did not focus his attention on this problem it seems appropriate to present both my own interpretation and the disparate quotations from Mosca.

First, as in the case of a ruling class, the existence of the second stratum is an empirical matter. Similarly the composition of the second stratum is an empirical matter—that is, whether it is related to particular social forces or whether it is a structure or class. Where such a significantly empirically distinguishable second stratum exists, we have to consider how far Mosca's description is true and what the political consequences of the composition of the second stratum may be. I think it will be found that there is at least a class of countries in which the second stratum exists, that the second stratum is particularly important in the developing countries, that the second stratum can often be identified in terms of certain traditional characteristics, that the second stratum is of particular importance in achieving national cultural integration, and finally that one of the most significant processes of change in this class of countries is the transformation of the character of the second stratum. The urbanization, bureaucratization, and intellectualization of the second stratum will have profound consequences for the political development of this class of countries, but for the moment it is important to distinguish between the second stratum in these developing countries and the group referred to as the new middle class. I believe it can be shown that there is a politically significant second stratum in Egypt and I believe it possible to make reasonable projections of what will happen to this second stratum. It is also possible to speculate comparatively concerning the three-way relations among the rulers, the second stratum, and the new middle class in Middle Eastern countries. Finally, it appears to me that the prevalence of military oligarchies renders the long range analysis of the second stratum more important even than study of the rulers themselves.

Let us go back to Meisel and Mosca for their statement of the theory of the second stratum.[30] For this we have to rely on Meisel's extensive survey, because the English version of Mosca's work is composed of parts written at different times. We must remember, however, that Meisel was hostile to what he thought was Mosca's elitist theory even though sympathetic to Mosca. At times, therefore, Meisel's rendering will seem gratuitously polemical, as in the following:

> The New Conservatism, of which one hears so much nowadays, surely derives much of its *raison d'être* from the very sense of importance which the elitist writers assign to this secondary stratum of the ruling class: the all-important subelite which rationalizes what the rulers do today and articulates what will be public opinion tomorrow. [**P. 3**]

But Mosca's second stratum is not merely the bureaucracy or feudal functionaries as revealed in these passages of political-sociological import:

> If there is a plurality of potent social forces, the political class will do well to mirror at least those that cannot be repressed. [P. 42]
> But since that excellence is varying in character, depending on the period and the country, Mosca decides, just like Aristotle, that "no single criterion for the forming of, and admission to, the ruling class can be established". The decisive factor is the paramount need of society at a specified stage of its development. Put differently: the specific "virtue" will be its ability to perform an essential social function, which, in turn will be that of the most important *social force* or forces of society. [P. 43]

The social origins of Mosca's elite are elaborated in the following passages which will be found to have particular relevance to modern Egypt:

"We find many instances in which elective offices have constantly remained the property of one and the same family." To characterize that fact, Mosca makes use of the happy term of "infeudation."
[P. 47]
"Elites do not grow overnight, they need an incubation period which lasts longer than one generation." [P. 48]

And more specifically regarding the second stratum:

The intelligentsia is, and is bound to remain (for some time? forever?) a subsidiary element of the political class. But that fact hardly detracts from the importance of the new elite of merit. For it is precisely from its ranks that the decisive second layer of the dominant class is composed. [P. 50]

Again in Mosca's words:

"In the last analysis . . . the stability of any political organism depends on the level of morality, intelligence and activity that this second stratum has attained; and this soundness is commonly the greater in proportion as a sense of the collective interests of nation or class succeeds in exerting pressure on the individual ambitions or greeds of this class." [P. 51]

Meisel adds as though he were talking of modern Egypt:

In no sense, therefore, could Mosca's second stratum be considered secondary in importance to the first . . . it is they who have to make those policies concrete and palatable to the public . . . the subelite stands in a much closer relationship to the ruled people than to its superiors in the higher ruling stratum. At first glance this contention does not seem to be borne out by the appearances—particularly in countries where the administrative class has a special social status unknown in those countries which are democracies. But even in those which are not, the public functionaries are recruited for the most part from the people and remain to some extent susceptible to pulls of their old milieu. To be sure their new function and environment will weaken the old influences. But to some degree, at least those members of the subelite who come in daily contact with the people may be said, in an informal way to represent them. [Pp. 51–52]

Despite the readiness of some commentators to equate Mosca's second stratum with the bureaucracy, the intellectuals, or the clerks, he has something else in mind as shown in the following passages.

"[Napoleon's] political class consisted exclusively of the bureaucracy
. . . and all political activity of other social classes showing indications of political maturity was savagely repressed. Such a system
could not fail to produce the most ruinous effects inasmuch as it
gradually separates the ruled from the rulers, instilling in the former
an indifference toward and even a hatred of, the latter." [P. 103]

Mosca believed that the political class, or at least its second stratum
ought to be a cultured and leisured class, but his description seems to
accord less with a landed aristocracy than a rural middle class:

There was in Rome, the "teeming plebs of small property owners."
There was "England's numerous gentry," once made up of "moder-
ately rich landowners," and now of "moderately rich businessmen."
[P. 155]

And Meisel adds, paradoxically,

The disinterestedness of all those classes may be questioned, but not
the fact that the economic climate of the middle class was favorable
to the rise of that "aristocratic" public mindedness that makes for
civic greatness. [P. 155]

More clearly still:

The new historian will do well to focus his attention on the second
stratum of the dominant minority: "We must, without denying the
great importance of what has been done at the vertex and at the base
of the pyramid, show that, except for the influence of the intermediate strata, neither of the others could have accomplished very
much . . ." The middle class character of Mosca's elite theory has
never before emerged as clearly as in this statement. His political
class is not actually the ruling class, but rather the class without
which society could not be ruled. [P. 194]

On political culture and on national integration:

Close intellectual and moral ties, we are informed, connect the first
and second strata of the ruling class, the top group being "more or
less imbued within the ideas, sentiments, passions, and therefore
policies" of the secondary level. [P. 217]
. . . the connection between masses and the second layer of the ruling
class [is] even "more certain and less varying than the other" (the
connection between the two strata of the ruling class itself). [P. 218]

After telling us all this, Meisel appears to cite with approval Antonio
Gramsci's criticism of Mosca's central idea:

Antonio Gramsci feels that Mosca's main sin is conceptual vague-
ness: "His political class . . . is a puzzle. One does not exactly
understand what Mosca means, so undulating and elastic is the
notion. Sometimes he seems to think of the middle class, sometimes
of men of property, in general, and then again of those who call
themselves 'the educated.' But at different occasions, Mosca has
apparently the 'political personnel' in mind [the parliament]. In
various instances he seems to exclude the bureaucracy, even its higher
stratum, from the ruling class which is assumed to control all appointments and all policy." [P. 315]
Some years later, Gramsci thought he had solved the "puzzle" and
noted in his diary: "Mosca's so-called 'political class' is nothing but
the intellectual section of the ruling group. Mosca's term approaches
Pareto's *elite* concept—another attempt to interpret the historical
phenomenon of the intelligentsia and its function in political and
social life." [P. 315]

Gramsci's apparent solution to the problem of identifying the members of the second stratum is obviously too simple. While his answer
has the virtue of pointing to the significant political role played by the
intelligentsia, especially in modernizing countries, the difficulty with this
solution is that by identifying the "political class" with the ruling group,
nothing seems to be said about their social origins. This apparent omission is important because it disregards what was crucially important
for Mosca. But the omission is evidently apparent only, for in other
sources Gramsci describes the relationship between the bourgeoisie and
its intelligentsia in terms of social mobility, though without specific
reference to the "ruling group."[31]

Every social class, coming into existence on the original basis of an
essential function in the world of economic production, creates
within itself, organically, one or more groups of intellectuals who
give it homogeneity and consciousness of its function not only in the
economic field but in the social and political field as well. [P. 118]
It should be noted that in reality the elaboration of intellectual
groups does not take place on an abstract democratic basis, but
according to very concrete traditional processes. Classes have been
formed which traditionally "produce" intellectuals and these are the
same as those who are commonly noted for "thrift", i.e. the rural
petty and middle bourgeoisie in the cities. . . . Thus in Italy the rural
bourgeoisie produces especially state officials and free professionals,
whereas the city bourgeoisie produces technicians for industry; and
therefore Northern Italy produces especially technicians and Southern
Italy especially officials and professional people. [Pp. 123–24]

What remains unclear in this abridged exposition is whether we are to understand that Southern Italy produces intellectuals who serve the ruling elite of Italy or whether the second stratum is in fact the intellectual segment of the rural bourgeoisie of Southern Italy. Even if these two alternatives are somehow reconciled theoretically, it seems likely that the second stratum, mediating between the most powerful stratum and the masses, would not entirely or immediately forget its origins in the rural bourgeoisie even while responding to the interests of the ruling elite or group whom they serve and to the ideal of a still emerging national community whose integrated culture will symbolize the vital link between country and city that these intellectuals have forged biographically.

Mosca was more concerned with the preservation of liberal government than he was with the forging of a national community. His notion of the political formula goes beyond the idea of nationalism, which is a particular type of solution to the question of the political community. Insofar as the political formula defines the political community it entails cultural, ideological, and legitimating elements as well as identitive designations. For Mosca social types can differentiate segments within a single ethnic group.

Mosca's concept of the social type, as we have seen, was broad enough to include not only nationality but also social class. If social class differences are paralleled by cultural differences, or as Mosca might say, differences in civilization, is it not reasonable to expect that not only habits and sentiments will differ (as in the case of bourgeois and working class patterns of life) and not only will material interests differ (as in the case of the interests of landowners and tenants) but that beliefs about the nature of authority and the duties of government will differ also? More importantly at this point in our inquiry, is it not possible that the definition of the nation or community or social type will differ?

If nationalism need not be essentially and a priori a bourgeois sentiment, does it follow that there is a nationalism which corresponds to the consciousness of each class, or that there are several types of nationalism corresponding to sections of the bourgeoisie, or that there is only one class-interested nationalism which is historically valid? Mosca evidently felt that each political formula would reflect a particular combination of identitive and materially interested elements, but his formulation does not help us to understand why it should have been the rural notability rather than the urban bourgeoisie that became the political class or the second stratum in Egypt, nor why their political infeudation could be termed a revolution. Marx discusses relevant matters in ex-

plaining the nature of a partial revolution in an early essay where he
seems to argue that there is a sequential relationship between the appearance of certain types of class-based nationalism and various stages
of the class struggle:[32]

> It is not *radical* revolution, *universal human* emancipation, which is
> a Utopian dream for Germany, but rather a partial, *merely* political
> revolution which leaves the pillars of the building standing. What is
> the basis of a partial, merely political revolution? Simply this: *a
> section of civil society* emancipates itself and attains universal domi-
> nation; a determinate class undertakes, from its *particular situation*,
> a general emancipation of society. This class emancipates society as
> a whole, but only on condition that the whole of society is in the
> same situation as this class; for example, that it possesses or can
> easily acquire money or culture.
>
> No class in civil society can play this part unless it can arouse, in
> itself and in the masses, a moment of enthusiasm in which it asso-
> ciates and mingles with society at large, identifies itself with it and is
> felt and recognized as the *general representative* of this society. Its
> aims and interests must genuinely be the aims and interests of society
> itself, of which it becomes in reality the social head and heart.
> [Pp. 55–56]

The role of this "section of civil society" which undertakes the
emancipation of society as though all of society were in its "particular
situation" has both a dialectical and a sequential character.

> For one class to be the liberating class *par excellence*, it is necessary
> that another class should be openly the oppressing class. The nega-
> tive significance of the French nobility and clergy produced the
> positive significance of the bourgeoisie. . . .
>
> . . . In France every class of the population is *politically idealistic*
> and considers itself first of all, not as a particular class, but as the
> representative of the general needs of society. The role of liberator
> can, therefore, pass successively in a dramatic movement to different
> classes in the population until it finally reaches the class which
> achieves social freedom. [Pp. 56–57]

From Marx's perspective on the French Revolution, we are carried
beyond Gramsci's characterization of the bourgeoisie. It is not simply
a matter of the conflict of the divergent interests of these bourgeois
segments and their intellectual allies. Marx shows how it is possible for
one such segment to seize power with the enthusiastic support of the
masses, and to dominate over the society, including other bourgeois
segments, for a time, at least.

For Marx, this phenomenon is only temporary, the consequence of a moment of enthusiasm which may be succeeded by counterthrusts of political disillusion and alienation. The sequential perspective is more problematical. Marx is comparing France and Germany in this passage, and his point is that Germany is not like France, that it will not pass through a sequence of class-based liberations until a final and complete liberation is achieved. Moreover, in this essay, Marx does not suggest that the process of which he writes is inevitable nor determinate. The role of liberator *can* pass successively, and it may well do so in France, but not in Germany. In Germany there is, nevertheless, a *possibility* of emancipation, but not a certainty, and this possibility depends upon the formation of a particular class. Ultimately, world-wide emancipation may depend upon emancipation in one country, and that country's emancipation may depend upon the actions of a particular class, but there is no argument, in this essay, that the development of the class struggle will be identical either phenomenally or sequentially in all countries.

It is tempting, indeed, to conclude that the rural middle class in Egypt was able to capture the support of the Egyptian masses in a moment of enthusiasm. This traditional, local, elite produced its own intellectual segment which became a new political class. The rural bourgeoisie then took on some of the tasks of the second stratum and helped in the repression of the urban bourgeoisie and the large landowners while presenting itself as the general representative of the Egyptian people. This at least is the idea which has to be tested empirically as far as we can. Yet, there is here an anomaly, for Marx had no great expectations regarding the role that the rural bourgeoisie might play in the emancipatory dialectic which he described. In fact, he writes off the peasants as competitors and as potential successors to the urban bourgeoisie in his analyses of the politics of mid-nineteenth-century France.

In the *Eighteenth Brumaire*, Marx identifies the lumpenproletariat who support Louis Bonaparte, he identifies the proletariat who fought in 1848 but were betrayed by the National Assembly, he identifies the petite bourgeoisie represented by the Montagne and also betrayed by debtor's laws passed by the Assembly, and he identifies the bourgeoisie proper, the party of order. A segment of the bourgeoisie is in reality monarchist and this segment is divided into the landed proprietors and the industrial-mercantile-financial bourgeoisie. Marx is at his most brilliant in describing the conflict among these groups and in describing how bourgeois fears of the proletariat led them to self-contradiction and political immobility in the face of the challenges of Napoleon III.

Napoleon III, he points out, was elected by the votes of the peasants who were given landed rights after the revolution and he was installed as emperor by the lumpenproletariat. Marx's least satisfactory analysis regards the role of the peasantry, not only because they are largely ignored, but because his view of the role of the peasantry is inconsistent. It is apparent that Marx treats the small holding peasantry as undifferentiated. They are a rural proletariat, holding barely enough land to feed themselves, but retaining a sentimental loyalty to the name of the emperor who gave them title to the land and who reduced their taxes. This peasantry should have realized that its interests were common with the urban proletariat, and, in fact, a few peasants did. The majority of the peasants were afflicted by false consciousness, however, and had no sense of themselves as a class with specific interests. Even Marx himself doubts that the peasants constituted a class, and he wrote in what is perhaps the most often quoted section of the *Eighteenth Brumaire*:

> The small-holding peasants form a vast mass, the members of which live in similar conditions but without entering into manifold relations with one another. Their mode of production isolates them from one another instead of bringing them into mutual intercourse. The isolation is increased by France's bad means of communication and by the poverty of the peasants. . . . Each individual peasant family is almost self-sufficient. . . . In this way, the great mass of the French nation is formed by simple addition of homologous magnitudes, much as potatoes in a sack form a sack of potatoes. Insofar as millions of families live under economic conditions of existence that separate their mode of life, their interests, and their culture from those of other classes, and put them in hostile opposition to the latter, they form a class. Insofar as there is merely a local interconnection among these small-holding peasants, and the identity of their interests begets no community, no national bond and no political organization among them, they do not form a class.[33]

When he is talking of the small holding peasant, Marx's definition of class links interest, community, and national bond coordinately. Marx is ambivalent about whether the peasants form an independent class. The structure of the small-holding peasantry is so weak that others must represent their interests. The bourgeoisie and Napoleon I represented their interests under the first empire. They thought Napoleon III and the lumpenproletariat represented their interests in 1850, but their true ally was the urban proletariat. To further confuse the issue of the class identification of peasants, Marx differentiates among them along ideological lines without reference to material interests, writing that "The Bonaparte dynasty represents not the revolutionary but the conservative peasant."[34]

In any case, the peasantry are a passive element in the dialectic of history. The first empire and its petty bureaucracy was based upon a small-holding agriculture, and that empire "was necessary to free the mass of the French nation from the weight of tradition and to work out in pure form the opposition between state power and society. With the progressive undermining of small-holding property, the state structure erected upon it collapses. The centralization of the state that modern society requires arises only on the ruins of the military-bureaucratic government machinery which was forged in opposition to feudalism."[35]

This last statement has important implications for interpreting the Egyptian situation. The parallel argument for Egypt is that the Nasserist regime and its military-bureaucratic machinery, forged in opposition to the monarchy, was based upon a small-holding agriculture. Thus far, the state apparatus has not undermined small-holding property, and so the Nasserist structure has not collapsed—although we shall have to watch Sadat's policies in this respect. What we do not learn from this passage though is how the demise of small-holding property came about. This was the result of the increasing political and economic domination of the urban bourgeoisie, a process which was certainly well advanced in Egypt in 1952, but which was stopped and then reversed by the revolution. This reversal was possible because of the links between the military-bureaucratic machinery of the state and the rural bourgeoisie—links which can be defined in terms of the function of the second stratum, its intergenerational mobility, and its potential as a general representative of a population which was, in 1952, still about 70% rural.

In the *Eighteenth Brumaire*, Marx does not offer us an incisive class analysis of rural France. Instead, his treatment of the political role of the peasantry in the last chapter of that work comes to explain away the failure of the bourgeoisie on the one hand and of the proletariat on the other. Throughout the first five chapters Marx was meticulously concerned with describing the shifts within the parallelogram of urban class forces, but in the last chapter he brings in the peasantry as a crucial but opaque element. Without knowing more about it than the mere fact that the peasantry can play an important role at critical developmental junctures, we are unable to draw any conclusions from descriptions of the Egyptian peasantry.

In his recent work subtitled *Lord and Peasant in the Making of the Modern World*, Barrington Moore, Jr., it seems to me, starts out from the contradiction between Marx's last chapter and the rest of his study of the *Eighteenth Brumaire*. Moore sets himself the task of explaining modernity in terms of the conflict between the pre-modern segments (classes?) of the landlords and the peasants and in his hands the situation of the peasants of France takes on a more familiar shape.

> As the revolution approaches, more details appear until at least some of the main outlines of peasant society become reasonably distinct. In the absence of the kind of commercial revolution that took place in England or of a manorial reaction such as that which happened in Prussia and also in Russia for quite different reasons, many French peasants had become in effect small property owners. Though it is impossible to give precise numbers of these *coqs de paroisse*—their counterpart will be called kulaks at a later stage in Russia—they were certainly a substantial and very influential minority. The large majority of the peasants trailed off beneath them by imperceptible gradations, through those who had tiny *lopins de terre*, down to those who had none at all and lived as agricultural laborers. One gets the impression—but it is no more than an impression—that the number of the land-short and the landless had been slowly and steadily growing for at least two centuries.[36]

Despite Moore's important emphasis upon the differentiated property position of the peasants, his analysis of peasant political motivation is still essentially simple. Historically or objectively, peasant political action might be prodemocratic or proaristocratic, but that action is at least subjectively based on the amount of land each peasant holds and upon the legal nature of his title.

Moore's amplification of Marx's brief discussion of rural social stratification in France might have been intended to supplement Marx's explanation of the rise of Napoleon III. At the same time, Moore, in effect, disposes of the question of whether the peasantry constitutes a class. But Moore's purpose goes beyond a mere apologetic for Marx's analysis. He argues that the impact of the rural strata on the political struggle in Paris was not merely epiphenomenal, leading to a merely temporary deviation from the ultimate confrontation of the bourgeoisie and the proletariat as seemed to be the case in the commune. Moore holds the view that these rural developments are really central to the theory of political modernization.

It is often true that economic conditions and cultural orientations change more slowly in rural areas, or, at least, that a greater effort is made by alien and indigenous modernizers alike to change conditions in urban centers. From this perspective, it is easy enough to conclude that the prevailing flow of political and cultural influence is from the city to the country; and, therefore, any counter current, even that expressed in an alliance of urban and rural political elements, must be a temporary aberration. Moore appears to reject this view, not only by referring to nineteenth-century France, but more significantly with reference to contemporary India. Moore's central argument has two major propositions which may be simplified as follows:

1. The agricultural classes must be mobilized and agricultural production must be rationalized in order that any political-social entity attain modernity and the potential for providing a high material standard of living for its people.

2. Although the transformation of agricultural society and production is an inevitably violent process, there will be crucially differentiated political-institutional consequences dependent upon the way in which the transformation is accomplished and upon whether the agents of the transformation are a "traditional" aristocracy using the rationalized instrumentalities of a bureacracy or a "modern" bourgeoisie using the instrumentalities of political participation.

Essentially, the difference between the outcomes is that aristocratic and bureaucratic transformations are likely to lead to dictatorships while participatory transformations lead to democratic regimes. While democracies are preferable to dictatorships, the more important point is that modernity is preferable to traditionalism when judged in terms of the ultimate value of material welfare. The greatest problem with participatory transformations is that important participatory segments may retain cultural and material attachments to and investments in the maintenance of certain traditional structures. Insofar as these participatory segments are rural, it is unlikely that the process of modernization will be complete and, consequently, it is unlikely that the violence attendant upon modernization will be compensated for by a step-level improvement in material well-being for the society as a whole.

If there is any validity to Moore's extension of Marx's analysis of French political development, then it follows, under circumstances that are notably nondeterministic, that it is important to learn whether there are significant rural segments that are mobilized or participant. It is similarly important to learn whether these or other rural groups are linked with mobilized or participant urban segments. Only on the basis of such knowledge can we assess the possibilities for a modernizing transformation of agriculture. Without such a complete transformation, urban industrialization will be incomplete and the development of a mobilized and participatory (though not necessarily a liberal-democratic) proletariat will be retarded or even inhibited.

Applying these insights to the Egyptian situation, we are able to juxtapose the political role of the second stratum as defined by Mosca with the alternative definition of Barrington Moore. There is, of course, no necessary contradiction between the two. Mosca describes the prerequisite of a stable and legitimate regime, wherein there is a consensual bond between the rulers and the ruled. Moore describes the possibly undesirable consequences of such an arrangement for the transformation of agriculture and, hence, for modernization. Is it possible that elements of the second stratum, as defined by Mosca, should be sufficiently mobilized and bureaucratized that they might perform the role envisioned by Moore, overcoming the opposition of the agrarian segments of the second stratum?

For Egypt that question is still open. Moreover, in prerevolutionary times (i.e., before July 1952) there were important urban bourgeois elements that were not closely linked with the Egyptian second stratum as we define it. Modernization in accordance with Moore's definition and stipulated prerequisite might be accomplished by a resurgent urban bourgeoisie even more readily than by the deruralized descendants of "kulaks." The required transformation of agricultural production may be easier for the bourgeoisie now that it has lost its agricultural property than it was during the era of the great absentee landlords. There are some who would argue, on the basis of such premises, that Sadat is more "progressive" than Nasser was.

But Moore's prerequisite, it must be remembered, is a radical transformation of the organization of agricultural production; so the question is, has anything like that taken place in Egypt? In fact, the rationalizing and the increasing of agricultural production has been one of the central goals of Egyptian policy since the early part of the nineteenth century. Gabriel Baer, in his important book on the history of landownership in Egypt, shows that the most important consequences of this policy were the gradual spread of private ownership, the enhanced administrative and social power of the 'umdah, the increased stratification of rural society, the increased concentration of ownership, the creation of a new class of absentee landowners, and the impoverishment of the great majority of the peasantry.[37] Throughout the nineteenth century, Egyptian agriculture became tied to world markets and dependent upon international financial institutions. Agricultural methods were also changed as perennial canal irrigation replaced basin irrigation and as increased use of fertilizers allowed for more intensive farming and multiple cropping. But the concentration of ownership did not lead to widespread mechanization, nor to the breakup of the traditional village.

Baer was concerned primarily with the emergence of a class of landed grandees, but Hasan Riad pointed to an equally significant alternative development. Discussing rural stratification, Riad shows that, despite the Islamic provision for the equal division of legacies among all sons (and half-shares to each daughter) the proportion of all landowners holding from 5 to 20 feddan has not changed since late in the nineteenth century.[38] The position of these middling landowners may well have become more difficult during the first half of the twentieth century, but there is some evidence that the political competition between the Court and the Wafd party after 1924 resulted in the increased mobilization and participation of the rural middle class. After 1952, tension between the large and the middling landowners was mostly eliminated as a consequence of the implementation of a moderate land reform law. The great absentee landowners who were connected with the palace or with the Wafd were deprived of part of their wealth and most of their political influence, leaving the more traditional rural segment of the second stratum in virtually undisputed dominance. The ministry of land reform set up its own bureaucratic apparatus in the villages where the reform was applied, but these areas amounted to approximately 10% of the agricultural lands of Egypt. The land reform laws as promulgated in 1952 and as later extended in scope have not brought about a radical transformation of agricultural organization and production in Moore's sense. If anything, they may have removed the only forces that were violently and cruelly transforming Egyptian agriculture. Nasser's land reform mitigated that violence and led to the temporary improvement of the material condition of the peasant small holder. Most of the members of the rural middle class and many large landowners were unaffected by the land reform except insofar as some of their competitors were eliminated from the political scene.

From the point of view of Barrington Moore, the political limitations which have been maintained in the transformation of the agricultural sector constitute a decisive barrier to modernization even though they may preserve an inclination toward liberal parliamentary government. It is from this perspective that it is easiest to understand the regime-level consequences of the responsiveness of the regime to the interests of the second stratum. The second stratum, it must be remembered, is not the "ruling class." The second stratum does not rule but is the stratum without which the rulers cannot rule. The role of the second stratum is expressed neither in collective action nor consciously—certainly not "class-consciously." To attempt to understand the political significance of the second stratum in the context of the analysis of elites within the pluralist theory which is so popular among American political scientists is to miss the point of this argument. Nevertheless, the concepts of participation and mobilization, which are widely employed by American political scientists, are relevant to our analysis. In Egypt the influence of the rural bourgeoisie is most clearly to be seen in the type of mobilization which has been sought and in the limited form of participation which has been allowed.

Mobilization is a term that has been widely used in studies of development, notably by Karl Deutsch and by David Apter. Deutsch tells us that "within any geographical setting and any population, economic, social, and technological developments mobilize individuals for relatively more intensive communication."[39] Deutsch does not stress purposeful political mobilization. By contrast, Apter defines the mobilization system as one in which "new values are being created" and in which "political leaders are trying to work out a moral system of authority."[40] It is evident that Apter's mobilization begins where Deutsch's leaves off.

Although the distinction between the types of mobilization is important, that distinction is often lost in much academic discourse. The importance of the distinction extends not only to the different strata which may be mobilized under the two types of situation indicated, but also to the varieties of political process that may be associated with each. Mobilization in the Deutsch sense, or social mobilization, is often associated with processes of participation, while mobilization in the Apter sense, or political mobilization, is often associated with processes of rationalization. Huntington's central thesis in his theory of political development was that if the political institutionalization of participation did not proceed apace with social mobilization then political decay rather than development would ensue.[41] The Comparative Politics Committee view was that social mobilization (or ECD) would give rise to a participation crisis which could be dealt with either by expanding the opportunities for democratic participation, by admitting new groups to participatory legitimacy, or by strictly regulating and controlling participation, thus preventing undesirable forms of participation from emerging.[42] Social mobilization is more often identified with explanations of the emergence of liberal parliamentary political regimes, while political mobilization is more often linked with explanations of the working of one party systems or authoritarian regimes.

From this theoretical perspective, Egypt appears to be an anomaly. Egypt has both elements that have been mobilized in the Deutsch sense and some that have been mobilized in the Apter sense. Supporters of the regime have tended to stress the significance of mobilized and participant elements while critics have tended to emphasize the importance of the mobilized and rationalized elements. Rodinson, for example, wrote that after 1954, "it seemed on the surface at least, that the internal political struggle had come to an end. The rulers were no longer concerned with securing the adhesion of this or that group. They had only to rule and to protect themselves."[43] For Rodinson, the basis of the regime was the complete domination of coercive force, so that even if there was some consensual support it was superfluous theoretically, and practically without any serious impact on policy. Rodinson's position is that mobilization within a rationalized bureaucratic framework does not result in high political costs in the form of admitting new groups to political participation. But is it equally true that a rationalizing bureaucracy may restrict the participation of an already mobilized (in the Deutsch sense) elite with impunity? I think that the answer for Egypt must be no. It is true that the former Wafdists and the Muslim Brethren were politically repressed, but it is apparent that they have outlasted Nasser and it is also known that they were politically active, as an illegal opposition, during his rule. More important is the question of the participation of the rural bourgeoisie. As we shall see, there is substantial evidence that the active participation of the rural notability was growing apace during the two decades preceding the revolution. The creation of the National Union and then the Socialist Union allowed this trend to continue, even under a mobilizational system of the Apter variety, and the remarkable thing is that there was little friction resulting from this ambiguous policy. The reason there was so little friction is, of course, the connection that exists between the rural bourgeoisie and the military bureaucratic apparatus of the state. In a later chapter we will have occasion to present some statistical data illustrating the nature of this connection but for now it may be sufficient to describe that linkage in the following propositional form.

1. The predominant social characteristic of the Egyptian elite is its derivation from the rural bourgeoisie, rural notability, or well-to-do peasants.
2. The rural notability characterizes the origin of the ruling elite and not its present status.
3. The rural notability is not the ruling class of Egypt, but provides the pool of qualified persons from among whom the important and not so important officials are chosen. It is the second stratum in Egypt.
4. Important segments of the urban educated middle "class" have more or less important links, economic, social and cultural, with members of their own families who are still members of the rural middle "class."

5. As the numbers of the urban middle class increase, the proportion of those with significant rural links (i.e., more than a nostalgic memory) declines.

6. The interests of the urban middle class are to be identified with their current largely bureaucratic functions, but their cultural values are still importantly traditional or rather derived from the life experiences of the rural middle class.

7. The rural bourgeoisie or notability can be identified as those persons or families holding more than 10 feddan of land, and more likely those holding from 30 to 50 feddan. These people usually include the village headman or 'umdah, the shuyukh of districts, and other village notables.

8. Such families are usually able to afford educating at least some of their sons, and thus help them to attain urban, educated middle class status and even render them eligible for cooptation by the government into positions of responsibility.

9. These village notables usually dominate village affairs including political affairs.

10. These village notables are "mobilized" in Deutsch's terminology, or politically aware, as Rodinson puts it.

11. While much of the urban population is mobilized in the same sense, they do not have the same influence because of the higher degree of political rationalization or bureaucratic control in the cities.

12. The second stratum has a higher tendency to be participant as well as mobilized than does the urban middle class.

13. The urban middle class is participant only in the limited and formal ways of voting in plebiscitary elections or of engaging in bureaucratic politics within their own organizations.

14. Borrowing from Almond's and Verba's volume on the civic culture, we can subdivide the mobilized rural middle "class" into a participant group and a subject group. Membership in the village committees of the National Union or the Socialist Union may be of either the participant or subject variety.[44]

15. Participant members' families are constantly being differentiated into urban and rural segments, while subject members are slowly becoming participant.

16. Rationalizing policies are either not extended to villages or are mediated and transmuted by village elites except in villages where land reform has been implemented.

Much of the rationalized apparatus of government and economy in Egypt is superstructural and possibly even a barrier between the leaders

of the regime and the most persistent parts of the sociopolitical substructure. The mobilizational efforts of the regime run counter to the
orientations of this substructure, while these substructural segments are
prevented from realizing full participation or citizenship. The issues
which confronted the Nasser regime as a consequence of this situation
were substantial. The most comprehensive problem was not whether
reactionary, capitalist, and urban-pluralistic social segments were to be
suppressed. It was rather whether mobilization and rationalization from
above could better achieve development than might allowing citizenship
and participation to a minority which is mobilized now and which is the
bearer of a distinctive national political culture. Can a useful political
structure be organized by first atomizing and then rationalizing the
associations of the entire population? Does the regime need an effective
mass party, or is the party only needed to prevent the formation of
opposition groups? The loose way in which the National Union and
the ASU were formed permitted some aspects of rural social structure
to show through. These characteristics once revealed are not changed
by simply becoming obscured organizationally because the organization
is directed at mobilization without participation. It is, in fact, the
strength of the regime that it has relied on this social segment for
support and for manpower, but it is the weakness of the regime that it
does not allow full participation to these elements.

During the last twenty-five years many important events have occurred in Egypt. Wars were fought, new institutions were set up, a
Bonapartist leader gained power, and important segments of the landed
classes and the haute bourgeoisie were put under pressure. Nevertheless, from the theoretical perspectives we have adumbrated, the most
important event has been the emergence of a new second stratum in a
moment of revolutionary enthusiasm. After a quarter of a century this
emergence has become the "pratico-inerte" of history in Egypt, and its
meaning for the future of Egyptian politics does not depend upon any
deterministic and sequential theory of political development or emancipation.[45] The meaning of this enigma will not be found in the experience of any other country, nor will the meaning be exhausted by either
a further radicalization of the Egyptian revolution or a continuation of
the present counterrevolutionary tendency. The historical slate is never
wiped completely clean, and historical "totalizations" are never general;
they are particular and they frequently take the form of processes of
social typification.[46]

The emergence of the sociopolitical phenomenon which we have
called the second stratum is significant whether one is primarily con-

cerned with the relationship between elite and mass, with national cultural integration, with class conflict, with development or with bureaucratization. Moreover, the significance of this phenomenon is not
contingent on a single ideological or even methodological perspective.
No single paradigm exhausts the possible political relevance of the
second stratum. Throughout this study the concept social class is used
with relative frequency, but in so doing neither Karl Marx nor Lloyd
Warner is being invoked. Instead, social class is used as a bit of "ordinary language," and, of course, not only ordinary English language but
ordinary Arabic as well. In this loose sense, social class is meant to
function linguistically and methodologically without ideological or empirical presupposition. More specifically it should not be expected that
the Egyptian second stratum, insofar as it may be empirically established that there is in Egypt a second stratum, will conform to some
extant definition of one or another social class which may in turn be
part of an explicit or implicit theory of elites, of class conflict, or of
social revolution. The empirical evidence of the existence of a second
stratum is not to be tested by means of social theory, but the opposite
might be a methodologically sound procedure.

It follows, to the extent that the variety of theoretical proposals
examined may be deemed to be nondeterministic, that the relevance of
the second stratum in any of the alternative paradigms will vary with
the empirical configuration of the second stratum itself. I have tried to
use the limited and varied data available to construct as objective a
statement of that configuration as possible. Because of the nature of the
data available, I have started with a snapshot of the second stratum in
1959. Thereafter I have tried to trace some of their historical roots as
well as to carry the analysis forward as close as might be to the present.

In the chapters that follow we are going to look carefully at the rural,
participant segment of the National Union. The social composition of
the membership of the National Union committees in Egypt's sixteen
agricultural provinces will constitute the basis of the analysis. Starting
with occupational distributions, the study will proceed to identify influential families, the occupational clusters within such families, the influence of landownership, the traditional origins of these elites, and
their intergenerational mobility. In the second section of this work, the
analysis will concentrate on the geographical distribution of rural elites
at the provincial, district, and village levels. With our group divided
into geographical units, it will be possible to venture some statistical
correlations as explanations of the peculiarities of geographical distribution, concentrations of elite statuses, and the prevalence of elite indi-

viduals and families. In the third section of the book, the elite composition of the Socialist Union of 1964 will be compared with the National
Union of 1959, and a similar comparison will be made with the Socialist
Union of 1968. Finally the political strategies of Sadat will be described
and his regime will be compared with that of Nasser.

Part One

The National Structure
of the Rural Elite

Two

Participation and Representation in the National Union

According to the census of 1897, the dwellers in Egypt were at that time 9,734,000 in number. These 9,734,000 souls may be classified in various ways.

The Earl of Cromer, *Modern Egypt*

In the *Philosophy of the Revolution*, the late President Gamal Abd al-Nasser expressed his disappointment with the nature of the popular response to the initiative taken by the Free Officers in July of 1952. The conspirators expected that the people would immediately rally behind the revolution and support the reforms which all knew were necessary. But this assumption was doubly naive, for it presupposed, first, that the amelioration of Egypt's social and economic problems could be accomplished by the negative act of removing the evildoers of the old regime and, second, that the people of Egypt comprised an integrated and mobilized community.

These two presuppositions define the empirical relationship between party organization and development in the new state. The people of Egypt did not rise as one man to the support of the new regime. Egyptian political and social life was not transformed overnight. The problem of what to do with the supreme authority once it had been attained was not resolved by a self-evident solution. The new regime had to find

A portion of this chapter has been reprinted by permission from my "Political Recruitment and Participation in Egypt," in *Political Parties and Political Development*, edited by Joseph LaPalombara and Myron Weiner (Princeton: Princeton University Press, 1966), pp. 217–40. Copyright © 1966 by Princeton University Press.

a way to mobilize support and to break down mass indifference while containing elite opportunism. The very difficulty of attaining this end revealed the nature of political underdevelopment in Egypt: the illiteracy and inaccessibility of the peasant masses; the sharp differences in income and styles of life between the urban upper class and the middle classes of both town and country; the inarticulateness of the urban proletariat; and the parochialism of the lower middle classes, the artisans, and the small-scale bazaar merchants. The revolutionary government came to feel that in order to achieve development it should increase the political participation of certain groups and restrict the participation of others. In general it sought to increase the symbolic participation of the masses, whom it intended to benefit but who made few concrete demands other than that their government be an Islamic-Egyptian one. It also sought to limit the political participation of the urban political elite of the ancien régime, which was likely to make the greatest demands.

Nasser sought to achieve these ends through the establishment of three successive political organizations, the Liberation Rally, the National Union, and the Socialist Union. The government of Egypt was reluctant to call these organizations political parties although they resembled single mobilization parties in almost every way. Their creation coincided with certain phases of policy orientation. The Liberation Rally was established after all political parties were banned and while revolutionary control of the bureaucracy was still limited. It was meant to fill the gap left by the previous parties and to mobilize support for Nasser immediately after his victory over Naguib, who had been the nominal leader of the revolution and had the support of the Wafd and some middle class urban groups such as the lawyers and students. The National Union was organized after the Sinai-Suez invasion and represented an attempt at unifying the Egyptian population behind a narrowly preserved regime. The National Union, unlike the Liberation Rally, was not meant merely to block the formation of other parties. The founding of the Socialist Union coincided with the adoption of a socialist ideology and the growing realization that mass cooperation and not merely moral support would be necessary if development goals were to be achieved.

Each successive organizing effort has revealed new dimensions of Egyptian policy regarding political participation. Each of the three political parties was organized as a pyramid of committees paralleling the village, district, province, and national levels of government. At the higher levels, as might be expected, members have sought effective rather than merely ceremonial political participation. There has been tension between the various committees of the parties and the parallel levels of the service branches of the bureaucracy. Each successive organization has recruited persons more sympathetic to the aims of the revolutionary regime into its upper ranks; and, as the rationalization of the economy outside of agriculture has proceeded, each successive organization has included more members of the government establishment in its higher echelons.

The dilemma of all populist regimes bent on development is posed by the need, both ideological and pragmatic, to mobilize a total population behind the goals of development and, at the same time, to prevent a premature diversion of resources from development to the satisfaction of immediate popular needs. Complicating this problem is the issue of how to cope with existing articulate demands for effective political participation by groups which have already become in some degree modernized—what we would term the participation crisis.

According to a largely implicit theory of evolutionary democracy, the participation crisis should be resolved by the gradual attainment of universal participation. A similar orientation prevails among parties asserting a nationalist ideology. Even though such parties are non-Marxist (though not necessarily anti-Marxist) or at least deny the existence or significance of class distinctions within their own nations, their "national" quality is measured by the degree to which all classes and social segments are represented in their ranks. The participation crisis is therefore often viewed as an historical sequence of demands by groups, ever lower on the social scale than their predecessors, for admission to legitimate participation in the political system.

The first important participation of indigenous Egyptians was under the French during the Napoleonic occupation. The French made use of 'ulama' and urban dignitaries to govern the cities after they had defeated the Mamluks. The French neither controlled the countryside well nor did they encourage the political assertion of the rural notables. This rural notable class was later strengthened by the increasing transfer of public and communal lands to private ownership and by the increased authority granted to the 'umad under the centralizing administrative reforms of the nineteenth century. The most dramatic evidence of the rising influence of this class occurs in the establishment of an advisory council by Khedive Isma'il in 1866. This council, the forerunner of the later parliaments, was comprised for the most part of 'umad. The tension and even open hostility that prevailed between the Khedive and the advisory council from its founding to the Khedive's deposition in 1879 is the first confrontation in a sequence which we have referred to as the participation crisis.

The tension between the council and the Khedive culminated in the 'Arabi revolution when the Khedive attempted to dismiss a large number of indigenous officers from military service. It is fairly well established that both the members of the council and these officers were drawn from the same class of rural notables and headmen. Indigenous (i.e., not Turkish, Circassian, Syrian, Mamluk, or Albanian) rural dignitaries made a bid for political participation and succeeded so well that they undermined the stability of a regime which they were incapable of running and whose security depended upon a very delicate international arrangement among Britain, France, and the Ottoman Empire. The British occupation of 1882 set the entire movement back on its heels.

Advisory councils of somewhat varying responsibilities continued to meet during the ensuing occupation, but no political parties were formed within these mock parliaments. The earliest parties were small ideological or conspiratorial bodies, more like clubs than political parties, comprised of urban groups. It is important to note the significant difference of interest and activity between the very small group of urban radicals (liberals) and the rural notables. The urban radicals sought a fundamental change of regime and a policy of cultural and administrative reaction to the West. The rural notables mainly sought effective political participation. It is further important to note that during this same period, as a result of irrigation improvements, fiscal stabilization in Egypt, and new administrative regulations, there was created a new class of urban absentee landowners of great wealth. From this time on it is possible to refer to the rural notables as a rural middle class.

The revolution of 1919 will bear much new scholarship and reinterpretation, but the least that might be argued is that all three groups, the urban radicals, the rural middle class, and the large landowners, combined for a time to produce an overwhelming protest against continued British occupation. Since the 'ulama' and even the humble fellah participated in the revolution, it is not easy to judge whether it had a more modernizing or traditionalizing thrust.

At any rate, the events of 1919 could be taken as an expression of broadly based national unity, and the Wafd was subsequently able to associate itself exclusively with this expression. The Wafd became the Egyptian equivalent of the Indian National Congress, the Muslim League, and the Convention Peoples Party. Because the image of the party was associated with the revolution, with adamance on the question of British imperialism, and with opposition to the throne, it was able to insist that it alone stood for Egyptian nationalism.

The Wafd may have been associated with the idea of comprehensive national unity, but it did not otherwise represent all classes. It might be argued that the Wafd and the Wafd alone in the 1920s and 1930s could have resolved Egypt's participation crisis by expanding its own ranks and interests. The Wafd was not unaware of these possibilities but did not emphasize the recruitment of peasants or members of the urban lower middle classes and proletariat because of the organizational and tactical problems such a policy would entail. The Wafd was not often in power, and when it was the king constantly harassed it. In struggling to maintain itself the Wafd preferred issues of national unity rather than controversial issues of social and economic reform. Aside from the tactical preference to avoid vulnerability on divisive issues, had the Wafd leaders sought to encourage effective political participation by peasants, workers, craftsmen, and the like, they would have alienated their strongest support. Wafd support might be described as a coalition of the rural middle class and certain high-status urban groups. The predecessors of these urban groups might have been called radicals twenty or thirty years before, but now they are often thought of as conservatives. They were the professionals (lawyers and doctors in particular), nonbazaar businessmen and financiers, industrialists, and intellectuals (professors, students, authors, newspaper editors). Under the Wafd, the rural middle class was strongly represented through the regional constituency system; and it was the support of this class that guaranteed electoral success for the Wafd whenever the king was unable to control the returns completely.

From a certain point of view it is possible to see the three-way struggle between the Wafd, the king, and the British as a continuation of the old struggle of the rural notables for political participation. The Wafd, rather than the parliament as a whole, was the vehicle of the demand for participation. It is possible, however, to see other things going on at the same time. In the first place, all that the Wafd could do for the rural middle class was to see to the reelection of loyal 'umad, prevent land reform, and extend irrigation facilities. The Wafd did not provide adequate credit facilities; it did not expand the educational system rapidly enough to accommodate the sons of the rural notables; it did not protect the rural middle class from the manipulations of Alexandria cotton merchants or the fluctuations of the market. Above all, the Wafd did nothing and probably could have done nothing to prevent the gradual breaking up of holdings through inheritance and hence the steady decline in wealth and social status of rural middle class families.

By contrast, merchants, industrialists, financiers, transporters, professionals, and the newer class of absentee landowners were direct beneficiaries of Wafd policies. The Wafd paid lip service to the need for land reform, for labor legislation, and for expanding the system of rural cooperatives while, in fact, acting to benefit the urban upper middle classes by means of administrative action and the use of influence. The king, of course, was capable of competing for the support of these urban groups, but his greatest reliance was placed upon a few landowners, industrialists, members of the military, and the 'ulama'. His methods were not conducive to continuous cooperation with the throne. Even though the king's friends were not a negligible group, their influence was intermittent, surreptitious, illegitimate, and insecure.

At the same time, the demands and frustrations of the lower urban classes were growing. Increasingly difficult economic conditions and the pressure of population growth drove many peasants to the cities. Their demands were largely unarticulated except when student riots or similar events gave occasion and outlet to the expression of their plight. Far more important was the growing protest of a new group of urban radicals. This group has sometimes been referred to as a lower middle class, and it did include teachers, students, journalists, 'ulama', shopkeepers, junior army officers, civil servants, and some skilled craftsmen.

The distinction between these members of the lower middle class and the proletariat on the one hand and the urban upper middle class (the old urban radicals) on the other is crucial. For the most part, this urban lower middle class was educated, though not so highly as the urban Wafdist elite. They were also immigrants to the city from rural hometowns. In other words, there were and are kinship links between the rural middle class and the urban lower middle classes. The kinship links are to be contrasted with the political links between elements of the rural middle class and the Wafd leadership. If we assume, as I think we must, that the downward social and economic pressure upon the rural middle class continued and that there was a consequent steady increase of rural middle class immigration to the cities, we can conclude that there has been an almost irresistible pressure upon educated members of the urban lower middle classes to desist from identifying their interests with their rural origins and to seek political participation in their own right. Developments of this kind have led to increasingly frequent demonstrations, to widespread political alienation, to the growth of system-challenging organizations (the Muslim Brethren, the Young Egypt movement, the Communist party), to numerous efforts to reinvigorate the Wafd, to the formation of the Free Officers organization, and to the near collapse of the old regime upon the burning of Cairo on 26 January 1952.

Obviously the participation crisis was but one aspect of the difficulties of the Egyptian political system on the eve of the revolution; nevertheless, we can conclude that the Wafd had not measured up to the task of resolving or easing that crisis.

The revolutionary regime of Egypt did not consider that one of its major tasks was to resolve a participation crisis. Certainly many more Egyptians, peasants, workers, civil servants, and teachers felt that the revolutionary government was more truly Egyptian than any they had known. Many more came within range of the propaganda network of the government and in this sense became participants in the political system. In addition we have already noted that under the constitution of 1956 every Egyptian was to be a member of the National Union and hence a participant. Still the first problem faced by the Revolutionary Command Council was not how to admit new groups to the political process but how to break the virtual monopoly which the Wafd was found to hold when the king abdicated.

The purpose behind the establishment of the Liberation Rally and its successors was to block the effective participation of the prerevolutionary elite. There has never been any intention of granting an effective voice to the members of the mass party. The mass parties were means of mobilizing sentiment for the regime and means of rendering the masses unavailable to alternative leaders. Later, when the security of the regime was better established, additional uses of the mass party were recognized. Only in the fields of interest-group coordination and the redress of individual grievance did the mass party appear to serve anyone but the government itself.

We can learn a few things about the limits and the possibilities of the use of the mass mobilization party by examining the experience of Egypt. It should be remembered that Egypt had had its mass party with an authentic grass roots base in the Wafd. The National Union (here using the term for its predecessor and successor as well) was an artificial creation based upon a composite of Indian, Ghanaian, Guinean, and above all Yugoslav models. In all of the parallel cases the national mobilization party was organized in preindependence times and was so influential politically that it has been interesting to discuss the distribution of administrative tasks between party and government in these countries, but not in Egypt. Furthermore, regardless of how tightly the leadership controls these parties, it is apparent that they represent significant power structures that may not be whimsically altered despite superficial organizational manipulation.

The Egyptian mass party differs on all these points. There is no revolutionary aura about it. Loyalty to the state cannot be equated with loyalty to a party which did not create that state but is its creation. The mass party may be changed at will, and it has been changed at times significantly. Its members approach it pragmatically. For those who are not on the inside, membership or, better still, holding office in the mass party is the only way of making one's voice heard. It is not a very effective way, but it is worth a try. For rural dignitaries, officeholding is a necessity if they are to retain their local prestige and function of seeking redress for their aggrieved neighbors. But when none of the really important members of the regime is willing to give the organization much time, when others become suspicious that the party may be used as a means of building an independent power base, when the benefits the regime gets from the party fall below the favors that must be done, or when a new political crisis requires a renewal of enthusiasm, then the whole ceremony of establishing a mass popular political organization may be repeated. If a popular organization is to be the repository of legitimacy, such an organization cannot be frequently or radically changed without mitigating its legitimizing effect. Finally, a mass political organization cannot serve as a legitimizing symbol without also serving as an effective means of popular political participation.

Another point that emerges from the experience of the National Union is that the effective building up of a mass political organization requires time and skill. The Egyptian government has demonstrated its ability to organize a mass party in a very short time. There have been two important consequences of this procedure. First, because of the rapidity of organization it is clear that effective organization must depend upon exploiting (or subordinating organizational purposes to) the existing social structure; second, the selection of organizational elements from among existing structures is a most direct form of recruitment into political participation. As indicated, membership or even officeholding in the National Union did not convey much political influence, but given the close control over the distribution of political values in Egypt, this is the only manner in which participation by outsiders is possible. Redress of grievance, protection of existing rights, retention of social prestige, and attainment of minimal qualifications for cooptation into higher political echelons—these are the benefits of membership in the mass political party.

With the elaboration of these general considerations it is possible to understand the very difficult nature of the participation crisis after the revolution of 1952. The revolutionary regime did not wish to permit the political participation of other system-challenging parties any more than it did the Wafd. The new regime was favorably inclined toward organized labor because of its assistance against Naguib in 1954; it favored the peasant through its insistence on land reform and the breaking up of the large estates. It was suspicious of students and lawyers because of their support for Naguib. It generally favored (until 1958 at any rate) businessmen, financiers, and industrialists because of the importance of economic development. The rural middle class and the urban lower middle class were favored by policies that limited the applicability of land reform to the largest holdings and enhanced the job security of the bureacracy. The Liberation Rally was to organize the entire nation. Members of the Revolutionary Command Council toured the country and established branches by investing various notables with responsibility and office in local branches. Offices and clubhouses were opened in existing facilities. The Rally did nothing except express its approval of Nasser's ouster of Naguib, the proposal to postpone elections for three years from early 1954, and similar things. The Rally was not organized systematically, but branches were established in all the major centers. Responsibility for the Rally was borne by Anwar al-Sadat, and his temporary decline from influence coincided with the demise of the Rally.

The Rally was allowed to die after the announcement that the National Union would be founded under the Constitution of 1956. The National Union was made the responsibility of Kamal al-Din Husayn, minister of education at the time. The National Union was established in more systematic fashion even though in most cases its officers were the same as those who served under the Liberation Rally.

The National Union was organized in 1958 and 1959, in accordance with the Egyptian constitution of 1956, in both Egypt and Syria. In Egypt, the organization of the National Union followed the precedent set by the Liberation Rally. The general pattern was for organizers to visit a village whereupon they would summon the peasants to register themselves as members of the Union. Not every village was visited, but a great many were, that is, over five thousand. Not every adult joined, but nearly six million, mostly males, did. Following the registration of ordinary members in these basic units, as they were called, each basic unit elected a committee to run its affairs. The size of the committee varied with the size of the village, but none seem to have had fewer than three members and the average was around seven; provincial seats had committees as large as twenty-five or thirty. In addition to these village committees, other governing committees were elected at the district (markaz) and provincial levels and an annual congress was to be held at the national level.

At the district level, there was, in fact, not a governing committee, but a bureau comprised of four officers, a president, a vice-president, a secretary, and a treasurer. The district might include anywhere from a handful to forty or fifty villages. Our data are limited to the members of the committees of the basic units and the officers of the district bureaus. A list of these committee and bureau members' names was published and it included almost 30,000 names.[1] A little more than 2000 of these members were from the urban provinces of Egypt and they will be left out of account in this analysis because they do not show any of the characteristics of the rural data. The urban committees were, of course, elected by much larger constituencies, designated by quarter, and comprised of persons who did not know one another, and the urban elections were often dominated by well-known national political personalities.

In the villages, it has frequently been reported that the elections were more or less free, but it must be remembered that voting was influenced by existing status differences, by the experience of the Liberation Rally, and by the fact that some central organs of the National Union had already been created in order to regulate the 1957 elections to the National Assembly.[2]

The central secretariat of the National Union persisted through the union with Syria to preside over the parliamentary elections of July 1959. Thus when the local elections of the village or basic unit committees of the National Union were held in July and November 1959, those elections were presided over by the central secretariat of the NU and by the Ministry of the Interior.[3] It is also noteworthy that the provincial councils were all elected in July while apparently only half of the basic unit committees were elected in July and the other half in November.[4] In other words, the elections were not exactly, or not entirely, from the bottom up. Since half of the members of the National Assembly of 1959 were to be chosen from the Assembly of 1957, and the other half chosen from the nominees of the National Union, there was additional incentive for influentials to seek election in the National Union. Furthermore, though the relationship between the basic units of the National Union and the formal structures of local government, or the more informal agricultural unions or cooperatives, was not yet made clear, it was becoming more apparent that National Union membership might be a necessary prerequisite to holding any local office of influence or power.

To sum up, the National Union was locked into existing status and authority structures. Even while the functions of the National Union were not clear, the consequences of election to a local committee were obviously significant. The ruling group in Cairo, at the center, had rather definite expectations regarding the persons who would become politically responsible locally, and the local influentials were relatively serious about getting or retaining political prestige. Despite central co-ordination of the elections, the fact that these village elections were held on only two designated days suggests a minimum of central control and a high degree of local control. It is also worth remembering that elections are not new to Egypt, where there have been forms of parliamentary elections since 1866. This history led the military regime to redraw the constituency lines in the parliamentary elections of 1957 with the specific aim of weakening the chances that the former Wafdists might prevail.[5] Elections to the basic unit committees within single villages would not be affected by such gerrymandering, and fifteen years after the "revolution," 'Abd al-Malik, the chastened Egyptian Marxist, could lament that "between 1952 and 1967 the single-party method put the men of the old order back into power in all areas."[6]

The NU elections of 1959 greatly underrepresented the urban segments of the party relative to the rural branches. Rural representation, as measured by the number of members of the basic units, ranged between one member per 600 to one member per 809 of population. Significantly, the largest "constituencies" were in al-Jizah province, just across the river from Cairo and highly urbanized also. By contrast Cairo was represented by one member (of the basic unit committees) per 4,611 of population. These proportions were calculated on the basis of the census of 1957 (see table 1).

There is no reason to believe that this was a deliberate attempt to exclude urban social groups, although a great deal of ideological importance was and is attached to the peasant as a symbol of the best in the nation. It is further true that some negative value was associated with certain aspects of urban life. It is, however, probable that this disproportionate representation of rural segments was due to the unarticulated belief that the regions of the country and the villages represent more meaningful or significant diversities, while the cities are not thought of as diverse but as largely identical. This feeling is sustained by the fact that there is little variation in occupational structure among Egyptian cities. Another explanation for disparate representation may be found in the simpler fact that the units represented—the urban quarter on the one hand and the village on the other—are greatly disparate in population. Most villages are far smaller in population than most urban quarters. Hence it would be incorrect to draw too many conclusions regarding the purposeful political calculations of the leadership from the urban/rural disparities in the composition of the National

Table 1   Proportion of NU Committee
                                       Members to Population

	Province	Population in 1957	Number of Members in NU	Proportion
1.	Cairo	2,877,200	624	1:4,611
2.	Alexandria	1,277,800	323	1:3,956
3.	Canal	416,300	194	1:2,146
4.	Suez	162,800	58	1:2,807
5.	Dumyat	332,800	460	1:723
6.	al-Daqahliyyah	1,838,800	2,713	1:667
7.	al-Sharqiyyah	1,672,600	2,661	1:629
8.	al-Qalyubiyyah	880,600	1,332	1:611
9.	Kafr al-Shaykh	843,300	1,355	1:622
10.	al-Gharbiyyah	1,579,800	2,244	1:704
11.	al-Manufiyyah	1,252,700	2,074	1:604
12.	al-Buhayrah	1,479,700	2,467	1:600
13.	al-Jizah	1,122,400	1,388	1:809
14.	Bani Suwayf	807,000	1,424	1:567
15.	al-Fayyum	763,700	1,161	1:658
16.	al-Minia	1,444,600	2,321	1:622
17.	Assiut	1,212,900	1,817	1:668
18.	Suhaj	1,450,300	2,178	1:666
19.	Qena	1,224,900	1,821	1:673
20.	Aswan	338,700	548	1:618

Note: The urban provinces are Cairo, Alexandria, and the Suez Canal area; the rest are rural. The variation in representation between the relatively narrow limits of 567:1 and 809:1 seems to have more to do with the number of villages or population units than with the density of population.

Union. Nevertheless, the great disparity revealed in the elections of 1959 (which was in part corrected in the 1964 elections to the Socialist Union) corresponds to some political, social, and cultural realities prevalent at that time. Essentially those realities were:

   1. The regime had not yet developed a socialist program beyond the nationalization of foreign property.

2. The regime had attained a measure of urban control during the period of internal strife in 1954.
3. The regime sought the supportive, formal, participation of the rural areas at a time when it was feuding with the Iraqi government of Abd al-Qarim Kassem and Kassem's Communist allies.
4. But the regime wished to avoid the risk of mobilizing urban political elements into a new and untried structure.
5. The regime tended to think in regional rather than occupational (corporativist) terms when it came to organization because that was the basis of administration and in particular was the way in which the Ministry of the Interior functioned.
6. Many of the members of the urban segments most favored by the regime were, in fact, elected as rural representatives because they presented themselves for election in the village where their families had some traditional standing even though they were now urban residents, and often were residents of Cairo itself and not merely of provincial cities.
7. Parliamentary elections had always been dominated by the rural electorate.
8. The cities were identified with the prevalence of minorities, with ideological politics, with organized religion and religious politics, with alien political and diplomatic influence and with moral corruption.

If the representation of the agricultural provinces was preferred above that of the urban provinces, the urban or modern or educated segments of the participant population of the agricultural provinces appears to have been favored above the rural, agrarian, and uneducated. In table 2 we have juxtaposed the percentage of the population of each province which is rural with the percentage of the members of the committees of the basic units of the National Union whose occupations were either rural (farmer, 'umdah, etc.) or traditional (man of religion). The most obvious characteristic of this comparison is the disproportion of modern or urban occupations among the members of the NU committees in contrast to the general population. It is clear that the electoral process for the committees of the National Union favored the more educated, more modernized, and more urbanized social segments of the Egyptian population insofar as these resided in or were at least legal residents of the predominantly agricultural provinces. Other important patterns emerge in this table which we shall find to be fundamental to the geographical pattern of the distribution of elites and to the occupational distribution of elites in Egypt: The modernized sector is exaggerated most in the Delta and least in upper Egypt. The modernized

sector is most disproportionately manifest in the representation of the
two agricultural provinces which are contiguous to Cairo and in the
Delta, that is al-Qalyubiyyah and al-Manufiyyah.

Table 2   Percentage of Rural Population and
                                     Traditional Occupations in the NU

Provinces	Rural Population	Traditional and Agricultural Occupations
Lower Egypt		
Dumyat	73.1%	50.9%
al-Daqahliyyah	81.7	75.3
al-Sharqiyyah	85.2	63.1
al-Qalyubiyyah	80.0	47.5
Kafr al-Shaykh	83.6	66.9
al-Gharbiyyah	73.0	59.0
al-Manufiyyah	86.8	47.0
al-Buhayrah	82.0	69.7
Upper Egypt		
al-Jizah	70.2	56.9
Bani Suwayf	80.5	68.8
al-Fayyum	80.0	70.6
al-Minia	82.9	79.4
Assiut	80.6	73.9
Suhaj	80.7	73.5
Qena	86.0	73.4
Aswan	79.3	58.0

Even though the agricultural provinces of lower Egypt are not very
different in terms of gross occupational statistical patterns from those
of upper Egypt, they differ substantially in terms of representation.
Several tentative explanations may be offered for this disparity:

1. While the occupational patterns of the agricultural provinces are
   not very different, the major urban centers are almost all in the
   north of the country (in lower Egypt).
2. The greater proximity of the urban centers, and especially Cairo,
   allowed candidates resident in Cairo but native to villages in
   lower Egypt to run in their native villages.
3. Not only are urban rural links stronger in lower Egypt, but the
   modernized segment is more politically influential in the villages
   of lower Egypt.

Damietta (Dumyat) and especially Aswan, neither of them close to Cairo, but each with an important urban center of its own, show the modern occupations greatly overrepresented. Both had a relatively small number of committee members (Damietta with an n of 460 and Aswan with an n of 548), a fact which may account for some of the distortion. In both cases it would appear that remoteness from Cairo coupled with the availability of capital and employment opportunities has led to a local urbanization based on commerce in Damietta and on hydrology, engineering, and hydroelectricity in Aswan.

Let us turn, now, to a more precise consideration of the occupational distribution of the members of the committees of the basic units of the National Union. We have already referred to the distinction between urban or modern and rural or traditional occupations. This distinction was based on the names of the occupations listed in the *Golden Register*. There are 21 occupations listed in the register, and of these only five were recorded as traditional/rural occupations: (*a*) member of a local (district or town) council, (*b*) "man of religion," (*c*) 'umdah or shaykh (village headman or assistant headman), (*d*) farmer or agriculturist, (*e*) unknown or not listed (when found in an agricultural village). All other occupations are, somewhat arbitrarily, listed as urban/modern, as are all women and all "unknowns" found in urban centers. These occupations do not accord with the categories used by the Egyptian Government Statistical Bureau, nor with the classifications employed from time to time by various development agencies. It seems that the classification scheme used by the officials of the National Union is a combination of terms preferred by the registrars and those used by committee members to describe themselves. Table 3 presents the breakdown of all committee members by occupation.

These occupations are not represented in proportion to their number in the population as a whole (as we shall see later in this chapter), but some effort was made to get a spread of occupations while still reflecting certain social class biases, not only of the regime but of the prevailing culture. By and large only three broad groups are represented: the western-educated, professional middle class; the employee or functionary lower middle class; and the middling or well-to-do peasant class.

A few occupational categories require some explanation. Of particular note is the category "former members of parliament," which refers to those elected in 1957, most of whom were reelected in 1959. Since there were 350 M.P.'s in 1957, nearly 83% of all former members of the National Assembly were elected locally to the committees of the basic units of the National Union. This very high rate indicates the political importance attributed to the committees at the local political level, even if the government in Cairo had a more ceremonial idea of the purposes of the National Union.

Table 3   Occupational Distribution of Members of NU Committees

Occupation	Number of Members	Percentage
Urban/Modern		
High official	17	.06
Cabinet minister	26	.09
Doctor	258	.87
Lawyer	848	2.87
Businessman	356	1.21
Teacher	2,892	9.80
Former M.P.	290	.98
Engineer	586	1.98
Merchant	2,473	8.38
Student	386	1.31
Journalist	52	.18
Ex-army officer	48	.16
Ex-police officer	41	.14
Civil servant	2,186	7.40
Worker	394	1.33
Woman (double counted)	53	(.18)
Unknown (urban)	19	.06
Rural/Traditional		
Local council member	326	1.10
Man of religion	463	1.57
ʿUmdah or shaykh	5,588	18.93
Farmer	10,733	36.36
Unknown (rural)	1,538	5.21
Total	29,520	100.00

High officials include officials of the National Union or former members of the Revolutionary Command Council or heads of large government agencies such as the Suez Canal authority. It is likely that all those recorded as doctors, lawyers, and engineers include those employed by the government or armed forces as well as those in private practice. Very few professionals in Egypt are exclusively engaged in private practice, anyway. This circumstance results in a lowering of the category of civil servant, and permits us to take "civil servant" as meaning at least nontechnical and probably only middle-ranking government employees as the referent of this category. Since the entries "former army officer" and "former police officer" are found without any further indications of current occupation (as in the case of former members of the National Assembly), we do not know whether these are also landed notables or not. It is, furthermore, quite possible that a good many former army officers or police officers have recorded their current occupations and so we cannot tell how many ex-officers are in the National Union committees.

It is generally assumed that the Egyptian government is dominated by the military. This popular conception is true insofar as members of the cabinet and other very highly placed personages are concerned. It is somewhat surprising that only 48 of the 29,520 committee members recorded their former occupations as military, and only 41 recorded their previous occupations as police. Members of the armed forces were not allowed to run for political office, so only retired officers could be elected. Although the number of ex-officers among the committee members is not small in comparison with the number of former officers in the total population, their modest numbers give no evidence of a permeating influence. It is only through their kinship ties with others that the military could have direct influence in the National Union committees as opposed to having political control from the center.

Occupations such as teaching and civil service are respected, relative to other positions, but they tend to represent the lower part of the spectrum of modern occupations requiring some, at least, western-style education. The large numbers of teachers and civil servants seem more to represent the large numbers of available candidates who are loyal ideologically, who are directly subordinated to the authority of the governmental executive, and who are educated enough to "get the message." If the relatively large numbers of teachers and civil servants do not establish the prestige of these occupations, then the influence of particular teachers and civil servants will also have to be referred to kinship or to some other individual characteristic.

If the situation of retired officers and of government employees is ambiguous, that of the agriculturists is even more so. The category farmer, or agriculturist, does not tell us whether the individual referred to is landless or not or what size holding he might have. The 'umdah or shaykh until recently was required to have a minimum holding of about 10 feddan (10.1 acres approximately). Not all of the 'umad, shuyukh, and local council members were members of the a'yan class, or the class of small landed notables who did not work their own land,

but nearly all were, as were most of the men of religion and a large
number of those listed simply as farmers.

One third or more of the agriculturists are 'umad, a fact which
weakens the significance of the very large number of ordinary farmers
on the committees. Since there is one 'umdah for every two farmers,
and an 'umdah for nearly every village, it is likely that the farmers will
be serving with their 'umdah on these committees. The 'umdah is, of
course, the civil authority in the village, and he has been the traditional
exponent of governmental authority in the village. Most political parties, when there was party competition in Egypt, did rely on the 'umdah
to deliver the votes in his village. The large number of 'umad elected
indicates that the government approved of the large representation of
traditional authority. It indicated that, insofar as it was serious about
mobilizing the population, the government intended to do so primarily
through traditional structures. And it indicated that the locally influential 'umdah thought it worth the while and the effort to run and win
the election.

The 'umad appear to be the key element in the representation of
diverse segments in the National Union. They hold together the village,
and to a surprisingly great extent, as we shall see, they hold together
the modern and the traditional.

In addition to listing the names and occupations of the members of
the NU committees, the *Golden Register* has also recorded the names
of those elected to the district offices of the National Union. Since we
have been given the name, occupation, constituency, and office of each
officeholder, it will be possible to use officeholding as a measure of
influence or prestige. In pursuing this line of inquiry it is important to
remember that officeholding may indicate that the officer is personally
influential, that his occupation is a highly respected one, that his occupation is functionally significant to the economic order, or that his
occupation (or the occupation of someone closely related to him) is
particularly important in the region from which the officer has come.

The election of district officers was more important to the central
government than either the enrollment of ordinary members (about 6
million) or the election of village committees (over 29,000 members).
There were altogether only 820 district officers. The number of district
officers was surprisingly small, bearing in mind that the number of
members of parliament in Egypt was 350 in 1957 and only 400 in
1959. Egyptian political organization is, thus, highly peaked. The Central Committee of the National Union paid closer attention to the election of district officers, but there is no suggestion that they departed
from a general preference for those who were locally respected and

influential. Nevertheless, the occupational structure of the district officers is greatly different from that of the committee members.

Despite the larger number of rurals in the National Union, the officers were predominantly urban or engaged in modern occupations.
Using the same breakdown of occupations employed earlier, table 4
illustrates the difference. For slightly more than half as many "urban"
committee members there are more than twice as many officers at the
district level. Table 5 compares these categories for each of the occupations listed.

Table 4   Distribution of Occupations among
                                   Members and Officers of the NU

	Urban/Modern		Rural/Traditional	
	Number	Percentage	Number	Percentage
Ordinary Members	10,345	36	18,365	64
District Officers	580	72	230	28
Total	10,925		18,595	

Students, teachers, workers, and men of religion are all underrepresented at the district level. All of these groups have been the target of
government mobilizing activity: the teachers and students through the
bureaucracy, the universities and the student unions, the workers
through trade unions and social welfare administration, and the men of
religion through al-Azhar University and a number of organizations
such as the International Islamic Conference. In all cases the goal of
government organization was regulation and control and not representation. It follows that no effort was made to give special salience to
these groups at the district level, and their relatively low social status
and relatively small numbers among NU committee members resulted
in very few being elected as district officers. The modern or urban
occupations of lower or moderate status—the employment of the bulk
of the "middle class" whether modern or traditional—are not salient
among the district officers. There is a clear difference of order of magnitude if we compare professionals, businessmen, journalists, ex-army
officers, and ex-police officers as a single group with teachers, merchants, and civil servants: the former are overrepresented while the
latter are roughly in the same proportion as district officers and as
committee members.

Among these groups the small differences in proportion generally
coincide with social prestige rankings—businessmen first, doctors sec-

ond, lawyers third, and engineers fourth. After the promulgation of the
July Socialist Laws (1961), businessmen may have declined in status
while engineers have improved. Journalists are not generally of high
status, but the five elected to district offices were. Ex-army officers
generally enjoy a higher status than do ex-police officers (a distinction
which has increased over the years since 1959). About 32% of all

Table 5   Comparison of Occupational Distri-
                                                bution of NU Members and Officers

Occupation	Ordinary Members	District Officers	Total Membership
Urban/Modern			
High official	.02%	1.46%	.06%
Cabinet minister	.07	.85	.09
Doctor	.81	3.17	.87
Lawyer	2.70	8.78	2.87
Businessman	1.10	4.51	1.21
Teacher	9.91	4.87	9.80
Former M.P.	.41	20.85	.98
Engineer	1.90	4.51	1.98
Merchant	8.37	8.17	8.38
Student	1.34	--	1.31
Journalist	.16	.61	.18
Ex-army officer	.14	.85	.16
Ex-police officer	.10	1.22	.14
Civil servant	7.35	8.90	7.40
Worker	1.35	.85	1.33
Woman (double counted)	.15	1.22	.18
Unknown (urban)	.04	.85	.06
Rural/Traditional			
Local council member	1.03	3.54	1.10
Man of religion	1.59	.61	1.56
ʿUmdah or shaykh	19.08	12.07	18.93
Farmer	37.06	9.39	36.36
Unknown (rural)	5.27	2.68	5.21
Total	99.95%	99.96%	100.00%

district officers are 'umad, a'yan, local council members, or farmers.
It is, however, extremely important to note that relatively few of these
people have been listed simply as farmers. More than twice as many
(relative to the NU Committee base from which they are drawn) are
'umad. The proportion is about five times as high for those who are
members of local governing councils, and about 25 or 30 times as high
for the former M.P.'s.

Of 290 former members of the National Assembly (former M.P.'s)
171 (59%) are officers. This figure suggests that there is a close link
between the NU elite and the parliamentary elite of Egypt. The former
M.P.'s are drawn from many occupations, but about 35% of the 1957
parliament were professionals, about 20% were members of the rural
middle class, 15% were from the army and the police, and 17% were
high government officials. In other words, the district officers reflect
not the composition of the NU committees, and certainly not the occupational distribution of the whole population of Egypt, but rather that
of the parliamentary elite.

Since four officers were elected in each district, the number of officers elected is a product of the number of districts into which the
province was divided. The agricultural provinces were divided into
relatively few districts and the urban provinces and the deserts into a
proportionately larger number.

In Cairo, Alexandria, the Canal cities, Suez, and the deserts, once
elected to a unit committee, a member has more than seven times as
many chances to become an officer than does a member elected in one
of the agricultural provinces (see table 6). Only 2% of the committee
members in the agricultural provinces were elected as district officers.
Almost 30% of all the district officers were from the urban provinces
and the deserts. The consequence of this circumstance is that the prestige or political importance assigned to each occupation in accordance
with the number of persons so occupied who were elected to district
office reflects also the special pattern of occupational prestige and availability in each province. For example, the desert regions have about
.5% of the teachers who are ordinary members and 10% of the teachers who are officers. For merchants, the figures are 2.5% compared
with nearly 27%, for civil servants almost 1.5% compared with 24%,
for 'umad about 1% compared with 18% and for farmers about .5%
compared with almost 8%. All the workers elected to district office
were from the deserts.

In comparing the distribution of occupations among the population,
the committees of the National Union and the district officers, and in
drawing conclusions regarding the political ranking of occupations,
statistical constraints have not been taken into account. For the membership of the NU committees that assumption is probably correct because of the large number of such members, even though their total
amounted to only a little over .1% of the population of Egypt. Such
confidence is less warranted for the urban provinces and for Dumyat
and Aswan, where the total number of committee members was small.
It is even more apparent that the restricted number of district officers

Table 6 Percentage of Officers

Province	Ordinary Members	Officers	Percentage
Cairo	540	84	13.5
Alexandria	279	44	13.6
Canal	166	28	14.4
Suez	50	8	13.8
Dumyat	444	16	3.5
al-Daqahliyyah	2,669	44	1.6
al-Sharqiyyah	2,618	43	1.6
al-Qalyubiyyah	1,304	28	2.1
Kafr al-Shaykh	1,323	22	2.3
al-Gharbiyyah	2,200	44	1.9
al-Manufiyyah	2,042	32	1.5
al-Buhayrah	2,419	48	1.9
al-Jizah	1,356	32	2.3
al-Fayyum	1,137	24	2.1
Bani Suwayf	1,392	32	2.2
al-Minia	2,277	44	1.9
Assiut	1,777	40	2.2
Suhaj	2,134	44	2.0
Qena	1,785	36	1.9
Aswan	528	20	3.7
Deserts	280	77	21.6

greatly vitiated any assumptions of hypothetical randomness against which the actual distribution of occupations might be compared. In order to test the statistical significance of the presumed political preference for certain occupational categories, the proportion of officers to members for each occupation was stated as a ratio where the random expectation is 1:1. Any ratio higher than 1 (if statistically significant) will be taken as a measure of political preference.

The ratios for Cairo and for the agricultural provinces were tested for significance by calculating the random error (at the .05 level) that might be expected if the process of election to district office were hypothesized to be no more than a random sampling process. It is to be expected that the smaller the occupational category from which officers are to be drawn, the more likely is it that the representation of that group will be distorted either up or down. This error factor was in turn converted to a number comparable to the ratio of actual to expected occupational representation. Thus, in Cairo, for those holding high positions, we expect a ratio of 1:1, though we actually get a ratio of 7.46:1—strong evidence of political influence. We note, however, that the number of those in high positions was very small (n = 7), so that the random error might be ±2.03; that is, the ratio might be as high as 3.03:1 (1 + 2.03) or as low as 0:1 without indicating any conclusion regarding political influence. Table 7 presents the ratios and error margins for Cairo.

For Cairo none of the standard occupational categories shows any statistical significance. Only those in high positions and former M.P.'s show political strength, while even cabinet ministers (obviously politically influential) and those in the miscellaneous category are only minimally above the line of significance. This striking finding requires some explanation. It would be quite wrong to assume that occupation has no significance in terms of deference behavior, accepted ideas about social structure, and the requirements of an adequate system of representation. There is no reason to assume that there was any randomness involved in the selection of officers. The only question is whether that selection was in any way influenced by occupation or whether it was influenced by other considerations. Consideration of other criteria, such as loyalty to the regime, political skill, particularistic and traditional status, and the like, might result in a nonrandom pattern of occupational distribution insofar as there might be distinct and special patterns of occupational distribution among those enjoying traditional prestige, for example, or if there were an obvious or manifest class basis for the recruitment of district officers.

The standard error calculation is much more important for the agricultural provinces than for Cairo because the number of officers in each occupational category is quite small relative to the total of members. Table 8 reveals some important differences when compared with the ratios for Cairo (table 7). The agricultural provinces show positive ratios for doctors, lawyers, and businessmen; and engineers are not far behind. Former M.P.'s are much more important in the agricultural provinces than in the cities. The other groups showing positive ratios are former army and police officers and local councillors. The army and police officers are relatively few even though "overrepresented," but the local councillors comprise a substantial proportion of the members of the rural middle class. In contrast to the local councillors,

Table 7   Significance Test of Occupational
                                               Distribution for Cairo Officers[a]

Occupation	Ratio	Error	Minimum Significant Ratio
Urban/Modern			
High official	7.5 : 1	2.0	4.4
Cabinet minister	3.1 : 1	1.8	.3
Doctor	.8 : 1	1.4	.0
Lawyer	.4 : 1	1.4	.0
Businessman	.9 : 1	1.3	.0
Teacher	.7 : 1	1.4	.0
Former M.P.	5.0 : 1	1.7	2.4
Engineer	1.4 : 1	1.6	.0
Merchant	1.2 : 1	1.3	.0
Student	.0 : 1	5.5	.0
Journalist	1.8 : 1	1.7	.0
Ex-army officer	1.2 : 1	2.1	.0
Ex-police officer	2.0 : 1	2.4	.0
Civil servant	.5 : 1	1.2	.0
Worker	.0 : 1	1.6	.0
Woman	2.0 : 1	1.5	.0
Unknown (urban)	4.0 : 1	3.0	.0
Rural/Traditional			
Local council member	--	--	--
Man of religion	1.2 : 1	2.1	.0
ʿUmdah	.0 : 1	1.7	.0
Farmer	--	--	--
Unknown (rural)	1.0 : 1	1.4	.0

[a]Formula for significance test:

$$\frac{\text{officers}}{\text{all members}} \times \frac{\text{each occupation}}{\text{all members}} = \text{probable percentage of members} = P$$
for each occupation among
officers

$$\frac{\text{officers in each occupational group}}{\text{all members in province}} = 00$$

$\frac{00}{P}$ = ratio of actual representation of each occupation among officers
to probable representation

among the more traditional occupations, the village chiefs and "men of
religion" not to mention farmers were all underrepresented. We can
conclude that there is some evidence here for the limited and not surprising findings that the free professions are less evenly distributed but
more highly regarded for political purposes than are the occupations
associated with government employment such as teaching and civil

service. It is also apparent that the free professions are more highly regarded and a more effective base for gaining political power where they are in the smallest supply. Access to those professions is hard to achieve, and therefore the prestige associated with these professions may derive from the economic or cultural resources of the families who were able to acquire such an expensive education for at least one of their sons.

The occupational categories employed in the National Union data are so general that they are inappropriate as indicators of social stratification. The designation "agriculturist" or farmer does not differentiate among landless laborers, smallholders, tenants, rich peasants, plantation owners, and the rest. The term civil servant does not differentiate among postal clerks, bureau chiefs, and deputy ministers. Furthermore, occupation is only occasionally informative regarding the education of the relevant individual and even less frequently does it suggest the amount of property which the individual owns. Despite these limitations,

Table 8   Significance Test of Occupational Distribution for Agricultural Province Officers

Occupation	Ratio	Error	Minimum Significant Ratio
High official	17.8 : 1	11.8	5.0
Cabinet minister	8.0 : 1	6.8	.2
Doctor	4.1 : 1	2.0	1.1
Lawyer	3.8 : 1	1.5	1.3
Businessman	3.9 : 1	1.9	1.0
Teacher	0.4 : 1	1.1	0.0
Former M.P.	29.2 : 1	3.0	25.2
Engineer	2.2 : 1	1.5	0.0
Merchant	0.6 : 1	1.1	0.0
Student	0.0 : 1	1.0	0.0
Journalist	0.0 : 1	1.4	0.0
Ex-army officer	7.5 : 1	4.4	2.1
Ex-police officer	8.5 : 1	4.8	2.7
Civil servant	1.1 : 1	1.2	0.0
Worker	0.0 : 1	1.1	0.0
Woman	1.6 : 1	2.6	0.0
Unknown (urban)	0.0 : 1	2.4	0.0
Local council member	4.3 : 1	1.8	1.5
Man of religion	0.3 : 1	1.2	0.0
ʿUmdah or shaykh	0.7 : 1	1.1	0.0
Farmer	0.3 : 1	1.0	0.0
Unknown (rural)	0.4 : 1	1.1	0.0

we cannot dismiss the discrepancies between the occupational composition of the National Union and that of the labor force as without meaning, for it is no accident that the occupational categories employed by
the National Union do not readily lend themselves to an analysis of the
class basis of that organization.

As we have seen, liberals and Marxists alike stress the significance
of the middle sectors, the cadres, the rural middle class, and the petite
bourgeoisie not merely as part of a ruling elite, but for their role in a
dynamic process of transition to either liberal democracy or socialism.
From the point of view of the regime, the National Union was not to
be an instrument of class domination, but rather a model or a representative of the whole nation. The reason why the occupations of the committee members were listed was in order to demonstrate that all classes
were indeed represented. The spirit in which stratification was approached was that of harmonizing diverse groups and affirming the
Egyptian gemeinschaft. Stratification was not seen as processual, dynamic nor as essentially transitive.

There is, of course, considerable difference in the ideological, and
hence definitional, designations of class between liberal and Marxist
theorists. Among those concerned with Egyptian affairs, liberal economists and other social scientists have preferred to use labor force statistics, landownership statistics, and categorizations by productive sector
(primary, secondary, etc.) without reference to class. Marxist writers
have been more inclined to make risky leaps from this kind of data to
the allocation of Egyptians to various social classes. Western liberal
observers use this sort of occupational data to measure economic development while Marxists are trying to measure both economic development and the exacerbation of class conflict. It may therefore be
expected that each side will tend to distort or ignore data that conflicts
with their expectations, or, if the data is of dubious validity or non-
existent, they may propose "educated" guesses which accord with their
own educational experiences. In point of fact, the weakness of the data
on occupational and social stratification and the great differences in
the interpretation of the social history of Egypt after the 1952 revolution pose a continuing challenge to the governmental statistical institute,
which, unfortunately, fell under the sway of the secret police.

In comparing the occupational composition of the National Union
with a composite of labor force statistics and with at least one Marxist
classification scheme, no attempt is being made to offer a definitive
analysis of Egyptian social classes (table 9). Nor should it be thought
that a collation of diverse schemata will provide us with a "moderate,"
nonideological, consensus on the matter. On the contrary, the labor

Chapter Two

Table 9 — Class and Occupations

National Union 1959 Occupational Distribution		Labor Force Statistics, Various Sources 1957/58		Mahmoud Hussein's Contending Classes 1950s	
1. *Political Elite*					
High official	.06%	Higher bureaucracy			
Cabinet member	.09	(grades 3 to minister)	.12%		
	.15		.12		
2. *Haute Bourgeoisie*					
Businessman	1.21	Managerial official	.83	"Big Bourgeoisie"	.88%
		Industrial firms	.05		
		Commercial firms	1.82		
	1.21		2.70		.88
3. *Professionals*					
Doctor	.87	Doctor	.16		
Lawyer	2.87	Lawyer	.11		
Engineer	1.98	Other professional	1.21		
	5.72		1.48		
4. *Educated Middle Class*					
Civil servant	7.40	Civil servant	1.14	Cadres	2.27
Teacher	9.80	Teacher	1.40		
Journalist	.18	Employee (private sector)	1.73		
Man of religion	1.57				
	18.95		4.27		2.27
5. *Merchants*					
Merchant	8.38	Small merchant	2.12	Traditional entrepreneur	2.72
	8.38		2.12		2.72
6. *Working Class*					
Worker	1.33	Industrial worker	14.77	Proletariat	3.00
		Transportation worker	2.98	Subproletariat	.70
		Retail employee	5.68	Unskilled worker	1.50
		Service employee	7.57	Minor employee	4.14
				Servant	3.70
				Urban unemployed	11.00
	1.33		31.00		24.04
7. *Rural Classes*					
Local council member	1.10	Owning less than: 1 feddan	32.16	Less than 1 feddan	3.98
ᶜUmdah	18.93	1-5 feddan	10.00	Petty bourgeoisie	10.55
Farmer	36.36	5-10 feddan	1.23	Rich peasant	3.24
Unknown occupation	5.21	10-20 feddan	.74	More than 20 feddan	.55
		Landless	13.31	Landless	51.85
	61.60%		57.97%		70.17%
Total	97.34%		99.66%		100.08%

force data[7] tends to justify the structure of the National Union and may even have been used, in part, to "construct" the National Union. The Marxist schema is a device for criticizing the regime and its policies.[8]

These divergences do not, however, make the task of comparison hopeless. There is also a certain amount of categorical convergence, as we should also expect, given that the various protagonists are discussing the same phenomena. Most observers concur in dividing Egyptian class structure into rural and urban segments. There is, furthermore, broad agreement with regard to the urban middle classes. Many analysts would divide these middle strata into three or four groups including the petite bourgeoisie of petty traders, craftsmen, and employees, the educated middle class of functionaries (civil servants), professionals and military officers, and the haute bourgeoisie. Some would separate the professionals from the bureaucracy and the military.

There is less agreement about the rural classes. Generally, rural stratification is based on the size of landholding, but Hasan Riad would add trees, machinery, and improvements, or cash to finance entrepreneurial renting as capital. There are differences of opinion regarding the coincidence of intervals between rural strata and particular sizes of holding. Usually 5 feddan has been taken as the prototypical smallholding below which it is culturally and economically undesirable to go. Some Egyptian leftists believe that 2.5–3 feddan is usually enough to support a family. Hence, they assert that those who hold 5 feddan or more are actually members of the agrarian middle class, while those who hold less are members of the agrarian proletariat.

While it is doubtful that this synthetic estimate of the size and composition of the Egyptian labor force in 1957/58 is accurate, these data, drawn from a variety of official and semiofficial sources, appear to provide a reasonable approximation. Since the size of families throughout Egypt is roughly the same and since women are employed in small numbers, the labor force statistics may be taken as a rough guide to class membership. From these data we can estimate the urban upper middle class at roughly 4.5%. The critical lower middle class might be estimated at about 6.5% of the total population. The lower classes, agricultural and nonagricultural, come to more than 85%. The rural middle and upper classes are notable for their small size—between 1.5 and 3.5%, depending upon the definition used. The labor force determination of the size of the proletariat is surprisingly large and in sharp contrast with the Mahmoud Hussein estimate or the representation of the working class in the National Union. If correct, these data suggest that the Marxist lament regarding the immature character of Egyptian class structure was unwarranted. It may well be that too many of the proletariat, subproletariat, and minor employees were located in rural areas or in small towns and were therefore not sufficiently class conscious from the Marxist perspective. This may have been the fault of the feudally oriented notables or of the pedantic communists themselves.[9] Nevertheless, Egypt was socially far more "transitional" than indicated by Mahmoud Hussein's analysis. It is, furthermore, evident that the bourgeoisie has a more rational understanding of the political potential of the Egyptian working classes than have some Marxist theoreticians.

Mahmoud Hussein departs from the usual classification system by including urban and rural groups which he calls the "proletarianized masses." Essentially these are the unemployed, the underemployed, and the landless. The greatest difficulty that we have with Hussein's breakdown is that he does not differentiate between male and female nor between young children and the working age population. A substantial proportion of his unemployed and landless categories include those who are not "heads of households" and many under fifteen years old. There are other discrepancies, too, for Hussein greatly exaggerates the number of landless peasants, while the labor force statistics disregard many of the urban unemployed. Hussein leaves out the small but important governmental elite as well as the politically significant professionals and he underestimates both the subproletariat and the proletariat. It is evident that he has also underestimated the number of fellaheen owning a fraction of a feddan. In general, Hussein has underestimated the urban segment of the labor force and he has overestimated the size of the rural "proletarianized masses." Mahmoud Abdel Fadil argues that the estimate of Samir Amin (alias Hasan Riad), on which Mahmoud Hussein based his own guess on the size of the landless agricultural labor group, was off by two million. Abdel Fadil holds that the total agricultural population was 16 million rather than 19 million, thus accounting for the discrepancy.[10] Apparently, the rural "proletarianized masses" were a residual group. Nevertheless, Hussein's separate designation of the class of owners of more than 20 feddan is strongly supported by what appears to be the quite objective study by Abdel Fadil.[11]

When we compare the National Union data on occupations with the labor force data, we find, despite efforts to make it appear that the National Union represented all classes and despite the opaque quality of a merely statistical analysis, that many groups are grossly underrepresented. Women, industrial workers, students, landless labor and others were hardly represented at all. For the most part, National Union members were drawn from the educated middle class, the "middle" and "rich" peasantry, the professionals and the merchants, representing about 10% of the labor force.

These data strongly suggest the political use to which the National Union was put. The occupational breakdown of the members of the National Union committees enhanced the representation of "safe" elements while gaining the legitimacy that followed from the appearance that all classes were represented. This end was achieved, primarily, by exaggerating the representation of the rural middle class and asserting that they represented all agrarian classes. By contrast, Mahmoud Hussein's criticism of the revolution is most strongly expressed in his minimization of the size of the proletariat. This analytical approach leads him into hopeless ideological confusion, however, when he tries to assure us and himself that Egypt is, nevertheless, ripe for a Maoist revolution. Presumably that revolution will be accomplished by the spontaneous outburst of the proletarianized masses.

Three

Traditionally Influential Families

Une trentaine de noms se répar-
tissent ainsi la communauté. Chacun
couvre un groupe qui possède son
habitat et dispose, si l'on peut dire,
d'un équipement économique et
rituel. L'établissement de ces groupes
. . . se mesure en siècles.

Jacques Berque, *Histoire sociale d'un
village égyptien au XXème siècle*

The ubiquity and historical persistence of a segment of rural influentials is the characteristic political-sociological feature of modern Egypt. The importance of the 'umdah or of the middle-sized landholders has been frequently remarked, and it is all too easy to draw an analogy with the English gentry, the French *coqs de paroisse*, or the Russian *kulaks*. The significance and the political role of each of these types varies with the structure of rural society and with the political opportunity structure in which they find themselves.[1] It is, furthermore, misleading to think of these people as a class, least of all as a ruling class. Their peculiar role is always, it seems to me, one of sustaining, resisting, mediating, interpreting or transforming power. They are not always passive instruments, but their power is usually local, their solidarity cultural, and their political aspirations oriented to the microtimocratic. In a sense, they are ideal members of parliament—the parliaments of notables described by Duverger.[2] They are only loosely bound by party, have but a vague sense of ideological commitment, disdain organization, and count votes in terms of traditional deference patterns. The political salience of such groups has everywhere been a passing phase, for while people of this type retain a modicum of influence in many countries, they and their rural settings have changed so much that often their importance now resides in the explanatory significance of their previous existence for understanding the contemporary political configuration.

There is no validated theory that can tell us, prior to any empirical investigation, what the political significance of a group of rural influentials will be. Their significance depends upon their characteristics and upon their setting—and this would likely be the case even if the existence of such a group were a necessity. But it is not a necessity, and therefore its existence as a significant political phenomenon in contemporary Egypt must be established. Existence and significance are both stressed, for in dealing with a sociopolitical category of this type, we are not merely concerned with its existence "for us," but its empirical incontrovertibility. This empirical "tangibility" is to be described both statistically and in terms of important political consequences.

The importance of the rural notables might well have been expected from reading Rafi'i's history, the Earl of Cromer's *Modern Egypt*, Landau's *Parliaments and Parties in Egypt*, or Vatikiotis's *The Egyptian Army in Politics*; but the impressionistic discussion of the rural middle class in these and many other works provides no operable empirical referents that might be used in rigorous analysis. The definition of the rural notable remains loose and inexact. There is uncertainty about how much land he must have, about the nature of his traditional role and authority, and about his relationship to the 'amudiyyah (office of the 'umdah). Landau describes the notables as wealthy.[3] Cromer saw them as well-to-do gentry.[4] Baer is concerned to explain the "dissolution of the village community" in terms of the decline of the economic and administrative functions of the 'umdah[5] while Berque writes that one of the major questions of Egyptian sociology is whence the cohesiveness of the village? Berque suggests that the answer may be found in "La façon dont le village se dirige, et les hiérarchies internes qu'il reconnaît."[6] Baer believes that the position of the village shaykh fluctuated in importance over the last century, experiencing "a tremendous rise under Isma'il; a decline during the British occupation . . . ; and a further decline under the constitutional monarchy (except for the shaykh's political power, which was bolstered by the parliamentary system)."[7] Berque, by contrast, emphasizes the patriarchal power of the shaykhs and their clan-based authority as symbolized in their maintenance of and presiding over the clan duwwar and madyafa (guest houses).[8] By contrast, Mahmud 'Awda, in discussing the rural notables declares that, "During the nineteenth and the first half of the twentieth centuries, the rural population was clearly divided into two opposed segments, the rich notable families and the simple peasant families."[9]

It is, in fact, possible to discern in the literature at least four perspectives on the rural notability, each with its own limited observational base, each with its own political-ideological inclination, and each with its own interpretation of the implication of recent changes in the status and the role of that rural notability. None of these views is wrong, but one has the sense that each represents only that part of the elephant's anatomy rendered accessible by the observer's method of inquiry. Baer's historical method emphasizes the administrative regulations and economic policies of the various governments of Egypt, and his historical analysis describes the secular decline in the administrative and economic functions of the village shaykh over the last century. Baer attributes this decline to two developments. The first was the enrichment of the 'umdah in the period of Isma'il and after, resulting in the removal of many village shuyukh to the city. The second was the restriction of the administrative authority of the 'umdah under the British. The first development compelled the appointment of less affluent village worthies as 'umad, and the second prevented those who were appointed from enriching themselves. Baer concludes: "The large landowning 'umda, so frequent in the days of Isma'il, became a rare sight in mid-twentieth century Egypt."[10]

Berque's view is based on his anthropological orientation, and he finds clan organization and traditional cultural patterns the central feature of the village he studied. Berque describes the village as a collection of families or clans of diverse size, each linked to the others in a system of spatial, lineage, ritual, and economic relations. The larger of these clans, numbering hundreds, are more or less dominated by the authority of affluent elders, the patriarchs of the traditionally most-respected families. These leaders are the rural notables, and they have traditionally controlled all aspects of village life as well as the external relations of the village. The traditional patterns and identifications are changing, but modern influences have not destroyed the family. Berque writes: "Bien que menacées par la montée des forces et des formes nouvelles, les familles sont encore puissantes. Elles ont gardé, tout au long du dernier demi-siècle, le pouvoir réel. Il s'exprimait, tour a tour ou simultanément, sous les espèces de l'instruction, de la fortune, ou de l'action politique."[11]

Berque's view is largely sustained by Hamed Ammar, another anthropologist. Ammar's purpose was to describe the socialization of the young, but he does give a brief description of the social, economic, and political order of Silwa village. Unlike many villages in the delta, Silwa, in Aswan, was not highly stratified. Furthermore, Ammar describes (and Baer quotes) the economic, administrative, and status decline of the 'umdah.[12] Nevertheless, Ammar affirms the significance of kinship ties in political, social, and some economic relationships. For example, in politics,

> There is strong evidence that kinship relations, and not party politics, decide the issue of the elections in this community. [P. 47]

And in social structure,

> This pattern of social structure does not apply merely to the Silwa community and the G'afra, but applies in varying degrees to the whole province of Aswan, and in many other provinces that are known to the writer in upper Egypt. In all this, the bond of common descent in family connections is one of the strongest factors as well as the most socially effective force in the social structure. [P. 48]

But in economic structure,

> The writer is under the impression, from his general observation, that the extended family seems to be stronger and more effective as an economic unit amongst bigger landowning families, as distinct from what obtains in Silwa, a community of small owners. [P. 44, n.1]

The third perspective may be described as individualistic and pluralistic, employing the methods of survey research and the intellectual perspective of social psychology. The two most important relevant works are Luwis Kamil Malikah's study of the same village that Berque observed, and Iliya Harik's study of a village near Damanhur. Malikah does not indicate that he knew of or was influenced in any way by Berque's research. Harik's study was, in part, influenced by the sociometric methodology of the Malikah work. Malikah's research was accomplished in 1960 and Harik's in 1967 and 1968. Among other academic purposes, Malikah was concerned to describe the structure of the village in order to assist government "field workers" in bringing about the changes sought by the regime. Harik described the subsequent bureaucratic and media penetration of the village and the changes achieved. Both take a favorable view of the government's mobilizing efforts and both are optimistic about the growth of democratic, individualistic, interest maximizing, participatory attitudes among the villagers. Both describe the decline of the political influence of the traditionally influential families and they describe the new bases of political influence in terms of personality characteristics, problem solving capacities, education, and social skills. Both minimize the significance of class differences in the villages they studied.

Malikah does not find evidence of intense political competition. Unlike Berque, he identifies only one important "family," which comprised 28.4% of his research sample.[13] This family had dominated village life, and had controlled the 'amudiyyah until recently. The "Shaykh" family lost the 'amudiyyah to Mr. "Manufi," who had been deputy 'umdah and acting 'umdah, because he was deemed more capable, more responsive to the needs of the villagers, and more personable.[14] Malikah argues that "Manufi's" election signifies (*a*) the decline of nonrational family ties and the growth of pragmatic and community-interest oriented attitudes; and (*b*) that the new leadership has attained its current position as the result of a multiplicity of personality and policy factors, including its concern to involve the largest number of citizens in village affairs.[15]

Malikah states that these are hopeful tendencies, but he does not refer them to two anomalous findings. His sociograms reveal that while "Manufi" is the center of the largest social network in the village, the second, third, and fourth largest networks are led by members of the "Shaykh" family.[16] The largest network is not described in terms of its component families, though it must represent a partial coalition of the smaller families, which comprised more than 70% of the research sample. The second and more important anomaly is Malikah's attribution of an oligarchical or "power elite" structure to the village leaders despite his individualistic and pluralistic biases. The various sociograms reveal that the village elite tended to select one another as members of the power, influence, and affective elites of the village.[17] This leads Malikah to speculate whether this mutual selection is caused by the "extension of or vestiges of the previous class thinking."[18] Malikah concludes that there is a mutual selection process among the elite which suggests that they look upon one another as members of a single group. Malikah, citing Hunter and Homans, evidently believes that the mutually supportive behavior of the village elite is modern and rational rather than a reflection of traditional class attitudes. Malikah finds that economic stratification is not an important factor in determining elite roles.[19]

Harik's village has felt the full impact of bureaucratic, political, and economic intervention under the socialist reforms of the 1960s. He reports that the government's efforts diffused political leadership, dispersed economic resources, encouraged popular political participation, and diminished the alienation of the peasant from the revolutionary leadership.[20] This village, which he calls Shubra al-Jadida, had no middle-sized landowners, but it did have several large landholdings owned by absentees and by two residents. Even though one of the two major social clusters revealed by Harik's sociograms is centered upon one of the resident large landowners, Harik denies the significance of traditional family influence in Shubra in 1967.[21] He also denies that there was a mutually supportive oligarchy or power elite or that social class counted for anything.[22] The competitive and only temporarily ascendant leaders are often described in terms of their personal characteristics.[23]

Harik draws the extreme conclusion that, "In Shubra, the political system has, by and large, replaced the kinship system."[24]

> These observations suggest that any effort to make sense of the current Shubra scene has to focus on individuals rather than on social classes or primary groups. The sense of social superiority recently acquired by some individuals has been the product of personal achievements such as skill, education and political involvement or rank . . . neither the size of landownership nor family background account for differences found in the political attitudes of villagers toward social esteem and political participation.[25]

The fourth perspective on the village notability is expressed in the writings of Mahmud 'Awda, in the books of Hasan Riad and Mahmoud Hussein, and in the columns of *al-Tali'ah* magazine. This view holds that the notables were an exploiting class and not the patriarchal leaders of the large clans referred to by Berque. The leftist writers do not generally discuss lineage structure in detail, preferring to base their analysis of rural exploitation on economic and political structure, rather than upon traditional culture. In this predilection, they are joined at least by Harik in distinguishing between the "landowning family" and Berque's "family of identity." In a very perceptive passage, Harik wrote,

> The term "landowning family" . . . is often used without precision in Egypt to refer to a group varying in size from the nuclear family to a larger group, including paternal uncles and second cousins but not including all the members of a patrilineal kinship group. The Samads, for instance, are known in Shubra and in the district as a landowning family, but only five individuals of more than 100 carrying the surname Samad were landlords.[26]

Leftist observers are, however, likely to disagree with Harik's assessment of the nature of the political influence of the rival landowning family. Some of the votes for the Kura family "also came from employees on their estate, estimated in 1967 to be about 160 persons during the peak season. These, however, were not clients; they were wage laborers in a free labor market and had no personal relations with their employers that would entail responsibility and dependency."[27] For the leftist writers, and for many liberal critics of the Nasser regime, the continued disparity in landownership and in the access to capital for purposes of agricultural exploitation, defines rural class structure and has significant political consequences. Hence, the specification of the size of landholding and the role in agricultural production is an indispensable part of the interpretation of rural politics as class struggle.

Writing about the situation in 1959, Hasan Riad estimated that the rural population of Egypt was about 19 million persons.[28] He stated that there were about one million holdings or farms owned by one million families averaging five persons each.[29] The rest, comprising 74% of the population, were landless and were employed less than one third of the time. Riad's figure of 10 million landless laborers available in the labor market with no more than 3 million jobs available accords with Ibrahim 'Amr's estimate of over 2.5 million full or part time hired agricultural laborers in 1952.[30]

The next group above the landless laborers are owners of less than one feddan, called simply poor farmers by 'Amr.[31] Riad estimates their number at 215,000 families, or 5% of the rural population. This size holding is not enough to support a family nor to maintain a grown male laborer in full employment for a year. Many poor peasant owners will accept wage employment when it is available.

Riad then describes as a middle income group those owning or working from one to five feddan. Those owning less than three (for an average size family of five) are in constant economic difficulty while those owning about five feddan usually hire seasonal workers to help them with the planting and harvesting. ('Amr refers to Riad's intermediate group, approximately 15% of the rural population, as only the *lowest* level of his three-level category of middle income peasants.)

For Riad, all those who own or work more than five feddan are members of the "privileged" rural classes. These number 217,000 families, or 5% of the rural population. They own or work 76% of the agricultural land with the aid of hired labor, and they "earn" 65% of the agricultural revenue.[32] (Most of those whom Riad refers to as privileged are included in 'Amr's and in Baer's middle group.)

The first of Riad's privileged agricultural classes exploit (owning or not) from 5 to 20 feddan.[33] He suggests that the renters might be called kulaks and the owners petty feudalists, but concludes that both are rooted in village life and are true peasants.

The second of Riad's privileged groups exploits more than 20 feddan, uses capital, if sparingly, engages in marketing, transport, and other commercial activities connected with their agricultural production, and generally lives in the town or city. The third group also owns more than 20 feddan, works part of the land directly and rents the rest, but often maintains a home in the village. Riad states that the upper strata of this group, owners of more than 200 feddan, comprised the landed aristocracy which the revolution has tried to deprive of political influence.[34]

In general, 'Amr is more concerned with the connection between types of agricultural activity and political consciousness than he is with distributive shares of agricultural income. Nevertheless, he is also interested in the impact of cultural affinities across class lines on political consciousness. 'Amr distinguishes among three kinds of middle peasant, two kinds of rich peasant, and between these and agricultural rentiers. The rentiers are most condemned, but they are not distinguished by size of holding. They include wealthy absentees, town merchants, and even civil servants and professionals living in the cities, as well as the government itself, all of whom rent land to the peasant and exploit his labor.[35] The rich peasants are not described in terms of size of holding either but rather are differentiated qualitatively and politically in terms of whether they produce raw materials for export or commodities for local, direct consumption. These rich peasants or agricultural entrepreneurs (and 'Amr suggests both) are allied to local finance capital and are only reluctantly competitive with imperialist interests. The two upper classes of the middle peasants are distinguished in that the highest receives a surplus and its members are always striving to enrich themselves while the second is self-sufficient but its members are constantly aware of the ever worsening conditions which make it more difficult for them to maintain their status.[36] It is evident that this middle peasant group was thought to have important political potential.

Both Baer and Riad point out that the relative size of the middle landowning group did not decline through the first half of the twentieth century, even though 'Amr cited the downward economic and social pressure on the lowest of the middle groups as the cause of their political activism and their opposition to the regime and its imperialist allies.[37] Mahmud 'Awda explained the origin of the middle group as the consequence of the distribution through inheritance of large estates. He further shows that the percent of middle holdings has declined even though the average size holding has remained constant. 'Awda does not attribute deeper or more authentic village roots to the middle owners. 'Amr's description lacks the specificity of reference to size of holdings that Riad offers, and neither is very clear about whether the wealthier groups have strong cultural and familial connections with the village.

For Riad, it appears that the group most closely connected with the village is the lowest of the privileged classes:

> Malgré leur hétérogénéité, les classes privilégiées sont solidaires sur le plan politique. De tous temps, les *omdeh*, les maires de village nommés par l'administration, ont été recrutés parmi les propriétaires d'exploitation de 5 à 20 feddans. Comme il n'y a généralement pas plus d'une ou deux familles de cette catégorie par village, l'intégration de cette sous-catégorie dans le système politique général est presque parfaite . . . . [38]

In his history of landownership in Egypt, Baer makes a fairly clear distinction between those who became large landowners in the nineteenth century as a consequence of their prerogatives as 'umad and those who were the recipients of royal grants or who purchased (generally uncultivated) land from the government. It would appear that many 'umad became owners of hundreds of feddan up through the 1870s, but a variety of forces broke this trend and brought about a considerable reduction in the size of these holdings.[39]

Baer makes a most important distinction in this way: "The higher officials' large estates were, as we have seen, created chiefly by means of grants from the ruler. Not so the landed property of village notables. This group owed its origin chiefly to the process of differentiation within the village itself, and was made at the expense of the fellah holdings."[40] But after the British introduced a new administrative system, and as a result of the division through inheritance, "Most 'umdas today are medium landowners with properties of 10 to 50 feddans."[41]

Following Baer, large landowners may be divided into two groups, the first having its origin in the village or in the settled tribe, and the second having its social origin in some urban setting. The first group was comprised of 'umad and shuyukh, and they emerged into positions of influence and wealth in the nineteenth century. Most of the members of this group have declined in property, wealth, and status, and many have removed to Cairo and Alexandria—but not all of them have lost their rural elite status. The second group may be further divided into two: those who acquired large holdings before the British occupation and those who acquired them afterward. The first group was composed of officials, servants of the court and members of the royal family, while the second group included an increasing number of entrepreneurs, merchants, and speculators, who purchased large estates. The latter group included foreigners and members of the minorities as well as Egyptian capitalists, rentiers, and officials, too. A substantial portion of the largest estates were investments held by joint stock corporations.

It seems apparent that there are or were such people as rural notables, but it is equally clear that different persons in different places and
at different times might qualify as such in the eyes of particular observers. The personal characteristics, social composition, and political
and economic roles of those who might be called a'yan, shuyukh, or
the rural bourgeoisie in all of their observed diversity are admitted, in
addition, to have changed. Each of the four perspectives or paradigms
that we have examined is based on empirical evidence of some sort, on
documents, on questionnaires, or on aggregate statistics. Each presents
a partial reality which serves only to enhance its ideological character
and to sharpen the challenge to objective analysis. The issues involved
are, moreover, of central significance in determining whether the regime
is a tutelary dictatorship on the road to democracy or simply a military
oligarchy; or whether it is a national and popular movement on the
noncapitalist path of development or simply a collection of administrative fiefdoms directed by the "new class." These issues have not been
resolved by reference to social and economic statistics, to macrohistory,
or to microcultural observation.

It might be preferable to start with some empirical unit of analysis
which would be of such manifest relevance for structures of rival political influence that the measurement and comparison of such units might
be used to test the arguments presented in these four paradigms and
their related developmental theories. One obvious starting point would
be to examine the social composition of the National Union committees
to see whether it was possible to discern a political elite which could be
characterized as a distinctive social type, as a social formation, or as of
a particular class. Although occupation alone was of limited value in
analyzing the political character of the National Union committees, a
preliminary examination of the National Union lists did reveal an alternative feature which offered the possibility of an analytical break-
through, even if of an unconventional sort.

It was noticed that, in some of the village committee lists, several
of the committee members had similar names. It was hypothesized that,
if those with similar names were from the same family, the presence of
two or more members of the same family in a village committee might
be the consequence of the persistence of the traditional influence of
rural notables in that village. Much of the remainder of this book is
devoted to testing that hypothesis, to providing an empirical definition
of the social, economic, and geographical characteristics of the stratum
thus identified, and to applying the resultant data configuration to a
critique of the self-presentation of the regime in the light of rival, non-
indigenous theoretical interpretations of Egyptian politics.

In the lists for the sixteen agricultural provinces, and generally for the villages rather than the district centers, it was found that, with some frequency, two or more members had quite similar names. Egyptians do not use last names, although occasionally they may employ a family name which refers to a trade, a locality, a distinguished ancestor, or something of that sort. Usually a person is known by three "first" names: his own, followed by that of his father and then that of his father's father.[42] A great many names listed in the register of the National Union included a fourth element, probably referring to the paternal great-grandfather. Not infrequently, one of the equivalents of a family name (i.e., a nisbah) might be added as a fifth element.

Clan names (laqab) are also sometimes used in Egypt, and a single clan might include a large part of the population of a village.[43] Generally, however, clan names are not recorded in the National Union register. Members of the committees evidently preferred to identify themselves in ways that would more easily distinguish them from their neighbors. Only on a very few occasions did it appear that a single family so dominated the village committee that it was possible that we were dealing with a clan name and not a family name. The distinction is important, for if a large clan has two or more seats on the village committee, that may indicate no more than that the clan is proportionately represented on the committee. If a family, even a large one, is represented by two or more committee members, we have a strong prima facie case for the belief that such a family is politically influential in the village.

In some villages it may be sheer coincidence that two members of a single family were elected, while, in other villages, two family members may not have stood for office. Nevertheless, it seems that there is a significant variation by province, by occupation, and by other characteristics, of those who appear to come from the same family. There is empirical support for the view that the members of committees who are related to one another are not randomly chosen representatives of large village clans since their occupations and prestigeful positions make it clear that they are at least leading members of the clan.

There are, in fact, two broad categories of name groupings included in the designation "family." In the first of these there are identical names in the second (father) and third (grandfather) position with or without any "family" name. Such persons are probably brothers. In these and similar cases (e.g., names are moved up one position) we know that the relationship is of the first degree. In the second category there is a distinctive "family" name with perhaps only one other similar "given name," or there are nominal elements that are frequently used by Egyptian families as a set for brothers or for father and son. In the end, after much study of the list of names, and after a good deal of consultation, it was decided to define as members of the same family (to the exclusion of the other members of that National Union committee) those who had a number of identical nominal elements, usually two or more, to give us confidence that they were closely related. The data were examined by three different persons and only those agreed to by all three were accepted. We only considered persons listed on the same village committee, excluding those from neighboring areas as more likely distant clan members or even having coincidentally similar names. To further ensure no exaggeration of this group, we excluded all those cases in which there was no decisive evidence and those in which the similar names were very common ones. It is likely that many related committee members, especially those related on the maternal side, were missed, but probably very few unrelated groups were identified as related. That brothers, sons, cousins and other close relatives were actually on the same village committee is further corroborated by interviews, by independent data such as obituary notices, and by the fact that membership of two or more close kin in a basic unit committee was expressly prohibited by a Socialist Union regulation of 1968.

We proceed then with the notion that those persons having significantly similar names who are members of the same village committees are closely related to one another. It is further hypothesized in a preliminary way that such persons are members of a family which is influential in village affairs. This hypothesis is also confirmed by interviews with well informed persons. In some cases, not many to be sure, more than one set of members who were related were found. In nearly all cases, the majority of the members of the committees were not members of these families. While there might be many more individual members from notable families, those families that were able to get two or more members on the village committee would seem to be more influential or more politically effective. Hereafter, two or more members of the same family who were members of the same basic unit committee will be referred to as a "family set."

The minimum set of family members was, of course, two. The largest set was ten. In the sixteen agricultural provinces, of the total committee membership of 27,936 there were 2,223 family sets comprising 5,498 individuals. The 2,223 family sets were found among a total of 4,191 villages and towns throughout the whole country, but, of course, these were not evenly distributed. The average village committee was made up of almost seven members. In a bit more than half of the committees there was a family set, usually composed of two closely related committee members. More significantly yet, of the 559 district officers in the agricultural provinces, 249 were members of family sets; and of the 249 former M.P.'s, 110 were members of family sets. Members of family sets made up 43% of district officers and 44% of all former M.P.'s, even though members of family sets comprise just under 20% of the total membership. There would seem to be a strong inferential basis for the conclusion that individual members, operationally defined as members of family sets, are influential in their own villages and members of a middle level elite segment with prestige and/or influence at the district and at the national level.

These dimensions of elite status converge further in that 71 members of the National Union committees were former members of the National Assembly and also district officers and also members of family sets. Hence, 64% of all former M.P.'s who were members of locally influential families were also district officers. While only 12% of all officers were both former M.P.'s and members of family sets, nearly 29% of the officers in family sets were former M.P.'s, and 41% of officers who were former M.P.'s were members of family sets.

Presumably, these 71 individuals who enjoy all three statuses, family-set membership, district officeholding, and former membership in parliament, are the most influential, or have the most prestige of all members of the village committees in the sixteen agricultural provinces of the National Union. Still, not all family-set members are officers, and not all officers are former M.P.'s. It would appear that it is possible to have party or parliamentary elite status without being a member of a locally influential family or, more likely, that not all influential families elected more than one member to the village committee. There are also many family sets that did not place one of their members in district office nor in parliament. There were 2,223 family sets and only 657 persons were chosen as district officers, M.P.'s, or both.

These statistics do not show whether there is a particular subset of family sets which enjoys elite status, or whether the elite status is to be attributed to the family set as a general class from which party and political elites are selected. I am inclined to accept the latter, broader, sociological interpretation, and not only on the basis of collateral knowledge, interviewing, and general familiarity with the situation, but because the probabilistic logic on which statistical inference is based strongly supports that view. Both the number of district officers and the number of members of parliament are limited by conventional constraints such as the number of districts, the relative population of provinces, and the optimum size of a district bureau and a national parliament. The number of family sets is determined by historical and social processes and not by convention.

If we accept this reasoning, however, we need to explain why some officers and some former M.P.'s are not found in family sets. It seems that not every family set has been turned up by our screening procedures, that there may even be one or more influential families in every village, that where there is more than one influential family they may have tended to cancel out one another's prominence, and that in smaller villages with smaller committees it was less likely that even an influential family would get two or more seats. An alternative explanation is simply that not all members of these party and parliamentary elites are drawn from this social elite, a conclusion which is not surprising. Both explanations are probably true for the most part.

Analysis of the occupational distribution of the membership of the village committees of the National Union failed to produce clear occupational indicators of elite status. In examining the significance of the family set as an indicator of elite status, we have established that family-set membership and status as a former member of the National Assembly or as a district officer correlate strongly. The occupations of family-set members may define the economic and class interests of the second stratum. As the analysis of family-set occupations proceeds, it should become clear that membership in a family set alone or identification with a given occupation alone are insufficient indicators of social position; nor, if taken in the aggregate, are they sufficient indicators of the broader pattern of social structure. This pattern will be revealed by an accumulation of several elements: occupation, traditional status, geographical location, sociohistorical continuities, and regional economic structure—all of which are to be plotted against party and parliamentary elite standing.

In table 10 the frequencies of all occupations among all members of the village committees of the National Union are compared with the occupations of members of family sets, and those absolute frequencies are converted into percentages. The base for all members has been changed to include only the members for the sixteen agricultural provinces, or 27,936. Family-set members, over 19% of the total, constitute a sufficiently large number to impose few statistical constraints on direct comparison of the percentages in each column. Furthermore, there being no institutional or a priori limit on the number in family sets, but simply a limitation of the evidence available to us, it need not be assumed that the size of the total number of members of family sets has had a

Table 10   Distribution of Occupations for All
                                      NU Members and for Members of
                                      Family Sets

Occupation	All Members		Family-Set Members	
	Number	Percentage	Number	Percentage
Doctor	197	.7	36	.7
Lawyer	739	2.6	205	3.7
Engineer	518	1.9	160	2.9
Teacher	2,773	9.9	364	6.6
Civil servant	1,945	7.0	410	7.5
Merchant	2,206	7.9	259	4.7
Businessman	219	.8	45	.8
Man of religion	450	1.6	59	1.1
Student	382	1.4	82	1.5
ꜥUmdah	5,473	19.6	1,540	28.0
Shaykh	--	--	57	1.0
Worker	311	1.1	32	.6
Farmer	10,632	38.1	1,837	33.4
Former M.P.	249	.9	110	2.0
Local council member	316	1.1	88	1.6
Army	33	.1	12	.2
Police	33	.1	8	.1
Unknown	1,432	5.1	177	3.2
Rare	8	.0	8	.1
Cabinet member	20	.1	9	.2
Total	27,936[a]	100.0	5,498	99.9

[a]This total will vary slightly depending on whether we use the official totals or summations of our analyzed breakdowns.

limiting effect on the distribution of occupations among family-set members in our "sample."

Once again, a familiar pattern emerges. Former members of parliament are strongly represented among family sets, establishing a firm link between the party and parliamentary elites. Note that all of those designated as having rare occupations, usually a high administrative post but not a cabinet ministry, are members of family sets; and nearly half of the cabinet ministers are in family sets. Table 11 presents the percentage of each occupation among the family members as a percentage of the corresponding percentage for all members, and, dropping the percent sign, records the resultant as an index.

$$\text{index} = \frac{\%\ \text{occup/family-set}}{\%\ \text{occup/all members}}$$

The listing of occupations in Table 11 has been slightly rearranged to bring out certain patterns. The professionals emerge as strongly represented among families except for the traditionally prestigeful profession of medicine. It is not clear whether the medical profession suffered some decline in prestige as a consequence of the expansion of medical training in Egypt, or whether there was more than a proportionate number of members of the minority communities in medicine. At any rate these provincial families of status do not show a particular preference for the medical profession. Law and particularly engineering stand out as preferred professions.

Table 11   Index Comparing Family-Set and
                                       Nonfamily-Set Occupations

Occupation	Index	Occupation	Index	Occupation	Index
Doctor	1.00	Merchant	.59	ʿUmdah	1.43
Lawyer	1.40	Businessman	1.02		
Engineer	1.57	Man of religion	.68	Farmer	.88
		Student	1.09	Local council member	1.41
Teacher	.66	Army	1.67		
Civil servant	1.07	Police	.83	Former M.P.	2.25
		Worker	.55	Rare	3.33
		Unknown	.62	Cabinet member	2.85

Note: Index = $\dfrac{\text{\% occupation/family set}}{\text{\% occupation/all members}}$

Of the two most widely chosen professions of the so-called new intellectual segment of the middle class, teachers and civil servants, the civil service emerges as clearly more prestigeful. This distinction is upheld in more casual observation, but it must be emphasized that by civil service here we do not mean merely employed or salaried by the government, but rather a ranked functionary attached to a specific administration by means of a position designated on an official table of organization. In general, we will find that civil servants are more salient in or near major administrative centers, while teachers are more frequently elected to National Union committees in areas more remote from such administrative centers.

On the basis of the occupations of the district officers, it is not surprising to see the low preference for merchants, for those described as men of religion, and for workers, and the high preference for former army officers, for municipal councillors, and, of course, for former M.P.'s, for cabinet ministers, and for other high officials. What is surprising is the relatively moderate preference for businessmen, the surprisingly high proportion of students in family sets, and the low preference for former police officers. The ratios of *occupational preference* of those elected as district officers (see table 8) are compared with the index of family-set occupational preferences in table 12.

The fact that the number of officers was so small tended to exaggerate the higher and lower ratios; nevertheless the smaller index of businessmen may be explained by the fact that they are more often found in provincial centers which are quite urbanized and less frequently family dominated. The higher index of men of religion and especially of students suggests that while these people were not elected to district office they are related to those who were. They probably represent special segments of the 'ulama' and of students who are more influential politically because of their family connection. Student status, in particular, as a transitional situation for most, is too undifferentiated to mean very much in stratificational terms although it may mean a great deal in political, cultural, or ideological terms.

The low index for police officers among family sets is very surprising and may be the consequence of their small numbers over all in the National Union. Still, small numbers have usually resulted in an opposite tendency toward exaggerating the importance of favored groups. The obvious conclusion is that former police officers have been favored for party-elite positions regardless of traditional family status.

The high prevalence of 'umad in the family sets contrasts with the relatively low ratio of 'umad among the district officers. This contrast points to the need to treat the family set as a set or group and not in the aggregate as individuals. There is a surprisingly large number of 'umad in the National Union committees, and they seem to have substantial influence in their own villages. The relatively large numbers in family sets indicate that their relatives are frequently also elected. Fewer 'umad are now elected to higher office than used to be the case, but it may be that their relatives, especially those who have a "western" education, are preferred for higher positions.

Approximately 70% of the members of family sets are engaged in traditional or rural occupations. These are the farmers, 'umad, municipal councillors, and 'ulama'. But this rural-traditional character of the second stratum is substantially diminished when these individuals are grouped as families. It might be expected that members of the same family set would all be engaged in either modern-urban or traditional-rural occupations. To test this hypothesis three categories of family set were distinguished: (*a*) where all occupations are modern (or urban), (*b*) where all occupations are traditional (or rural), and (*c*) where the occupations are both modern and traditional, or simply mixed. Only

Table 12

Ratio of Occupational Preference of
District Officers and Index of
Family Occupational Preference
Compared (559 officers/5,498
family members)

Occupation	District Officers	Family Sets	Occupation	District Officers	Family Sets	Occupation	District Officers	Family Sets
Doctor	4.1	1.00	Merchant	0.6	0.59	'Umdah	0.7	1.43
Lawyer	3.8	1.40	Businessman	3.9	1.02			
Engineer	2.2	1.57	Man of religion	0.3	0.68	Farmer	0.3	0.88
			Student	0.0	1.09	Local council member	4.3	1.41
Teacher	0.4	0.66	Army	7.5	1.67			
Civil servant	1.1	1.07	Police	8.5	0.83	Former M.P.	29.2	2.25
			Worker	0.0	0.55	Rare	17.8	3.33
			Unknown	0.4	0.62	Cabinet member	8.0	2.85

about 40% of all family-set members are members of wholly traditionally occupied families. The most significant finding is that 48.7% of all
families are mixed—that is, these families are composed of at least one
member who has a modern occupation and one who has a traditional
occupation. Contrary to the hypothesis that elite families will be occupationally homogeneous, the modal family has both moderns and traditionals in it.

The classification of moderns and traditionals has a certain arbi-
trariness about it. The explanatory power of categorical classifications
is less decisive when it is understood that there are few ideal typical
moderns or traditionals, and that those in between are often not in
"transition" at all, but simply neither wholly traditional nor wholly
modern. Occupation is, furthermore, but one ambiguous indicator of
attitudes and ideology, and even more obscure as an indicator of elite
status. The picture is even more complicated when we have to take
account of what the rest of the family is doing before we can make
serious predictions regarding political behavior or political status. The
mixed family itself is a broad class of types, some of which are more
mixed than others.

Members of family sets make up 43% of all district officers of the
National Union, and about 4.5% of all family members are district
officers. If holding district office is an indicator of elite status, then the
fact that proportionately more family-set members hold office than do
others indicates that they constitute a pool or aggregation from which
officers may be chosen. The small number of officers leaves open the
question of whether these officers were chosen from among 5,498 persons, all of whom have the same status, or whether there is an even
more elite segment among the family members.

A consideration of the level of office further strengthens the importance of family-set membership and bears upon the question of stratification within this elite segment. There were four district offices:
president, vice-president, secretary and treasurer. The distribution of
these offices among the members of family sets illustrates that the
family-set members were proportionately stronger in the more prestigeful offices since they comprised 48% of the presidents, 46% of the
vice-presidents, 40% of the treasurers, and 37% of the secretaries.

Regardless of whether the officer group is representative of all the
family-set members, officers who are in family sets comprise a very
special group of 249 members of the party elite, and we can learn more
of the composition of that elite by examining some other characteristics
of the "family officers." At this point we will look at their occupations.

Table 13 lists the occupations of the 249 family officers, and it compares the percentage of these officers in each occupation with the percentage of all officers and then of all members in each occupation. The
pattern of proportionate increase or decrease for each occupation is
graphically presented in figure 1.

From table 13 we learn that there is much greater differentiation of
occupations, in terms of elite significance, than we found for either
officers alone or families alone. The preference for the professionals,
especially lawyers, is much more marked. The proportion of doctors
hardly changed from all members to family-set members, but among
family officers that proportion increased more than fourfold. The increased proportion of lawyers appears to grow by geometric progression, while the proportion of engineers does not quite double as we
move from all members to family-set members to family officers.

Teachers, civil servants, merchants, and farmers all show a decline
in status. These groups are all substantially represented among the
family sets, but they are clearly lacking in status when compared with
other members of their own kinship groups. It appears that these persons have been elected to the National Union committees because they

Table 13   Occupations of Family Officers

Occupation	Number	Percentage of Family Officers	Percentage of Family-set Members	Percentage of NU Members
Doctor	8	3.2	.7	.7
Lawyer	23	9.2	3.7	2.64
Engineer	14	5.6	2.9	1.85
Teacher	4	1.6	6.6	9.93
Civil servant	14	5.6	7.5	6.96
Merchant	9	3.6	4.7	7.89
Businessman	4	1.6	.8	.78
Clergy	--	--	1.1	1.61
Student	--	--	1.5	1.37
ʿUmdah	39	15.6	28.0	19.59
Shaykh	8	3.2	1.0	
Worker	--	--	.6	1.1
Farmer	37	14.8	33.4	38.06
Former M.P.	71	28.5	2.0	.89
Local council member	12	4.8	1.6	1.13
Ex-army officer	2	.8	.2	.12
Ex-police officer	1	.4	.1	.12
Unknown	3	1.2	3.2	5.13
Rare	--	--	.1	.03
Cabinet minister	--	--	.2	.07
Total	249			

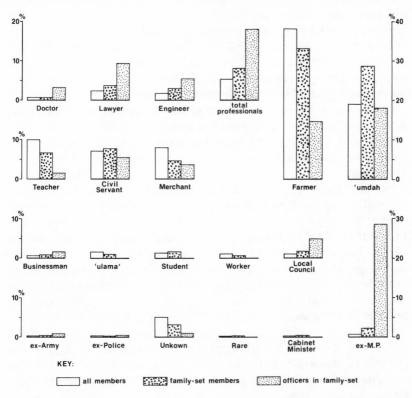

Fig. 1   Percentages of Occupations and
                                              Political Status

are related to someone of impressive influence, but they themselves do
not carry the prestige of the family.

There are, of course, fewer teachers, proportionately, among family
members than among all National Union members, and their recruitment in substantial numbers in certain regions may be taken as coun-
terbalancing traditional influences and strengthening the centralizing
bureaucratic influence of the government at Cairo. Among family officers, the proportion of teachers drops dramatically.

For civil servants the pattern is different, because the proportion of
civil servants increases slightly among family sets, but declines noticeably among family officers.

The proportion of merchants declines steadily, and though the number of merchants among the "family officers" is not negligible, they do
not appear to constitute a characteristic or fundamental component of

the party elite. There is a small group of merchants who are connected
with rural, agricultural, traditionally influential families, but the rest are
from small and large towns without important rural connections. The
relative unimportance of merchant kinship connections for elite role
recruitment is illustrated in the decline of the proportion of merchants
among members of family sets. The decline in percentage of all members to family-set members is almost three times as large as the decline
in percentage of merchants in family sets to the percentage of merchants
among family officers. It is probable that some merchants have wider
kinship, social, cultural, and economic networks in the rural areas, and
these have a much better chance of being elected to higher office than
do the rest.

Farmers, the largest group among the members and the largest occupational group in Egypt, decline sharply from their large numbers
among all family members to only 14.8% of family officers. Still,
14.8% is the third largest occupational group among the family officers.
The decline is not as drastic as that of the teachers. Hence, a farmer
who is not also an 'umdah or a member of the local council is far less
likely to be chosen as an officer than one of his relatives who is an
'umdah or a local councillor or, perhaps, a member of parliament. The
persistently large number of farmers is a clear indication that landholding is the basis of elite status, while recruitment to party elite positions
is further channelled through kinship structures, which have their own
patterns of status differentiation (sex, age, personality, etc.) and then
selection is channelled through the prestige and skill structures of education and occupation.

The 'umad are a subset of farmers, of middle-sized landholders who
have been selected, usually for several generations, as a special lineage
within a broader kinship group. The number of 'umad was second only
to the number of farmers among all members of the National Union,
but that proportion increased dramatically from 19.6% to 29% of all
family-set members. Thus, the 'umdah, with his combination of land
and administrative influence, is the mainstay of the elite family. The
elite family has a rural base and urban links. Farmers, professionals,
'umad, and M.P.'s are all linked in families with others who pursue still
other occupations, but selection for political office among the members
of these families is not random, just as occupational selection by members of these families is also not random. It is, therefore, instructive
that the proportion of 'umad among the family officers declines just as
dramatically to 18.8% after having risen to 29% of all family-set
members. Control of village administration is closely held by these elite

families, and 'umad are the second largest group among the family officers and among family-set members, but it is fairly frequently the case that the 'umdah will be left in charge of village affairs while another member of the family accepts a higher political position. If we bear in mind the large number of 'umad among all family-set members (1,540 in 2,223 family sets), it is clear that many of those who are elected to district office who are not 'umad are related to 'umad. These include a good many of those engaged in modern occupations: professionals, teachers, and civil servants, rather than other farmers.

The most important group of family officers is made up of former M.P.'s. Former M.P.'s comprise the largest occupational group among family officers, 71 or 28.5% of the total. Nearly 65% of the former M.P.'s who are family-set members are also district officers. Once again we can discern the continuity between the party elite and the parliamentary elite and between the parliamentary elite and a broad stratum of society. Kinship is a crucial variable while occupation is an important secondary variable. The peaking of former M.P.'s as members of family sets and as district officers strongly sustains these categories as indicators of elite status.

Members of local councils (singular: majlis al-balad) are also favored among members of family sets for district office. The local council evidently coincides with an area larger than the village but smaller than the district (markaz), and it is apparent that members of these councils have been able to use their positions in the district administration to get themselves elected to district office in the National Union. At the very least, they have achieved positions within the party apparatus which parallel their positions in the administrative apparatus of the Ministry of the Interior. Manifestly, local councillors represent the same social segment as the 'umad, the a'yan, and many of the farmers and former members of parliament.

We note, finally, the exclusion of 'ulama', students, and workers, even though some are members of family sets. Those of unspecified occupation (probably farmers but not certainly) decline considerably, while the increased proportion of former army and police officers is unimpressive. Businessmen, or entrepreneurs as opposed to merchants, increased their proportion, but their number is so small that it lacks political significance.

These patterns may be more easily comprehended by looking at the several diagrams included in figure 1. Each occupational group's percentage of all members, all family-set members, and family officers is charted from left to right, showing at a glance whether that group's elite status increased with each level of recruitment selectivity. Note also that all professional groups have been charted together as well as separately.

The family set has been shown to be a useful empirical referent for the rural elite. Comparing the occupations of the members of family sets with those of other groups has made it possible to confirm certain hypotheses regarding the status of some occupations and to explore the possibility that the members of family sets are themselves stratified. In particular, the finding that members of family sets have a dispropor- tionately large share of district offices and were disproportionately rep- resented in the previous parliament establishes the empirical utility of this group as an indicator of elite status. Our understanding of the phenomenon "the traditional notability" has been enhanced by review- ing the observations and conclusions of others, but it has been possible to avoid relying on these reports and their potentially ideological in- clinations. It is, for example, most important to bear in mind that members of family sets engage in a wide variety of modern and tradi- tional occupations. It is similarly significant that the modal family set includes persons engaged in both modern and traditional occupations as well as occupations of both high and low status. These findings are promising, and it is to be hoped that further investigation of the char- acteristics of this empirically defined segment will reveal to us some of the political and social characteristics of Egypt that might have been misunderstood had we relied on conventional histories, the usual aggre- gate statistics, the ideologically grounded theories of development, or the microanalysis of a single community at a given moment in time.

Four

Differentiation among Elite Families

The *'izba* is inseparable from any large property. It constitutes a hamlet for the workers which is the estate owners property. . . . Before the revolution there were more than fifteen thousand *'izbas*.

However, there is a rural middle class, consisting of medium landowners. Gain-loving, conservative and unpretentious, they live in the country and keep a close eye on the yield of their feddans. . . . From this class are drawn the pupils of the provincial secondary schools, the students of the religious institutes dependent on Al-Azhar, many of the government employees and police officers. It has produced contemporary Egypt's most notable men.

Henry Habib Ayrout, *The Egyptian Peasant*

Thus far all members of family sets have been treated as members of a largely homogeneous elite, although it has been suggested that these individuals might be further differentiated in terms of their occupations. Occupation, however, is an ambiguous guide, for, despite all the writing about the new middle class, membership in such a middle group does not seem to mean much unless one is also connected with a family which has local, rural, and traditional influence. It appears that such influence is both qualitatively and quantitatively highly structured as a consequence of the highly structured patterns of rural society, economy, and administration. Particular emphasis must, once again, be placed on the role of the 'umdah. Nevertheless, it is obvious that some families are more influential than others, even though most appear to have about the same socioeconomic base. Without abandoning interest in occupational distribution, we shall try to uncover more decisive evidence of elite differentiation, such as the number of family members in the National Union, the continuity of elite status, and geographical concentration and dispersion. Granted that not all members of the second stratum have the same influence, we shall ask whether there are discrete and

89

well-demarcated segments among the second stratum or whether its
members are differentiated only in degree. The data make it easiest to
ask whether the party and parliamentary elites are easily differentiated,
but we will also attempt to differentiate between those with the larger
landholdings and those with smaller estates. In this chapter we will be
primarily concerned with the number of family members holding party-
elite positions and with size of landholding as indicators of influence.
The problems of historical continuity and geographical location will be
taken up in subsequent chapters.

The typical or modal family set is comprised of two members, but
the size of family sets varies from 2 to 10. Table 14 presents the dis-

Table 14   Distribution of Family Sets by Size

Size	Number	Percentage	Size	Number	Percentage
2	1,570	70.6	6	20	0.9
3	418	18.8	7	9	0.4
4	139	6.3	8	4	0.2
5	59	2.7	9	2	0.1
5+	96	4.3	10	2	0.1

tribution of family sets by size. Family sets including more than five
names are rare, constituting less than 2% of the total number of families and 4.5% of all members of family sets. The group may be important, but the larger the family set in the larger (ten or so members)
village committees, the greater the suspicion that it is a predominant
clan and not merely a family. Still, it seems unlikely that the small
number of very large family sets will constitute a well-demarcated segment of the party elite rather than a few special cases of a much more
widespread phenomenon. In addition, the small number of very large
family sets limits the possibility of useful statistical analysis. Hence all
family sets of five and above have been combined in a single category,
designated as 5+.

Our problem is to discover whether the size of the family set is politically significant and, if so, in what way. Our hypothesis is, of course,
that the larger the family set, the more likely is it that the members of
the set will have prestige occupations, will be officers at the district
level, will hold higher offices, and will be members of the National
Assembly.

Family-set size, according to our preliminary and simple hypothesis,
is determined by political influence or elite status (and competition with
others) but an additional and important constraint is the size of the

village committee. Manifestly, it is impossible to have a family set of
five in a village committee of three. Presumably, the larger the village
committee, the easier it is to elect two or more members of the same
family. Presumably, the larger the village committee and the smaller
the family set, the less influence should we attribute to that family. But
the social and economic patterns which give rise to family dominance
may occur only in certain parts of the country and may occur only in
villages of a certain size, that is, in villages which are differentiated in a
somewhat significant manner. Leaving the geographical question aside
for the moment, we must account for size of village committee as an
influential variable.

The average size of the 4,191 village committees surveyed was 6.7,
and 95% of the villages had committees of 10 or fewer members. The
size of the village committee was related to the size of the population of
the village, but only in a rough way. The crudeness of the relationship
of committee size and village population is apparent from the nonrandom distribution of committee sizes. Three-member and ten-member
committees were clearly preferred, as is shown in figure 2.

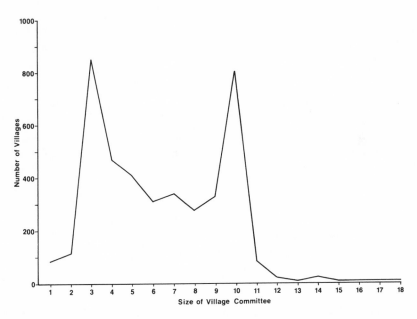

Fig. 2   Distribution of Villages by Size of
                                        Village Committee

The largest village, or rather unit, committee was 35, but the very large committees occurred in the highly urbanized provincial capitals or secondary centers which are referred to administratively as the bandar as opposed to the markaz within which the villages are grouped. There are no villages within the bandar since it usually comprises a small city, and unlike Cairo, the bandar is not broken up into sections. The result is that the bandar has the largest committees, but is still relatively underrepresented. As a consequence, the largest village committees are special cases for us. There are, however, so few committees in each of the larger categories that we have compromised and grouped all village committees with 12–29 members and labelled them all as "twelves," and all committees of 30–35 have been labelled as "thirteens."

The assumption that the size of village committee and the size of population of the village were correlated is somewhat upset by the unexpected bimodality of the distribution of village committee sizes. In order to test our preliminary assumption and to establish the level of correlation, a sample of the villages was tested. Selecting every tenth unit, whether village or bandar, the actual population size for that unit was obtained from the published census for 1960. Of the 420 villages included in the sample, census data were available for 405. The distribution of the villages among the various categories of committee size was close enough to indicate that elaborate randomization of sampling was, as expected, not necessary.

There was a surprisingly large range of variation, however, within each committee size category. Table 15 gives the average and the minimum and maximum size of population of each committee size.

While these figures indicate that there was much overlapping of population categories, the progression of average sizes indicates that some rule of thumb did prevail. Furthermore, the only census figures available to the organizers of the National Union were those of 1947, which may account for part of the distortion. It also appears that the village committees having only a single or two members were probably incorrectly reported in the National Union documents—this is particularly likely in the cases of a committee of one. It may further be noted, in the cases of the committees of 3 and 10, sizes clearly preferred by the National Union organizers, that there is a greater range of population than for any of the others except for the clearly aberrant group of 6 villages in category 12. It was apparent that the exclusion of categories 1, 2, 12, and 13 and the elimination for each category of the smallest and the largest village would have given us a very good correlation, but even as it is the Pearson correlation coefficient for all 405 villages (and cities) with all 13 committee size categories was .6705 (significant at the .001 level). It is, therefore, safe to conclude that village population and village committee size are roughly correlated over the whole of the sixteen agricultural provinces.

Table 15   Population and NU Committee Size

Committee Size	Average Population	Minimum Population	Maximum Population
1	2,011	118	4,263
2	1,722	514	4,382
3	1,434	202	5,458
4	2,199	1,460	4,860
5	2,832	1,063	5,723
6	3,919	2,782	8,468
7	3,844	2,769	5,105
8	5,036	3,476	12,581
9	5,805	3,817	10,285
10	8,182	2,303	27,810
11	9,223	2,825	20,502
12	45,015	5,629	178,288
13	64,745	35,074	83,128

Note: Sample villages only.

The effect of village committee size on the probability of finding a family set is apparent from figure 3, showing the distribution of village committee sizes by the number of villages having from three to eleven committee members. Alongside of that bimodal curve, familiar from figure 2, we have also plotted the number of family sets found in each size category of village committee (including some multifamily-set committees). It is obvious from figure 3 that as village committee size increases, the probability of there being a family set in the village committee increases until it is virtually certain that a family set will be found in all committees of more than eleven members. In table 16 we have converted the findings of Figure 3 into percentage terms.

From these decisive statistics it is possible to conclude that increasing the size of the village committee in any village would probably lead to the election of more than one member of a single family. It would appear that the political influence of traditional elite families would assert itself equally in all villages regardless of size. That is to say that there is a good probability that village size as indicated by village committee size has little effect on the elite pattern we have been uncovering.

In the larger village committees, family-set members were differentiated from others within the same committee in order to identify the

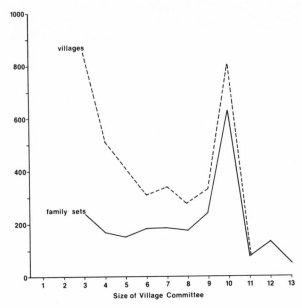

Fig. 3   Number of Family Sets in Each Size
                                              of Village Committee

rural political elite. In village committees of size three, however, where
only 28% of the committees had family sets, we are essentially differentiating sets of villages (with a family set as opposed to without a
family set) rather than social strata or status groups. If we assume that
an increase in the size of the committee would increase the number of
family sets, it follows that we must assume that more of those who were
not of family sets in committees of size three really belong to the elite
group. There is, however, no indication of which of the three committee members belongs to our second stratum where there are no family
sets.

We may be able to clear up this problem somewhat by examining
the village committee sizes as discrete collectivities having their own
elite characteristics. Presumably, if rural Egypt is a homogeneous entity, and particularly if sociopolitical structure does not vary much with
village size, and if it is true that the prevalence of family sets is a function of village committee size, then it follows that the proportion of
family-set members will not vary from village size to village size. In
table 17 we present the percentages of family-set members by committee size. Note how little variation there is from category to category,

and in particular how well the smallest categories, 3 and 4, stand up. There is a substantial decline for the two largest categories 12 (12–29) and 13 (30–35). Since we assume that the smallest village committees preside over the most rural and traditional communities and that the largest committees are located in the largest, most modern and most urbanized communities in the agricultural provinces, it follows that in the most traditional and rural communities status differentiation is not very great, just as economic differentiation is not very great, but even the limited distinction is statistically discernible to a substantial degree. In the most modern and urban communities, the traditionally influential families are very important, but their influence is evidently limited by and shared with the influence of culturally modernized, educated, individuals who may or may not have originated in traditionally influential families, but who now have achieved some political standing on their own. Furthermore, the constituency of each member of a bandar committee averages about 4,000 persons, while each member of a three-person committee represents only about 500 persons on the average. The high correlation of committee members and family-set members ($r^2 = .99$) shows (a) that elite patterns are consistent throughout the agrarian districts, and (b) that the distinction between family-set members and others is both politically and statistically significant.

Figure 4 contrasts the percentage of all members and all family-set members with the percentage of district officers by village committee size. Figure 4 shows us that there are substantially more officers drawn from the larger and more urban units and proportionately fewer drawn from the smaller committees. The decline in the percentage of family sets in the larger units is to be considered in relation to the sharp increase in the percentage of district officers, raising the question of

Table 16   Family Sets as a Percentage of NU
                                           Committees

Village Committee Size	Family Sets as a Percentage of Committees
3	28
4	35
5	36
6	55
7	55
8	62
9	75
10	79
11	90

Table 17   Percentage of Family-Set Members
                                               by Committee Size

Size of Village Committee	Number of Committee Members	Number of Members of Family Sets	Percentage
3	2,556	538	21
4	1,856	386	21
5	2,055	354	17
6	1,920	413	22
7	2,310	435	19
8	2,200	445	20
9	2,907	617	21
10	7,990	1,618	20
11	792	171	22
12	2,139	345	16
13	883	117	13

whether elite status as measured by officeholding is to be correlated with size of unit alone and not with membership in a family set?

The percentage of officers in family sets is always much higher than the percentage of family-set members in the total membership. In the two smallest units and in the two largest, the percentage of officers in family sets declines to less than 50%, suggesting that family-set membership is not as effective a manner of identifying the elite in the smaller units because of the constraints of small committee size, nor is it in the larger units because of the influence of a more differentiated occupational structure. Together these four categories of village size account for 26.7% of all our National Union committee members, so this is an important finding. Still the significance of the finding should not be exaggerated. Family-set membership has been shown to be a strong indicator of elite status for all committees, and it is a much stronger indicator for committees having from five to eleven members. If there are fewer district officers in family sets in the smaller units, that is because there are fewer family sets. Despite these considerations, the family-set members retain their proportion of officer positions in both the larger units and the smaller units (see table 18).

While it is likely that different socioeconomic considerations apply in the larger units, it is apparent that the traditional families have not lost all influence in these larger units. In fact, it is difficult to say whether they have gained or lost influence relative to the position these families formerly enjoyed in the district capitals. In just about every bandar, except for some provincial capitals, we find at least one family set. Hence, even if a traditional family formerly *dominated* the politics of that bandar and though that traditionally influential family must now share power with others, it has been able to hold its own and to assert its own interests.

Out of more than 2,200 villages or National Union basic units, 294 or about 13% had more than one family set. Of these 294 villages, 40 were banadir or district capitals. Since there are 144 districts in all, this amounts to almost 28% of the banadir. As we would expect, the larger the unit committee, the more likely are we to find a family set. Sampling ten multifamily-set banadir and comparing them with a sample of ten single family-set banadir, we find a striking contrast. The average size of multifamily-set committees is 22.9 while the average size of single family-set bandar committees is 10.6. Family-set members comprise a smaller proportion of the larger unit committees, for even when we have two family sets of three members each in a committee of 23 members, they will comprise 26% of the members, whereas a single family set of three will comprise 30% of a committee of ten.

The question now arises whether there are no more than two family sets in some of these larger units because there are no more traditionally influential families of the necessary degree of influence, or because there are competing influential interests among the educated middle

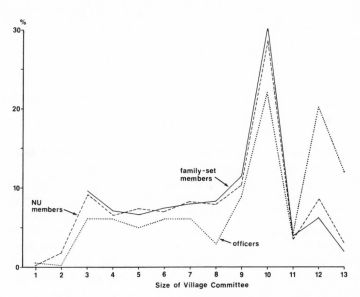

Fig. 4   Village Committee Size and Political
                                        Status

class. Sampling every tenth village committee having multifamily sets from among those which are not banadir, we found that the average village committee size was 10.52. In other words, the average size of a multifamily-set unit which was not a bandar is roughly equal to the average size single family-set bandar committee. This finding seems to indicate that multifamily sets are not a function of village committee size, but of other factors. The lower percentage of family-set members in the larger committees may be related to the smaller than expected number of multifamily-set bandar committees. It is more likely that the political interference of Cairo, or of the provincial governor, restricted the influence of certain families, rather than that there simply are not as many members of the second stratum in the banadir.

Table 18   Proportion of Family-Set Officers to Family-Set Members by Committee Size

Village Committee Size	Percentage of Family Officers / Percentage of Family Set Members	Percentage of Officers / Percentage of All Members
3	.57	.65
4	.69	.91
5	.81	.68
6	.85	.87
7	.96	.72
8	.44	.38
9	.86	.87
10	.91	.77
11	1.55	1.43
12	2.62	2.60
13	3.62	3.75

It is undeniable that the probability of any set of two or more individuals being elected is increased by increasing the size of the village committee, assuming the same size of village population, but it is also reasonable to assume that the influence and prestige of individual families vary. Some being more influential than others, those families will tend to get extra seats as the size of committee increases. This is even more significant politically when the village committee size is not increased beyond the arbitrary limit of ten, even though not all such villages have the same population. The implication is that political influence is unevenly distributed in all villages but that, in general, there is a threshold below which such influence was not decisive for membership in the National Union committees. Some families were not influential enough. Some were not influential enough to get seats on a small committee, and still others were not influential enough to get two or more seats on a small committee. We have been able to separate out only those enjoying a somewhat higher status by the method of identifying family sets. But this method does not argue that there are no members of the second stratum where we do not have family sets, or that where we find one family set that there are not other traditionally influential families which are either competing, cooperating, or otherwise present in the same village. This perspective is the logical counterpart of the statistical pattern which we have found, since we have strong probabilistic evidence for the existence of a rural elite but no evidence of an absolute separation of elite from nonelite. It would, of course, be astonishing to find such a castelike absolute separation in Egypt.

It is to be expected that the distribution of occupations will vary in accordance with village committee size. We would expect to find more traditionals and rurals in the smaller village committees and more moderns and educated in the larger committees. Similarly, we would expect to find slightly more of the occupations found more frequently among the family sets in the village committees where family-set members are more frequently found. We do, in fact, find that there are proportionately more professionals and more civil servants in family sets in committees of ten and fewer members than for nonfamily-set members. The fact that there are slightly fewer professionals and civil servants in family sets in the largest committees might argue for the existence of a politically influential, but nontraditional, group in the largest of the towns and cities in the sixteen provinces.

There are some family-set occupations for which it is possible to discuss a skewing toward the larger committees. The tendency is not strong, and it may be explained in different ways for different occupations. Merchants are underrepresented among family-set members, and they are underrepresented among family-set members in the smallest committees. Surprisingly enough, however, there are more than twice as many merchants among family-set members than might have been expected in the largest village committees (category 13) controlling for both number of family-set members and for the number of merchants in the largest committees. Obviously, here we have a high status component of the largest family sets which does not show up when we look simply at the percentage of merchants among family-set members in all committees. Businessmen are also much more strongly represented among family sets in the largest committees than might have been expected. Bearing in mind that there are few family sets linking merchants and farmers or 'umad, it appears that, in some cases, urban family sets have no significant link with the rural, agricultural notability. Yet 'umad are also overrepresented in the largest committees, allowing for the possibility that there is an incipient link between the rural notability and a nascent provincial capitalist segment.

The three most politically relevant "occupations" are former member of the National Assembly (former M.P.'s), member of a local council, and 'umdah. All are substantially overrepresented among the family-set members, but none of these show that political influence is tied to a particular size of committee, nor that there is a skewing toward either larger or smaller committees (see table 19).

Table 19   Proportion of Family-Set 'Umad,
                                           Local Council Members, and Former
                                           M.P.'s to Members of Family Sets

Village Committee Size	Former M.P.	Local Council Member	ʿUmdah
3	.37	1.88	.81
4	.54	.60	1.01
5	1.59	.76	1.00
6	1.20	2.79	1.06
7	.89	.74	1.06
8	1.45	2.41	1.03
9	1.08	.65	.94
10	.96	1.11	1.00
11	1.27	1.09	1.16
12	1.05	1.00	1.06
13	.99	.59	1.08

The data we have examined thus far indicate that village committee size, reflecting the size of the village or town, does not greatly affect elite status. District officers are more frequently found in the larger units. Former M.P.'s and local councillors are also more frequently found in the larger units. 'Umad and shuyukh are more frequently found in the smaller units. The professionals are more frequently found in the larger units. Nevertheless, the prevalence of these occupations among family-set members does not correlate with the frequency of family-set members in each committee size. If we can conclude that family-set membership is an independent variable, indicating a measure of political influence, does it follow that the larger the family set the more influential that family set is? If this hypothesis is *untrue*, it follows that family-set size is, in substantial part, a function of village committee size.

The largest family sets, those made up of 5 or more members, were not outstandingly more influential than the smaller family sets, possibly even less influential, as measured by ability to elect district officers. Table 20 compares the percentage of family-set members in each size family set with the percentage of officers in family sets for each size family set. The percentages are astonishingly similar.

Table 20   Percentage of Family-Set Members and Family Officers by Family-Set Size

	Family-Set Size			
	2	3	4	5+
Family-set members	57.1%	22.8%	10.1%	10.0%
Family-set officers	53.4	24.1	11.6	10.8
Officers as percentage of all members (family sets in both cases)	4.5	4.8	5.0	4.9

The largest family sets in the largest units were more influential than the largest family sets in the middle-sized units (5–10) but they were not more influential than the smaller family sets in the largest units. Similarly, the largest family sets in the middle-sized units numbered 447, or 12% of the total of family-set members in that group, and they elected 12% of the officers who were elected from family sets. More than 1 in 10 of all the family-set members of the largest villages was elected to district office, whereas the overall average was less than 5%, and the average for the largest family sets in units of 5–10 was 4%. Clearly, village committee size is more significant than family-set size, as an indicator of influence once we know that the individual is a member of a family set.

There are, in addition to the number of officers elected, other measures of influence which might be examined before we decide to disregard family-set size altogether. The first of these is the office itself. Remembering that the district officers were a president, a vice-president, a secretary, and a treasurer, we assume that the president and vice-president are more influential than the secretary and treasurer. Table 21 breaks down the district officers by office and by family-set size.

Manifestly, family-set size is significant with regard to the allocation of district offices. Members of larger family sets who are district officers are more likely to be presidents and vice-presidents than they are to be secretaries or treasurers. Family-set size makes a difference, but the difference is not as great as that between membership in a family set of any size and nonmembership in a family set.

Table 21   Percentage of District Officers by
                                      Family-Set Size

Office	Family-Set Size			
	2	3	4	5+
President	24.1%	25.0%	41.4%	40.7%
Vice-president	27.1	23.3	34.5	25.9
Secretary	23.3	23.3	13.8	18.5
Treasurer	25.6	28.3	10.3	14.8
Total	100.1%	99.9%	100.0%	98.9%

When we examine the data for the distribution of occupations among family-set members in terms of family-set size, we find a similar significance. For the three professions of medicine, law, and engineering, only family sets of four are substantially higher than the average for all family-set members. The larger family sets have fewer teachers, merchants and 'umad, but more students, farmers, and former members of the National Assembly. It is not surprising to find more farmers in the larger family sets (4 and 5+) and fewer 'umad, since this further confirms that it is the family and not the occupation which determines elite status.

In table 22 we have brought together the data for both office-holding and occupation among the members of family sets to show the overall pattern of the significance of family-set size. Considering only those who are officers and also family-set members, table 22 shows the distribution of these members by family-set size, office, and occupation.

Table 22 contains some rather striking patterns, the most important of which is the distribution of former members of the National Assembly. Former M.P.'s tend overwhelmingly to be presidents and vice-presidents, that is, 65 out of 70 of them. This high concentration of political status is not strongly related to family-set size, but would appear to be linked to political factors which are operative outside of the village itself. Family-set size, though in part dependent upon committee size, is still essentially a measure of influence within the village rather than of influence in Cairo.

The occupational composition of the officers in the largest family sets is predominantly traditional—suggesting that the traditional seg-

Table 22   District Officers in Family Sets by
                                      Occupation and Family-Set Size

Office/Occupation	Family-Set Size			
	2	3	4	5+
President				
Former M.P.	20	8	7	8
Professional	2	3	2	1
Civil servant	2	-	-	-
Teacher	1	-	-	-
Local councillor	1	1	-	1
ʿUmdah	5	-	1	-
Farmer	1	2	2	1
Businessman	-	1	-	-
Vice President				
Former M.P.	12	5	4	1
Professional	5	2	-	3
Civil servant	3	1	2	1
Teacher	1	1	-	-
Local councillor	2	-	-	-
ʿUmdah	5	3	2	1
Farmer	5	-	1	-
Merchant	2	1	-	1
Ex-police officer	1	-	-	-
Ex-Army officer	-	1	-	-
Unknown	-	-	1	-
Secretary				
Former M.P.	2	1	1	-
Professional	9	4	1	-
Civil servant	1	-	1	-
Teacher	1	-	-	-
Local councillor	2	-	-	-
ʿUmdah	8	2	1	2
Farmer	4	4	-	2
Merchant	2	-	-	-
Businessman	1	-	-	1
Ex-Army officer	1	-	-	-
Unknown	-	3	-	-
Treasurer				
Former M.P.	-	1	-	-
Professional	8	4	-	-
Civil servant	2	1	-	-
Teacher	-	-	-	-
Local councillor	3	-	-	1
ʿUmdah	11	3	1	2
Farmer	7	5	2	1
Merchant	1	2	-	-
Businessman	1	-	-	-
Unknown	1	1	-	-

ment of these families is dominant and/or that the basis of the family's political influence is traditional: notability and landowning. The smaller the family set, the more likely is it that its members who are officers are professionals and 'umad. If a member of a two-person family set becomes a district president, he is likely to be a former M.P. by about 2 to 1. If a member of a two-person family set holds some other office, he will be a professional or an 'umdah in 46% of the cases. Forty percent of the nonpresidents are professionals or 'umad in family sets of three, and 39% of the nonpresidents are professionals or 'umad in family sets of four and above. Hence, traditional status as represented by the office of 'umdah and a more traditional pattern of modernization as represented by preference for the professions, stands out strongly as the basis of political influence in the sixteen agricultural provinces. The political elite is more closely linked to a traditional class of notables than it is to the modernized and urbanized middle class.

It appears from this data that there is only a difference of gradation of elite status and not of kind among family-set sizes. While there are some significant differences, family-set membership is more important than family-set size. We have not, however, taken account of differences in the size of landholdings among the family sets.

The land reform of 1952 did eliminate many large landowners as significant political protagonists, but it did not end the political involvement of all the old and wealthy rural families. In many cases it was possible to divide the family holdings into units of 300 feddan (200 in the name of the male head of household and 100 in the names of his dependents) and thus to survive the reform without any diminution of holdings. In other cases the family holdings had already been divided through inheritance. In still other cases, only some members of the family were forced to sell or dispose of surplus land, while the rest remained unaffected. Hence, even after the land reform, there were important differences among the remaining landowners in terms of size of holdings, and in terms of the historical circumstances in which they acceded to their agricultural property.

Though Baer argues that the holdings and social position of the earliest group of indigenous rural landowners declined after 1882, he and Riad both tell us that the proportion of middle holdings (either 20–50 feddan or 5–20 feddan depending upon the source) has not changed since the 1880s or 1890s. Hence, even though many members of these families have migrated to the cities, many of their relatives have remained behind, and others have arisen to take their leading positions in the villages. This persistence of rural property and the durability of the 'umdah class provide the backbone of the second stratum.

On the other hand, Baer gives us little basis for differentiating among the members of the second stratum in terms that might relate size of holding to the degree of elite influence. It is true that there is a substantial range of difference between the extremes of 5 and 50 feddan, and both Riad and 'Amr would put owners of such estates in different categories. Riad goes on to differentiate the largest exploiters-owners in terms of the level of capitalization, and 'Amr refers to the balance of instrumental and prestige values in their attitudes toward the land.

These considerations incline us toward the view that political elite stratification within the National Union may be related to the existence (persistence, emergence) of a group of large landowners who are of rural origin, who are not completely absentee, and who tend to exploit their holdings by traditional methods. These traditional methods, alluded to by 'Amr, include renting their latifundia in small plots to peasant sharecroppers rather than working it by means of labor-saving methods.

This hypothesis was somewhat strengthened when some of the names mentioned by Baer were traced in the *Golden Register*. Baer gives two examples of "notable families, known as *mashayikh* . . . (who) came to control a large part of village lands, which they converted into private property."[1] Descendants of both of these are found as members of family sets and officers in the National Union. He gives additional examples of 'umdah families that were appointed in the nineteenth century and retained that post for several generations.[2] The descendants of three of the four of those whose villages could be located are found in the National Union list, and two are members of family sets including 'umad. All three of the others mentioned as retaining the 'amudiyyah down to the middle of the twentieth century are also found in the NU register, and all are members of family sets. Two of the family sets include 'umad. Yet, of the eight 'umad mentioned by Baer as having held the largest estates (800 to 2000 feddan), only two were found, but both were former M.P.'s.[3]

These few names cited by Baer and drawn from the *Khitat* of 'Ali Pasha Mubarak cannot provide a systematic test of our hypothesis. Nevertheless, there is enough evidence to suggest that even if the great majority of 'umdah families do not own a great deal of land, it may be possible to distinguish between those families which once held large

estates and enjoyed substantial political influence and those which have
never been large landowners and have only recently become politically
participant.

Unfortunately the kind of information we would like to have is simply
not available. We would like to know the history of the landownership
status of each of the high-ranking officers and family-set members of
the National Union. It would even be sufficient to know how much land
each member owned in 1959, so that we could judge the influence of
landownership on political elite structure.

While this sort of information has nowhere been recorded, other
relevant information on prerevolutionary landholding of the sort that
interests us was discovered and analyzed by Sidney Chesnin.[4] He found
some solid evidence for the existence of precisely the type of rural,
landed, and politically influential segment that might be differentiated
as having an elite standing above that of the average member of the
second stratum.

Chesnin found a series of large-scale maps of Egypt which recorded,
in addition to the names of towns and villages, the names of farming
communities constructed on large estates adjacent to the village lands.
Estates on which such communities were built are called 'izab. Some of
these 'izab were named after the family of the estate owner, and so it
was possible to seek the name of the owner or of his relatives in the
National Union register list for the relevant village and to construct a
set of descendants or relatives of large estate owners who were members of the National Union committees. By law, an 'izbah could not be
constructed on less than 50 feddan.

Chesnin hypothesized that 'izbah owners or their descendants would
tend to hold higher political office (i.e., district officer or former M.P.),
to be members of family sets, and to be members of larger family sets.
He found that

> At every level on the elective status scale, there is a much higher
> percentage of the ezba-owners among the family-set members than
> among those not members of family-sets. The key figures to note are
> that ezba-owners comprise 22.9% of the family-set members in the
> largest class—the ordinary members of the village committees—but
> of those not members of family-sets only 3% are ezba-owners. This
> means that unless you are a member of a family-set elected to a
> village committee, your chances of being a member of the ezba-
> owning group are minimal. This strikingly confirms Binder's hypoth-
> esis that the family-set members form a special, key segment of the
> rural elite.

On the elective status scale, the ezba-owners make up an increasingly greater proportion, the higher up the status ladder one proceeds. (Only in the ex-MP group were the expectations reversed, with ex-MP's who are also district officers having fewer ezba-owners among them than the remaining ex-MP's.) This confirms the validity of the elective scale generally. Moreover, the greater proportion of ezba-owners at the highest levels of elective status reinforces our view of the ezba-owners as the upper segment of the rural elite.[5]

Chesnin's data is presented in table 23.

Table 23   Distribution of 'Izbah Owners by
                                        Elective Status and Family-Set
                                        Membership

Elective Status	ᶜIzbah Owners	
	Family-Set Members	Not Members of Family Set
Ordinary members	22.9%[a] (N* = 1,236.6)	3.0%[b]
District officers	33.8% (N = 81)[c]	10.3% (N = 30)
Former M.P.'s--Ordinary members	61.0% (N = 25)	15.4% (N = 8)
Former M.P.'s--District officers	50.0% (N = 35)	18.9% (N = 14)
Former M.P.'s--Total	54.1% (N = 60)	17.7% (N = 22)

Source: S. Chesnin, "A Subclass of Egyptian Rural Elites" (M.A. Thesis, University of Chicago, 1974), following p. 2-1.

[a]Confidence interval at 95% level = ±1.2%. N* = weighted total for all Egypt based on samples.

[b]Confidence interval at 95% level = ±1.9%. Chi-square for difference between percentages a and b = 63.29 with 1dF. P = .0001. Source of percentage was independent nationwide random sample with n = 303.

[c]N = number of ᶜizbah owners.

Chesnin also found, in comparing 'izbah-owner family sets with non-'izbah-owner family sets, that the former sets were systematically larger for all political levels. The relevant data is presented in table 24.

In considering the significance of these findings, Chesnin's own caveat is well worth bearing in mind:

It should be noted that the class of ezba-owners is not exactly identical with the class of all landowners of more than 50 feddans.

Not all large landowners built ezbas. Not all large landowners were
politically influential in the post-revolutionary Egypt of 1959. In this
study we have identified only those who were politically influential
in 1959 and who had been ezba-owners in 1930. (They might or
might not have been ezba-owners in 1959.) We have no information
regarding politically influential large landowners who did not own
ezbas. Despite the possible omission of a group of large landowners,
it has been possible to establish a clear relationship between the
ezba-owning elite and the group which Binder has identified as the
second stratum.[6]

Table 24   Average Size of Family Sets by
                                      'Izbah Ownership and Elective Status

| | Average Size of Family Set | |
Elective Status	ʿIzbah Owners	Non-ʿizbah Owners
Ordinary members	2.9	2.3
District officers	3.4	2.5
Former M.P.'s--Ordinary members	3.6	2.1
Former M.P.'s--District officers	3.6	2.9
Former M.P.'s--Total	3.6	2.6

Source: S. Chesnin, "A Subclass of Egyptian Rural Elites" (M.A. Thesis, University of
Chicago, 1974), following p. 2-2.

In this chapter, additional evidence supporting the major hypothesis
that family-set members constitute an elite segment within the National
Union has been presented. The case for identifying family sets with the
rural notability has been greatly strengthened by establishing that the
breakdown by size of village committee, a relatively arbitrary statistical
exercise, did not weaken the statistical weight of our findings. This sort
of analytical test will be found to have been even more valuable when
the data is broken down and differentiated by politically relevant categories such as geographical region. Nevertheless, our findings with regard to the significance of family-set size and with regard to the stratification of the rural notability itself are somewhat ambiguous. The data
on village committee size, on occupation, on district officers and former
M.P.'s suggested that there were no significant typological or class differences among the rural elite and that family-set size did not count
for much. The data on the 'izbah owners very strongly suggests the
opposite. Hopefully, further investigation will elucidate these issues.

Five

Nineteenth-Century Origins
of the Second Stratum

Urabi's advent as head of an Egyptian national movement had been due to the coming together of three groups. . . . They were: the would be constitutionalists, who were wealthy fallah notables, and members of the Turco-Circassian aristocracy; the reformers, who were mainly fallah intellectuals; and the fallah officers in the army. The terms 'Turco-Circassian' and 'fallah Egyptian' were not only used as ethnic labels, but also carried a connotation of class.

Afaf Lutfi al-Sayid,
Egypt and Cromer

British apologists, Egyptian nationalists, leftist critics of imperialism, and many others have narrated the astonishing series of changes that occurred in Egypt during the nineteenth century. Few historians could wish for a more dramatic story to tell, even if most have failed to convey the sweep and intensity of those events. The century opened with the French invasion and it closed with the British occupation. In between, a series of gubernatorial dynasts, owing nominal allegiance to the Ottoman Porte, attempted to modernize and aggrandize their provincial domain. Muhammad Ali tried to build both a modern industry and a modern army. Isma'il strove to build modern institutions reflecting the contemporary culture of Europe. The westernizing efforts of the alien dynasty were challenged by two of the new institutional groups. The parliament of rural notables and the new corps of low-ranking indigenous army officers joined in an ambivalent political protest which precipitated the occupation. For some, the period was a series of failures, when measured, at least, in terms of what the rulers of the day sought to achieve. For others it was primarily a tale of the denaturing of the ancient Egyptian people. Yet others discerned in the political frustrations of nineteenth-century Egypt the stubborn persistence of an indigenous cultural authenticity. If the Egypt which emerged at the end of the century was a new Egypt, it was nevertheless one in which the indigenous mass was to play a far more important political role than ever before.

The changes which the rulers of Egypt sought to bring about rendered Egypt extremely vulnerable to foreign economic intervention. Nearly all "third world" countries were open to imperialist influences during the nineteenth century, but in few cases were there concomitantly extensive native efforts being made to transform indigenous social and economic structures. The Mamluk fief-holders were eliminated and taxes were imposed directly on the peasants. The village headman's position was enhanced as administrative agent of the government. Virtually complete rights of ownership of land were granted in a series of regulations promulgated throughout the century. Egyptian agriculture became tied to world markets and international capital followed swiftly, linking the Nile Valley and Manchester. Age-old irrigation systems were changed, at least in the northern part of the country. A new rural elite came into existence, became enriched, and moved to the cities, and its second generation succeeded in gaining employment in the army and in the bureaucracy. On the eve of the British occupation, rival forms of large-scale landownership emerged, reflecting both the traditional rewards to the khedivial courtiers and the irresistible drive of contemporary entrepreneurship.

The value of Egyptian agricultural production increased sixteenfold during the nineteenth century while the population increased less than five times. This virtual windfall growth contributed to the creation of a new class of agrarian magnates, but it also attracted foreign investors and it encouraged profligate government spending. The Egypt of Isma'il fell heavily in debt to European lenders and lost control over its own financial policies to a consortium of European powers. Ultimately, international financial and political pressures to increase the transfer of Egypt's new agricultural wealth abroad reached the crisis point. The 'Arabi "revolution" and subsequent British invasion and occupation illustrate that the struggle for power within Egypt was also a conflict over the distribution of this new wealth.

One of the consequences of this struggle was the stagnation and retrogression in the economic, political, and social standing of the rural elite. It is, perhaps, remarkable that the rural notability was not completely overwhelmed by the concentration of landownership, the increased capitalization of agricultural enterprise, and the restrictive practices of agricultural credit sources. Nevertheless, for a variety of political and cultural reasons, some half-hearted efforts were made to preserve and protect the class of small- and middle-sized landholders, most notably in the "Five-Feddan Law" and various amendments

thereto. In addition many writers argue that the class of middle owners
was continuously replenished by the testamentary distribution of large
holdings, so that, in one way or another, a class of rural notables persisted under the British occupation. Is there any reason to believe that
the persistence of this class has been characterized by continuities of
culture, of political orientation, and even of direct lineal descent?

The data presented in earlier chapters established the political influence of the family set, and it was safely hypothesized that such influence
is in part due to traditional factors, in the sense that kinship and status
in the peasant community are an expression of traditional values. To
establish the traditional influence of these families in the historical sense
—establishing the fact that these selfsame families, or rather their ancestors, were influential in the past, requires a different sort of data. It
requires a source of information on rural elites at an important period
in the past which can be compared with the identification by name and
place of the rural elite of the National Union. Such a source, it was
thought, might be found in 'Ali Pasha Mubarak's gazetteer of Egypt,
published from 1886 to 1889.

The family links we are to examine in this chapter are among members of a lineage; however, the great significance of geographical location and of landownership or an agrarian vocation are implicit. If the
second stratum in Egypt had lost its regional base, it might or might
not have retained influence, but we could not, in any case, trace it.
That they have not lost their rural base is not only fortunate for our
research, but it is a substantive datum of far-reaching political importance.

The *Khitat al-tawfiqiyyah al-jadidah* of 'Ali Pasha Mubarak has been
carefully studied by a number of scholars, and particularly by Gabriel
Baer, who made the work the subject of a detailed critique in the ap-
pendix to his *Studies in the Social History of Modern Egypt.* More
importantly, he used the *Khitat* for his *History of Landownership in
Modern Egypt, 1800–1950.* In the latter volume, Baer cited the names
of many prominent landowners, gleaned from the pages of the *Khitat.*
Faced with the problem of whether the family sets we found in the
register of the National Union represented traditional notable families
or a new class promoted by the revolutionary regime after 1952, it
seemed that one way of shedding light on the problem would be to
search the volumes of 'Ali Pasha's *Khitat* very carefully, to compile all
the names of prominent Egyptians from the provinces, and to see
whether their descendants were among our family sets.

Obviously, this method has shortcomings. The primary difficulty is
that an absence of a name in 'Ali Pasha does not necessarily mean that

a contemporary family set had no prominent ancestors. Baer's review
of the *Khitat* is replete with criticism of 'Ali Pasha's casual approach
to citation, his selective use of sources, and the unsystematic nature of
the compilation. Nevertheless, Baer writes,

> the work is rich in information on agriculture; land tenure and
> ownership; rural trade; the specific crafts of many of Egypt's villages,
> towns, and districts; and the general economic development of
> various towns. . . .
> Of major importance is Mubarak's material on the various social
> groups and classes in nineteenth-century Egypt. We find in the
> *Khitat* unique information on Egypt's tribes and the process of their
> settlement; on rural families and notables; on merchants, officials,
> army officers, physicians, engineers, and particularly 'ulamā'. A great
> part of this information is in biographies and autobiographies which
> shed light on the origin and social background of members of these
> groups, their position in society, and their rise and decline.[1]

'Ali Pasha's gazetteer is by no means a complete survey of the Egyptian countryside. Baer tells us that most of the *Khitat* was probably
written in the mid-1870s even though it was published ten years later.[2]
More important, however, Baer counted only 1,155 towns and villages
discussed by 'Ali Pasha as against the "3,651 towns and villages and
about 8,600 smaller places" in Egypt in 1882. Baer also points to some
errors in citing the names of places.

Nevertheless Baer and Anwar 'Abd al-Malik confirm that many of
the individuals mentioned in the *Khitat* as substantial landowners had
descendants who were still important landowners prior to the land
reform of 1952. Baer, in particular, tells us that "About thirty of the
large landowning families mentioned in this work were represented in
either the Lower or the Upper House [of parliament] between 1942
and 1952 (in many cases by more than one member of the family).
. . . Eighteen of the families provided Cabinet Ministers between 1924
and 1950."[3]

Baer cited approximately one hundred names of large landowners
mentioned in 'Ali Pasha's *Khitat*. He states that about half or more of
these families had acquired their primary holdings in the first half of the
nineteenth century, and many joined the Wafd after the signing of the
Anglo-Egyptian treaty of 1936. These families weathered the political
storms from the decline of Muhammad Ali through the adventures of
Isma'il, the British occupation, and the rise of Egyptian nationalism.
But these wealthiest and most influential landlords did not survive the
revolution of 1952, the first wave of land reform, and the abolition of
political parties in 1954.

It is over against these great landowners that we must compare the
rural notables, shuyukh, 'umad and a'yan. 'Abd al-Malik, following
Ibrahim 'Amr, categorizes this group as owners of from 5 to 50 feddan.[4]
'Abd al-Malik calls them the "kulaks of Egypt" and asserts that this
class had greatly benefited from Isma'il's support, after Abbas I and
Sa'id had attempted to weaken the village 'umdah.

> Isma'il, tout au contraire, s'appuie largement sur eux; la première
> assemblée consultative des Députés de 1866 est choisie, pour la
> meilleure part, parmi les *sheikhs* . . . plus, Isma'il en nomme un
> grand nombre au poste de *moudir* (gouverneur) contre l'aristocratie
> turco-albanaise; tout naturellement, ces hommes soutiennent la
> révolution de 'Arabi en 1882, et rallient les *fallahs* à la cause na-
> tionale.[5]

'Abd al-Malik goes on to argue that Cromer sought to weaken this
recalcitrant political element by having his governors assert greater control over the village chiefs. Many shuyukh moved to the cities and
rented out their lands. Of those who stayed on many regained their
influence during World War I as a consequence of their responsibilities
for the recruitment of peasants for the Labor Corps. "It was the sons
of these rural notables who furnished the national movement, and the
Egyptian state and society, too, the majority of their functionaries and
intellectuals."[6] 'Abd al-Malik reminds us that 'Ali Pasha mentioned the
names of some of the 'umad favored by Isma'il, and he cites ten names,
only three of which are found in Baer's list of wealthy parliamentarians.[7]

Isma'il established the National Assembly in 1866 in order to extend
his influence into the rural areas and to find there new sources of funds.
Isma'il was a modernizer and ambitious to undertake grandiose projects
which resulted in the hopeless indebtedness of Egypt. These projects
also required a broadening of the scope of Egyptian government and
increased penetration of the government into the lives and consciousness of the people of village Egypt. Through the establishment of the
assembly and through the recruitment of junior officers from among
the rural notability, members of this rural segment became true participants in the Egyptian political system. Many of these junior officers in
the army were implicated in the rebellion of 1879 led by 'Arabi Pasha.
This mutinous activity was paralleled by pressure from the National
Assembly. Hence it may be said that the National Assembly was but
an indication of the intrusion of a whole new class into Egyptian politics, a class of rural notables who have shared a political history.

The extent to which this group shared other characteristics is not
clear. There is some evidence that through meeting in the assembly, in

the army, or in the bureaucracy, members of a'yan families have in the last hundred years grown to comprise a cohesive segment. But in their villages they may still be closer to their own neighbors, the small land-holding peasant or even the landless laborer, than they are to the nota-bles in the next village down river. Mosca and Marx would both argue that the local notable was isolated and that, in the aggregate, the rural notables did not form a class. Jacob Landau writing about indirect elec-tions in the early assembly seems to agree in the following passage:

> As Cairo, Alexandria and Damietta together chose only six delegates, this electoral system was designed mainly for the rural population which, in certain parts, was almost entirely illiterate. Thus the people could only be expected to vote for personalities with whom they were acquainted in everyday life.[8]

The suggestion that the cultural and social context of the a'yan was in effect that of village society is also sustained by Hasan Riad:

> Homogène, cette catégorie l'est dans la mesure où tous, propriétaires ou non, sont authentiques "paysans", presque toujours originaires du village, de mentalité réactionnaire et de comportement tradi-tionaliste.[9]

This brief discussion established the following points:
1. Many students of Egyptian social history agree that there has been some continuity of status for those who acquired substantial land-holdings in the early part of the nineteenth century.
2. While some of the largest landowners started out as village nota-bles, it is, in fact, important to differentiate these two groups after the second third of the nineteenth century.
3. The two groups developed separately after 1865, with the large landowners being strengthened under British occupation and the village notables being weakened, but not eliminated nor uprooted.
4. 'Ali Pasha mentions the names of both first stratum and second stratum elite personalities in his gazetteer.
5. The class of village notables is culturally homogeneous to the ex-tent that it shares traditional peasant culture, that is, to the extent that it resides in the village, participates in rural social life, and directly administers its agricultural holdings.
6. It is to be expected that some descendants of those mentioned by 'Ali Pasha will still be resident in the same villages, still own middle-sized estates, still dominate village politics, and still share in peasant culture.

'Ali Pasha's information dates from the 1870s and the National Union data is from 1959. In 90 years many village notables may have moved to the city, may have moved to another village, may have become poor, may have become very rich, may not have had male off-spring, or may have chosen names that were not traditional in the family. Only if an ancestor of the same or similar name was found in the same village in the *Khitat* could we be absolutely certain of the lineal continuity of the members of the village committees of the National Union. A somewhat lesser degree of certainty could be maintained for cases in which persons with similar names were found within the same district but not in the same village (or when we could not find the village listed in the register of the National Union). Some validity could be asserted for lineal continuity in the case of unusual names found in nearby places, even if not in the selfsame village recorded by 'Ali Pasha. We have already noted that 'Ali Pasha made a great many errors and that he often discussed personalities in contexts other than descriptions of their villages.

These materials do not permit a systematic comparison of those believed to have been influential rural notables in 1959 and the persons named by 'Ali Pasha. The most that can be accomplished is to establish some link, for some names. In this way, it can be shown that at least a segment of the rural notables of today are descendants of rural notables of a century ago. We will then be able to make some guesses regarding the degree of continuity, guesses which will have to stand until additional data becomes available.

The names mentioned in 'Ali Pasha may be roughly divided into two groups: the landed grandees and the rural notables. Of about one hundred names recorded by Baer, he identifies about 45 as grandees. 'Abd al-Malik lists ten 'umad, and only three of these are on Baer's list. Six of the remaining seven are on the list that we traced. We are, obviously, interested in the small fry, who were not so important for Baer.

An effort was made to excerpt all the names of important personalities mentioned by 'Ali Pasha as residing in the villages he described. After much review, discussion, and uncertainty, a list of some 237 names was agreed upon as both complete enough to be traced and well enough identified with a geographical location to be found in the register. For 88 of these names nothing was found in the register that gave us any confidence at all of having traced the descendants of the notables of 1875. For 71 names in 'Ali Pasha there was the strongest confirmation of continuity in the discovery of members of the National Union committees with similar names in the same or virtually the same village in 1959. For another 37 where the village name as recorded in 'Ali Pasha's *Khitat* cannot be located in the much more comprehensive register, a second level of confidence was assigned to the affirmation of intergenerational continuity as a consequence of discovering (usually several) similar names in the same district in 1959. The remaining 41, although often including quite well-known or unusual names, could be traced only to the province and not to the district at all. Otherwise the names are so common or so incomplete that we could not be sure that we found real kin in the register. Hence, there is strong affirmation for only 71 names out of 237, and even of these, 9 names were from one family, 3 from another, and in four cases 2 names were from the same family. In other words, we really have 58 strong independent cases out of 223, or about 26%.

Before looking more carefully at our strongest cases, let us compare the two groups, that is those for whom no names could be found in the province, and those for whom at least a minimally plausible case could be made that their descendants had been found. In table 25 we have broken down both groups in terms of the titles or occupations recorded by 'Ali Pasha. We do not have information for all the names, but even from the spotty information we have it is clear that the group which we have been unable to trace held a higher social position than the ones we have traced. Obviously those of high status were not then and their descendants are not now rural notables of the middle class.

High status personalities moved out of the countryside to the cities. Furthermore, it is precisely these people who have been purged by the revolutionary regime. We, therefore, expect to be able to trace fewer titled dignitaries and many more 'umad.

The members of the rural middle class whose names were cited by 'Ali Pasha are more likely to have descendants still in the same village and still members of the same class. Not every relative or descendant of a pasha becomes a pasha. Many relatives of the same name will remain on the land, frequently on the estate of their illustrious kinsman, where they may serve as 'umdah or shaykh al-balad. Some "extended" families can dominate several adjacent villages or at least villages where land is owned by the same absentee owner. The register of the National Union is not likely to contain the names of aristocrats or former pashas, but it may, as in the case of the Shawarbi family of Qalyub and the Abaza family of Bilbays, include many "not-so-rich" individuals with these famous family names. Still, we should expect that most of those names that can be traced with confidence are those of nonaristocratic members of the rural middle class—notables with only moderate-sized landholdings.

Table 25   Comparison of First and Second
                                          Stratum Members Mentioned in the
                                          Khitat

Occupation or Title	Not Traceable (n = 88)	Traceable (n = 149)	
Titled (pasha, bek, effendi)	35%	28%	(24%)
ʿUmad	18	42	(44)
Landowners	15	10	(11)
Civil servants	7	10	(11)
Others	25	10	(10)
Total	100%	100%	(100%)

Note: Parentheses indicate percentages with 8 members of the Abaza family excluded.

Of the 58 strongly confirmed names, only nine, or less than 16%, are titled. With the whole Abaza family and two more members of the Sha'ir family we have 17 titled out of 71, or less than 24%. The Abaza family was of bedouin origin and, as tribal shuyukh, was able to gain many titles and control over a good deal of land in return for settling down in al-Sharqiyyah province during the nineteenth century. Its route to landed wealth is not atypical for the Middle East, but it is certainly atypical for Egypt in the nineteenth century. It is also apparent that the roots of this family in al-Sharqiyyah countryside cannot easily be removed. In general, the areas which have a stronger residue of tribalism and bedouin influence, areas settled in more recent times, still show a greater dominance of the traditional tribal chiefs, often as 'umad and M.P.'s.

Leaving the Abaza family out of consideration, we have 63 confirmed names. Of these, 35 or nearly 56% were listed as 'umad by 'Ali Pasha. Of those who were not 'umad in this confirmed group, 6 were merchants, 6 were district or section administrators, 5 were owners of land or "truck gardens," 3 were low-ranking military officers, 2 were members of an important bedouin family, and the rest were not clearly identified. In three or four cases persons otherwise employed can be identified as related to persons who were 'umad. On the whole, it would appear that it is easier to trace those mentioned in 'Ali Pasha who had only local influence, or who, like the Abazas or the al-Sawis, were bedouin chiefs. Those who held great administrative responsibility, who had landed estates with pumps and "castles" of their own, and those who were highly educated are all more difficult to trace in the register of the National Union.

We have no way of knowing what portion of the rural notables of the period were included in the *Khitat*, nor whether the present rural middle class is wholly or only in small part descended from the rural middle class of a century ago. We cannot tell whether new elements entered the stratum of rural notables nor whether older segments left that stratum. Our hunch, confirmed by Hasan Riad's data on the fairly constant number of middle-sized landholdings, is that there was less social mobility among the rural middle class than elsewhere in Egyptian society. Our best guess is that a very substantial segment of the rural middle class goes back about one hundred years, at least. Furthermore, as we have seen, our historians find no evidence that the Egyptian authorities have tried persistently during the last hundred years to change the families from which the 'umad are chosen.

Hopefully, we have established some plausibility for the assertion that the contemporary rural middle class has ancestral links with an earlier rural middle class, one which antedates the revolution by many years. We shall now turn to examine the characteristics of the members of the National Union whose ancestors we have found in 'Ali Pasha's *Khitat*. Our goal in this examination is to discover whether these descendants of the nineteenth-century rural middle class are now among the more influential members of the National Union or not.

Restricting our analysis to the most highly confirmed descendants of those mentioned in the *Khitat*, we find that 34% of the family names (not individuals) in 'Ali Pasha can be traced to 40 family sets in the register of the National Union. Twenty-five other names in 'Ali Pasha can be traced to 26 individuals in the register. Thus more than half of our small sample can be traced to the more influential segment of the National Union. Almost all the villages with descendants of those named in 'Ali Pasha have relatively large committees, and we have further shown that 'Ali Pasha did not cite names at random but that he selected some, though not all, of the prominent people in some, though not all of the villages he discussed. We are not surprised, therefore, to learn that the descendants of the notables of 1875 are found disproportionately among the more influential of the members of the National Union.

When we compare the family set members of the National Union committees which have descended from those mentioned in 'Ali Pasha with the individual names we have found, the difference is quite striking. These 40 family sets, traced back to the nineteenth century, come out as quite influential. The total number of family-set members is 113, or an average 2.82 members per family set. Table 26 compares the two groups.

Table 26   Members of NU Descended from
                                        Those Mentioned in the *Khitat*

Occupation	Individuals		Family-Set Members	
	Number	Percentage	Number	Percentage
Former M.P.	1	4.2	12	10.6
ᶜUmdah	3	12.5	28	24.8
Farmer	10	41.7	36	31.9
Local council member	2	8.3	5	4.4
Doctor	0	0	2	1.8
Lawyer	2	8.3	3	2.7
Engineer	1	4.2	7	6.2
Civil servant	2	8.3	9	8.0
Educator	1	4.2	3	2.7
Merchant	0	0	1	.9
Entrepreneur	0	0	1	.9
Journalist	0	0	1	.9
Worker	1	4.2	0	0
Unknown	1	4.2	5	4.4
Total	24	100.1	113	100.2

There were among the individuals only 3 officers, a district president and two treasurers. Among the family-set members 16 were officers, nine presidents (seven of them former M.P.'s), two vice-presidents, three secretaries, and two treasurers.

It is by now clear that those family sets that can be traced back to 'Ali Pasha's *Khitat* with precise confirmation of name and place have an even greater concentration of the marks of influence than does even the average family set. Still we see that some individuals can trace their families back through 'Ali Pasha and yet they lack substantial influence. Some of the family sets are not outstanding in their local influence. But on the whole those family sets that we have been able to trace back have not lost influence or status, and they have gained positions of political influence in the National Union and in the National Assembly.

Our search for links between 'Ali Pasha's *Khitat* and the register of the National Union has amplified our understanding of the nature and origins of the rural middle class, but it has also demonstrated that the family set remains an even more important guide to the Egyptian rural elite than does the collection of names of notables in the *Khitat*. If we can assume (and it is very dubious) that 'Ali Pasha was a good sampler of the rural elite, then we might say that his list would be divided about equally into three groups. The first is comprised of the names of grandees who have been purged. The second is comprised of lesser digni-

taries of the period who cannot be traced today. The third group still
seems to hold positions of some status in the villages, and a little more
than 60% of them can truly be said to have persisted and perhaps even
grown in political influence.

Clearly many factors must be taken into consideration in explaining
why some families have remained consistently influential from 1875 to
1959 and why some are no longer heard from. Part of the answer has
to do with the geographical location of the family estate, a subject
which we will discuss below. Something must be attributed to luck, and
no doubt much more must be attributed to political skill. Be that as it
may, our strongest conclusion is that some, not all, families have persisted in their status as rural notables, and those that have persisted are
more influential than many of those who have more recently come into
local prominence.

Six

The Formation of
the Second Stratum in
the Twentieth Century

The Delegation, thus, represented
all sections of the Egyptian population. In addition to the old nationalists and Copts, it consisted of Hamd
al-Bâsil, a representative of the
Bedouins, and Muhammad Mahmûd,
a representative of the aristocracy
from Upper Egypt. Ismâ'il Sidqi
represented big business.

Zaheer Quraishi, *Liberal Nationalism
in Egypt*

Sidqi at fifty was an elegant figure,
attractive to women, who with his
oval face, his lively bearing, the
reticent brilliance of his eyes, his
informality of manner contrasted
strikingly with his corpulent and
somewhat ungainly Egyptian
colleagues.

Jacques Berque, *Egypt,
Imperialism and Revolution*

British troops remained in Egypt from 1882 until 1956. For the first
forty years of this period, British political influence was exercised more
or less directly, but in a context of legal anomaly. Egypt was formally
a province of the Ottoman Empire, with which state Great Britain enjoyed normal, if not friendly, relations until the outbreak of World
War I. In 1914 the United Kingdom renounced its previous recognition
of Ottoman sovereignty and established a protectorate over Egypt. The
protectorate went virtually unchallenged until after the war and the
opening of peace negotiations. A new nationalist leadership, which had
emerged under the British occupation, now demanded to be heard at
the peace conference and insisted that Egypt be granted complete independence. Some of these leaders formed an Egyptian nationalist delegation, or Wafd, to present Egypt's case at Paris. British resistance led to
the "revolution" of 1919 and to a vigorous nationalist agitation which
lasted until the United Kingdom agreed, in 1922, to recognize Egypt
as a sovereign state. In fact Egyptian independence was to be limited
by a continued British military occupation, by the presence of British

advisers in the key ministries, by British control over the Suez Canal and over the administration of the Sudan, and by British administration of both foreign affairs and defense. For a variety of complex domestic political reasons, the Wafd, which had developed from a cabal of nationalist notables to a network of jacobinist committees to a mass national movement, agreed to accept the new constitution and to contest the elections as a political party. In its capacity as a political party, though still claiming to be the only genuine national movement of Egyptians, the Wafd dominated the stormy parliamentary history of Egypt from 1924 to the revolution of 1952.

The basis of the Wafd's great popularity was the adamancy of its first and greatest leader, Sa'd Zaghlul, in demanding complete independence in 1919. The reputation of the Wafd was established as a result of its total identification with the rising of 1919. Naturally, the Wafd was criticized when it compromised these demands, and when it agreed to work with both the palace and the British under the 1923 constitution. It was also criticized for failing to press sufficiently vigorously for a program of social and economic reform. The Wafd platform called for independence from the British, enforcing constitutional limitations on the power of the king, and improving the lot of peasants, workers, members of the middle classes, and even the new class of Egyptian capitalists. The Wafd managed only limited, for the most part symbolic, achievements in all three areas.

Critics of the Wafd, and they have been most numerous since the 1952 revolution, have attempted to explain the failures of the Wafd as consequences of the social bases of Wafd strength, the interests of the Wafd leaders, or the structure of Egyptian society or its "stage of development" at the time. Those who were most impressed by the electoral strength of the Wafd tend to point to its influence over or support by the 'umdah class. Those who were impressed by Wafd agricultural policies point to Wafd links with the owners of latifundia, the joint-stock agricultural companies, and the absentee owners. Others still, noting the origins of the Wafd in the growth of the liberal-nationalist ideology among educated groups between 1882 and 1919, and the ability of the Wafd to mount effective student demonstrations right up to the 1950s, point to the urban and middle class character of the Wafd. As a mass national movement, the Wafd tried to be all things to all groups all the time. In point of fact, the Wafd made frequent tactical shifts and changes of course. It contested elections and boycotted elections. It established secret committees and a terrorist wing and then it abolished them. It mobilized the rural masses and then it abandoned them. No simple nor a priori dialectical theory can explain all of these tactical turns, nor do all of them make political sense. Nevertheless, it is probably most sound to see in the Wafd a bourgeois national movement of a not untypical sort, influenced by the liberal ideology of its British rulers and exploiting the social resources which were available despite the deepening cultural gulf between leaders and mass.

Though the Wafd has frequently been identified with rural Egypt, it was not an agrarian party. It was neither dominated organizationally nor ideologically identified with the rural middle class. The Wafd was linked with rural Egypt because it presented itself as a mass movement and because it could often control the rural vote. Some observers state flatly that the Wafd never lost a "free election." Others have suggested that none of the elections were really free, but that, whenever the palace allowed the Wafd electoral machinery to operate, an overwhelming vote was delivered. That vote was a peasant vote, it was often cast for landowners, but it was mobilized by the 'umad and masha'ikh. Milner complained that the Wafd controlled the 'amudiyyah through the district councils and later authors have noted that 'umad are appointed and dismissed by the Ministry of the Interior. 'Umad might be influenced by locally based landowners as well. Even though the notables got out the vote for the Wafd, only some of the a'yan were committed to the Wafd—especially after Zaghlul's death in 1927. The devices by which the rural vote might be controlled were also accessible to the royal court and to the pashas who opposed the Wafd. Because of the Wafd's early popularity in the countryside, it tended to take the rural vote for granted. The neglect of its rural organization encouraged its opponents to compete for the rural vote, and this strategy, in turn, when coupled with the emergence of radical urban groups strained both the organizational and political-doctrinal capacities of the Wafd.

Neither the electoral machinery of the Wafd, its willingness to use shady political tactics, nor even the "bourgeoisification" of the party should obscure the important fact that right up to 1952 the Wafd was the most popular political party, and that it did command the loyalty of the majority of the rural classes as well as some very important urban segments. If, as we believe, the revolutionary regime established after 1952 was in part sustained by the traditional social structure of rural Egypt, it follows that the support of the Wafd and the support of the Nasserist regime should be compared to learn whether they were the same; and if they were not the same, how they differed. We will find that the formation of the rural parliamentary elite of prerevolutionary times was a complex historical process and not a simple process of nationalist mobilization behind the leadership of the Wafd.

The enthusiastic rural risings of 1919 were episodic, and they subsided quite as suddenly and decisively as they erupted. The Wafd, through its secret societies and through the family links between its urban members and the rural notables, had organized and encouraged, if not directed, those risings.[1] During the course of the 1919 revolution, there were also incidents of peasant violence against landlords and the seizure of lands. Baer and Berque have both refuted the view that the Egyptian peasant is essentially and always submissive.[2] Despite such manifestations of typical peasant protest and growing land hunger, the 1919 revolution in the countryside was initiated in Cairo and implemented through the notables; and it was turned off in virtually the same manner. Neither peasant violence nor rural middle class agitation counted for much during the ensuing three decades of parliamentary and party politics. Though the rural notables continued to be elected to parliament, as they had been under Isma'il, little attention was paid to their waxing and waning by the chroniclers of the period. There was, in fact, some decline in the representation of the rural notability in the decade of the 1920s, when the Wafd was at the height of its popularity and electoral strength, and there was a considerable increase in the proportion of rural notables in the National Assembly in the 1930s and 1940s. The rise and fall of the representation of the rural notability may not have been the major theme in Egyptian politics, but, in retrospect, those changes are evidence of a complex process of historical structuring which has produced the rural support of the postrevolutionary regime.

To discover the degree of historical and social continuity between the pre- and post-revolutionary rural elites, we will examine the occupational composition and the correspondence of family names between members of prerevolutionary parliaments and the members of the National Union committees. Data from two periods of Egyptian parliamentary history, 1866–82 and 1924–50, will be used. These periods were chosen because of the relatively easy access to data concerning the members of those parliaments, and because they were periods of relative political independence for Egypt. Before 1866 consultative councils had been summoned by Napoleon in 1798 during the French occupation and by Muhammad 'Ali Pasha in 1824. But the continuous parliamentary history of Egypt begins in 1866 with the convening of a regular, elected assembly by Isma'il Khedive. This assembly was renewed in 1870, 1876, and 1881. From 1882 to 1923, during the period of direct British control, Egypt's parliamentary institutions were established in accordance with British preference. From 1883 to 1912 a bicameral legislature, modelled on the Indian Viceroy's Legislative Council, served as the Egyptian parliament. In 1913 Lord Kitchener replaced this bicameral legislature with the unicameral Legislative Assembly, including 66 elected members, 17 nominated members, and the ministers. This assembly held only one session. It was not reconvened after the outbreak of World War I. A new bicameral legislature was provided for in the constitution of 1923. Elections to the lower house were held in 1924, 1925, 1926, 1929, 1931, 1936, 1938, 1942, 1945, and 1950. No new parliamentary elections took place until after the revolution in 1957.

Table 27 presents the breakdown of the occupations of the elected members of parliament (lower house only) for the four sessions preceding the British occupation and for all but the 1950 session during the period of the constitutional monarchy. It may be assumed that the categories 'umdah and shaykh refer unequivocally to the rural middle class. The beks might be of rural or urban origin. The efendis, even if of rural origin, are to be associated with urban residence, advanced education, and some administrative experience. For the post-1924 list, 'umdah and a'yan are the main categories of the rural notability, while the property owner should probably be taken to refer to an owner of urban properties or a large absentee landowner. For the parliaments of 1942 and 1945, the occupational categories change once again, and the large number of "others" does not permit us to do more than guess about the occupational composition of those parliaments.

The proportion of 'umad in the assemblies of 1866, 1870, 1876, and 1881 was very large but there was a noticeable decline in their number as tension between parliament and the Khedive increased. The shaykhs and beks in the assembly of 1881 are still mostly a'yan, so the decline is easily exaggerated. It is noteworthy that the number of efendis, who are probably urban, educated, and "bourgeois," increased greatly in 1881, that is, during the 'Arabi agitation. Landau believed that it was the efendis who gave Isma'il and Tawfiq most of the trouble.[3]

There was a gradual decline in the numbers of a'yan and 'umad from 1924 to 1929, and then an increase which is very marked after 1931. At the same time, we note a gradual increase in the number of lawyers; some of them, but certainly not all nor even the majority at this time, were connected with rural middle class families. Another group that makes an important appearance in the parliament of 1929 was the property owner.

The Wafd ministry of 1929 was supported by the largest majority ever won by the nationalist party. The Wafd represented an emerging coalition of liberal bourgeois elements, fewer rural notables but more lawyers and more absentee landowners. With 60% of the popular vote and over 93% of the seats, Nahhas Pasha led the Wafd in their greatest effort to use the electoral system, parliament, and democratic legitimacy to change the system. The three goals of the Wafd were to gain a new

Table 27

Occupational Composition of Members of Egyptian Parliaments

	Year of Parliament and Total Membership												
	1866	1870	1876	1881	1924	1925	1926	1929	1931	1936	1938	1942	1945
Total Members	75	75	75	80	214	211	213	235	150	232	264	265	264
ʿUmdah	58	64	59	29	19	22	8	4	7	5	1	2	0
Shaykh	1	1	0	5								26	20
Bek	4	1	2	14								55	53
Efendi	3	0	1	18									
Other			11	5								137	151
Aʾyan					100	100	82	65	82	96	156	9	
Lawyer					34	40	48	52	10	53	28	2	
Property owners					0	5	14	48	3	17	3		
Government official					13	9	12	16	17	20	27		
Estimated number in rural middle class	58	64	59	48	119	122	90	69	89	101	157	?	?
Percentage of rural middle class	77.3	85.3	78.6	60.0	55.6	57.8	42.2	29.3	59.3	46.1	59.4		

treaty from Great Britain, to assert ministerial control over appointments to the Senate, and to invoke legal retribution to forestall royalist ministers who might be tempted to subvert the constitution of 1923. Failing of an agreement with the British, Nahhas's assault on the powers of King Fu'ad were doomed, and he resigned at the end of 1930.[4]

In 1930, the king suspended the constitution, prorogued the Wafd-controlled parliament, and approved a new electoral law providing for indirect elections and more restrictive qualifications for the franchise. The Wafd boycotted the elections of 1931. The increase in the membership of a'yan in that year represents the efforts of the monarchy to undermine the source of the Wafd's strength in the villages and to build a counterweight to the Wafd's growing support among the urban bourgeois intellectuals and among the urban bourgeoisie. There is substantial evidence suggesting that the rural notables favored by Sidqi's 1931 electoral strategy were from families that had never been members of the parliamentary elite or at least were from rural strata which had never been politically influential outside of their own villages. It may well be that Sidqi tapped a political reservoir of owners of more modest holdings from more remote villages than had the Wafd heretofore. The successful electoral strategy of the monarchy forced the Wafd, eventually, to cultivate a similar or the same group of rural notables in order to win elections even while continuing to serve the interests of nonrural elements.

Figure 5 shows the opposing tendencies of the curves of representation for the a'yan on the one side and the lawyers and property owners on the other. The percentage of seats won by the Wafd in each of the elections from 1924 to 1950 was also plotted in order to show the relationship between Wafd electoral success and the representation of the rural middle class. While the percentage of rural middle class or a'yan was, in 1924, almost as high as it was in 1881, the decline of representation of a'yan from 1876 to 1881 is significantly related to increased nationalist agitation as well as to the institutional and educational reforms of Isma'il. Similarly, the percentage of rural middle class in the National Assembly was inversely related to Wafd electoral success during the interwar period. There was, however, no real continuity between 1881 and 1924 in this regard. It is sounder to note the rise of non-agrarian elites and to measure the change over four decades by a comparison of the average rural middle class representation for the two periods in question: 75.3% for the nineteenth century and 49.9% for the interwar period.

The wide fluctuation of the number of Wafd seats in the parliament can be contrasted with the gradually decreasing amplitude in the fluctuation of the percentage of rural notables in the assembly. Whenever there was a sharp decline in the number of Wafd seats, there was either royal interference in the election or a Wafd boycott of the election as an anticipatory protest. The boycotts of 1931 and 1945 account for the absence of Wafd seats. Although the representation of the Wafd and rural middle class are inversely related, there is evidence that the difference between the two was beginning to decline. There is also a suggestion of a secular decline in the size of the Wafd parliamentary party.

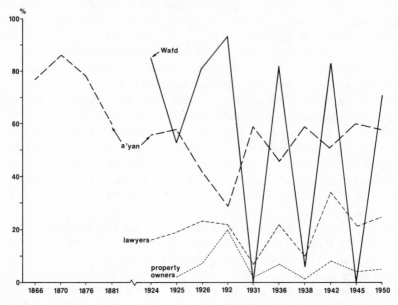

Fig. 5   Occupational Representation in
                                              Prerevolutionary Parliaments

The popularity of the Wafd is often exaggerated by historians of the interwar period, for its popular vote ranged from 6% to 40% less than the proportion of seats won in various elections. The largest disproportion was in 1924 and the smallest in 1925, yet the representation of the rural middle class changed only slightly in these two elections. We are led to the hypothesis that the Wafd and the palace drew on rival groups of the rural middle class for the first part of the period in question. There were frequently rival candidates for the position of 'umdah in many villages.

Had the Wafd succeeded after the elections of December 1929, it is likely that it would have concentrated its energies to a far greater extent on the urban classes. Efforts were made to instigate widespread opposition to the palace and to the government of Sidqi Pasha. The historian Rafi'i Bek even writes of 'umad resigning their posts in protest against the suspension of the 1923 constitution and the new electoral law of 1930.[5] Nevertheless, the Sidqi government mobilized strong support in the countryside.

Despite the ease with which the Wafd was defeated, Great Britain sought a more popular government with which it could sign an agreement legitimating its presence in Egypt. When the Wafd returned to power in 1936, it was to work out a treaty with Britain that would be acceptable to popular opinion, and that return to power was preceded by popular political disturbances in Cairo and other cities, as King Fu'ad was nearing death. Faruk, who ascended the throne in 1936, won amazing popularity as a young, pious monarch, and he was able to make short shrift of the Wafd. As soon as convenient after the signing of the Anglo-Egyptian treaty of 1936, the palace sought new elections. The Wafd suffered a humiliating electoral defeat in 1938, bringing the realization that the national party had lost part of the popular support which it had mobilized in the agitation in the cities in 1935/36.

In 1942 the Wafd was, in effect, installed by the British to prevent any Egyptian-German cooperation. The further loss of political popularity in the urban areas which this British support occasioned was exacerbated by the increasing responsiveness of the Wafd to the wealthy urban classes, to property owners, to carriage trade doctors and lawyers, and to the emerging group of indigenous banker-industrialists. In its victories in 1942 and 1950 the Wafd depended as usual upon its rural "machine" for electoral support, but the leadership in Cairo was increasingly forced to contend with a younger and more revolutionary group of urban intellectuals. The leadership of the Wafd was divided over the issues of reform and radical protest in 1950 as it had been in 1920 and 1933. The Wafd was constantly losing conservative members, even though it was radical only on the issue of relations with Britain. Nevertheless, the Wafd tended to do marginally better in the urban areas than in the rural areas in the elections. In fact some former Wafdists who felt that the revolution of 1952 was pressed too far by the army officers argued that, left to itself, the Wafd was on the verge of a truly far-reaching internal reform which would have provided for both the preservation of the parliamentary system and for extensive social reform in Egypt.

We cannot tell whether the Wafd would have given greater political expression to urban social development or whether it would have persisted in policies which favored the haute bourgeoisie. The Wafd pur-

sued a conservative economic policy while relying on the a'yan to serve
as the political buffer against social and economic change in the rural
areas and to provide the necessary legitimation of a majority vote.
There was considerable stability of the political process in the rural
areas from the 1870s to the 1930s despite significant economic and
social change in those areas. The a'yan still dominated the political
process.

Urban political patterns, as suggested by the growth of student agitation and the emergence of the Muslim Brethren, were increasingly di-
verging from rural politics during the interwar period. In the cities
agitational politics and an alienative political culture prevailed, while
in the country consensus politics and a deferential political culture
persisted despite the deepening economic decline. After the revolution,
the urban and rural processes remained apart, with mass mobilizing
politics characterizing the urban political process and traditional authoritarianism and consensualism dominating the rural process. Before
and after the revolution the keystone of the structure of rural politics
was the role of the rural notable.

This examination of the occupations of the members of the assembly
during the interwar period has revealed the changes in the class orientation of the Wafd, the recruitment of an apparently new rural segment
into political participation by Sidqi Pasha, and the subsequent competition of the palace and the Wafd for control of this pliable and relatively
undemanding group.

In the parliaments examined, that is, from 1866 to 1881, and from
1924 to 1945, including by-elections to those thirteen parliaments, 2400
seats were filled in the sixteen agricultural provinces. Of that number,
901 or 37.5% of the seats were held by ancestors of members of National Union committees. The 901 seats were held by about 400 or
450 individuals representing approximately 370 lineages. Some lineages
were elected to as many as 10 or 12 of 13 parliaments examined. Occasionally, and especially in the 1940s, more than one member of a family (lineage) held a seat in the same parliament.

These ancestors will be traced through the 13 parliaments and will
be compared with the rural middle class members and with the Wafd
parliamentary party. Table 28 shows for each parliament, the number
of M.P.'s who were a'yan or members of the rural middle class, the
total number of seats, and the percentage of all seats held by our "ancestors." Figure 6 compares the percentage of the rural middle class in
each parliament with the percentage having descendants in the National
Union.

Table 28   Proportion of NU Ancestors and
                                          Rural Middle Class in Prerevolu-
                                          tionary Parliaments

Year of Parliament	Ancestor Seats[a]	Total Rural Middle Class	Total Members (all provinces)	Ancestor Seats as Percentage of Total Seats
1866	31	58	75	41.3[b]
1870	45	64	75	60.0
1876	34	59	75	45.0
1881	31	48	80	38.8
1924	29	119	214	13.6
1925	40	122	211	19.0
1926	30	90	213	14.0
1929	41	69	235	17.4
1931	88	89	150	58.7
1936	114	101	232	49.1
1938	123	157	264	46.6
1942	138	?	265	52.0
1945	157	?	264	59.2

[a]Ancestor seats include all seats held by members of the same lineage but does not distinguish whether elected in a by-election or in the regular election. In 1945, of 157 seats, only 134 lineages were represented, but, e.g., in 1929, there were no multiple seat families. Ancestors were traced for the 16 agricultural provinces only.

[b]Percentage is based on all seats, disregarding by-elections. By-elections were not unimportant in number, but my data does not tell me whether the M.P.'s were reelected at by-elections or not. In 1931, for example, the election was, in effect, held twice, but most of the rural representatives were reelected.

From the figure we can see that for the four nineteenth-century parliaments there is a strong correlation of the percentage of the rural middle class in parliament and the percentage of M.P.'s having National Union committee descendants ($r^2 = .59$). During the interwar period it seems that there was a tendency for the percentage of M.P.'s having descendants in National Union committees to rise despite the sharp fluctuation of the proportion of the rural middle class in those parliaments. The continued rise of the number of M.P.'s with links to the National Union for the parliaments of 1942 and 1945, given that 1942 was a year of Wafd victory and 1945 a year of a Wafd defeat, is remarkable. We might have expected that 1942 would have been a year of decline for the rural middle class in parliament and 1945 would show the opposite tendency. It is widely believed that the Wafd did change its political direction after 1942, so we may not be far wrong in suggesting that as the reason for the continued upward trend of National Union-linked M.P.'s in 1942 and 1945 even under the Wafd.

This influence is further sustained by the coincidence of a Wafd victory in 1936, a high percentage of National Union-linked M.P.'s elected in that year, and a smaller decline in rural notable M.P.'s than in 1925 or 1926. Admittedly there is not much to go on, but it looks as though 1936 may have heralded the turning point in Wafd tactics which were more strongly manifested in 1942.

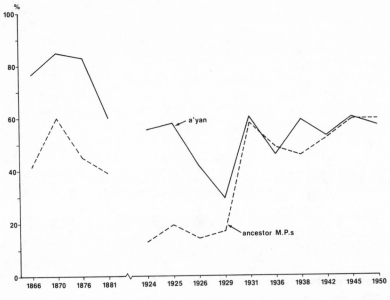

Fig. 6   A'yan and Prerevolutionary M.P.
                                               Ancestors of NU Members

It might be argued that the increase in National Union-linked M.P.'s in the more recent parliaments is a function of chronology and that those who were more recently influential are now more influential than those who were influential in more remote generations. This view might be translated as a theory of the "half-life" of elite status. Such an interpretation will not hold, however, because it does not account for the high percentage of those descended from the M.P.'s of the nineteenth century who are still political forces on the local scene. Furthermore, the sharp rise in National Union-linked M.P.'s in 1931 is the result of the political tactics of Sidqi Pasha, and his political legacy is still viable in Egypt today.

The evident success of Sidqi's political recruitment policies was not alone due to his "discovery" or creation of an important rural elite segment. There were, in addition, important new cultural movements developing in the urban areas which conflicted with the growing "liberalism" of the Wafd. In particular, middle class and lower middle class alienation began to express itself in radical movements which were influenced by European fascism, by religious fundamentalism, and to a lesser extent by Communism. Hence, the Wafd was drawn to a "rural strategy" for many reasons: to compete with the king, to strengthen its nationalist image by calling to mind the events of 1919, to win the support of the "grands bourgeois," and to reduce its dependence on the mobilized and "illegitimately" participant urban groups.

If our conclusions from this analysis are correct, it follows that the significant rise in political status of the rural middle class during the last phase of the prerevolutionary period (1931–52), after a substantial decline from the heights of 1870, was due less to the organization, initiative, ideological cohesiveness, or even the growing *urban* strength of the rural middle class, than it was to the competitive search engaged in first by the palace and then by the Wafd for quiescent and pliable political allies.

With the extreme fluctuation in the percentage of seats won by the Wafd from election to election in mind, it is interesting to find out whether the king and the Wafd were drawing on different segments of the rural middle class. Figure 7 compares the actual number of M.P. ancestors of National Union committee members in each parliament with the actual number of newly elected M.P. ancestors. There was a diminishing tendency for two groups of a'yan to alternate in incumbency depending on whether the king or the Wafd won. In terms of the National Union and the postrevolutionary parliament, however, the two groups are not easily distinguishable.

The divergence of the preoccupation, nineteenth-century pattern and that under the constitutional monarchy is striking. During the four nineteenth-century elections new membership fluctuated directly (with the percentage of rural middle class and) with the total of rural middle class seats, thus indicating, despite the decline in rural middle class representation, that there was keen competition and considerable turnover of such representation. During the interwar period, the total number of M.P. ancestors increased in every election except that of 1926, a Wafd victory. The election of 1929 was an even greater Wafd victory, and the relatively small increase in total M.P. ancestors indicates that the Wafd probably replaced some of the king's rural supporters with their own. The election of 1931, showing a sharp increase in both total M.P. ancestors and newly elected M.P. ancestors, reflects Sidqi Pasha's electoral strategy of recruiting a new rural elite and of preferring the

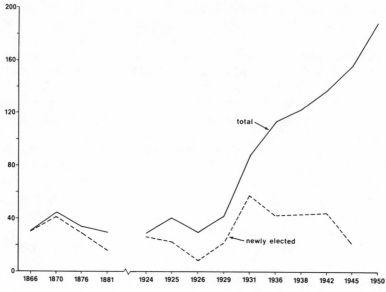

Fig. 7   Newly Elected and Cumulative Total
of Prerevolutionary M.P. Ancestors
of NU Members

rural middle class to the bourgeoisie and to the absentee landowners.
From 1931 on the total M.P. ancestors continues to increase while
newly elected members tend to decrease, thus showing that an increasing number of these M.P. ancestors were reelected. Since the Wafd
won more than 80% of the 265 seats in 1942, but only 6% in 1938
and no seats in 1945, it follows that the Wafd and the king were electing many of the same people. Looking back at figure 5 we can further
confirm the importance of the election of 1931, but the data on the
National Union ancestors renders 1931 a decisive turning point not
only for the interwar period but for the organization of the National
Union itself.

We have suggested that figure 6 allows the inference that the size of
the rural middle class continued to increase in the parliaments of 1942,
1945, and probably 1950. Unfortunately, we do not have good occupational data for 1942 and 1945, so our inferences regarding the 1942
and 1945 parliaments cannot be sustained decisively. Our projection
is, however, based on the assumption that the ancestors of National
Union committee members were for the most part members of the rural
middle class themselves.

For 1942 and 1945 we were able to trace the occupations only of those "ancestors" who were reelected in 1942 and 1945. The proportion of "ancestors" in the rural middle class in these parliaments is low for two reasons. First, we do not have information for any of the M.P.'s who were elected for the first time in 1942 or 1945 and, second, some of those who were elected in 1942 and 1945 were descendants of M.P.'s elected in the nineteenth century and might themselves be professionals or businessmen while their fathers or grandfathers were a'yan. Table 29 presents some data on the "ancestors."

The middle column shows us that a very large proportion of the ancestors of National Union members are from the rural middle class. There does appear to be some tendency for this proportion to decline from the heights of the nineteenth century, but we note the high level of 83% reached in 1931—our crucial year. In 1936 there was another decline with the Wafd victory, but in 1938 Faruk's victory brought the percentage up to 76%.

While most of the "ancestors" of the National Union committee members were a'yan, these ancestors did not make up the bulk of the a'yan group in parliament until 1931, even though they were gradually increasing their share of the rural middle class in parliaments after 1924. Despite the lack of information regarding the occupations of the "ancestors," and despite what appears to be a downward trend in the proportion of a'yan, we also note that in 1945 the proportion was up to

Table 29		Percentage of Prerevolutionary M.P.'s Who Were A'yan	
Year of Parliament	Number of Ancestors Who were A'yan	Percentage of Ancestors Who were A'yan	Percentage of A'yan Who were Ancestors
1866	27	87	46.5
1870	43	95	67.2
1876	30	88	50.8
1881	20	65	41.6
1924	22	76	18.4
1925	30	75	24.6
1926	21	70	23.3
1929	22	54	31.8
1931	73	83	82.0
1936	73	64	72.2
1938	94	76	59.2
1942	(61)	(44)	--
1945	(89)	(57)	--

57% from 44%. We note further that this increase took place in a year when the Wafd boycotted the elections. The pattern remains consistent.

Recently some new data has been published which allows some differentiation between the members of parliament who were large landowners and those who were of the rural middle class. 'Asim al-Dasuqi defined as large landowners those owning over 100 feddan, and he has given us the percentage of all M.P.'s who fell into that class for all the parliaments from 1924 to 1950.[6] On figure 8 his data are compared

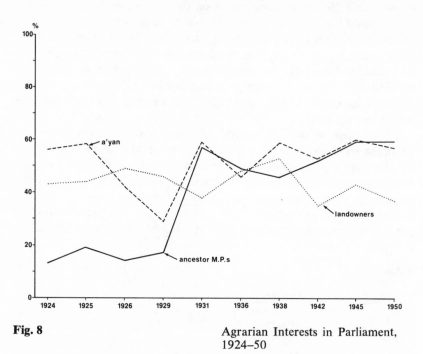

Fig. 8   Agrarian Interests in Parliament, 1924–50

with the percentage of ancestors and the percentage of rural middle class members. In interpreting figure 8, it is well to remember that most of the parliamentary ancestors of members of the National Union elite were a'yan and that the proportion of a'yan ancestors increases as we approach the revolution of 1952. Moreover, the proportions of both ancestors and a'yan are evidently increasing in the years before the revolution. Al-Dasuqi's data shows that, throughout the period there was a tendency for the proportion of ancestors to decline as the proportion of large landowners increased. The only exceptions were the elections of 1925 and 1945 and the 1925 case can readily be interpreted as sustaining the hypothesis that, for the most part, the largest landowners were not members of the rural middle class. The relatively high percentages for all three in 1936, converging at about 47%, together with the counter trend data of 1945 remind us that a substantial proportion of the ancestors were large landowners, or owners of 'izab and latifundia. Nevertheless, the downward trend of the large landowners and the upward trend of the ancestors and a'yan are clear. Earlier, it was suggested that in 1942 the Wafd may have adopted the 1931 strategy of Sidqi and the palace. Al-Dasuqi's data strengthen this hypothesis and further suggest that the coalition of anti-Wafdist parties which won in 1938 and in 1945, as opposed to Sidqi's virtual one-party domination of the 1931 elections, included more of the largest landowners. Finally, in considering the divergence of interests between the largest and medium landowners, al-Dasuqi also reports that only 55% of the members of the Agricultural Committee of the Parliament for the entire period 1924–50 were large landowners, while 80% of the members of the Committee on Cotton were large landowners.[7]

It is likely that the worldwide depression, which knocked the bottom out of cotton prices also had much to do with the political changes in Egypt which brought this group of "ancestors" to the fore. Little was done to relieve Egypt's economic problems, but Sidqi did set up a new agricultural bank and several types of loan remission and payment deferral were granted which hurt the financial groups, benefitted the middle-sized farmer, and probably kept the biggest landowners from gobbling up the middle-sized group. It would appear that the king needed the a'yan just when the a'yan needed the king most.

The reelection of many rural notable ancestors in the war years suggests that at least some were backed by both the king and the Wafd. Or, more accurately, some of the rural middle class candidates changed their party affiliations in accordance with their perceptions of who had the upper hand at the time of the elections. Nevertheless, it would be intriguing to learn whether there was some substantial differentiation between those a'yan who supported the Wafd and those who supported the king. In particular we want to know whether the second stratum which emerged after the revolution of 1952 developed from a rural stratum originally mobilized by a monarchist prime minister seeking to stem the political rise of the Egyptian bourgeoisie. In summing up his analysis of the party affiliations of the ancestors, John Anderson expressed the view that both the Wafd and the parties supported by the palace drew upon the same "broadly homogeneous rural class," but that it was possible to draw some significant political distinction between the two insofar as the ancestors of the National Union elite is concerned. Anderson shows that proportionately more of the descendants of the prerevolutionary M.P.'s who were members of the National Union committees were descendants of "anti-Wafdist" M.P.'s, as were more of the district officers, members of larger family sets, and members of the 1957 National Assembly (see table 30).

Table 30   Proportion of the Rural Middle Class among Wafdists and Anti-Wafdists in Parliament

Year of Parliament	Total Seats Won		Rural Middle Class[a] Wafd among All Wafd		Rural Middle Class[a] Anti-Wafd among All Anti-Wafd	
	Wafd	Anti-Wafd	Number	Percentage	Number	Percentage
1924	181	33	99/181	54.7	24/33	72.7
1926	172	42	77/172	45.6	24/42	57.1
1929	212	20	63/212	29.7	14/20	70.0
1936	180	52	80/180	44.4	27/52	51.9
1938	14	250	9/14	64.3	148/250	59.2
1942[b]	(203)	(30)	(99/203)	(49)	(19/30)	(63)
1950[b]	(157)	(79)	(78/157)	(50)	(58/79)	(73)

Source: John Anderson, "Representative Systems and 'Ruralizing Elections'" (M.A. thesis, University of Chicago, 1976), p. 121.

[a]Rural middle class occupation totals, based upon Subhi for 1924-38 and upon Subhi and *Le Mondain egyptien* for 1942 and 1950, are for the first-elected only, excluding by-elections.

[b]Party affiliation totals listed here are based for the most part upon immediate press reports (*al-Ahram* and *Egyptian Gazette*) and differ slightly from Quraishi's totals, which seem to include later changes, chiefly to the Wafd in landslide election years. Totals for 1942 and 1950 are incomplete because occupational data were unavailable. First and second ballot figures for 1942 give the Wafd 234 seats, versus 30 to Independent and minority party candidates; in 1950, these figures are 221 and 98, respectively.

The ancestor MPs (mostly a'yan) are consistently a larger proportion of the pro-palace deputies, though both groups continued to grow. . . . [Wafdist ancestor seats] total 398 or 29.9% of all Wafd won seats in the regular elections. Anti-Wafdist ancestors total 553 or 53.7% of all anti-Wafdists . . . . [See figure 9.] A number of these ancestors are the same for both groups, but these were mostly Sa'dists and other defectors to the King's camp, so we might consider the Wafdist ancestors even fewer if later party affiliations are given precedence.[8]

Anderson goes on to point out that the Wafd's electoral strength was actually much greater in the cities than in the countryside on the eve of the revolution, and that fewer Wafd candidates were elected unopposed in the rural areas than in the cities (see figure 10). In the election of 1950 he points out that the urban vote of the Wafd candidates was

57.6% in the largest cities and 53.4% in the provincial cities, but only
40.3% in the rural districts.[9] Anderson even found some evidence that
the elements of the rural middle class recruited to parliamentary politics
after 1931 were drawn from somewhat lower strata than those members of the rural middle class elected during the 1920s, and he was
able to show that there was a larger proportion of ancestors among
the Wafdist losers in the elections of 1942 and 1950 than among the
winners.[10]

On the eve of the revolution, Wafdist candidates were meeting with
increasingly tough competition in the rural areas and they seemed to be
trying to recruit notables who were influential in their own right—but
frequently these notables had little influence, as yet, beyond their own
village. These notables retained that local influence and so were elected
to the National Union committees, or else they were so little tainted by
their brief and unsuccessful association with the Wafd that the Nasserist
regime did not believe it worthwhile to prevent their candidacy or their
election.

The descendants of this important group of prerevolutionary members of parliament numbered approximately 800 or a little under 3%

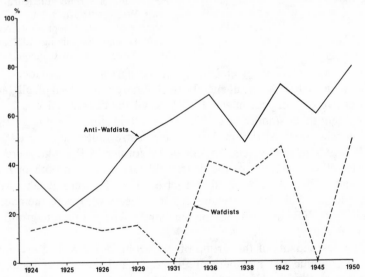

Fig. 9　　　　　　　Party Affiliations of Ancestors:
　　　　　　　　　　Proportions of Wafd and Anti-Wafd
　　　　　　　　　　Parliamentary Groups
　　　　　　　　　　John Anderson, "Representative
　　　　　　　　　　Systems and Ruralizing Elections"
　　　　　　　　　　(M.A. thesis, Univ. of Chicago, 1976)

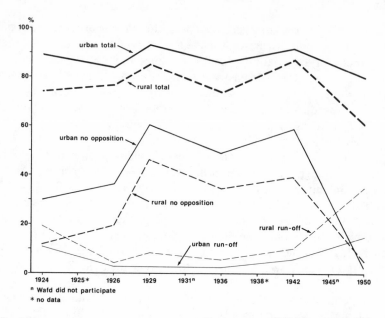

Fig. 10

Percentage of Urban and Rural
Seats Won by Wafd
John Anderson, "Representative
Systems and Ruralizing Elections"
(M.A. thesis, Univ. of Chicago, 1976)

of the National Union membership of the agricultural provinces. This
3% includes 17.3% of all members of family sets, 55% of all family
sets of five or more members, 17.2% of all the district officers, 29.7%
of all officers in family sets, 22.9% of all members of the National
Union who were M.P.'s in 1957 (i.e., postrevolutionary), 35.4% of
such M.P.'s in family sets, 55.7% of all former M.P.'s who were also
district officers, 31.5% of the district officers who were both in family
sets and M.P.'s, 42.3% of all district officers who were 'izbah owners,
and 48.1% of all 'izbah-owning district officers who were members of
family sets. The average size of the family set for this last group was
3.61 (figure 11).

The descendants of this group of prerevolutionary M.P.'s are among
the most influential members of the National Union, as measured by
family set, district office, 'izbah ownership, and membership in parliament. It is also the case that, among the descendants, the members of
family sets were also more influential than the individuals.

The descendants who were members of family sets comprise more
than 75% of the total descendants of prerevolutionary M.P.'s and therefore constitute the bulk of this elite segment, even though the indi-

viduals are not to be neglected. Furthermore, the average size of family
set for descendants is 3.22, while the average size of all family sets is
around 2.5. Family-set ancestors outnumbered the others in every election year except 1929 and 1931. There were more officers and more
former M.P.'s among the family-set descendants than in the nonfamily
group. The ancestors of this family-set group were reelected more frequently than the ancestors of the nonfamily group: ancestors of family-

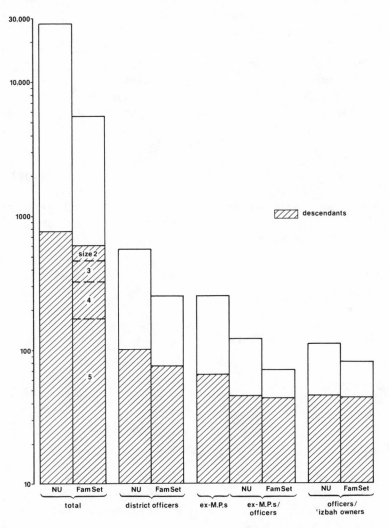

Fig. 11   Elite Status of Descendants of
                                         Prerevolutionary M.P.'s

set members were reelected an average of 2.57 times while ancestors of
individuals were reelected only 1.95 times. Family ancestors comprised
only 51.5% of the total but their descendants included 74% of the
district officers. Similarly there were 59 former M.P.'s, of which 39
were in family sets (66%) and 20 were not. In the election of 1931
and thereafter there was a steady increase in the number of ancestors,
and that increase was far more marked for the ancestors of officers and
former M.P.'s in family sets than for the ancestors of nonfamily-set
elite personnel. In order to grasp the relative influence of the family set
better, the percentage of family sets including a former M.P. can be
compared with the percentage of former M.P.'s among the nonfamily-
set descendants. The resultant percentages are 20.2% for family-set
members and 11.6% for individual descendants.

Family-set size is also politically important. Figures 12 and 13 show
that the descendants in family sets tend to come from the larger family
sets. Lineages of prerevolutionary M.P.'s account for 5% of family sets
of 2, 12% of family sets of 3, 25% of family sets of 4, and 55% of
family sets of 5 or more. Hence, for any family set of five or more, the
chances are better than 5 to 4 that the members of the family set are
descendants of a prerevolutionary M.P., and the chances are about 1 to
5 that one member of the family set was elected to the National Assembly in 1957. Chances of the average member of a National Union committee being a former M.P. are less than one in a hundred.

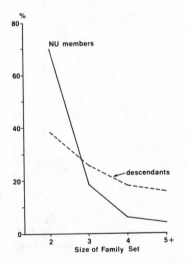

Fig. 12

Family-Set Size and Descent from
Prerevolutionary M.P.'s

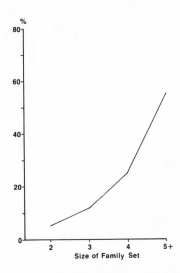

Fig. 13   Descendant Family Sets as a Proportion of All Family Sets

The political characteristics of the descendants, indicating a significant continuity of elite status at a specific level of the political regime,
throw retrospective light on the ancestors as a fairly distinct group,
but one that could not be known except as part of our category of the
rural middle class, were it not for the data on the National Union.
Reciprocally, our analysis of the political fate of these ancestors contributes to a diachronic study of the contemporary political elite. We
believe that the present influence of the descendants is due not only to
the status of their ancestors as M.P.'s, but even more to the political
purposes to which the ancestors responded. The political role of the
ancestors elucidates further the meaning of the second stratum, particularly insofar as there is ground for the hypothesis that the same sociopolitical element has structured regime level change processes both
before and after the revolution.

It seems inescapable that the most influential part of the second
stratum of the Egyptian revolutionary regime developed from the seed
planted in 1931, that it was formed in the image of the electoral struggles of the 1930s and 1940s, and that it was decisively defined by the
policy of excluding important former Wafdist politicians in the aftermath of the Naguib-Nasser dispute of 1954.

Seven

Occupational Configurations and Mobility Patterns in Elite Families

All the china and glass in the house
—save for the ceremonial black
coffee set which was kept for fu-
nerals—was now broken up, tram-
pled on, shivered to atoms. Everything that might suggest the order
and continuity of earthly life,
domestic, personal or social must be
discarded now and obliterated.

Lawrence Durrell, *The Alexandria
Quartet*

By and large the modernization literature has had an individualistic bias. Modernization and its political consequences have been attributed to the activities and ideas of individuals who have broken family ties, moved away from the old homestead to the city, acquired new ideas, and taken jobs in new institutional settings. The concepts of the "new man," the mobile empathetic individual, and the intelligentsia have all been used to describe the modernizing and rationalizing political elite. Both western liberal and communist theorists have been disposed, at times, to see these "new men" as individuals rather than as members of families. Consequently they have tended to view the modernizing elite in its urban setting without regard for its possible rural origin. They have also made it difficult, indeed, to take account of the tradi-tional and regional components of elite recruitment because they have considered, primarily, where the new men are now rather than where they come from.

While analysis of the data on the National Union has not allowed families to be traced beyond the village or town in which committee members resided, even a family in a single location has characteristics which are more revealing than those of individuals. The distribution of occupations within family sets will be used to make distinctions regard-ing the composition of the second stratum and to determine whether

144

the second stratum is comprised of several distinct social components or whether it is a homogeneous group.

We have already discovered that the members of family sets are more modern-urban than a random selection of members of the National Union committees. We have also discovered that only 51.3% of all the family sets are comprised of either wholly modern or wholly traditional members. The remaining 48.7% of all family sets include those engaged in both modern-urban and rural-traditional occupations. There are more influential mixed families than either modern or traditional family sets. The mixed family set is the mode, but man for man, given that there are far fewer moderns, the moderns are proportionately more influential in some urban areas. Nevertheless, insofar as the second stratum is concerned, there is no significant urban-rural break. On the contrary, there is an important and vital urban-rural link which is maintained by an influential social segment. Furthermore, in many cases, it will be more reasonable to argue that it was the priority of rural notability which was the precondition of elite status and the prelude to migration and the acquisition of a modern education.

An important if indecisive piece of evidence is family-set size. Family-set size is larger for the mixed family, averaging 2.8 against 2.3 for the traditional family set and 2.1 for the modern family set. We have already found that the larger the family sets are, the more influential and the more likely are they to be connected with the prerevolutionary parliamentary elite.

Insofar as occupation is itself taken as a measure of status and influence and simultaneously functions as the basis of determining whether the family sets are modern or traditional, a comparison of these two types (modern and traditional sets) is impossible. We can only compare the modern with the mixed and the traditional with the mixed, in turn. Even such a comparison will be complicated because the groups to be compared in each case will not have the same occupational categories. The mixed family sets will include all the occupations while the modern and traditional will be mutually exclusive. To cope with this problem, the mixed category was divided into two parts, corresponding to the two occupational subsets, and each subset was compared with the corresponding modern or traditional occupations of the nonmixed family sets. Table 31 compares the occupational distribution among modern family sets and among traditional family sets with the distribution of modern occupations only among mixed family sets. Also listed are the occupational distributions for all members of all family sets. The column headed "mixed unadjusted" under which the percentages for each occupation are enclosed in parentheses, gives the per-

Table 31   Occupational Distribution of Family-
                                          Set Members

Modern Occupation	Modern Family Set	Mixed Family Set	All Members of All Family Sets	Mixed Unadjusted
Doctor	1.6%	2.1%	.7%	(.9)
Lawyer	8.8	12.4	3.7	(5.8)
Engineer	6.6	9.8	2.9	(4.5)
Teacher	21.3	19.2	6.6	(8.8)
Civil servant	23.6	21.8	7.5	(9.9)
Merchant	16.8	12.8	4.7	(5.8)
Businessman	2.9	2.2	.8	(1.0)
Student	2.9	5.2	1.5	(2.5)
Worker	2.6	1.4	.6	(.6)
Former M.P.	4.9	6.6	1.6	(3.0)
Local councillor	5.6	4.4	1.6	(2.0)
Ex-army officer	.6	.7	.2	(.3)
Ex-police officer	.5	.4	.0	(.2)
Rare	.6	.3	.0	(.2)
Cabinet minister	.5	.5	.0	(.2)
Total	99.8%	99.8%	32.4%	45.7%

Traditional Occupation	Traditional Family Set	Mixed Family Set	All Members of All Family Sets	Mixed Unadjusted
Clergy	1.5%	1.8%	1.0%	(1.0%)
ʿUmdah	42.1	44.1	28.0	(24.1)
Shaykh	1.3	2.1	1.0	(1.2)
Farmer	52.0	45.6	33.5	(24.9)
Unknown	3.8	6.2	3.2	(3.4)
Total	100.7%	99.8%	66.7%	54.6%

centage in each occupation of all members of the mixed family sets, modern and traditional.

It is clear that the mixed family sets include more of the high status occupations than either the modern or traditional. There are more professionals and former M.P.'s among the mixed families, and fewer teachers and civil servants. There are also more students but fewer local councillors. The modern family set is almost always drawn from the largest and most urbanized units, where a disproportionate number of officers, former M.P.'s and high status professionals are found. But when the data are adjusted by occupation, the mixed family is more influential than the modern family set, even though offices are allocated by family rather than individual and, of course, there are more mixed family-set members. 'Ulama' are not of high status generally, but relative to farmers they are. More significantly 'umad and shuyukh are of higher status than farmers and there are proportionately more of them among the mixed family sets than among the traditional family sets.

Our argument may be buttressed by taking a different statistical perspective of the unadjusted data. Taking the ratio of 'umad to farmers for each of the mixed and traditional family sets, we find that the proportion of 'umad is higher for the mixed family sets (table 32). Taking civil servants and teachers together as the combined base of the most typical modern occupations, we can compare the ratios of professionals (doctors, lawyers and engineers) and former M.P.'s and local councillors for the modern and the mixed family sets (table 33).

Table 32

Ratio of 'Umad to Farmers for
Mixed and Traditional Family Sets

	Mixed (unadjusted)	Traditional
ʿUmdah Farmers	$\frac{24.1\%}{24.9} = .97$	$\frac{42.1\%}{53.0} = .79$

The importance of the mixed family stands out in both of these exercises, and lends credence to the view that the modal pattern of the second stratum is that of the family including members who have both modern and traditional or rural occupations. Nevertheless, the political and social importance of the mixed family is not so overwhelming as to disallow recognition of the probable significance of urban and "small

Table 33

Ratio of Former M.P.'s, Local
Councillors, and Professionals to
Teachers and Civil Servants for
Mixed and Modern Family Sets

	Mixed (unadjusted)	Modern
Professionals Teachers and civil servants	$\frac{11.2}{18.7} = .60$	$\frac{17.0}{44.9} = .38$
Former M.P.'s Teachers and civil servants	$\frac{3.0}{18.7} = .17$	$\frac{4.9}{44.9} = .11$
Local councillors Teachers and civil servants	$\frac{2.0}{18.7} = .107$	$\frac{5.6}{44.9} = .124$

village" subsegments of the second stratum—among other important segments such as the descendants of prerevolutionary M.P.'s.

These data do not preclude the possibility that there exists, in provincial cities as well as in Cairo and Alexandria, an elite segment which is modern, westernized, individualistic, dissociated from any rural or agricultural base, relatively well educated, secular, empathetic, and rationalistic. It is, nevertheless, clear that such a group is small.

The data in table 31 may understate the political precedence of mixed family sets, because we have, somewhat arbitrarily, assigned both former M.P.'s and local councillors to the modern category. Since there were 30 former M.P.'s and 34 municipal councillors among the 289 modern family sets, more specific occupational information (apart from political office) might shift some of these family sets into the mixed category.

Merchants, of whom there were 103 in the modern family-set category, were also identified as modern-urban in all cases. Clearly, not all merchants are modern, and it might have been better (but technically complicated) to assign all merchants from the smaller villages to the rural-traditional category, and all those from the larger towns to the modern-urban category.

While we could not recover the occupations of the local councillors, it was possible to ascertain the occupations or professional degrees of most of the former members of the 1957 parliament. With these occupations, rather than the designation "former M.P.," the occupational type of each former M.P. family set was more accurately identified (table 34).

Table 34   Number of Former M.P.'s in Each
                                    Type of Family Set

Family-Set Occupational Configuration	Number	Percentage	Percentage of Each Type of Family Set	Percentage of Expected Value
Modern	23	20.5	13.0	157.
Mixed	66	60.8	44.0	136.
Traditional	21	19.5	43.0	45.
Total	110	100.8	100.0	

There are approximately three times as many former M.P.'s in occupationally mixed family sets as in either modern or traditional family sets. We can compare the percentage of former M.P.'s in each type of family set with the percentage of family sets in each type for the whole

National Union. The percentage of family sets is preferred to the percentage of members because, generally speaking, the seat in parliament
is allocated to the family (whether reflected in a "political" family set or
not) and only a very few family sets had two former M.P.'s.

Table 34 shows that there are far fewer former M.P.'s in occupationally traditional or rural family sets than were to be expected on the
basis of the proportion of traditional family sets to all family sets. The
number of influential traditional family sets is small and it is growing
smaller. A more careful analysis of the occupations of the former
M.P.'s, for whom we often have more data, indicates that many of them
are engaged in some sort of agricultural enterprise involving marketing
or modern cooperative enterprise. Furthermore, many of these families
have near relatives in Cairo or in other cities, or they soon will have
them as opportunities arise. We cannot deny the possibility that there
may be a residual group of quite isolated and firmly rural traditional
notables who are part of the second stratum, but the significance of
such a group is not great and their persistence is much in doubt.

The prediction regarding the future decline in the influence of wholly
rural-traditional families is based on projections using the contemporary mixed family as a guide. Originally rural, these families have become partly urban and modern in recent decades. It is less certain,
however, that the modern family set can serve as a model for the future
development of the mixed family set, or that the modern family set was
originally a rural, agriculturally involved or otherwise traditional family. Our information regarding the occupations of the former M.P.'s
can tell us a little more about this important elite group than we know
about the generality of modern family sets. Of the 23 former M.P.'s in
modern families we can find some agricultural connection for five and
for five others there is evidence that they are related to families of descendants of prerevolutionary M.P.'s all of whom included members
who were occupied in agricultural or rural pursuits. Despite the strength
of this evidence for the rural-traditional notable origins of even the
modern family set, we cannot assume that those of lesser influence than
the parliamentary elite, who are also members of modern family sets
are necessarily drawn from the same social segments. Nevertheless, the
predominance of the rural middle class is manifest.

The distribution of district officers among the modern, traditional
and mixed family sets offers a pattern not dissimilar from that found in
the distribution of former M.P.'s. The modern family set has, proportionately, the largest number of officers, the mixed family set has the
second largest proportionate number, and the traditional family set has

the smallest number. Table 35 presents the data for the distribution of district officers, and it takes account of the specific occupational information for former M.P.'s.

Table 35   Distribution of District Officers by Type of Family Set of Which They Are Members (actual numbers)

Office	Modern	Traditional	Mixed
President	15	12	43
Vice-president	8	16	43
Secretary	15	15	24
Treasurer	7	21	30
Total	45	64	140
Percentage of total officers in family sets	18.3	25.7	56.0
Percentage of total family sets	13.0	43.0	44.0

Just about 15.5% of the modern family sets include a district officer, while 14.3% of the mixed families include district officers, but only 6.7% of the traditional family sets have officers. In this case the mixed family sets compare somewhat more favorably with the modern family sets. If we look at the distribution of officers who are also former M.P.'s among the three family-set types, we find results that are almost identical with those for the distribution of former M.P.'s. Table 36 presents that distribution.

Among those descendants of prerevolutionary M.P.'s who are found in the NU register, there were 190 family sets, comprised of 624 members of NU committees. Table 37 presents details of this segment of the second stratum. Some descendants who are influential and are en-

Table 36   Distribution of District Officers Who Are Also Former M.P.'s among Three Types of Family Set

Family-Set Type	Officers in Family Sets		
	Number	Percentage	Percentage of Expected Value
Modern	15	20.0%	154%
Mixed	44	58.7	132
Traditional	16	21.3	37

gaged in modern occupations are not found in family sets. The influence of a provincial urban elite will not be identified with the modern
family set.

The modest place of the modern family set within this historically
influential group is further evidenced by the distribution of district
officers who are descendants of prerevolutionary M.P.'s. There were,
in all, 73 officer-descendants, and of these, 24 (34%) were in village
committees of more than 10 members. In other words, about a third
of the district officers came from the larger units, and many might have
been expected to be in modern family sets. This was not the case.

Table 37   Family Sets among Descendants of
                                                Prerevolutionary M.P.'s

	Modern		Traditional		Mixed	
	Number	Percentage	Number	Percentage	Number	Percentage
Family sets	18	10	49	26	121	64
Members of family sets	40	7	125	20	454	73
Former M.P.'s	1	2.5	9	23	29	74

We broke down these family-officer-descendants into four groups,
mixed, modern, traditional (where we were certain of the occupation
of the former M.P. if a family-set member), and mixed-traditional
(where we were not certain, but where all other family-set members
had traditional occupations). Some families had two district officers in
them and these additional officers are noted in parenthesis for each
category in table 38. The modern family set, despite its influential profile does not include many influential descendants of the prerevolutionary parliamentary elite. This historically important segment is reflected to a small extent in the rural-traditional family set, but most
significantly in the mixed family set.

There were another 25 officer-descendants who were not family-set
members, but who were very influential, for 17 of them were former
M.P.'s. Only 11 of these were members of committees with more than
10 members. Hence, influential descendants do not loom large among
the more highly urban part of the political elite in the agricultural
provinces.

About one-third of all the officers in family sets in committees with
more than 10 members are descendants. Less than 10% of all the nonfamily-set officers in the largest committees were drawn from descendants. Insofar as the modern family sets are influential they are not
drawn from descendants of the prerevolutionary M.P.'s and insofar as

some nonfamily-set committee members are influential in the largest units they are also not descendants. If there is a social continuity between the urban and rural elements of the second stratum for the historically most persistent group, it is also clear that there remains an urban elite segment which is socially distinct and of more recent origin.

Table 38   District Officer Descendants of Prerevolutionary M.P.'s by Family-Set Type

Family-Set Type	Number of Officers	Percentage
Mixed	49 (+5)[a]	72
Traditional	7	10
Mixed-Traditional	15	7
Modern	5	7
Total	68 (+5)	96

[a]More than one district officer in 5 families.

The occupational configuration of the mixed family set is suggestive of a pattern of occupational mobility which must be supplemented by our knowledge, from other sources, of the geographical mobility of Egyptians from village to urban center. Of course, cross-sectional data of the kind we are now discussing cannot be used to prove assertions regarding diachronic mobility. It is because of our existing knowledge of these mobility patterns that we can make sense of our own data and that we can construct the family-set typology. Consequently, the three types of family set may represent three distinct components of Egyptian society, one mobile and two relatively immobile, from which elements of the elite are selected. Alternatively, the mixed family set may be a guide to the basis on which elite recruitment takes place. Following the former interpretation, the mixed family set may merely play a significant role in mediating between the two more isolated and homogeneous groups. Accepting the latter alternative, the mixed family set reveals what the data available do not show for most of the wholly urban or wholly rural family sets—that is, a more complete picture of rural base, urban scope, and a pattern of social, cultural, and political mobility.

It is our view that the three types of elite family are dynamically related. There are some important families which have for generations been resident in the large urban areas and which do not have any significant agricultural property. These families are few outside of Cairo, Alexandria and the Canal cities to which some Cairenes and Alexandrians have migrated. There are more families of the rural middle class without close relatives having a modern education and modern employment, but that group is rapidly declining. The mixed family set, which is the politically most important type, will be adding new recruits from the rural areas and will probably lose members to a new but growing class of urban residents whose ties with their rural origins are withering. If this view is correct, it probably matters less just how the elite positions are distributed among these three groups than it matters that there is a dynamic link among all three. Since the acknowledged pattern of mobility is from the country to the city and from traditional agricultural occupations to modern secondary and tertiary occupations, our only problem is to establish empirically such a pattern for elite families. If we can establish such a pattern, then the significance of the wholly rural and wholly urban segments will decline, and greater importance will have to be given to the rate of change and the significance of any political role differentiation between those who became mixed families earlier and those who made the transition later.

The mixed family set emerges as the prototype of the influential rural and traditional elite segment, but the definition of this segment, because of the limitations of the data, remains more formal and operational than empirical. The persuasiveness of the data available has been limited by four aspects of that data. The first problem was that we inferred the existence of a family set from the external evidence of names. The second problem was that we could judge the pattern of occupational distribution within a family set only by those relatives who were elected to committees and then only for family members resident in the same village or town. The third problem was that we had data only for blood relatives and not for relatives by marriage. The fourth problem was that we had little evidence of occupational mobility from generation to generation.

To increase our information regarding these points while gaining additional information on the parliamentary elite, a sample of obituary notices was collected and analyzed. The obituary of an important person is usually an advertisement taken in a newspaper with a large circulation listing, after the name of the deceased, his mourning relatives, their degree of relation, their occupations, and occasionally their place of residence. Ideally all of this information is present, but in practice many occupations are left out, most places of residence are omitted, and not all relatives of the same degree are mentioned. At times whole families are noted with a single reference to the family name. Not infrequently the obituary will reach out to a more distant relative who has achieved some political prominence.

Only obituaries including some reference to a former M.P. were selected. Only the obituaries printed in *al-Ahram* during a six-month

period in 1960 and 1961 were searched. The former M.P. mentioned
may have been a close relative of the deceased, and in a few cases he
may have been the deceased himself, and in yet other cases he was a
distant relative.

As we have seen, the parliamentary elite, at least in its agrarian-
linked segment, is not distinctly separate from the second stratum. The
obituary notices, which do not usually take the former M.P. as the
central figure (i.e., the deceased) show even more clearly the mixed
nature of occupations and the firm connection between the parliamentary elite and the second stratum. Even though the parliamentary elite
looks, occupationally, like the rest of the second stratum, we have already found that an important segment of the parliamentary elite has
perpetuated its political precedence for two or more generations. We
will also find some evidence of intermarriage among these relatives of
M.P.'s, suggesting that there are some castelike qualities which may
distinguish the parliamentary elite families from the broader class of
rurally based families comprising the second stratum.

Over the sampling period, 157 obituary notices were found and analyzed. About 110 different former M.P.'s were mentioned, but many
were quite peripheral to the immediate family suffering the loss. The
immediate family or a close collateral branch was sought in the register
of the National Union, and in 99 of 157 cases at least one person mentioned in the obituary notice was found in the register. Of these 99, as
many as 60 were members of family sets in the register. In 42 cases
at least two members of the family mentioned in the obituary notice
were also found in the register as members of the same National Union
committee. Hence, in 70% of the relevant cases it was possible to confirm that the family set is indeed a family set. In the remaining cases
there is only the dubious negative evidence of omission. The fact that
there are 39 individual names (i.e., nonfamily set) in the National
Union register is not problematical, since not all members of influential
families could be elected to the committees. Yet the evidence of the
obituaries shows these individuals also to be members of the second
stratum, linked to the rural middle class for the most part, and members
of influential families linked to the parliamentary elite. We cannot
account for the 18 cases where family sets were found in the register
but where only a single name corresponded to those listed in the obituary. It may be assumed that in such cases the family-set members were
more distantly related—bearing in mind that the obituaries vary greatly
in length and in detail.

In view of the link between the parliamentary elite and the rural
middle class, one that makes it difficult to distinguish sociologically

between the two, and certainly doubtful to distinguish culturally between the two, is it conceivable that there is a parliamentary segment distinct from the broader rural middle class? In attempting to answer this question, it is of particular interest to note the links that tie the M.P.'s to one another, in addition to those that tie them to the rural middle class.

Careful examination of the obituary notices revealed that the same names sometimes appeared in notices reporting the death of different individuals. Sometimes the "linking" name was the M.P. himself, but these were thought to be of little interest since the obituaries might only tell us of the kin-clientele of the M.P. and not of any connection among members of the parliamentary elite. To find "linked" obituaries, we selected those where identical non-M.P. names were found in obituaries mentioning different M.P.'s. A link of this sort does not necessarily indicate a very close family relationship, since the names may range over a considerable area of kinship: several generations and several degrees of relationship.

The linked obituary notices indicate, however, that, to some extent at least, some of the M.P.'s and their families are part of a distinct group, the character of which is somewhere between a class and a caste. The group is not closed to outsiders, but it has been remarkably persistent as a social group and clearly evident as a political group for over a century. Insofar as the parliamentary elite is not distinct from the rural middle class or the second stratum, these data give additional ground for inferring that the rural middle class itself is more than a mere categoric group. It would appear that the rural middle class has certain kinship, cultural and social ties that link it over areas of the country, despite or because of migration from village to city. Of course, we must also be open to the third alternative hypothesis, that there is a two-tiered system of rural middle class interconnections: locally between the elite and not so elite rural middle class, and interregionally among the more influential members of the rural middle class, who would really constitute the second stratum.

Of the 110 M.P.'s mentioned in the obituary notices, there were 65 mentioned in notices linked by at least one name to at least one other M.P. There are 17 linked groups of M.P.'s, and these 17 "chains" of closer or more distantly related M.P.'s included 74 M.P.'s, but 9 of the M.P.'s mentioned actually served in prerevolutionary parliaments. No M.P. is mentioned in two of these 17 chains, so that they have been constructed in as exclusive and extensive a manner as possible. The chains of M.P.'s, linked in the obituary notices, are distributed as follows:

8 sets of 2 M.P.'s   2 sets of 5 M.P.'s
4 sets of 3 M.P.'s   1 set of 8 M.P.'s
1 set of 4 M.P.'s   1 set of 24 M.P.'s

Nine prerevolutionary M.P.'s are mentioned by name in the linked notices, and of the 65 that remain, 35 or near 54% of the postrevolutionary M.P.'s were descendants of prerevolutionary M.P.'s. Of the 35 descendants, 31 were members of family sets, and four were listed individually. Ten of the 65 "linked" M.P.'s were actually among those family sets confirmed by comparing the obituary notices with the listing in the register of the National Union.

These data regarding the linked M.P.'s are very suggestive, but there are a number of considerations to be borne in mind in interpreting them. The obituary notice is usually not about the M.P. nor his *immediate* family. Since the M.P. has status, many distant relatives are proud to mention that someone in their family is an M.P. The link between the obituaries might be someone who is distantly related to both mourning families, and similarly distantly related to two M.P.'s. Furthermore, some obituary notices are quite complete, while others are very short. There might be many more such "chains" if all of the notices were complete, but, then, if all the information on everyone were available from such sources, we would be unable to differentiate anyone from anyone else. In other words, we are inclined to consider the fact of inclusion in an obituary notice in *al-Ahram* to be an indication of social status. In this regard, the obituaries mentioning M.P.'s are not much different from those not mentioning M.P.'s, except that they are somewhat longer. In terms of culture and social class, the parliamentary elite does not appear to be greatly differentiated from others whose names could or would appear in an obituary notice. But there may well be a subgroup of the second stratum which has been influential for several generations, has better access to political positions and also tends to be endogamous. If there is a distinct political subgroup of the rural middle class, it is not numerous. Based on the number of agricultural holdings of 20 to 50 feddan, and an average of 5 persons per family, one may estimate the number of members of the second stratum as between 700,000 and 1,000,000 persons in Egypt. The obituaries included mention of a little less than one-third of all the M.P.'s registered in the National Union. The number of employed male relatives mentioned in the obituaries was 3,131. Doubling this number to account for female relatives and adding a third to account for minor children we get 8,000. This figure is to be multiplied by about 3 to accord with the whole membership of parliament. The resultant figure of 24,000 is a generous estimate of the elite segment described in the obituary notices. This figure may be compared with the larger figure of 700,000 whence we derive that this political segment of the second stratum may include less than 3.5% of the total. The rural middle class is itself only about 3% of the total population of Egypt.

We turn now from this consideration of the castelike aspects of the more historically continuous part of the parliamentary elite to a consideration of the occupational characteristics of the whole group. Table 39 gives us a comprehensive picture of the occupational distribution among those who are related by blood *or marriage* to members of the Egyptian parliamentary elite. Heretofore our data has been restricted to members of the political elite (at any level) but not their relatives. It has been restricted to blood relatives and did not reveal those who were related by marriage, and it was restricted to residents of the same village or town. We see in table 39 that there is a considerable spread of occupations among those related to M.P.'s. There is strong representation of both urban and rural occupations, and there is a somewhat more elaborate breakdown of occupations into thirty-five categories, used in the obituary notices themselves. The relatives mentioned by name in the notices are broken down into two groups: those whose precise relationship is identified and those merely described as qarib wa-nasib, or relatives and members of the same lineage.

From table 39 we note how few are the traditionally occupied, and we also note the very large percentage of civil servants and military officers. Professionals of all sorts are also found in large numbers. It is obvious that, occupationally speaking, this group is not a cross section of the Egyptian labor force. There is not a great deal of difference between the close relatives and those designated as qarib wa-nasib. The qarib wa-nasib are presumably more prestigeful but more distant relatives. We should expect them to be older as well. Nevertheless the only occupations in which they exceed the close relatives, proportionately, are 'umdah, doctor, lawyer, and teacher. We can disregard the qarib wa-nasib without great loss to our analysis.

Table 40 compares the occupational distribution of the relatives of the former M.P.'s with that of the various categories of members of the National Union that we have already considered. In this comparison we have used only the specifically related individuals listed in the obituaries, and we have used the occupational categories employed in the National Union documents. The elite occupational configuration of the relatives of the former M.P.'s stands out. The agricultural and traditional occupations decline by about 80%, while the professions, the civil service, and the military and police increase greatly. It is also noteworthy that the proportion of businessmen increases while that of

Table 39   Occupations of Persons Mentioned
in Obituary Notices

Occupation	Near Relations	Qarib	Total
Traditional			
1. ʿUmdah	4.80%	9.27%	5.24%
2. Aʾyan	3.50	2.23	3.39
3. ʿAlim (religious scholar)	.28	.32	.29
4. Qadi (judge)	1.80	1.60	1.78
5. Man of religion	.49	1.92	.64
6. Muʿallim (teacher)	--	--	--
7. Muzariʿ (farmer)	.28	--	.26
8. Tajir (merchant)	2.94	2.24	2.87
Transitional			
9. Physician	5.89	11.82	6.48
10. Lawyer	6.53	7.35	6.61
11. Muwazzif (civil servant)	21.15	19.81	21.02
12. Prosecutor	1.17	.32	1.09
13. Mustishar (counsellor of ministry)	1.63	.32	1.54
14. Manager, commercial	1.84	1.28	1.79
15. Engineer, nongovernment[a]	6.60	6.07	6.55
16. Engineer, industrial	2.63	1.92	2.56
17. Engineer, agricultural	1.91	1.28	1.85
18. Engineer, government and nongovernment	8.84	7.03	8.66
19. Corporation employee	1.88	.64	1.76
20. Board director	.32	.64	.35
21. Private finance	1.10	.32	1.02
Modern			
22. Government finance	.60	.96	.64
23. Teacher	2.73	5.11	2.97
24. Student, secondary	2.06	.64	1.92
25. Student, technical college	.89	.32	.83
26. Student, liberal professions	2.20	1.60	2.14
27. Student, military or police	.78	--	.70
28. Student, commerce	.85	.32	.80
29. Commerce, urban private	.78	1.28	.83
30. Accounting	.85	1.92	.96
31. Army	9.40	8.95	9.36
32. Press or mass media	.57	.32	.54
33. Police	2.34	1.92	2.30
34. Scientist	.21	--	.19
35. University professor	.11	.32	.22
Total	99.95%	100.04%	100.15%

[a]Included in 18.

teachers decreases. Teachers are found in rural areas, but businessmen,
civil servants, and army officers are not. The rural-urban balance of
the National Union data is turned on its head, and we learn that the
families of the Egyptian parliamentary elite are overwhelmingly urban
and modern.

The original estimate of the size of the second stratum was based on
the assumption that for every rural member of the rural middle class
there was an urban relative, and that together they comprised the second stratum. It is evident that the names listed in the obituary notices
reflect the urban side of the second stratum more than do the family
sets in the National Union register. Nevertheless, it is only the urban-

rural balance that may be misrepresented and not the fact of the urban-rural linkage for most of the second stratum.

The 157 obituary notices yielded 166 family "trees." Of these 166 family trees, 69% included members engaged in traditional occupations, and even more importantly, 63% of the total (n = 104) included either an 'umdah or member of the a'yan or both. Slightly less than 30% of these families had no traditional or rural members explicitly listed. There were only 6 family trees that listed only traditional or rural members. Of the nearly 6.5% of the families including nonagricultural traditionals, nearly all (5.4%) included one or more merchants as the only traditionally occupied member in the family tree.

Since an obituary notice often emphasizes the older generation of any family—the generation of the deceased in most cases—it would be likely that traditional occupations would be found in considerable numbers. The relatively small number of traditional occupations mentioned may be due to the fact that many traditional occupations, and especially agriculture, are either not prestigeful or may be considered so generally known as not to require mention in a notice which does cost money.

It is likely that, in addition to the occupations of women (i.e., mostly housewives), the occupations of farmers and other low status occu-

Table 40   Occupational Distributions of NU Members and Relatives of the Parliamentary Elite

Occupations	All Members	Family Sets	Family Officers	Descendants	Obituaries
Doctor	.70	.7	3.2	.8	5.90
Lawyer	2.64	3.7	9.2	6.6	6.50
Engineer	1.85	2.9	5.6	5.0	13.38
Teacher	9.93	6.6	1.6	--	2.73
Civil servant	6.96	7.5	5.6	7.9	21.15
Merchant	7.89	4.7	3.6	2.9	2.94
Businessman	.78	.8	1.6	.9	4.04
Clergy	1.61	1.1	--	--	2.57
Student	1.37	1.5	--	1.0	6.78
'Umdah	19.59	28.0	15.6	21.6	4.80
Shaykh	--	1.0	3.2	--	3.50 (a'yan)
Worker	1.10	.6	--	--	--
Farmer	38.06	33.4	14.8	31.5	.28
Former M.P.	.89	2.0	28.5	7.4	--
Local council member	1.13	1.6	4.8	3.4	--
Ex-army officer	.12	.2	.8	1.0	9.40
Ex-police officer	.12	.1	.4	--	2.34
Other government	--	--	--	--	3.40

pations would not be mentioned. It is probable that the agricultural segment of this elite group has been understated. Nevertheless, it is apparent that the wholly local, completely agricultural elite segment which was evident in the National Union data as the traditional family set is either greatly restricted in its influence or is an artifact of our data source in the sense that the modernized segments of the family just did not turn up on the village lists of the National Union.

The parliamentary elite is to a substantial degree traditional, historically established, rural-agrarian in origin, but occupationally differentiated. The data from the obituary notices must lead us to lower yet more our estimate of the significance of the wholly agrarian component of the second stratum.

In order to get a better idea of occupational mobility, the occupations in the obituary list were broken into three groups: (a) the traditional-agrarian; (b) occupations which do not depend upon the latest technological or institutional developments (which we will call, suggestively if arbitrarily, transitional); and (c) the modern occupations which do depend upon contemporary technological and institutional developments. The transitional group includes physicians, lawyers, civil servants, government prosecutors, and mustasharun or counsellors of a ministry. Only 3% of the family trees examined included both traditional and transitional occupations but no modern occupations. Just over 60% (n = 100) of the family trees included all three types of occupations. Less than 2% were wholly modern, while 30% included both transitionals and moderns.

The heavy dependence of the postrevolutionary regime on the armed forces has made of army officers an important segment of the political elite. Army officers constitute a large component of the members of our parliamentary family trees, too, suggesting that the officers help to get their relatives elected to parliament and that the traditional influence of the notables helped to get these officers into the military academy. At any rate, 60% (n = 100) of all family trees include at least one army officer and many include several. The average is almost 3 officers for each family tree including army officers. Of these family trees, 66 also include at least one 'umdah or member of the a'yan, while 34 are wholly urban in occupational composition. The preponderance of the rurally based elite is once again established.

If we compare the actual number of officers in each type of family, we can discern some slight advantage in favor of rural families over urban families. We find 69% of the total number of military officers in rural-connected families and only 31% of the officers in wholly urban families, even though only 66% of families including officers are rural-connected, and though only 63% of all families are rural-connected.

The pattern remains nearly the same when we turn to the lower status position of civil servant. About 88% (n = 146) of all family trees included at least one civil servant and of these families, 63% (n = 92) also include at least one 'umdah or member of the a'yan, while 37% (n = 54) are wholly urban. Since 63% of all family trees include rural members, it follows that the differential distribution of high status military officers and lower status civil servants between urban and rural families has no apparent relationship to the elite or nonelite character of these occupations but is rather the consequence of the distribution of the parliamentary elite between urban and rural families. It is further likely that·elite family members are distributed among all of the preferred employments in accordance with prevailing opportunity structure. Family and status rather than occupation and class still appear to be decisive.

Since the most significant and most strongly represented occupations are pretty much similarly divided between our two types of family, it is reasonable to treat all of those mentioned in the obituaries as a single group for purposes of analyzing occupational mobility. In seeking information on occupational mobility for these elite families, two strategies were available. Each of those for whom the precise relationship to the deceased was given could be listed by generation, taking the generation of the deceased as the base or, more relevantly, taking the generation of the former M.P. as the base. In the following tables, the generation designated as zero is the base generation of the deceased or the former M.P. as indicated, and the generations marked $+1$, $+2$, $+3$ are those of descendants while those marked -1, -2, -3 are preceding generations.

Table 41 presents a breakdown of occupations by generation, using the generation of the deceased as the base. The entries are in percentages of each occupation. What is immediately apparent is that most of the individuals listed are of the generation of the deceased. There are practically no entries for two or three generations ago, and entries are relatively few for two or three generations after the deceased. Most data are available for the generation of the deceased, that of his father, and that of his son. As we might expect, the majority of the traditional occupations are held by generations 0 and -1. The transitional occupations are held about evenly between generations 0 and $+1$ with generations -1 and $+2$ having only a small number. In particular we note that most scientists, engineers, and managers (categories 34, 18 and 14) are found in the base generation. Government economists,

Table 41   Breakdown of Occupational Titles
by Generation with the Generation
of the Deceased as "0"

Occupation	Generation							
	-3	-2	-1	0	+1	+2	+3	Total
Traditional								
1. ʿUmdah	-	-	11.8%	60.7%	23.7	3.7%	-	99.9%
2. Aʾyan	-	-	16.1	45.4	36.3	2.0	-	99.8
3. ʿAlim	-	-	12.5	25.0	62.5	-	-	100.0
4. Qadi	-	-	1.9	56.8	37.2	3.9	-	99.8
5. Man of religion	-	-	-	64.2	35.7	-	-	99.9
6. Muʿallim	-	-	25.0	25.0	50.0	-	-	100.0
7. Muzariʿ	-	-	25.0	25.0	50.0	-	-	100.0
8. Tajir	-	1.2%	6.0	53.0	39.7	-	-	99.9
Transitional								
9. Physician	-	-	3.6	47.5	41.5	7.2	-	99.8
10. Lawyer	-	-	1.6	47.8	47.2	3.2	-	99.8
11. Muwazzif	-	-	4.5	42.9	48.1	4.3	-	99.8
12. Prosecutor	-	-	6.0	42.4	51.5	-	-	99.9
13. Mustishar	-	-	8.6	43.4	43.4	4.3	-	99.7
14. Manager, commercial	-	-	1.9	50.0	40.3	7.6	-	99.8
15. Engineer, nongovernment[a]	-	-	6.9	47.3	38.1	7.5	-	99.8
16. Engineer, industrial	-	-	6.7	52.7	36.4	4.0	-	99.8
17. Engineer, agricultural	-	-	7.4	48.1	40.7	3.7	-	99.9
18. Engineer, government and nongovernment	-	-	5.6	51.8	36.9	5.6	-	99.9
19. Corporation employee	-	-	7.5	35.8	52.8	3.7	-	99.8
20. Board director	-	-	33.3	44.4	22.2	-	-	99.9
21. Private finance	-	-	6.4	48.3	45.1	-	-	99.8
Modern								
22. Government finance	-	-	-	41.1	52.9	5.8	-	99.8
23. Teacher	-	-	3.8	40.2	50.6	5.1	-	99.7
24. Student, secondary	-	-	-	22.4	67.2	10.3	-	99.9
25. Student, technical college	-	-	-	24.0	60.0	16.0	-	100.0
26. Student, liberal professions	-	-	3.2	22.5	53.2	17.7	3.2%	99.8
27. Student, military or police	-	-	-	31.8	54.5	13.6	-	99.9
28. Student, commerce	-	-	4.1	25.0	66.6	4.1	-	99.8
29. Commerce, urban private	-	-	-	59.0	40.9	-	-	99.9
30. Accounting	-	-	8.3	29.1	54.1	8.3	-	99.8
31. Army	-	.3	4.1	43.3	46.7	5.2	-	99.6
32. Press or mass media	-	-	6.2	-	62.5	31.2	-	99.9
33. Police	-	1.5	6.0	36.3	48.4	7.5	-	99.7
34. Scientist	-	-	-	50.0	16.6	33.3	-	99.9
35. University professor	-	-	-	33.3	66.6	-	-	99.9

[a]Included in 18.

teachers, private employees, accountants, army officers, police officers,
journalists, and university professors all tend to prevail in generation
+1. Taking the deceased as the base generation, it appears that it
would be preferable to include all the occupations down to and including 21, that is, private finance, as "transitional." Most of those listed
from 22 to 35 have most of their number in generations +1 and +2.

Any choice of a base generation must be somewhat arbitrary since
death may occur at any age. As a consequence, all those that we have

included in the base generation may not be of the same generation. We assume that most are, however. In substituting the generation of the former M.P. for that of the deceased as the base generation, we hope to have narrowed somewhat the age variation of the base while relating occupational mobility somewhat more closely to the elite characteristics which were the basis of selecting this group for analysis in the first place. Table 42 is constructed just as was table 41, except that the base generation is that of the former M.P. While not all former M.P.'s were of the same generation, their ages evidently varied less than did

Table 42   Breakdown of Occupational Titles
                                 by Generation with the M.P. as "0"

Occupation	Generation							
	-3	-2	-1	0	+1	+2	+3	Total
Traditional								
1. ʿUmdah	-	-	20.1%	67.4%	12.4%	-	-	99.9%
2. Aʾyan	-	4.7%	25.0	52.3	17.8	-	-	99.8
3. ʿAlim	-	-	-	40.0	60.0	-	-	100.0
4. Qadi	-	-	26.3	47.3	26.3	-	-	99.9
5. Man of religion	-	-	-	100.0	-	-	-	100.0
6. Muʿallim	-	-	-	-	-	-	-	-
7. Muzariʿ	-	-	-	50.0	50.0	-	-	100.0
8. Tajir	-	1.5	12.3	81.5	4.6	-	-	99.9
Transitional								
9. Physician	-	-	15.3	56.9	27.0	.7%	-	99.9
10. Lawyer	-	-	6.5	70.2	22.6	.5	-	99.8
11. Muwazzif	-	.2	6.9	59.1	33.3	.4	-	99.9
12. Prosecutor	-	-	10.8	59.4	27.0	2.7	-	99.9
13. Mustishar	-	-	16.2	53.4	18.6	11.6	-	99.8
14. Manager, commercial	-	-	8.1	57.1	28.5	6.1	-	99.8
15. Engineer, nongovernment[a]	-	1.2	13.8	53.4	28.3	1.8	1.2%	99.7
16. Engineer, industrial	-	1.6	11.4	63.9	21.3	1.6	-	99.8
17. Engineer, agricultural	-	-	19.2	59.6	19.2	1.7	-	99.7
18. Engineer, government and nongovernment	-	.9	12.6	57.2	26.6	1.4	.9	99.6
19. Corporation employee	-	6.2	6.2	62.5	25.0	-	-	99.9
20. Board director	-	-	-	50.0	50.0	-	-	100.0
21. Private finance	-	-	9.6	70.9	19.3	-	-	99.8
Modern								
22. Government finance	-	-	23.0	38.4	38.4	-	-	98.4
23. Teacher	-	-	8.4	57.6	30.5	3.3	-	99.8
24. Student, secondary	-	-	-	28.8	68.8	2.2	-	99.8
25. Student, technical college	-	-	4.1	20.8	70.8	4.1	-	99.8
26. Student, liberal professions	-	1.6	6.5	42.6	34.4	11.4	-	96.5
27. Student, military or police	-	-	4.5	54.5	36.3	4.5	-	99.8
28. Student, commerce	-	-	9.0	45.4	40.9	4.5	-	99.8
29. Commerce, urban private	-	-	20.0	53.3	26.6	-	-	99.9
30. Accounting	-	-	-	55.0	35.0	5.0	5.0	100.0
31. Army	-	.8	6.2	55.8	33.9	3.1	-	99.8
32. Press or mass media	-	-	-	57.1	35.7	7.1	-	99.9
33. Police	-	-	13.8	52.3	33.8	-	-	99.9
34. Scientist	-	-	-	60.0	-	40.0	-	100.0
35. University professor	-	-	-	100.0	-	-	-	100.0

[a]Included in 18.

the ages of the deceased. Table 42 now shows us that the great majority of the traditionally occupied are now clearly in generations − 1 and 0, with the former much more numerous in the most important categories of 'umad and a'yan. We note that now over 80% of the traditional merchants are found in the base generation.

Among the transitional occupations we now find little variation, with most of them showing between 53% and 64% in the base generation and between 19% and 28% in the succeeding generation. The generation − 1 has relatively few among the transitionals except for physicians, counsellors, and agricultural engineers. Except for the very small number of members of boards of directors, we note that only civil servants and commercial managers among the transitionals show more than 29% for the generation + 1.

Among the modern occupations it appears that teachers and those engaged in urban private commerce are misplaced and might better be included with the transitionals. None of the rest have fewer than 34% in the generation + 1. It is important, however, to note that many of the military, the police, the journalists, and the students in the military and police academies are in the base generation. In each case more than 50% of the occupational category is in the same generation as is the member of parliament.

We might now revise our categories of the major occupations in three groups as follows:

Traditional

'umdah (village headman)	qadi (religious judge)
a'yan (notable)	tajir (traditional merchant)

Transitional

physician	corporation employee
lawyer	private finance
prosecutor	teacher
counsellor of ministry	commerce, urban, private
engineer	

Modern

civil servant	press or mass media
manager, commercial	student in military or police
accountant	academy
army	government finance
police	students

Our expectation is that in each succeeding generation there will be more moderns and fewer traditionals among the families of the political elite in Egypt. It is not clear whether there will be a decline in the number of transitionals, because that depends upon the occupations chosen by the students after graduation. I think it unlikely that these occupations should decline greatly, but it is worth considering the possibility that these elite families may be moving away from the free professions toward membership in the larger state bureaucracies and institutions. The set of occupations listed as modern is striking in its emphasis upon the administration of government, finance, coercive force, and information.

To get a clearer idea of intergenerational occupational mobility we have arranged these data in table 43 to present each occupation as a percentage of the generation. Each column in table 43 should total 100% or nearly that. The change from column to column tells us how the occupational distribution among the families of the parliamentary elite of 1959 has changed over the last few generations. Table 43 shows us, somewhat dramatically, how each of the traditional occupations declined from generation to generation with almost no exception. Among the professionals, both private engineers and doctors have increased in generation +2, as have media specialists, accountants, and police officers. Students in the liberal professions have greatly increased, but it is likely that they will find jobs with the government. The proportion of army officers has remained remarkably stable over generations 0, +1, and +2. We note also a modest increase in the proportion of commercial managers and a substantial decline in the proportion of lawyers.

The surprises found in table 43 are the unexpected increases for physicians and some engineers and the sharp increase in the proportion of students of the free professions. In general, table 43 sustains the view that there will be a shift toward the larger institutional bureaucracies by the members of politically influential families, but there is still some considerable attachment to the more "transitional" values of a liberal education and a professional career.

In order to find out whether this continuing transitional preference might be an expression of the values of a particular segment of the parliamentary elite, a separate tabulation of this data was made for the obituaries which were linked together in what we have called a "chain." While the evidence is not decisive, there is some basis for identifying the linked family members, 40% of the total, as a more transitional group which clings longer and more stubbornly to the liberal and bourgeois values of the pre- and early revolutionary periods.

There are substantially fewer 'umad and a'yan than expected among the family chains. There are also fewer members of generations −2 and +2 and more members of the base generation. Remarkably enough, there are almost no teachers, a low status profession, in this group. On the other hand, the proportion of almost every one of the transitional occupations, of the accountants, and of the students in the liberal professions is greater than was to be expected among this segment of the parliamentary elite.

Table 43   Breakdown of Generations by Occupational Titles with the Generation of the M.P. as "0"

Occupation	-3	-2	-1	0	+1	+2	+3	Qarib wa-Nasib[b]
Traditional								
1. ʿUmdah	-	-	9.9%	6.0%	2.2%	-	-	10.0%
2. Aʾyan	-	29.4%	9.2	3.5	2.4	-	-	2.4
3. ʿAlim	-	-	-	.2	.7	-	-	.3
4. Qadi	-	-	4.8	1.7	1.7	-	-	1.7
5. Man of religion	-	-	-	.5	-	-	-	2.1
6. Muʿallim	-	-	-	-	-	-	-	-
7. Muzariʿ	-	-	-	.3	.5	-	-	-
8. Tajir	-	5.9	2.2	2.5	.3	-	-	.3
Transitional								
9. Physician	-	-	9.2	6.3	5.9	3.8%	-	12.8
10. Lawyer	-	-	4.4	8.7	5.5	1.9	-	8.0
11. Muwazzif	-	5.9	15.1	23.6	26.0	7.7	-	21.5
12. Prosecutor	-	-	1.1	1.3	1.2	1.9	-	.3
13. Mustishar	-	-	2.6	1.7	1.2	9.6	-	.3
14. Manager, commercial	-	-	1.5	2.0	2.0	5.8	-	1.4
15. Engineer, nongovernment[a]	-	11.8	9.2	6.6	7.0	7.7	50.0%	6.6
16. Engineer, industrial	-	5.9	2.9	3.2	2.1	3.8	-	2.1
17. Engineer, agricultural	-	-	3.7	2.2	1.3	1.9	-	1.4
18. Engineer, government and nongovernment	-	11.8	11.8	9.6	8.7	7.7	33.3	7.7
19. Corporation employee	-	17.6	1.1	2.3	1.7	-	-	.7
20. Board director	-	-	-	.3	.7	-	-	.7
21. Private finance	-	-	2.6	.8	1.6	-	-	.3
Modern								
22. Government finance	-	-	1.8	.4	.8	-	-	1.0
23. Teacher	-	-	2.2	3.0	3.2	5.8	-	5.6
24. Student, secondary	-	-	-	1.0	5.3	3.8	-	.7
25. Student, technical college	-	-	.4	.3	2.4	1.9	-	.3
26. Student, liberal professions	-	5.3	1.5	1.8	2.8	17.3	-	1.7
27. Student, military or police	-	-	.4	.8	1.1	1.9	-	-
28. Student, commerce	-	-	1.1	.9	1.6	1.9	-	.3
29. Commerce, urban private	-	-	1.5	.8	.8	-	-	1.4
30. Accounting	-	-	-	.9	1.2	1.9	16.7	2.1
31. Army	-	17.6	5.9	9.9	11.8	15.4	-	9.8
32. Press or mass media	-	-	-	.6	.8	1.9	-	.3
33. Police	-	-	3.3	2.3	2.9	-	-	2.1
34. Scientist	-	-	-	.2	-	3.8	-	-
35. University professor	-	-	-	.2	-	-	-	.3
Total		100.0	100.2	99.9	100.4	99.7		99.6

[a]Included in 18.

[b]Relationship unspecified.

If we could separate out the families of those descended from pre-revolutionary M.P.'s, the orientation toward the free professions, toward private business and toward liberal education might be even more pronounced. These families have been established for a longer period of time and, despite their solid agrarian base, they have fewer family members engaged in agriculture. Despite the continuity of their influence and their extensive family links with other regional elites, and despite their political acceptability in 1959, they were not yet committed to the great institutional bureaucracies. It might be expected that many of these people would get caught in the economic and administrative squeeze with the passage of the Socialist Laws of July 1961.

The elite families which have a larger than expected proportion of 'umad and a'yan are probably poorer, of more local influence, and have only recently begun to participate politically. These families are only beginning to break out of their agricultural framework, and they have probably found their first good opportunities in the new revolutionary bureaucratic structure as well as in the new institutes which give specialized training rather than a liberal education.

It is likely that the rise of the rural middle class to political importance occurs in waves, with new families of a'yan coming up as social mobilization and political awareness strikes ever more remote villages. Each, in turn, attempts to exploit the opportunity structure provided by the regime of the day. To the extent that the families which rose earlier have not been politically excluded, the residues of each wave coexist like layers of a single political elite. In the rural areas these layers are geographically separated, but in the urban areas they are stratified in terms of their occupation, income, and education. It is still unclear whether the political fates of the urban and rural parts of each wave must be the same or whether they will be able to function separately from one another.

Part Two

The Geographical
Distribution of the
Second Stratum

Eight

The Provincial Distribution of the Second Stratum

In Miocene times the Mediterranean extended as far inland as Cairo and Siwa, and a number of small streams drained northwards from the African tableland to this sea. One such stream, the early, or proto-Nile, was strengthened in late Miocene times by a slight tilting of the plateau.

W. B. Fisher, *The Middle East*

The concepts of "center" and "periphery" predominate in the analysis of geographical differences in development theory. In modernization, the center leads and the periphery lags. Development proceeds in the main by diffusion; but the pattern and rate of diffusion are determined by the structure of transport, communication, population densities, and, of course, the competition of alternate centers. For the most part, geographical differences are taken as obstacles to be overcome by the development process itself. When regional differences in levels of development are accompanied by the uneven distribution of distinctive sociopolitical segments, the problem is exacerbated, but it does not change essentially. From the Marxist viewpoint, regional loyalties are manifestations of the interests of regional elites, and these, in turn, reflect the local relations of production and may be expressed in the distinctive ethnic or regional or national cultural terms which ubiquitously mask false consciousness. From the liberal point of view, despite the existence of theories justifying regional political pluralism, traditionalist geographical differences constitute obstacles to be overcome by social mobilization, by economic integration, and by the development of a strong, "penetrative," administrative system.

The geographical characteristics of significant sociopolitical segments are, consequently, not taken as essential or central to theories of devel-

171

opment. Geographical distribution may complicate matters, but what is most important is that there exist, somewhere, groups or strata capable of initiating and directing the development process. For the Marxists these groups are the party cadres and the proletariat or the proletarianized peasants; and for the liberals they are the members of the new educated middle class—for the most part members of the state cadres. The geographical origin of these cadres is thought to be far less important than the modernization role they are to play. Geographical differences pose severe problems if they are manifested in the concentration of unassimilated cultural or racial communities which may resist modernization in order to preserve their distinctiveness. The situation is quite different where a particular regional group contributes more than its share to the composition of the modernizing elites and cadres. In the latter case, which is closer to the Egyptian situation, regional elites may encourage modernization while seeking to preserve the traditional bases of their local influence if such a strategy will help expand their opportunities for political influence or economic aggrandizement at the political center.

The Egyptian rural elite has been described in terms of its historical origins, its evolving political role, and its position in the structure of Egyptian society. Though the political role of the agrarian notability has changed in substance, its steady emergence into the political role of the second stratum has been marked. The utility of the second stratum in sustaining the regime is, of course, related to its ability both to mediate governmental political penetration of the countryside and symbolically, or culturally, to represent at least some segments of the rural population. Since an important part of whatever the a'yan do politically is carried out in face-to-face situations, the effectiveness of the second stratum will be limited by its location. If it is rural in any significant way, then its geographical distribution will be influenced by the mode of agricultural production, by the fertility of the land, by the availability of water, by the proximity to markets and transportation, and by many other factors governing the agricultural economy. There are also social factors that may influence the geographical distribution of the elite. The size of village may determine the number of elite families, and the presence of large clans may provide the support necessary for holding certain types of leadership positions.

The peculiar configuration of the settled area of Egypt greatly limits the possible patterns of distribution. Only about 5% of the surface area of Egypt is inhabited and cultivated. Except for some recently discovered petroleum, no important natural resources have been found outside of the settled areas. These settled areas lie along the Nile, in the delta between the Rosetta and Damietta branches of the Lower Nile, and along the Suez Canal. There are small settlements in the oases in the Western Desert and along the coast near Libya. There are also some small settlements in the Sinai Peninsula. Our data relate only to the sixteen agricultural provinces of the delta and Nile valley, excluding the oases, the canal cities, and the two largest metropolises, Cairo and Alexandria. The sixteen provinces included about 80% of the population of Egypt in 1960.

Egypt has enjoyed internal political unity for centuries, particularly when it lacked independence. In earliest times the unity was not so complete as it later became, and there prevailed at times a substantial political separation of north and south, of lower and upper Egypt. North of Cairo, the provinces of lower Egypt fan out like a broken portion of a wheel with its hub at the capital. South of Cairo, the villages and towns cling closely to the Nile as it winds its devious way between the harsh granitic cliffs of upper Egypt. Only the small province of al-Fayyum and its lake stand apart from the Nile, an easy stage from Cairo, and a westward extension of the fertile valley into the hostile desert. Lower Egypt was not always the more dominant area politically, as Luxor and Karnak testify, but for millennia the north has prevailed. The power of the central government of Egypt did not always extend as far to the south, the north, and into the desert fringe as it now does. The growth of ancient and medieval imperial power led to a gradual extension of political control, but the largest strides in administrative and political penetration were made as late as the nineteenth century.

Surrounded by desert and bound by the Mediterranean and Red seas, Egypt is rather more isolated than other countries from neighborly contact. Though the seat of empires and the victim of alien imperial expansions, the great mass of the Egyptian population was directly but little touched by outside influences. During the Hellenistic period the center of Egypt's political gravity was moved north to Alexandria, where it remained for several centuries. Cairo, a restored inland capital, was established by the Arabs and maintained thus throughout the Ottoman period. Alexandria declined in importance while some provincial capitals increased in size and influence. Mansurah, Tanta, and Assiut, all important seats of Mamluk governorships, and other lesser towns emerged to political significance under the decentralizing influence of the pluralistic praetorianism of pre-nineteenth-century Egypt. Under Muhammad 'Ali, the Mamluks were destroyed, local elites and dignitaries were allowed to convert influence into private landownership, and a new Ottoman segment of the central political elite was encouraged to settle in Egypt and gradually merged with the indigenous elites. The traditional Egyptian isolation was ended in the nineteenth century, at the same time that the introversion of the provinces was being altered. As the origin of foreign influence shifted from Istanbul to Europe, Alexandria became more than a gateway. Alexandria became the second city of Egypt, and for many Egyptians it was the cultural and commercial capital. The forces of European influence, sometimes mediated by Lebanese immigrants, and local notables and landowners met at Cairo, where the indigenous forces were at least temporarily defeated in the crises of 1879 and 1882. For the next seventy years Egypt was decisively open to foreign influence and the major channel for that influence was Alexandria.

Cairo is the most important city in contemporary Egypt, and its political predominance has been enhanced by the extreme centralization of authority and decision making. While such centralization may have been aspired to under the British, the pre-1952 regime was essentially pluralistic, oligarchical, and multipolar. Cairo was the center of everything, but it was more responsive to the forces converging on it than it was the source of decisions to be implemented elsewhere. Hence, when we look for a geographical diffusion pattern of political status and influence, we should expect to find influential persons closer to Cairo and concentrated along the most efficient and frequently used means of transportation and communication. This expectation is not the result of the impact of Cairo on its surroundings, but, on the contrary, the result of the impact of nearby centers of power on Cairo. The pattern of diffusion will not necessarily be symmetrical, as it would be if it were centrifugal. On the contrary, it will depend upon the social structure and agrarian structure of the surrounding areas. Until very recently, Cairo has tended to confirm existing local authority.

This pattern of diffusion, based upon the accessibility of Cairo to provincial influence and upon the strength of the base of that influence, was modified by the intrusion of European influence by way of Alexandria. European influence was, of course, much more powerful than that of any indigenous social segment. Europeans also cooperated with Egyptians and so tended to strengthen some and weaken others. The consequence of this influence was to distort the diffusion pattern so as to render the most politically influential rural area that which lies along a line stretching from the northeast of Alexandria to the northeast of Cairo.

The ways in which modernity may have become diffused are greatly limited by the configuration of the provinces of Egypt. Except for al-Fayyum, all the provinces south of Cairo, stretch in a long line. There

is but a single possible pattern of diffusion from Cairo. A half-serious
alternative is diffusion from the secondary center of Assiut, the so-
called capital of upper Egypt. To the north of Cairo, within the delta
there are a number of important towns, eight provincial capitals, and a
couple of industrial centers. Roads lead to Alexandria, to Damietta,
and to the Suez Canal. The two branches of the Nile, parting just north
of Cairo, diverge to the northeast and the northwest. But Alexandria
has come to outweigh Damietta by far. From the time of the construction of the canal up to 1967, the canal cities grew in population and
political importance, but these cities have no agricultural hinterland
and have been populated by immigrants from other parts of Egypt.
Thus the possible diffusion patterns of the delta have been affected by
the dominance of the Cairo-Alexandria line, and this powerful political
axis has been influenced by the presence of important secondary centers
of political influence. The delta does not have good east-west communications. It is easiest to travel to Cairo first and then from Cairo to
other distant points in the delta, if one's desired destination is not on
the line to Cairo. The western branch of the Nile is the more developed
one from Rosetta down to Tanta, but from Tanta south to Cairo, the
Damietta or eastern branch is the more important.

There is a good road across the desert from Alexandria to Cairo,
which bypasses the delta. This road and the development of air transport and telecommunications have brought Cairo into direct contact
with the world. With the decline and then the termination of British
influence, Alexandria has also declined. Cairo has become the true
center of power and decision making in Egypt. But the governments
that have resided in Cairo have not yet proven themselves powerful
enough to penetrate the countryside effectively or to dispense with the
support of rural influentials. In time, I suppose, with the progress of
modernization, the pattern of diffusion of all things in Egypt may become truly centrifugal, but this is not yet the case.

Given the diversity of Egyptian ecological conditions and the vicissitudes of its history, it is not surprising that social conditions, rates of
development, and political structure should vary from region to region.
More specifically, it should be no surprise that the size of the second
stratum would vary from region to region. Despite the reasonableness
of such expectations, the contrary hypothesis was entertained until the
immovability of the empirical made it clear that the percentage of members in family sets varied from province to province. It is interesting to
consider why this hypothesis, unreasonable as it seems in retrospect,
was pursued. In the first instance, as a practical if myopic device, it was
assumed that the percentage of members in family sets in each province

was roughly the same, and that if a province had too many or too few, that was probably due to errors in data (i.e., name) analysis. Second, it was assumed that the social and cultural homogeneity of Egypt would produce only marginal regional differences. Third, it was naively assumed that to be effective as a second stratum, the rural middle class had to be more or less the same everywhere. Fourth, it was assumed, in accordance with the consensus of development theorists, that the only important regional differences were differences in degree of modernization and that these differences were determined by a pattern of linear diffusion from the center to the periphery. From this point of view, it was easy to jump to incorrect conclusions: that the second stratum represents an exclusively traditional social force, that it is not at all structured by development or modernization, and, perhaps most important of all, that the regionally differentiated size and character of the second stratum cannot itself serve as a measure of political development. Indeed, for the most part, political development is defined as a qualitative aspect of the political process and it is usually measured only in terms of its presumed aggregate statistical correlates or in terms of the political attitudes of participants (as reported by themselves) along dimensions postulated to comprise a developed political orientation.

These presuppositions were overcome by the facts. There is significant variation in the percentage of members in family sets in the provinces as table 44 shows. Family-set members are found in substantially greater proportion in lower Egypt, in the delta, and near Cairo. The percentage in family sets is higher in the west delta and lower in the east delta. There is an obvious decline in the proportion of family-set members as one proceeds southward from al-Jizah and al-Fayyum. Once these striking statistics were established and reconfirmed, many plausible explanations presented themselves and an effort was made to test those that seemed most sensible and for which there was data available at the province level. The data which could be used was essentially of two kinds, provincial breakdowns of various dimensions of the NU data and official government statistics.

The most important alternative hypotheses were that the percentage of members in family sets, that is, the degree of *prevalence* of the second stratum, is a function of the level of modernization attained; or that it is a function of the agrarian characteristics of each region; or that it is a function of the historical and social characteristics of the rural bourgeoisie in each province. These three and other subordinate hypotheses were explored, if not tested, by means of a correlational analysis. The percentage of members in family sets, and various subcomponents of this general measure of prevalence were correlated with measures of diverse dimensions of development.

There is no single measure of development, acknowledged by all or deemed to have broad theoretical implications. Nor could we employ an ideal set of dimensions. We were compelled to use those province level statistics which are published by the government of Egypt. From these available statistics measures of literacy, education, social services, and industrialization were tried. A number of measures of agrarian development such as land rents, crop mixes, and rural roads were used to measure a type of development that is often ignored in the moderni-

Table 44   Percentage of NU Members in
                                        Family Sets

Province	Members of Family Sets
al-Qalyubiyyah	24.5%
al-Sharqiyyah	19.5
al-Daqahliyyah	16.7
Dumyat	12.6
Kafr al-Shaykh	26.1
al-Gharbiyyah	27.4
al-Manufiyyah	22.4
al-Buhayrah	25.9
al-Jizah	27.1
al-Fayyum	25.5
Bani Suwayf	13.4
al-Minia	16.9
Assiut	15.3
Suhaj	11.4
Qena	9.5
Aswan	3.8

zation literature. Occupational differentiation is another measure of modernization, and we have already noted that the members of family sets tend to have more urban-modern occupations than other National Union members. It follows that the second stratum may be more numerous in those provinces where the labor force has a similarly larger proportion of urban-modern occupations. Consequently, a comparison of the occupational characteristics of the labor force as a whole, of the National Union membership, and of the members of family sets was undertaken at the province level even though at the national level, occupation alone did not count for much. Finally, it was hypothesized that the stratification of the second stratum itself, in terms of size of family sets, occupational mix of family sets, 'izbah ownership, descent from the prerevolutionary parliamentary elite, incumbency in district level office, and membership in parliament, might not be randomly distributed among the provinces. It might well be that the second stratum in certain provinces was more influential, of longer standing, of greater agricultural wealth, or the like, and that these characteristics might help to explain the size of the second stratum in the province as well. Throughout the statistical explorations that follow, it should be noted that, in addition to explaining the variance in the province level prevalence of the second stratum, we are also interested in describing its provincial characteristics. In this last regard, it should be noted further that we have developed no measure of proximity to Cairo for statistical purposes. Such a measure would be complicated to devise and would likely suggest more than it could convey. Nevertheless diagrammatic maps will be used to give the reader some idea of where the provinces are, and the diffuse significance of the introductory discussions of some of the geographical characteristics of Egypt should be borne in mind. The most apparent differences will be those between the delta and upper Egypt, but interesting and more subtle differences will emerge when these two large regions are disaggregated by province and, in a later chapter, by district.

Two indices relating to health distinguish upper Egypt from the delta region. The index of sick persons treated at government clinics and the index of the distribution of pure-water projects in villages show that health care and pure water are more generally available in lower Egypt than in upper Egypt. The more urbanized and industrialized Aswan is better situated than most southern provinces. Al-Jizah does not show up well because its sick use the facilities available in Cairo (see table 45).

Two measures of educational attainment are available, both of which show that lower Egypt is more advanced than upper Egypt (table 46). First we have the percentage of population, 15 years and older, who are university graduates. The percentage is very small in all these provinces, and much less than we would expect in Cairo, Alexandria, and the canal cities. The disparity between the north and south is not so great, because university students tend to migrate to the cities to become educated and then they stay on. It is noteworthy that even Assiut, which has a university of its own, has a lower percentage than does Aswan, a center of immigration. Dumyat and, of course, al-Jizah, the two most urbanized areas, stand out from the rest, while the more rural Kafr al-Shaykh looks like it should be in upper Egypt. For the rest the delta has more university graduates than upper Egypt.

The second measure of education is the index of illiteracy. There are proportionately more illiterates in upper Egypt than in lower Egypt.

Kafr al-Shaykh is joined by al-Buhayrah in exceeding its expected
share of illiterates among the delta provinces, while all the provinces
of upper Egypt except for al-Jizah and Aswan have somewhat larger
numbers of illiterates in proportion to their population.

Table 45   Measures of Standards of Public
                                          Health

Province	Index of Patients Treated	Index of Pure-water Projects
al-Qalyubiyyah	1.73	.99
al-Sharqiyyah	1.59	1.05
al-Daqahliyyah	.90	1.69
Dumyat	2.36	--
Kafr al-Shaykh	.98	1.04
al-Gharbiyyah	1.24	.83
al-Manufiyyah	.57	1.08
al-Buhayrah	.46	1.20
al-Jizah	.75	.66
al-Fayyum	.53	1.66
Bani Suwayf	.59	.81
al-Minia	2.17	.89
Assiut	.58	.77
Suhaj	.55	.93
Qena	.49	.66
Aswan	1.26	.30

Table 46   Measures of Standards of Education

Province	University Graduates	Index of Illiteracy
al-Qalyubiyyah	.32%	.92
al-Sharqiyyah	.34	.97
al-Daqahliyyah	.45	.87
Dumyat	.60	.81
Kafr al-Shaykh	.26	1.08
al-Gharbiyyah	.52	.92
al-Manufiyyah	.35	.94
al-Buhayrah	.28	1.03
al-Jizah	1.66	.90
al-Fayyum	.26	1.07
Bani Suwayf	.27	1.06
al-Minia	.27	1.07
Assiut	.33	1.05
Suhaj	.18	1.10
Qena	.17	1.11
Aswan	.45	1.00

To measure industrialization, two statistics can be used, the percentage of the labor force (15 years and older) employed in establishments with more than 50 employees and the percentage of the labor force employed in industrial installations of the private sector (table 47). While the percentage employed in the larger enterprises does not seem to be very great, it represents a very large segment of all those who are employed outside agriculture. The contrast between the provinces with some industrial development and those without is obvious. Al-Qalyubiyyah, al-Gharbiyyah, al-Buhayrah, al-Jizah, and Aswan are the only provinces with a substantial industrial base. Al-Qalyubiyyah is near Cairo, al-Buhayrah is near Alexandria, al-Jizah is near Cairo, Aswan is at the High Dam, and only al-Gharbiyyah seems to have an important, independent industrial sector.

Three more statistics, the registration of motor vehicles (automobiles and motorcycles), the number of persons per television set, and the per capita budgets of the provincial governments, allow us to measure social differentiation (table 48). Motor vehicle registrations were measured as an index stating the ratio of the percentage of registrations to the percentage of population. Al-Qalyubiyyah has surprisingly few automobiles registered, but that may be explained by the fact that many of those who can afford an automobile can afford to live in Cairo or at least maintain a second residence there. The large number of automobiles registered in al-Jizah and Aswan is no surprise, but that al-Daqah-

Table 47   Measures of Industrialization

Province	Work Force in Establishments of 50 or More Employees[a]	Employees in Private Sector[a] (Industrial)
al-Qalyubiyyah	6.42%	8.95%
al-Sharqiyyah	.35	2.05
al-Daqahliyyah	.33	2.53
Dumyat	.37	4.72
Kafr al-Shaykh	.15	1.68
al-Gharbiyyah	3.25	6.60
al-Manufiyyah	.12	1.63
al-Buhayrah	2.35	3.96
al-Jizah	2.43	4.74
al-Fayyum	.19	1.94
Bani Suwayf	.25	1.57
al-Minia	.38	2.10
Assiut	.23	1.72
Suhaj	.10	1.44
Qena	.61	1.84
Aswan	2.39	3.52

[a]Percentage of population, male and female, above age of 15.

Table 48   Measures of Amenities

Province	Index $\dfrac{\text{Percentage of motor vehicles registered}}{\text{Percentage of population}}$	Number of Persons per TV Set	Per Capita Budget (LE)
al-Qalyubiyyah	.60	5,818	3.760
al-Sharqiyyah	.91	6,030	3.122
al-Daqahliyyah	1.21	2,674	3.223
Dumyat	1.09	3,724	4.299
Kafr al-Shaykh	.83	13,329	2.233
al-Gharbiyyah	1.48	1,772	3.387
al-Manufiyyah	.77	9,761	3.233
al-Buhayrah	.83	5,306	2.461
al-Jizah	2.93	215	3.214
al-Fayyum	.91	5,506	3.408
Bani Suwayf	.61	8,926	2.972
al-Minia	.87	42,162	3.057
Assiut	.74	66,250	2.720
Suhaj	.40	524,667	2.262
Qena	.41	450,000	2.375
Aswan	1.17	--	5.267

liyyah should have so many registered is surprising. Note again, the substantial number of vehicles registered in al-Gharbiyyah, which emerges as the most developed of those delta provinces which are not also in part suburban.

The number of persons per television set describes a broader stratum than those who can afford an automobile, but the distribution of television registrations is also influenced by the effectiveness of the reception of the TV signal. It was obviously impossible to catch the broadcast in Aswan, and probably exceedingly difficult to do so south of Bani Suwayf. Al-Jizah has the most sets per capita, and al-Gharbiyyah the next largest number.

Per capita provincial budgets vary from 2.233 Egyptian pounds per annum (1961/62) to 5.267. There is no budget breakdown available so we don't know whether the budget is used for the same things in all cases or not, nor even what these budgets are theoretically for. These per capita budgets do, however, coincide with some general notion of development, industrialization or urbanization in that Aswan and Dumyat have the highest budgets, Suhaj, Qena, and Kafr al-Shaykh have the lowest budgets, while Al-Qalyubiyyah and al-Gharbiyyah are relatively high. Al-Buhayrah is surprisingly low. It is not unreasonable to assume that provincial budgets are expended on civil servants, urban-type amenities, and on the infrastructural needs of industry, all of which tie in with indices of social differentiation.

Thus far we have considered various aspects of development excluding agricultural development. We have several measures of diverse dimensions of agricultural development, almost all of which are largely unrelated to the welfare of the poorest peasants. Most of these measures are of greater significance for the owner of 10 feddan or more land and hence indicate which provinces are likely to have more of such middle-sized landholdings.

The average rent per feddan reflects the fertility of the land, its proximity to urban markets, and its suitability for truck gardening. High rental lands are usually owned in larger plots by wealthier landlords who have easier access to credit. The highest land rent provinces are al-Qalyubiyyah, al-Manufiyyah, al-Jizah, all near Cairo, and al-Minia.

We have constructed an index measuring the ratio of agricultural and desert roads in each province to that province's taxable agricultural land. That index shows the provinces around Cairo to be best endowed with such roads, thus enhancing the influence of the Cairo market over agricultural production in these areas. In upper Egypt, we note that Assiut is much better supplied with these roads than is al-Minia.

A third measure of agricultural development is the prevalence of agricultural cooperatives. Such cooperatives, in areas where no bureaucratically controlled land reform took place, are generally dominated by the middle-sized landowners and village headmen. Hence, unless it is a "land-reform cooperative," an agricultural cooperative is also likely to be a vehicle of political and economic dominance by the local a'yan. From table 49 we note that the co-ops are widely distributed.

These data, presented in an effort to draw distinctions among the various provinces of Egypt, do not show the kind of decisive differences that are exhibited in contrasting urban and rural or highly developed and less developed regions. In some cases the data are anomalous in purport, but for the most part they simply show that there is no consistent hierarchy of development among the agricultural provinces of Egypt. Some of the provinces reflect the influence of their proximity to Cairo or Alexandria, others reflect the influence of a high level of rural development in their own hinterland. Consequently, it is difficult to draw general conclusions without some idea of the relationship of these measures of development to one another. In order to get at this problem, selected indices of development have been correlated and stepwise multiple regression analyses have been run on them.

The strongest indicator of overall development for these provinces is the index of illiteracy. When correlated with a number of alternative indices, it gave the results found in table 50. From the list of correlations we learn that where illiteracy is greater, health services will be lower, large industrial establishments fewer, automobiles fewer, provincial budgets lower, agricultural rents lower, and the number of farmers in the NU committees higher.

Table 49   Measures of Agricultural Development

Province	Average Rent per Feddan in LE	Index of Agricultural and Desert Roads	Index of Agricultural Coops by Population
al-Qalyubiyyah	32.9	1.44	1.03
al-Sharqiyyah	20.5	.98	1.20
al-Daqahliyyah	26.1	.98	1.01
Dumyat	20.1	.79	.75
Kafr al-Shaykh	17.1	.76	1.00
al-Gharbiyyah	28.0	.78	.97
al-Manufiyyah	32.6	1.03	1.14
al-Buhayrah	17.8	.84	1.07
al-Jizah	29.8	1.39	.66
al-Fayyum	13.3	1.28	.98
Bani Suwayf	25.7	1.53	1.27
al-Minia	28.6	.68	1.11
Assiut	23.5	1.27	.90
Suhaj	23.5	.90	.90
Qena	17.8	.92	.77
Aswan	9.3	1.08	.92

The illiteracy index, as expected, gives us the highest multiple regression coefficient when taken as the dependent variable, and it is, otherwise, always the most influential independent variable in explaining the indices of patients, industrial workforce, and motor vehicles. Table 51 shows how much stronger is the regression with illiteracy as the dependent variable.

Table 50   Correlation Coefficients of Measures of Development and Illiteracy

	Index of Illiteracy
Index of patients treated	-.47201
Percentage of work force employed in establishments of 50 or more	-.33533
Motor vehicles per capita	-.52298
Provincial budgets	-.55096
Average rent of agricultural land	-.37370
Index of farmers in NU	+.62315

Despite the strength of illiteracy as a general index of development, we must carefully note that the remaining indices do not correlate well with more than one or two of the variables chosen. Just as we have seen in examining the indices one by one, there does not appear to be a uniform pattern of distribution of the provinces for all fields of development.

Table 51   Comparison of Indicators of
                                      Development

Dependent Variable	Multiple R
Illiteracy	.80071
Motor vehicles	.57865
Patients	.54797
Work force	.36640

It might well be hypothesized that this rather complex pattern of rural provincial development, as revealed by the aggregate data at hand, would be reflected in the provincial distribution of occupations among the members of the National Union committees. It would also be expected that, to the extent that National Union committee members reflect distinct social and political strata, there would be significant divergences by province between the distribution of urban and rural occupations among the population and the National Union members.

With few exceptions only adult males were chosen as NU committee members. Assuming that adult males constitute less than half of all those 15 years or older, then the social pool from which NU committee members were chosen was about 25% of the total population. Nevertheless, for purposes of statistical computation it is important to note that the number of committee members of the NU in the provinces and the total of those 15 years and older in the population are correlated at .972 (significance level .001).

When we compare the percentage of professionals in the NU committees with the percentage in the population of all those 15 years and older, we find that the professionals are overrepresented by some two to twenty times. Lawyers are better represented in committees than either doctors or engineers, although engineers are more numerous than doctors or lawyers. More professionals are found in lower Egypt than in upper Egypt. The southernmost provinces have the fewest professionals except for Aswan, which has a large number of engineers working on hydraulic and electricity projects. The number of doctors and lawyers, but not engineers, elected to the NU committees in each province has some relation to the number of professionals living in each province, as shown in table 52.

The percentage of the actual number of professionals living in each province elected to the NU committees was surprisingly high. Table 53

Table 52   The Representation of Professionals in NU Committees

1. Absolute number in each profession in the population and in the National Union, by province

   Doctors   .5305   significance level   .017
   Lawyers   .7312   .001
   Engineers .1936

2. Percentage of each profession in each province and in the National Union committees in each province

   Doctors   .4234   significance level   .051
   Lawyers   .4925   .026

Table 53   Percentage of Each Profession Elected to Committees of the NU in the Provinces

Province	Doctor	Lawyer	Engineer
al-Qalyubiyyah	7.3%	72.9%	15.4%
al-Sharqiyyah	6.5	51.8	20.1
al-Daqahliyyah	10.1	29.7	15.5
Dumyat	4.2	31.6	29.6
Kafr al-Shaykh	9.7	59.8	125.8[a]
al-Gharbiyyah	6.2	27.2	12.4
al-Manufiyyah	13.3	51.9	52.5
al-Buhayrah	9.2	43.1	13.7
al-Jizah	4.6	29.0	2.6
al-Fayyum	2.5	42.9	14.1
Bani Suwayf	1.9	32.5	13.6
al-Minia	7.5	43.5	2.3
Assiut	4.6	26.7	11.2
Suhaj	3.7	33.9	7.3
Qena / Aswan	24.5	33.9	3.9
Mean	7.7	40.7	22.0[a]

[a]Without Kafr al-Shaykh the mean for engineers is 15.3.

shows these percentages. Professionals are generally more readily elected in the less urbanized delta areas or the more advanced of the more agricultural areas. It appears that there are fewer important rural families in upper Egypt, but they are probably of longer standing. Being more distant from Cairo, they were slower to seek professional degrees; being wealthier, they were less in need of professional incomes, and being fewer, they comprise a smaller segment of the total number of professionals to be found in the provinces of upper Egypt.

Teachers and civil servants are more evenly distributed over the provinces, although here, too, we find fewer in the southern provinces. Teachers and civil servants are also generally overrepresented, but more strongly in the urbanized provinces, near Cairo. Though there are somewhat fewer teachers and civil servants in the NU in upper Egypt, there are also fewer teachers and civil servants in the population as a whole. Provincial differences in elite occupational structure may be due to differences in the size of the rural middle class, or to regional characteristics of the rural middle class. The relative wealth of the rural middle class in each province may be a factor determining whether family members become lawyers or civil servants. Nevertheless, the distribution of civil servants and teachers in the NU is also strongly influenced by their distribution in the population as shown in table 54.

Table 54   Teachers and Civil Servants in NU
                                       Committees

1. Number of teachers and civil servants in NU committees and in the population of each province

	Pearson r^2	Significance Level
Teachers	.7080	.001
Civil servants	.6183	.007

2. Percent of all teachers in each province and in NU committees in each province

Teachers	.5707	.010
Civil servants	.5720	?

The agrarian segment of the NU committees is represented by the two categories of 'umdah and farmer. 'Umad are not ordinary farmers, but since they are numerous in the NU committees, they will add to the weight of agrarian representation while indicating the extent to which the representatives of the rural areas are differentiated from their constituents. A large part of the rural population, women, landless laborers, and children, are not represented by the NU data. When farmers and 'umad are taken together, they greatly overrepresent the agrarian population in the NU committees. Farmers alone tend to be overrepresented in upper Egypt and to be approximately justly proportionately represented in the delta.

It is unlikely that 'umad or even 'umdah families constitute more than 1% of all the landowning farmers, yet they frequently constitute a third or more of the agrarian members of the NU. The proportion of 'umad to farmers is highest in the most urbanized areas and the areas closest to Cairo.

When the number of farmers in the National Union committees is correlated with the number in the population, the $r^2 = .9007$ (significance level .001), so that most of the NU variance from province to province is accounted for by the number of farmers in the population. The residual does not seem to be of great political significance. When we correlate the percentage engaged in agricultural production with the percentage of 'umad in the NU in each province, we get the low r^2 of .0377; hence there is no apparent link between the two.

The distribution of most occupations follows roughly the distribution of the population group from which the NU members are drawn. By "roughly" we mean that from 40% to 70% of the variance in the provincial distribution has been accounted for (except in the case of engineers) by the distribution of members of the identified category in the population. The remainder is likely to be accounted for by the distribution of these occupations among rural elite families. This distribution varies from province to province in such a manner that various modern occupations can be taken as functional equivalents. If modern occupations were to be ranked in terms of prestige, income, and required schooling, we would probably find that the highest ranking would appear in the largest numbers in lower Egypt, near Cairo, and the lowest ranking would be more frequent in upper Egypt. We would also find that the proportion of modern occupations as a whole would be smaller in upper Egypt.

The large proportion of 'umad in the NU committees, and especially in those areas closest to Cairo, is an indication of the way in which the distribution of occupations in the NU may have been skewed by the distribution of occupations among the rural middle class. The excess of 'umad near urban centers, in more developed provinces, is something of an anomaly, however, for the occupational configuration of the more influential members of the National Union committees is somewhat more modern-urban than for the average committee member. This paradoxical situation is congruent with findings regarding the occupational characteristics of family sets, and especially the most influential family sets, most of which include 'umad and farmers.

Since it is a fact of Egyptian political life that although 'umdah fathers tend to "produce" sons who become professionals and civil servants, the urban middle class does not "produce" 'umad, even though some 5% of agricultural land is held by the effendiyyah, it follows that the second stratum has a rural-agrarian base. The word "base" is meant to refer at once to historical or rather generational priority and also to the base of power or influence, where we are concerned to explain why someone was elected to an NU committee. A base is, however, only a base; and it is apparent that urban occupations are extremely important. Nevertheless, these correlations suggest that, at least, 'amudiyyat determine access to professional and bureaucratic positions for rural-based aspirants.

A second important statistic to keep in mind is the distribution of family sets by family-set size in the provinces. Table 55 presents the breakdown of family-set size by province. It is readily apparent that there is great variation in the distribution of family-set members by family-set size. In general, those provinces with a low percentage of

Table 55   Distribution of Family-Set Members by Family-Set Size and by Province as a Percentage of Family-Set Members in the Province

| | Family-Set Size | | | |
Province	2	3	4	5+
al-Qalyubiyyah	57.5	22.0	9.8	10.7
al-Sharqiyyah	61.7	(30.1)	6.9	(1.3)
al-Daqahliyyah	64.8	21.8	9.7	3.7
Dumyat	77.6	(9.0)	(6.0)	7.5
Kafr al-Shaykh	50.1	24.5	(16.9)	8.5
al-Gharbiyyah	48.8	25.4	11.1	14.8
al-Manufiyyah	60.6	18.1	8.6	12.7
al-Buhayrah	47.3	23.5	13.2	16.0
al-Jizah	(45.2)	(29.5)	9.6	15.7
al-Fayyum	(42.7)	26.2	15.4	15.7
Bani Suwayf	(71.2)	(12.2)	7.2	9.5
al-Minia	57.3	21.5	9.2	12.0
Assiut	64.0	23.7	8.6	3.6
Suhaj	(71.0)	18.1	(4.8)	6.0
Qena	(76.5)	(13.2)	7.8	2.5
Aswan	(73.5)	18.4	8.2	(0)
All agricultural provinces	57.1	22.8	10.1	10.0
Standard deviation	11.31	5.96	3.34	8.2

family sets of size 2 and high percentages of family sets of size 5+ have a higher percentage of the second stratum among all members of the National Union. We note that none of the northern provinces falls outside of a single standard deviation from the mean of family sets of two, while all but two of the southern provinces do. It is apparent that the structural differences between the northern and southern provinces are not only relevant to modernization and urbanization, but also to the stratification and composition of the political elite.

Third, the larger the average family-set size, the larger will be the provincial percentage of family-set members. Since the larger family sets are located in the larger committees it might be expected that the provinces with the larger committees will have higher percentages of the largest family sets. In fact, this is exactly *not* the case. The variation in the prevalence of the second stratum is not due to any arbitrary statistical ordering of the data, but rather to significant sociopolitical factors.

The apparent relationship between development and the distribution of the second stratum suggests that we will find the key to that distribution in the occupational distribution of the family-set members of the National Union. Commencing with the "free" professions, it may be recalled that all three are greatly overrepresented in the National Union but only lawyers and engineers are overrepresented among family-set members. Despite the statistical similarity in the distribution of lawyers and engineers, they are differentially distributed over the provinces. Lawyers and engineers are overrepresented in the family sets in nearly every province of upper Egypt. Despite this overrepresentation, the percentage of professionals tends to decline as one moves from north to south, and from east to west. Professionals constitute 9.6% of all family-set members in al-Gharbiyyah but decline to 4.9% in Qena. While both professions remain overrepresented in comparison with the whole population, in some provinces they are underrepresented among family sets.

The aggregated statistics for all sixteen provinces showed that while civil servants enjoyed a somewhat higher status than did teachers, neither group was of very great prestige in itself. When these data are disaggregated by province, a somewhat different picture emerges. For the teachers, we find slightly higher percentages among family-set members in Suhaj and Qena only. These differences are significant, given the low percentages of doctors and engineers. It is possible, therefore, that where other professionals are in short supply, teachers will enjoy greater political influence.

For civil servants the picture is very different from what was expected. Since the difference between the percentage in all the National

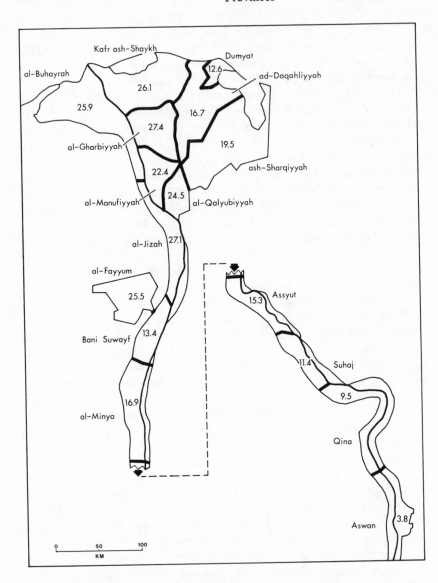

Union committees and the percentage in family sets was so small (6.96%
and 7.5%), it was not assumed to be politically significant. In 9 out of
16 provinces, however, the percentage in family sets is higher, and it is
higher by more than one standard deviation in al-Qalyubiyyah, al-

Manufiyyah and in Aswan. The percentage of civil servants in family sets is also moderately higher in al-Jizah and in Bani Suwayf and so it is probable that proximity to Cairo accounts in part for the larger number of civil servants in family sets.

'Umad are the key occupational or status group differentiating agrarian elite families from others. Farmers related to 'umad remain an important group and they are generally more numerous than the 'umad, but in five provinces, four of them in lower Egypt, 'umad are actually more numerous than farmers among family-set members. The percentage of 'umad increases from committee members to family-set members in all but one province, but the increase is not the same in all. The range is from a 20.6% increase in Bani Suwayf to a 69.6% increase in al-Daqahliyyah (see table 56).

Our data show unequivocally that the basis of the National Union elite or of the second stratum is agrarian local notability, manifested in most cases by control of the post of 'umdah. The 'umdah himself may not be the most influential member of the notable family, but the

Table 56   Percentage of 'Umad and Farmers
                                        in the NU and in Family Sets by
                                        Province

Province	'Umad			Farmers		
	NU	Family Sets	Increase	NU	Family Sets	Decrease
al-Qalyubiyyah	18.0	29.1	61.0%	24.1	19.9	17.4%
al-Sharqiyyah	22.2	26.8	20.7	32.6	29.1	10.7
al-Daqahliyyah	20.4	34.6	69.6	30.9	27.8	10.0
Dumyat	16.0	22.4	40.0	21.7	25.4	-17.1
Kafr al-Shaykh	20.5	30.4	48.3	38.5	34.6	10.1
al-Gharbiyyah	20.6	31.4	52.4	27.0	28.9	- 7.0
al-Manufiyyah	17.8	27.7	55.6	25.5	25.4	0.4
al-Buhayrah	21.5	31.3	45.6	40.3	36.4	9.7
al-Jizah	19.1	26.6	39.3	30.4	30.9	- 1.6
al-Fayyum	21.1	31.5	49.3	44.1	43.0	2.5
Bani Suwayf	22.8	27.5	20.6	39.7	36.0	9.3
al-Minia	26.9	38.7	43.9	44.3	38.2	13.8
Assiut	19.6	29.5	50.5	47.2	41.7	11.7
Suhaj	13.1	16.5	26.0	52.8	44.0	16.7
Qena	11.0	14.1	28.2	59.6	55.3	7.2
Aswan	10.4	8.2	-22.2	39.7	38.8	2.3
Mean	18.8	26.6	39.3	37.4	34.7	6.0
Standard deviation			(27.1) 13.98[a]			7.82
Total[b]	19.5	29		38	33.4	

[a]Without Aswan.

[b]Total = percentage for whole country.

'umdah component is the most consistent, while other occupations vary
somewhat more from province to province. It is also clear that there
are fewer members of the second stratum in the far south, and that the
agrarian element in the National Union is about 15% greater in upper
Egypt than it is in lower Egypt. The size of the second stratum *and*
the occupational composition of the second stratum vary with level of
development and geographical location. Despite its agrarian base, the
second stratum is larger where the nonagricultural component is largest.

The 'umad are the key to influential political status, and the 'umdah
is the most important occupational category among those having a
larger percentage among family sets than in the membership of the NU
committees. There were, in fact, 3,081 members of 'umdah family sets,
or 56% of all family-set members. In table 57 we see how the various
provinces differ in this regard.

Table 57   Percentage of Family-Set Members
                                    in Family Sets with 'Umad

Province	Percentage	Province	Percentage
al-Qalyubiyyah	27.8	al-Jizah	55.9
al-Sharqiyyah	50.1	al-Fayyum	64.3
al-Daqahliyyah	67.0	Bani Suwayf	51.8
Dumyat	47.7	al-Minia	70.8
Kafr al-Shaykh	56.9	Assiut	57.2
al-Gharbiyyah	65.7	Suhaj	33.8
al-Manufiyyah	58.3	Qena	29.6
al-Buhayrah	65.2	Aswan	20.4

The general pattern of occupational distribution within the second
stratum may be described as follows: in the less developed provinces
more members of family sets will be farmers and teachers. Family-set
size will be smaller. The percentage in family sets will also be smaller.
Paradoxically, where there are more farmers in the NU, there will be
more farmers among family-set members, but the number of family-set
members will be relatively smaller.

This pattern is nicely illustrated when we try to use occupation as an
explanation of the size of the second stratum. In table 58 the percentage
in family sets in each province is correlated with the percentage who
are lawyers, teachers, civil servants, and farmers among the NU committee members. The percentage of farmers in the NU committees is
the most important independent variable. In the multiple regression,
the influence of lawyers is considerably reduced, to the point that it is

about equal to that of civil servants. The percentage of teachers retains
no influence when all occupations are taken together to explain the
percentage in family sets.

In this chapter aggregate statistical data bearing on the level of development, industrialization, or modernization of the sixteen agricultural
provinces have been analyzed. An attempt was made to determine
which are the more and which the less "developed" provinces, but it
was found that the rankings produced by different statistics made a
single scale problematical. Nevertheless, two indices were found to
correlate best (negatively) with the other indices of development: the
percentage of illiterates in each province and the percentage of NU
members listing their occupations as farmers.

Table 58   Occupation as Determinant of Per-
                                      centage in Family Sets

Percentage Who Are	Correlation Coefficients (% in family sets)	Percentage Who Are	Multiple R (% in family sets)
Lawyers	.402	Farmers	-.484
Teachers	.126	Lawyers	.562
Civil servants	.185	Civil servants	.641
Farmers	-.484		

The NU members, already identified as having more modern occupations than the population as a whole, are distributed geographically
by occupation roughly in accordance with the prevalence of the occupations among the larger population. The most important exception in
this regard is the larger than expected number of 'umad in the developed provinces near Cairo. There is a high positive correlation between
farmers in the National Union and farmers in the population, but no
significant correlation between the number of 'umad in the NU and the
farmers in the population. This anomaly was further sustained by the
finding that the members of family sets are more prevalent in the more
developed provinces, and especially in a belt of provinces from al-
Buhayrah south to al-Fayyum. The proportion of both farmers and
'umad among family-set members in the more developed provinces was
also higher than expected. We find, therefore, that the second stratum
is more prevalent in the more developed provinces, that it includes
more individuals with high status occupations but also more of those
engaged in agriculture than expected. 'Umad are particularly prevalent
among family-set members in al-Buhayrah among the developed provinces but also in al-Minia.

The prevalence of the second stratum is not determined by the occupational characteristics of its members. The outstanding characteristic of the second stratum is its agricultural base. For the rest, the occupational characteristics of the second stratum are determined by the level of development of the province. These structural characteristics are clear, but they may or may not have consequences for the political influence of the second stratum in the various provinces.

Nine

The Provincial Distribution
of Second Stratum
Influentials

One is not surprised to find that no
elaborate electioneering campaign is
required to persuade the G'afra
villages to vote for the candidate
who belongs to their stock. In fact,
the same candidate for Silwa constituency has won the last three
elections with a sweeping majority.

H. Ammar, *Growing up in an
Egyptian Village*

With the fact established that the second stratum is differentially distributed among the provinces, it may be further hypothesized that the
influence of the second stratum differs from province to province. It
has already been established that there are important differences of
status, influence, and economic circumstances among members of the
second stratum. Furthermore, if it is true that the political influence of
the second stratum varies by province, it will be desirable to seek
an explanation of the variation, at least in terms of the data available.
Insofar as the political influence of the second stratum varies geographically, it will be important to inquire, first, whether a part of the second
stratum performs the role we have attributed to the entire stratum and,
second, whether that part is geographically concentrated.

The procedure in this analysis will be to see how many officers and
former M.P.'s were members of family sets in each province and to
differentiate the statuses and influence levels of these elite members in
terms of family-set size, 'izbah ownership, descent from members of
prerevolutionary parliaments, and other relevant indicators. It is to be
expected that the analysis will become more and more complicated
as additional differentia are included. To some extent the complexity
and detail have been simplified by omitting some breakdowns that

proved insignificant, by combining several breakdowns in the same table, and by constructing composite indices.

While the central government at Cairo always takes a keen interest in provincial politics, it seems reasonable to assume that there are differences in the degree to which it is prudent to impose candidates on local communities rather than accepting those who enjoy traditional status and influence in each constituency. We have hypothesized that, for the most part, local notables have been sustained in their influence by the generally socially conservative policy of the Nasser regime. M.P.'s individually, and the parliament collectively, may not have wielded much influence, but it is clear that a member of the National Union who was elected to parliament was at least acceptable to the central governmental authorities. District officers also had to be acceptable, but since their tasks were local, they seemed to represent not merely a lower level of elite standing—below that of the parliamentary elite—but they also represented a different kind of influence—more localized than national. Of course, we shall find some individuals who are both district officers and former M.P.'s enjoying strong national influence in addition to, or because of, their strong local influence. There were also, doubtlessly, some areas in which such a policy could not or did not work, either because the local influentials were hostile to the "revolution," or because they were not really very influential.

Table 59 presents the distributions of district officers and former M.P.'s in family sets for all the agricultural provinces. Since some of the former M.P.'s are also officers, a third distribution of both groups (without duplication) is also presented. The fourth percentage is the number of former M.P.'s who were officers divided by the total of all officers and former M.P.'s—and thus is an index of the concentration of elite status in that province. The last column in table 59 is an index of the dominance of the second stratum in each province and it has been derived in an arbitrary manner by multiplying the third column by the fourth. The index of dominance reflects both the concentration of officeholding and the prevalence of family-set members among the officeholders.

There is virtually no correlation between the percentage in family sets and the percentage of former M.P.'s and officers in family sets in those provinces where family-set members are most prevalent. The more regularly the same individuals hold both membership in parliament and district office in the National Union, the more likely they are to be members of family sets. Al-Fayyum has a relatively large percentage of the members of the NU in family sets (prevalence of the second stratum) and it also has a high concentration of elite statuses (former

M.P.'s who were also officers) and a high index of dominance (former M.P.'s/officers in family sets). Contrarily, provinces in which a large second stratum seems to have resulted in a greater dispersion of elite positions are al-Qalyubiyyah, Kafr al-Shaykh, and al-Buhayrah. Those provinces with a relatively small second stratum which have a high percentage of district officers and former M.P.'s in family sets are al-Sharqiyyah, al-Minia, and Suhaj.

Table 59 Distribution of District Officers and Former M.P.'s in Family Sets by Province

Province	District Officers	Former M.P.'s	District Officers and Former M.P.'s Without Duplication	Index of Concentration of Elite Status	Index of Dominance of Second Stratum
al-Qalyubiyyah	50%	75%	56%	.12	.0672
al-Sharqiyyah	53	57	57	.26	.1482
al-Daqahliyyah	36	33	36	.15	.0540
Dumyat	25	20	24	.19	.0456
Kafr al-Shaykh	38	42	38	.16	.0608
al-Gharbiyyah	43	43	42	.20	.0840
al-Manufiyyah	56	32	49	.20	.0980
al-Buhayrah	63	45	53	.15	.0795
al-Jizah	44	57	47	.22	.1034
al-Fayyum	58	67	61	.23	.1403
Bani Suwayf	38	30	35	.12	.0420
al-Minia	64	68	63	.27	.1701
Assiut	23	28	20	.21	.0420
Suhaj	52	55	51	.20	.1020
Qena	22	35	25	.15	.0375
Aswan	25	0	23	.05	.0115
All 16 provinces	44.5%	44%	43.5%		
Mean	43.1%	43.5%	42.5%	.18	.0804

It is worth noting which provinces show substantial differences between the percentages of district officers and of former M.P.'s in family sets, since the district officers may represent local influence while the former M.P. may more likely have some national influence. Comparing the first column and the second of table 59, we find that those provinces are al-Qalyubiyyah, al-Manufiyyah, al-Buhayrah, al-Jizah, Qena, and Aswan.

Just about every province with a relatively numerous second stratum also has high percentages of district officers and former M.P.'s in family sets, but the fact that there are provinces with a relatively small second stratum with high elite percentages indicates that the election of family-set members to district office or to the National Assembly does not depend upon a constituency of members of the second stratum. On the contrary, there is some indication that wherever the second stratum is larger, there is more competition for office among members of the rural middle class.

Provinces with the highest percentages of elite family-set members include two with important bedouin elite elements: al-Sharqiyyah and al-Fayyum; and two with important numbers of influential 'umad from large villages: al-Buhayrah and al-Minia, al-Qalyubiyyah, which is adjacent to Cairo, and Suhaj.

The distribution of influential members of the second stratum among the provinces is obviously interesting, but also problematic. The elements of a provincial configuration which have been derived from table 59 do not conform to the distribution of percentage in family sets, nor do they reflect the general pattern of the decline of the second stratum from its peak in the northwest sector of the delta. In order to explain this difference between "prevalence" and various measures of elite status, we shall require more information about the differential composition of the second stratum and its most influential members in the sixteen provinces.

In assessing the political influence of the rural middle class as measured by family-set control of elite positions, we have not taken into account the ratio of family-set members to all members in each province, nor the ratio of elite positions to family-set members, nor the difference between small family sets and large family sets. These considerations may be of importance in the following ways. First, if there are more family-set members in any given province, there is a higher probability that an officer or former M.P. will be a member of a family set. Second, the larger the constituency of each incumbent, the more influence may be attributed to him. Third, we have found some connection between family-set size and political influence, and even more between family-set size and historical continuity of elite status. Thus, if we trace the differences in family-set size down to the province level, we may be able to determine whether elite segmentation is regional or stratal.

In table 60 we list by province the total number of National Union committee members, the total of family-set members, the number of district officers, the average constituency per officer, the proportion of family-set officers to all officers, the proportion of family-set members to all members, and the ratios of family-set officers and family-set members to the *mean total* of each. We have already noted that the percentage in family sets varies importantly from province to province

Table 60

Distribution and Ratio of Family-Set Members, Officers, and Constituencies by Province

Province	Total Members	Family-Set Members	Percentage	District Officers	Average Constituency	Percentage of Family-Set Officers	Family-Set Members: Mean Total (19.5%)	Family-Set Officers: Mean Total (44.5%)	Constituency: Mean Total (50)
al-Qalyubiyyah	1,323	327	24.7	28	47	50	1.25	1.12	.94
al-Sharqiyyah	2,642	519	19.6	43	61	53	.99	1.19	1.22
al-Daqahliyyah	2,696	454	16.8	44	61	36	.85	.81	1.22
Dumyat	457	67	14.7	16	29	25	.75	.56	.58
Kafr al-Shaykh	1,354	355	26.2	32	42	38	1.33	.85	.84
al-Gharbiyyah	2,245	615	27.4	44	51	43	1.39	.97	1.02
al-Manufiyyah	2,073	465	22.4	32	65	56	1.14	1.26	1.30
al-Buhayrah	2,467	638	25.9	48	51	63	1.31	1.42	1.02
al-Jizah	1,386	376	27.1	32	43	44	1.38	.99	.86
al-Fayyum	1,162	286	24.6	24	48	58	1.25	1.30	.96
Bani Suwayf	1,426	222	15.6	32	45	38	.79	.85	.90
al-Minia	2,339	393	16.8	44	53	64	.85	1.44	1.06
Assiut	1,822	278	15.3	40	46	23	.78	.51	.92
Suhaj	2,223	248	11.2	44	50	52	.57	1.17	1.00
Qena	1,770	173	9.5	36	49	22	.48	.49	.98
Aswan	549	23	3.8	20	27	25	.19	.56	.54
All 16 provinces	27,907[a]	5,439[a]	19.5	559[a]	50	44.5	1.00	1.00	1.00
Mean	1,744	340	19.5	35	48	43.1	1.00	1.00	1.00

[a]Total.

and that this variation does not coincide with the percentage of officers in family sets. The average constituency varies quite considerably also, there being one officer for every 65 members in al-Manufiyyah and one for only 27 members in Aswan. Taking these ratios, we can construct a scale of relative influence of the family-set officers in each province. Since the higher the ratio of family-set members, the easier it is for a family-set member to be a district officer, we divide the ratio of family-set officers by the ratio of family-set members. Since the higher the constituency ratio, the more difficult it is to become an officer, we multiply the quotient by this ratio. The resultant scale is given in table 61.

Table 61   Scale of Family-Set Officer Influence
                                       by Province

Province	Scale	Province	Scale
al-Qalyubiyyah	.84	al-Jizah	.62
al-Sharqiyyah	1.46	al-Fayyum	1.00
al-Daqahliyyah	1.15	Bani Suwayf	.97
Dumyat	.43	al-Minia	1.79
Kafr al-Shaykh	.53	Assiut	.59
al-Gharbiyyah	.71	Suhaj	2.05
al-Manufiyyah	1.44	Qena	1.00
al-Buhayrah	1.10	Aswan	1.09

As we might expect, those provinces which are high on this elite scale have scores which are in inverse order when compared with the percentage in family sets. The influence of the family-set officer is roughly inversely proportioned to the size of the second stratum.

To complete our scale of family-set officer influence we have to take account of family-set size and the office itself. We will do so in the following way: assuming that presidents are more influential than vice-presidents, and vice-presidents more influential than secretaries, and secretaries more influential than treasurers (the order listed in our source), we give a score of 4 to a president, 3 to a vice-president, 2 to a secretary, and 1 to a treasurer. Assuming further that the larger the family set, the greater the political influence, we give a score of 1 to family sets of two, 2 to family sets of three, 3 to family sets of four, and 4 to family sets of five and more. Multiplying these scores for each officer, adding the total for each province, and finding the mean for the province, we arrive at a crude score of family-set officer influence by family-set size and office as given in table 62, where the score is also converted into a ratio by dividing each by the mean (7.21). The two scales from tables 61 and 62 are combined by multiplication in table 63 for a comprehensive scale of family-set officer influence by province.

Table 63 presents a dramatic contrast with the distribution of family-set members. The influence of family-set members does not appear to depend upon the size of family-set constituency. Instead we find that six of the eight provinces of upper Egypt are relatively high on the influence scale, whereas only three of the provinces of lower Egypt emerge with a score above 1.00. Table 63 illustrates the highly concentrated influence of a small segment of the second stratum.

Table 62   Family-Set Officer Influence Score and Ratio by Family-Set Size and Office by Province

Province	Score	Ratio	Province	Score	Ratio
al-Qalyubiyyah	7.86	1.09	al-Jizah	7.00	.97
al-Sharqiyyah	6.96	.96	al-Fayyum	9.46	1.31
al-Daqahliyyah	5.81	.81	Bani Suwayf	9.00	1.25
Dumyat	5.00	.69	al-Minia	7.14	.99
Kafr al-Shaykh	6.42	.89	Assiut	7.56	1.05
al-Gharbiyyah	8.26	1.15	Suhaj	6.88	.95
al-Manufiyyah	7.28	1.01	Qena	7.88	1.09
al-Buhayrah	8.77	1.22	Aswan	4.00	.55

Table 63   Comprehensive Scale of Influence of Second Stratum at District Office Level by Province

Province	Scale	Province	Scale
al-Qalyubiyyah	.92	al-Jizah	.60
al-Sharqiyyah	1.40	al-Fayyum	1.31
al-Daqahliyyah	.93	Bani Suwayf	1.21
Dumyat	.29	al-Minia	1.77
Kafr al-Shaykh	.47	Assiut	1.06
al-Gharbiyyah	.81	Suhaj	1.95
al-Manufiyyah	1.45	Qena	1.09
al-Buhayrah	1.34	Aswan	.87

Earlier we raised the question of the possibility that the political influence of provincial elites may be differentiated into at least two types: local influence based on traditional economic and deference arrangements and central influence based on service to and cooperation with the central authorities in Cairo. Of course these two types of influence may be found in the same family or individual. In order to get some idea of this difference it was decided to use the position of district officer as an indicator of local influence and that of former M.P. as an indicator of central influence. In table 64 we have compared the number of former M.P.'s in each province with the number of former M.P.'s who are officers, the number who are not officers, and the number in family sets.

We can take column 2 to represent those with both local and central influence while column 3 represents those with central influence only. The provinces where central influence appears to be more important are al-Daqahliyyah and Qena, especially where family-set membership is low both among the National Union members and among elite incumbents. Central influence is also substantial in al-Qalyubiyyah, al-Manufiyyah, al-Buhayrah, Bani Suwayf, and Suhaj. The question now arises whether those who wield (or are wielded by) central influence are from the second stratum or not. Column 8 gives us column 7 as a percentage of column 1 and is a summary indicator of central influence. Only in al-Qalyubiyyah, al-Sharqiyyah, and al-Fayyum are the majorities of the centrally influential former M.P.'s from family sets. Elsewhere the nonfamily-set former M.P.'s are the majority of those former M.P.'s who do not hold district office. In particular, the parliamentary elite of al-Daqahliyyah, al-Manufiyyah, al-Buhayrah, Bani Suwayf, Assiut, and Qena appear to be more than ordinarily influenced by the center because more of their former M.P.'s hold no district office and are not members of family sets which are dominant at the village level.

To complete the picture, we should also consider the number of district officers in each province who were not former M.P.'s. The more district officers who are not former M.P.'s, the more can we assume a measure of local influence which is not centrally determined. Since there were fewer former M.P.'s than officers, we shall have to measure this difference taking account of the ratio of officers to former M.P.'s. We have calculated the expected number of officers who are not former M.P.'s for each province assuming that the number of officers and former M.P.'s were the same. The ratio of the actual number to the expected number of officers who are not former M.P.'s (under the aforementioned assumption) was calculated. Table 65 presents these ratios. These results confirm some of those of table 64.

Tables 64 and 65 have been labelled scales of central and local influence, respectively, but table 64 measures central influence in terms of the parliamentary elite whereas table 65 measures local influence in terms of the district officers. Five provinces are high on both scales, thus suggesting that in these five provinces the selection of the two

Table 64

Scale of Central Influence
(distribution of former M.P.'s among district officers, nonofficers and family sets by province)

	1	2	3	4	5	6	7	8
Province	Former M.P.	Former M.P. Officer	Nonofficer	Former M.P./Family Set	Former M.P./Officer/Family Set	Former M.P./Family Set/Nonofficer	Former M.P./Nonofficer/Nonfamily Set	7/1
al-Qalyubiyyah	8	4	4	6	2	4	0	0
al-Sharqiyyah	23	17	6	13	8	4	2	8.7
al-Daqahliyyah	24	10	14	8	3	5	9	37.5
Dumyat	5	4	1	1	1	0	1	20.0
Kafr al-Shaykh	12	7	5	5	3	3	2	16.7
al-Gharbiyyah	21	13	8	9	6	4	4	19.0
al-Manufiyyah	19	10	9	6	4	2	7	36.8
al-Buhayrah	20	10	10	9	8	4	6	30.0
al-Jizah	14	10	4	8	5	2	2	14.0
al-Fayyum	12	8	4	8	5	3	1	8.3
Bani Suwayf	10	5	5	3	2	1	4	40.0
al-Minia	19	17	2	13	12	0	2	10.5
Assiut	18	12	6	5	5	0	6	33.3
Suhaj	22	13	10	12	8	5	5	22.7
Qena	20	8	12	7	3	4	8	40.0
Aswan	2	1	1	0	0	0	0	0

levels of the elite is most differentiated between the center at Cairo and the local community, with Cairo picking more M.P.'s without reference to local influence and with more district officers being chosen who are unable to secure their election to parliament. There are also four provinces, al-Qalyubiyyah, al-Sharqiyyah, al-Fayyum and al-Minia, in which the party and parliamentary elites are most similar, that is, where central selection and local status are most in agreement.

Table 65   Scale of Local Influence
                                               (ratio of expected district officers
                                               who are not former M.P.'s to actual
                                               number by province; mean = 1.05)

Province	Scale	Province	Scale
al-Qalyubiyyah	.93	al-Jizah	1.00
al-Sharqiyyah	.93	al-Fayyum	1.00
al-Daqahliyyah	1.20	Bani Suwayf	1.09
Dumyat	1.00	al-Minia	.89
Kafr al-Shaykh	1.08	Assiut	1.02
al-Gharbiyyah	1.05	Suhaj	1.06
al-Manufiyyah	1.09	Qena	1.21
al-Buhayrah	1.13	Aswan	1.05

When the elite positions of district officer and former M.P. were analyzed, it was found that second stratum influence could be measured in terms of the proportion of officers and former M.P.'s who were members of family sets, the ratio of officers and former M.P.'s in family sets to the total membership in family sets, and the degree of overlap or joint incumbency between officers and former M.P.'s who were at the same time members of family sets. Using these distinctions, it was possible to determine that though the second stratum holds most elite positions where it is most prevalent, its influence is most concentrated where it is proportionately smaller. Hence, in the northern provinces, the second stratum has more of the characteristics of a constituency, while in the southern provinces it is more of an elite. An alternative hypothesis might explain the provincial differences in the concentration of the elite statuses among the second stratum in another way. It is possible to argue that the second stratum is itself stratified, that there are among the members of the second stratum segments in almost every province which are highly influential. The differences among the provinces would then be accounted for by the size of the "surplus" members of the second stratum who are not as influential.

There is, in fact, quite impressive evidence that there may be a rural segment of the second stratum which, while sharing many characteristics with the rest of the family-set members, exhibits greater coherence of elite characteristics including size of family set and occupations. This particularly influential segment has been identified by means of three indicators: (1) descent from prerevolutionary M.P.'s; (2) kinship with the contemporary parliamentary elite as evidenced by the obituary notices sampled; and (3) ownership of an 'izbah as evidenced by the 1930 survey of Egypt maps. We shall next examine the geographical distribution of these three groups.

A recapitulation of some of the national findings regarding the parliamentary ancestors of members of the National Union committees may prove helpful. Of the total of twenty-four hundred parliamentary seats filled in regular and by-elections to the Egyptian National Assembly in sixteen agricultural provinces in thirteen elections 892 seats (37.2%) were filled by 370 ancestor M.P.'s for an average of 2.41 seats per parliamentary ancestor. The total number of incumbents was 653, and they held an average of 3.67 seats. Hence it is clear that the ancestors of National Union members were not in most cases the most influential of the prerevolutionary elite. So, while there is important continuity before and after 1952, evidence of this social and political continuity ought not to mislead us into believing that the revolution brought no change.

The number of seats held by an ancestral line (i.e., all the ancestors of a 1959 member of the National Union) may be used as an indicator of traditional influence. We have disregarded the question of whether a single individual incumbent was actually reelected, especially because the elections in question span a period of several generations, but have instead considered whether a single family of descent held seats in more than one parliament. In table 66 the average number of seats per ancestral family is presented in a provincial breakdown. The average is largest in Suhaj, Qena, and al-Manufiyyah; nevertheless, it nowhere reaches the average of 3.67. In fact, with a standard deviation of only .206 (calculated without Dumyat), it is clear that there is no great variation among the provinces. In political-sociological terms, we can say that if there were two groups of M.P.'s, one that included most of the ancestors of the contemporary second stratum and another that included most of the prerevolutionary bourgeois landowning elite, then it is unlikely that many descendants of the latter are to be found concentrated in particular provinces as members of a present-day political elite. Only the ancestors of the present-day elite of Suhaj are likely to have been drawn from the latter segment.

Table 66   Distribution of Seats Filled by
                                            Ancestor M.P.'s by Province

Province	Average number of seats	Percentage of seats
al-Qalyubiyyah	2.59	47.9%
al-Shariqiyyah	2.38	40.5
al-Daqahliyyah	1.96	26.8
al-Dumyat	3.00	25.0
Kafr al-Shaykh	2.38	[30.2
al-Gharbiyyah	1.89	
al-Manufiyyah	3.10	43.3
al-Buhayrah	2.29	37.2
al-Jizah	2.33	46.3
al-Fayyum	2.35	37.7
Bani Suwayf	2.54	26.9
al-Minia	2.50	35.1
Assiut	1.88	32.4
Suhaj	3.19	53.1
Qena	1.40	39.8
Aswan	1.40	16.7
Mean	2.41	35.9
Standard deviation	.206[a]	9.78

[a]Without Dumyat.

The total seats won by ancestors of National Union members can be used as a measure of the provincial level political influence of this group when taken as a percentage of the total number of seats available, bearing in mind that the total seats varied in different parliamentary periods. Table 66 also lists the percentage of all seats (elections and by-elections) filled by ancestor M.P.'s for each province for all thirteen elections considered. The provinces in which the ancestors of our National Union members were most influential were Suhaj, again, al-Jizah, al-Qalyubiyyah, al-Manufiyyah, and al-Sharqiyyah. The thirteen elections have been divided into three periods as follows: the first including the elections of 1866, 1870, 1876, and 1881; the second including 1924, 1925, 1926, and 1929; and the third including the elections of 1931, 1936, 1938, 1942, and 1945. The findings for each of the three periods are presented in percentage of total seats to be filled for each province (table 67).

The middle period, including the elections of 1924–29, has, as expected, a substantially lower percentage than the other two periods. In the earliest period the provinces which have the strongest showing are the mostly high prevalence provinces of al-Qalyubiyyah, al-Buhayrah, al-Fayyum, Qena, al-Manufiyyah, and al-Jizah. For the second period, the ancestors of the postrevolutionary elite are nowhere very strong, except perhaps in Suhaj. In this second period, it may be remembered, the Wafd succeeded in three of the four elections.

In the third period the proportion of ancestors increases and it is more evenly divided among all the provinces. The strongest province is Suhaj, where it appears the rural elite has been least challenged for the last one hundred years. For Qena we note some attrition in the position of the traditional rural elite, whereas for Assiut and more especially for al-Minia the rural notables seem only more recently to have emerged as a substantial force.

In order to illustrate more clearly the changes over time, table 68 gives the rank order of each province in each of the three periods. The lower the rank, the greater the influence of these ancestors; and the lower the sum of the rankings the more historically consistent has been that influence. It is apparent that the provinces with the most persistently *and* recently high influence of ancestor M.P.'s are grouped about Cairo (al-Jizah, al-Manufiyyah, al-Qalyubiyyah, and al-Sharqiyyah) in addition to the first ranked province of Suhaj.

Turning our attention to the descendants of this segment of the prerevolutionary parliamentary elite, we will first consider whether the

Table 67   Percentage of Available Seats Filled
                               by Ancestor M.P.'s by Period and
                               by Province

Province	1866-81	1924-29	1931-45
al-Qalyubiyyah	78.3%	23.1%	54.4%
al-Sharqiyyah	25.7	28.8	55.0
al-Daqahliyyah	41.7	2.8	39.4
Dumyat	0.0	33.3	50.0
Kafr al-Shaykh al-Gharbiyyah	38.1	4.2	45.3
al-Manufiyyah	56.0	26.3	51.8
al-Buhayrah	88.5	7.7	43.0
al-Jizah	50.0	26.3	56.5
al-Fayyum	71.4	23.7	42.6
Bani Suwayf	25.0	5.7	41.5
al-Minia	21.4	14.8	51.7
Assiut	25.0	17.8	44.0
Suhaj	42.9	35.5	66.7
Qena	62.5	22.0	46.9
Aswan	0	0	29.2
Mean	44.6	17.0	48.6

Table 68   Rank Order of Provinces by Percentage of Seats Filled by Ancestor
M.P.'s

Province	1866-81	1924-29	1931-45	Mean
al-Qalyubiyyah	2	6	4	4.0
al-Sharqiyyah	10	3	3	5.3
al-Daqahliyyah	8	13	14	11.6
Dumyat	13[a]	2	7	7.3
Kafr al-Shaykh al-Gharbiyyah	9	12	9	10.0
al-Manufiyyah	5	4[c]	5	4.6
al-Buhayrah	1	10	11	7.3
al-Jizah	6	4[c]	2	4.0
al-Fayyum	3	5	12	6.6
Bani Suwayf	11[b]	11	13	11.6
al-Minia	12	9	6	9.0
Assiut	11[b]	8	10	9.6
Suhaj	7	1	1	3.0
Qena	4	7	8	6.3
Aswan	13[a]	14	15	14.0

[a-c] Same rank.

family-set descendants are found unequally distributed among the provinces. Of the total ancestor seats about 60% correspond to family-set
descendants and 40% can be linked with individual descendants.

It is surprising to find (table 69) that there are only two provinces
falling substantially below the mean level of 60% ancestors of family
sets. The provinces where the family-set descendants of the prerevolutionary parliamentary elite appear to be very strong the al-Qalyubiyyah,
al-Buhayrah, and al-Fayyum. In each of these three provinces one or
two highly influential families were able to establish their political positions in the nineteenth century and to maintain at least one parliamentary seat throughout the prerevolutionary period.

It is to be expected that the occupations of the descendants will vary
by province because of modernization differentials. From table 70 we
find that this is the case but to a lesser extent than was anticipated.
Each province deviates importantly in only one or two occupations,
and were we to divide the table into equal quadrants, it would show
that the largest number of deviations occur in the upper left-hand
quadrant and in the lower right-hand quadrant. That is to say that the
lower Egyptian provinces deviate by the greater percentage of modern
occupations, while the upper Egyptian provinces deviate by the greater

percentage of farmers, former M.P.'s, and local councillors. The upper
Egyptian provinces have fewer 'umad and they have more former M.P.'s
and local councillors.

Together the percentage of 'umdah descendants and the percentage
of former M.P. descendants can tell us about the degree of the concentration and the continuity of elite statuses in each province. A simple
index combining both characteristics can be constructed by taking the
proportion of former M.P.'s to 'umad: the more former M.P.'s the
greater the continuity and concentration, the more 'umad the greater
the dispersion of authority. Table 71 gives us the proportions for each
province.

Table 71 gives striking evidence of the difference between lower and
upper Egypt. The more developed the province, the more likely is it
that more of its 'umad will be descendants of prerevolutionary M.P.'s
and fewer of its former M.P.'s will be descendants of prerevolutionary
M.P.'s. There is, thus, some evidence of greater downward political
mobility in the more developed northern provinces where the second
stratum is larger. It is also true that large numbers of the second stratum
in the north are politically active and that the regime draws more of its

Table 69   Distribution of Seats Held by
                                     Family-Set Ancestors (Prerevolu-
                                     tionary M.P.'s) by Province

Province	Seats Held by Ancestors of Family Sets	Seats Held by Ancestors of Individuals	Percentage of Ancestors of Family Sets
al-Qalyubiyyah	44	14	75.9%
al-Sharqiyyah	47	36	56.6
al-Daqahliyyah	16	39	29.1
Dumyat	0	3	0.0
Kafr al-Shaykh		8	65.0
al-Gharbiyyah	67	28	
al-Manufiyyah	59	34	63.4
al-Buhayrah	54	17	76.1
al-Jizah	33	23	58.9
al-Fayyum	28	12	70.0
Bani Suwayf	17	11	60.7
al-Minia	39	21	65.0
Assiut	27	41	39.7
Suhaj	67	35	65.7
Qena	40	28	58.8
Aswan	5	2	71.4

Table 70

Distribution of Occupations of Descendants of Prerevolutionary M.P.'s by Province (in percent)

Province	Total Descendants	Professional	Civil Servant	Teacher	Merchant	Businessman	M.P.	Local Councillor	'Umdah	Farmer	Other
al-Qalyubiyyah	53	17.0	9.4	7.5	0.0	3.8	3.8	3.8	26.4	22.6	5.7
al-Sharqiyyah	63	11.1	3.2	6.3	1.6	1.6	6.3	4.8	25.4	28.6	11.1
al-Daqahliyyah	53	3.8	9.4	11.3	1.9	0.0	5.7	3.8	22.6	30.2	11.3
Dumyat	1	--	--	100.0	--	--	--	--	--	--	--
Kafr al-Shaykh	34	17.6	5.9	0.0	2.9	2.9	5.9	0.0	23.5	35.2	2.9
al-Gharbiyyah	94	13.8	8.5	4.3	8.5	1.1	4.3	0.0	23.4	29.8	6.4
al-Manufiyyah	66	12.1	16.7	6.1	7.6	1.5	3.0	1.5	19.7	27.3	4.5
al-Buhayrah	87	14.9	5.7	1.1	2.3	0.0	4.6	0.0	28.7	37.9	4.6
al-Jizah	46	13.0	15.2	6.5	4.3	0.0	8.7	2.2	23.9	19.6	6.5
al-Fayyum	39	12.8	5.1	2.6	2.6	0.0	10.3	7.7	15.4	43.6	0.0
Bani Suwayf	33	15.2	15.2	6.1	0.0	0.0	3.0	0.0	21.2	39.4	0.0
al-Minia	52	15.4	3.8	3.8	0.0	1.9	13.5	1.9	17.3	32.7	9.6
Assiut	53	13.2	7.5	1.9	1.9	0.0	9.4	15.1	22.6	24.5	3.8
Suhaj	64	7.8	1.6	1.6	1.6	0.0	17.2	7.8	15.6[a]	37.5	9.4
Qena	52	11.5	7.7	7.7	0.0	0.0	9.6	1.9	15.4	38.5	7.7
Aswan	3	33.3	0.0	0.0	0.0	0.0	33.3	0.0	0.0	33.3	0.0
Total	793										
Mean[b]		12.8	8.2	4.8	2.5	.9	7.5	3.6	21.5	32.2	6.0

[a] Includes 3 a'yan.

[b] Aswan and Dumyat have so few descendants that they need not be considered, and they have not been included in calculating the mean percentage for each occupation.

support from the delta regions. Similarly, the greater part of the "loyal opposition," insofar as oppositional pressures can be brought to bear, is also located in the north.

It seems reasonable to argue that wherever the second stratum is more numerous, as measured by family sets, it is more modernized occupationally, and more politically influential in the aggregate, but the influence of the second stratum is also more widely dispersed (among more individuals), and, hence, more beset by intragroup competition.

Table 71   Index of Continuity and Concentration of Elite Statuses

Province	Index	Province	Index
al-Qalyubiyyah	.14	al-Jizah	.36
al-Sharqiyyah	.24	al-Fayyum	.67
al-Daqahliyyah	.25	Bani Suwayf	.14
Dumyat	--	al-Minia	.78
Kafr al-Shaykh	.25	Assiut	.42
al-Gharbiyyah	.18	Suhaj	1.10
al-Manufiyyah	.15	Qena	.62
al-Buhayrah	.16	Aswan	--

In upper Egypt a different sort of situation prevails. Political influence is more concentrated and often identified with families that were prominent before the revolution. Less prominent segments of the second stratum are more politically apathetic both with regard to influencing their own clients and pressing demands on the central government. The important families of the parliamentary elite still appear to be the most important power brokers and it makes most sense to orient oneself politically toward them.

If we take the position of district officer to be an indicator of local influence and the position of former M.P. to be an indicator of central influence, it follows that, for officers who were also former M.P.'s and descendants, central and local influence are conjointly wielded. Such a group, really only a handful of families, exists especially in al-Sharqiyyah, al-Fayyum, al-Minia, Assiut, and Suhaj.

The prerevolutionary and the postrevolutionary parliamentary elites are conjoined in the group of descendants who are themselves former M.P.'s. Altogether there were 62 such descendants and about two-thirds of them were members of family sets, as shown in table 72. The 62 former M.P.'s comprised nearly a quarter of all the former M.P.'s in the National Union, thus indicating considerable continuity at the highest levels in our investigation. These descendant former M.P.'s were

212   Part Two

not evenly distributed over the provinces; the largest percentages were
to be found in upper Egypt and the lowest in the west delta and Bani
Suwayf. The provinces showing the greatest transrevolutionary continuity of the parliamentary elite are Suhaj, al-Minia, al-Fayyum, al-
Jizah, Assiut, al-Sharqiyyah, Qena, and al-Qalyubiyyah.

That there is substantial evidence of the similarity among elements
of the parliamentary elite in various parts of Egypt, and further evidence of transrevolutionary continuity of elements of that elite raises
the question of the possibility of social linkages among members of this
elite. We have already described some of the characteristics of these
"linked" M.P.'s and their related families, but it remains to be seen
whether these linked families are concentrated in a few provinces or
whether they are spread throughout the country. A further consideration is whether they are linked within a single province or whether they
have significant kinship ties to parliamentary families in other parts of
the country.

In five provinces a number of M.P. families were linked together.
Table 73 lists these provinces and gives the number linked as opposed
to the total for the province and the total mentioned in the obituaries.

Table 72   Distribution of Proportion of For-
                                        mer M.P. Descendants

| Province | Former M.P. Descendants | | | Former M.P.'s in NU | Percentage of Descendants of Former M.P.'s |
	Family Set	Nonfamily Set	Total		
al-Qalyubiyyah	1	1	2	8	25.0%
al-Sharqiyyah	6	-	6	23	26.1
al-Daqahliyyah	2	1	3	24	12.5
Dumyat	-	-	-	5	(0.0)
Kafr al-Shaykh	2	-	2	12	16.7
al-Gharbiyyah	3	1	4	25	16.0
al-Manufiyyah	1	2	3	19	15.8
al-Buhayrah	2	2	4	21	19.0
al-Jizah	1	3	4	14	28.6
al-Fayyum	3	1	4	12	33.3
Bani Suwayf	-	1	1	11	9.1
al-Minia	5	2	7	19	36.8
Assiut	3	2	5	18	27.8
Suhaj	7	4	11	25	44.0
Qena	4	1	5	20	25.0
Aswan	1	0	1	2	50.0
Total	41	21	62	258	--
Percentage	66.1%	33.9%	100%	--	(mean) 25.7%[a]

[a]Excluding Aswan.

Table 73   M.P.'s Linked in the Same Province

Province	Number Linked in Province	Total M.P.'s in Obituaries	Total M.P.'s
al-Qalyubiyyah	0	3	13
al-Sharqiyyah	2+2[a]	7	25
al-Daqahliyyah	0	8	30
Dumyat	0	2	6
Kafr al-Shaykh	0	5	20
al-Gharbiyyah	0	6	27
al-Manufiyyah	0	6	23
al-Buhayrah	3	9	25
al-Jizah	0	1	15
al-Fayyum	6	11	15
Bani Suwayf	0	8	15
al-Minia	4	16	23
Assiut	6	11	22
Suhaj	0	10	28
Qena	0	3	23
Aswan	0	2	9

[a]Two groups of 2 M.P.'s.

Only a few provinces have many linked M.P. families and those are two provinces in the heart of upper Egypt, al-Minia and Assiut (but not Suhaj), and two tribally influenced provinces, al-Sharqiyyah and al-Fayyum. The highest proportion of linked M.P.'s are in al-Fayyum and Assiut. Since less than half of the total number of M.P.'s from these provinces were in our obituary sample, there is the further possibility that even more of the parliamentary elite may be related.

Other family links are geographically more distant. Seven linked M.P. families are in neighboring provinces, as illustrated in figure 14. All of these are found in lower Egypt, and we note that the geographically central province of al-Gharbiyyah is the subject of five of those linkages.

Five linked M.P. "chains" are in nonneighboring provinces. For upper Egypt, these chains link parliamentary families in al-Fayyum and Assiut and Suhaj and al-Minia. Also linked are al-Fayyum and al-Qalyubiyyah, Assiut and al-Buhayrah, and al-Jizah and Kafr al-Shaykh. Even more distantly linked are a chain in Bani Suwayf, Alexandria, and Assiut, and another in al-Buhayrah, Qena, and al-Daqahliyyah; the largest of them all includes 23 M.P.'s:

Assiut	6	al-Buhayrah	2	Suhaj	1
al-Minia	3	Qena	1	al-Qalyubiyyah	1
al-Gharbiyyah	3	al-Fayyum	1	al-Daqahliyyah	1
Aswan	2	Kafr al Shaykh	1	Bani Suwayf	1

This largest chain strongly suggests the castelike quality of the parliamentary elite, and its homogeneity on a country-wide basis. At the very least this list accounts for 20% of all the M.P.'s in our sample.

Table 74 shows that the percentage of linked M.P. families is somewhat larger in upper Egypt than in lower, suggesting that the endogamous status group tendencies of the parliamentary elite are waning characteristics found more prominently in the more highly stratified and more traditional provinces.

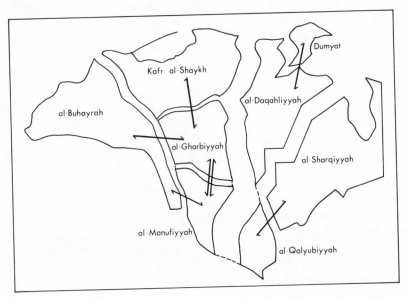

Fig. 14   Linkages among Prerevolutionary
                                     M.P.'s in Neighboring Provinces

These suggestions can be tested to a limited degree by seeing how many of the linked M.P.'s in each province had ancestors in the prerevolutionary parliaments. From table 75 we find that this segment (more traditional? more status oriented?) of the postrevolutionary parliamentary elite is strongly related to the prerevolutionary elite in nearly all provinces except for the most urbanized. It also appears that this descent pattern is somewhat stronger in upper Egypt than in lower Egypt.

The last segment of the rural elite to be considered from the perspective of geographical distribution is the 'izbah owner. This group of members of the National Union are related to, or descended from, a group of landowners who had established a type of latifundium on

estates of at least 50 feddan in area. These latifundia were identified
from 1930 maps, but they may have been established much earlier. We
know only the minimum but not the maximum area of these estates.

Table 74   Linked M.P.'s as Percentage of All
                                      M.P.'s and M.P.'s in Obituaries

Province	All M.P.'s	M.P.'s in Obituaries	Percentage in Obituaries	Linked M.P.'s	Percentage Linked	Linked in Province
al-Qalyubiyyah	13	3	23.0	3	23.0	0
al-Sharqiyyah	25	7	28.0	5	20.0	2+2[a]
al-Daqahliyyah	30	8	26.6	3	10.0	
Dumyat	6	2	33.3	1	16.6	0
Kafr al-Shaykh	20	5	25.0	3	15.0	0
al-Gharbiyyah	27	6	22.2	6	22.2	0
al-Manufiyyah	23	6	26.0	3	13.0	0
al-Buhayrah	25	9	36.0	7	28.0	3
al-Jizah	15	1	6.6	1	6.6	0
al-Fayyum	15	11	73.3	9	60.0	6
Bani Suwayf	15	8	53.3	2	13.3	0
al-Minia	23	16	69.5	7	30.4	4
Assiut	22	11	50.0	9	40.9	6
Suhaj	28	10	35.7	2	5.1	0
Qena	23	3	13.0	2	8.6	0
Aswan	9	2	22.2	2	22.2	0

[a]Two groups of 2 M.P.'s.

Table 75   Percentage of Linked M.P.'s De-
                                      scended from Prerevolutionary
                                      M.P.'s

Province	Number of Linked M.P.'s	Number Descended from M.P.'s	Percentage
al-Qalyubiyyah	3	1	33.3
al-Sharqiyyah	5	2	40.0
al-Daqahliyyah	3	2	66.6
Dumyat	1	0	0
Kafr al-Shaykh	3	1	33.3
al-Gharbiyyah	6	3	50.0
al-Manufiyyah	3	1	33.3
al-Buhayrah	7	4	57.0
al-Jizah	1	0	0
al-Fayyum	9	5	55.0
Bani Suwayf	2	0	0
al-Minia	7	3	42.8
Assiut	9	4	44.0
Suhaj	2	1	50.0
Qena	2	2	100.0
Aswan	2	2	100.0

In attempting to determine the reasons for the peculiar distribution of 'izab, we are handicapped by the limited data available. Chesnin's data is comprised of three parts: (a) complete data on 'izbah ownership for former M.P.'s and district officers, (b) a substantial sample of all family-set members in each province, and (c) an inferential distribution of 'izbah owners among nonfamily-set members. The distribution of 'izbah owners among nonfamily-set members was inferred from the basic finding that about 3% of nonfamily-set members, countrywide, were 'izbah owners. Controlling, then, for the percentage of nonfamily-set members in each province, it is possible to arrive at an estimated number of nonfamily-set owners for each province.

Table 76 shows that a greater proportion of family-set members are 'izbah owners than are nonfamily-set members. The proportion of family-set 'izbah owners to nonfamily-set owners varies considerably from less than 2 to 1 in Assiut to a high of almost 20 to 1 in al-Qalyubiyyah, Kafr al-Shaykh, and al-Fayyum.

Table 76   Number and Percentage of Members
                                          of the NU Who Are 'Izbah Owners

Province	Family-Set Members		Nonfamily-Set Members	
	Number	Percentage	Number	Percentage
al-Qalyubiyyah	136	41.6	158	2.16
al-Sharquiyyah	90	17.3	188	4.56
al-Daqahliyyah	62	13.7	170	4.80
Dumyat	8	13.8	12	.87
Kafr al-Shaykh	142	40.0	163	2.10
al-Gharbiyyah	137	22.3	193	3.45
al-Manufiyyah	114	24.5	169	3.42
al-Buhayrah	249	39.0	320	3.90
al-Jizah	31	8.2	53	2.16
al-Fayyum	104	36.4	120	1.86
Bani Suwayf	30	15.7	63	2.64
al-Minia	63	16.0	142	4.08
Assiut	17	6.1	67	3.27
Suhaj	27	10.9	107	4.14
Qena	27	16.2	85	3.51
Aswan	0	0.0	6	1.11

It is not at all clear that these two groups of 'izbah owners comprise two mutually exclusive segments of the rural elite. We know that family-set membership itself comprehends a number of strata, and it is fairly certain that many members of these strata did not turn up as family-set members of the National Union. It is, therefore, probably incorrect to assume a random distribution of nonfamily-set 'izbah owners among the provinces. It is more likely true that their numbers are proportionate to the numbers of owners in family sets. Nevertheless, we will proceed on the assumption that they may comprise a separate and nonintersecting social set. Table 77 shows the resultant percentage of the total membership of the National Union in each province who were 'izbah owners. It is this statistic (as a percent, Z score, or in absolute numbers) which will be used in searching for explanations of the distribution of 'izbah owners, bearing in mind that it minimizes the extent to which 'izbah ownership is thought to be characteristic of and proportionate to family-set membership.

Table 77   Percentage of All Members of the
                                          NU Who Own 'Izab

Province	Percentage	Province	Percentage
al-Qalyubiyyah	11.9	al-Jizah	3.8
al-Sharqiyyah	7.1	al-Fayyum	10.3
al-Daqahliyyah	6.3	Bani Suwayf	4.4
Dumyat	2.6	al-Minia	6.1
Kafr al-Shaykh	12.0	Assiut	3.7
al-Gharbiyyah	8.6	Suhaj	4.9
al-Manufiyyah	8.1	Qena	4.7
al-Buhayrah	13.0	Aswan	1.1

Using Z scores, Mr. Chesnin tried a number of regressions with a modification of this last statistic. Chesnin's percentages differed slightly in that he assumed a flat 3% of nonfamily-set members were 'izbah owners in each province. He tried to see whether there was any relationship between the percentage of 'izbah owners in each province and the following independent variables. The correlation coefficients are in percentages.

1. Owners of 50 or more feddan ($r^2 = .19$ sig. $= .05$)
2. Workers in establishments employing fifty or more ($r^2 = .10$ sig. $= .11$)
3. Male illiterates ($r^2 = .02$ sig. $= .28$)
4. Density of population per square mile ($r^2 = .12$ sig. $= .095$)
5. Feddan planted in fruits and citrus ($r^2 = .20$ sig. $= .04$)
6. Feddan planted in cotton ($r^2 = .006$ sig. $= .38$)
7. Percentage of family-set members in the National Union ($r^2 = .50$ sig. $= .001$)
8. Percentage of traditional occupations in the National Union ($r^2 = .01$ sig. $= .32$)

From these findings it is clear that the strongest determinant of the percentage of 'izbah owners is the percentage in family sets in the National Union. This high correlation is not surprising since Chesnin correlated the Z scores of two ratios of the same base, that is, total members of the National Union in each province. Nevertheless, this close association is upheld even when we use the number of members of family sets and the number of 'izbah owners. As we see in figure 15,

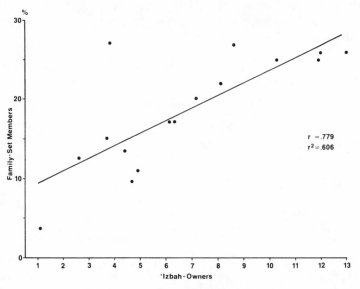

Fig. 15   Percentage of Family-Set Members
                                               and 'Izbah Owners by Province

the scattergram shows that the percentage of 'izbah owners is, to a very high degree, directly proportional to the percentage of family-set members. Chesnin's scattergram (fig. 16) of his correlation is similar, except that it indicates that there may be a curvilinear relationship suggesting that the number of 'izbah owners escalates sharply with each increment of family-set members beyond a certain critical point.

These findings argue against the notion that 'izbah ownership defines a quite separate segment of the rural middle class. That is to say that, by 1959, for the most part, only the owners of the smaller 'izab or their descendants were still politically viable. We should not forget, however, that in certain provinces the parliamentary and party elite is long-standing and has a high concentration of control over political office. In these provinces of high concentration and traditional continuity the percentage of family-set members is lower. Hence, 'izbah ownership does not coincide with the most influential and traditional stratum of the rural middle class, even though more former M.P.'s and more district officers are 'izbah owners than are not. 'Izbah ownership marks an intermediate stratum of the rural middle class, and insofar as we designate a segment of the members of the National Union by this term we are not referring

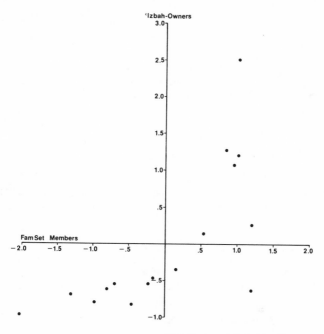

Fig. 16   Z Scores of Family-Set Members
and 'Izbah Owners by Province
S. Chesnin, "A Subclass of
Egyptian Rural Elites"
(M.A. thesis, Univ. of Chicago, 1974)

to the richest owners of the largest latifundia. Yet this group probably owns about 50 feddan, or less if the 1930 family holdings were divided upon inheritance. A further conclusion to be drawn from the scatter-grams is that, insofar as 'izbah ownership increases more rapidly than family-set membership, the prevalence of 'izbah ownership is probably the result of the diffusion of the practice of establishing 'izab after it had been adopted by a critical number of owners or wherever there were enough other owners and incentives to create a favorable social climate. In this last connection, the moderately strong correlations of both larger holdings and fruit growing (a high capital crop) are indicative of secondary influences.

We recall that about 60% of all former M.P.'s were also district officers, that is, about 27% of all district officers. Only 20% of the district officers owned 'izab, whereas about 45% were members of family sets. For former M.P.'s the figures are 33% 'izbah owners and also 45% members of family sets. These figures suggest that 'izbah ownership indicates higher political status. The percentage of former M.P.'s who are also district officers and who are members of family sets drops to 29% (13% of all district officers), not too far from the percentage owning 'izab. And finally the percentage of former M.P.'s who are district officers, members of family sets, and owners of 'izab is 14% (6.3% of district officers). The combined probabilities are about 9% for former M.P.'s and about 2.5% for district officers. That former M.P.'s and district officers are equally likely to be members of family sets indicates that the second stratum is a broad social layer including persons of varying levels of influence. Differences between the two groups emerge here only with regard to 'izbah ownership, and though relatively more former M.P.'s are 'izbah owners, there are nearly twice as many more 'izbah owners than expected among the district officers than there are among the former M.P.'s.

With these country-wide statistics in mind, let us now see whether these characteristics are to be found in every province in the same degree. Table 78 shows the percentage of district officers who own 'izab (for 555 district officers). Five provinces have less than 10%, six provinces have less than 21%, and five range from 28% to 43.8%. This distribution probably has something to do with the prevalence of 'izab, but since we don't know how many there are in each province we cannot check this hypothesis. At any rate, the provinces in which more district officers are 'izbah owners are al-Qalyubiyyah, al-Sharqiyyah, and al-Buhayrah, with al-Manufiyyah and al-Fayyum close behind. The provinces with the highest percentage of 'izbah owners among all members of the National Union were al-Qalyubiyyah, Kafr al-Shaykh, al-Buhayrah, and al-Fayyum.

Among owners there were higher percentages of family-set officers than nonfamily-set officers in every province without exception. The provinces in which the combination of family set/district officer/'izbah owner prevails most frequently are al-Qalyubiyyah, al-Sharqiyyah, Kafr al-Shaykh, al-Buhayrah, and al-Fayyum. There is a similar pattern for former M.P./'izbah owner, for former M.P./'izbah owner/family-set member, and for former M.P./'izbah owner/family-set member/district officer. Consistently, al-Sharqiyyah, al-Buhayrah, and al-Fayyum come through as the provinces in which there is the largest 'izbah-owning elite of the most concentrated influence. Al-Minia does not have so many 'izbah owners, but al-Minia's owners are relatively influential. These provinces have already been noted as having high percentages of family-set members, having many locally influential 'umad (al-Buhayrah and al-Minia) or having important tribal elements among the rural elite (al-Sharqiyyah and al-Fayyum).

Table 78   District Officers and 'Izbah Owner-
                                               ship

Province	Owners	Nonowners	Unknown
al-Qalyubiyyah	42.9%	57.1%	--
al-Sharqiyyah	37.2	51.2	11.6%
al-Daqahliyyah	18.2	75.0	6.8
Dumyat	0.0	93.7	6.3
Kafr al-Shaykh	18.8	81.3	--
al-Gharbiyyah	18.2	75.0	6.8
al-Manufiyyah	28.1	71.9	--
al-Buhayrah	43.8	52.1	4.2
al-Jizah	6.3	90.6	3.1
al-Fayyum	29.2	58.3	12.5
Bani Suwayf	15.6	71.9	12.5
al-Minia	20.5	79.5	--
Assiut	2.5	95.0	2.5
Suhaj	13.6	86.4	--
Qena	2.8	94.4	2.8
Aswan	0.0	100.0	--
All 16 provinces	20.0%	75.7%	4.3%

The countrywide ratio of former M.P. 'izbah owners to former M.P. family-set members is .73, but in six provinces the ratio is 1.0 or more (see table 79). In those provinces there are fewer 'izab, and 'izbah ownership appears to be an indicator of higher status rather than mere family-set membership. I would not be surprised to learn that the average size of 'izab is larger in those provinces of upper Egypt. In the provinces where family-set membership is more prevalent and where there are more 'izab, there are as many or more former M.P./'izbah owners as former M.P./family-set members.

Significant differences among the provinces appear more clearly when we turn to examine the relationship between 'izbah owners and descendants of the prerevolutionary parliaments. Table 80 shows the number of 'izbah owners found in the sample for each province and

Table 79   Comparison of Percentages of
                                            Former M.P.'s Owning 'Izab and in
                                            Family Sets

Province	A ᶜIzbah Owners	B Family Sets	A/B
al-Qalyubiyyah	75.0%	75.0%	1.00
al-Sharqiyyah	47.8	52.2	.92
al-Daqahliyyah	16.7	33.3	.50
Dumyat	0.0	40.0	--
Kafr al-Shaykh	50.0	50.0	1.00
al-Gharbiyyah	52.4	47.6	1.10
al-Manufiyyah	31.6	31.6	1.00
al-Buhayrah	55.0	50.0	1.10
al-Jizah	14.3	50.0	.29
al-Fayyum	58.3	66.7	.87
Bani Suwayf	20.0	20.0	1.00
al-Minia	26.3	68.4	.39
Assiut	5.6	27.8	.20
Suhaj	13.6	50.0	.27
Qena	25.0	40.0	.63
Aswan	0.0	0.0	--
All 16 provinces	33.0%	45.0%	33/45 = .73

the number of those 'izbah owners who were descendants. Not only
does the percentage vary considerably from province to province, but
we find the percentage tends to be lower where more 'izbah owners
were found. This paradox suggests that wherever 'izab were more rare,
there were 'izbah owners able to hold onto their influence longer. We
note that the average is brought down by al-Qalyubiyyah, Kafr al-
Shaykh, al-Buhayrah, and al-Fayyum, all provinces with larger numbers
of 'izbah owners of high status.

These statistics, drawn from a sample, are somewhat misleading.
The data on the district officers were complete, and therefore give us a
better picture. We know that 20% of all district officers were 'izbah
owners, and that 74% of these were members of family sets. Forty-five
percent of these 'izbah-owning district officers were descendants of
members of prerevolutionary parliaments. Of these district officer/'izbah
owning/descendants, 88% were members of family sets and 50% were
also former M.P.'s. Remembering that we have only 555 district officers, and only 111 district officer/'izbah owners, and only 98 district
officer descendants, the combined probability is only 3.5% of all district
officers. The actual percentage of 'izbah owning/district officer/de-
scendants is 9%, and, of course, family-set membership is well above

expectation, as is the percentage of former M.P.'s. This is clearly a very high status group. More than one half of all the officer descendants were 'izbah owners. Just about 75% of all the 62 former M.P. descendants were 'izbah owners. So many of these influentials are family-set members that it is clear that we are dealing with a very special segment of the second stratum, but then all of these people are 'izbah owners. It is clear that 'izbah-owning officers are more influential and have been influential longer than have been those district officers who do not own 'izab. These 20% of all district officers account for 33% of the family-set member/district officers, for 51% of the officer/descendants, and for 75% of the former M.P./officer/descendants. Chesnin's indices of 'izbah-owning former M.P.'s and 'izbah-owning district officers correlate at .865. There is a close relationship between 'izbah ownership and descent from prerevolutionary parliaments as we would expect given that the data on 'izbah ownership is from 1930.

With these countrywide statistics in mind we can turn to a provincial breakdown of some of this information to see if these associations hold throughout all the provinces. Table 81 gives us the percentage of 'izbah-owning district officers who were descendants, and, conversely, the percentage of officers and descendants who were 'izbah owners. The

Table 80   Percentage of Descendants of 'Izbah
                                       Owners by Province

Province	Number of 'Izbah Owners	Number of Descendants	Percentage
al-Qalyubiyyah	49	11	22.4
al-Sharqiyyah	12	5	41.6
al-Daqahliyyah	10	3	30.0
Dumyat	0	0	0
Kafr al-Shaykh	27	7	25.9
al-Gharbiyyah	14	7	50.0
al-Manufiyyah	13	7	53.8
al-Buhayrah	25	7	28.0
al-Jizah	7	0	0
al-Fayyum	26	5	19.2
Bani Suwayf	11	6	54.5
al-Minia	9	4	44.4
Assiut	5	3	60.0
Suhaj	7	4	57.0
Qena	11	7	63.6
Aswan	0	0	0
All 16 provinces	226	76	33.6

first column does not take account of the fact that the number of officer/descendants was limited, nor does the second column take account of the limitation of the number of 'izbah-owning officers. Taken together in the last column, by means of multiplication, we get an index of the strength of this segment in each province.

Table 81   'Izbah Owners, District Officers, and Descendants

Province	'Izbah-owning Officers Who Were Descendants	Officer/ Descendants Who Were 'Izbah Owners	Index
al-Qalyubiyyah	50.0%	100.0%	50.0%
al-Sharqiyyah	56.3	81.8	46.1
al-Daqahliyyah	25.0	50.0	12.5
Dumyat	--	--	--
Kafr al-Shaykh	0.0	0.0	0.0
al-Gharbiyyah	37.5	50.0	18.8
al-Manufiyyah	44.4	57.1	24.4
al-Buhayrah	38.1	88.8	33.8
al-Jizah	0.0	0.0	0.0
al-Fayyum	42.9	50.0	21.5
Bani Suwayf	60.0	75.0	45.0
al-Minia	66.7	54.5	36.4
Assiut	100.0	11.1	11.1
Suhaj	83.3	33.3	27.7
Qena	0.0	0.0	0.0
Aswan	--	--	--
All 16 provinces	45.0%	51.0%	23.0%

It follows from these statistics that 'izbah ownership is more prevalent in certain northern provinces than in the south. 'Izbah owners in the south are more likely to have higher status than in the north. The second stratum is larger in the north, and there is a more gradual slope of the status and influence pyramid among the rural middle class. In the south, it is more likely that there is a social hiatus between the top layer of the rural elite and the rest of the second stratum.

In spite of the high concentration of influence in an elite of restricted numbers in some southern provinces, the more interesting political phenomenon is the greater prevalence of 'izbah ownership in the north. This is borne out by some of the regression analyses run by Chesnin, where he was able to show that the percentage of former M.P.'s who were 'izbah owners correlates with the percentage of acreage in fruits and citrus at $.429 = r^2$. The same percentage of former M.P.'s who were 'izbah owners correlates with the percentage of family-set members in the National Union at $.517 = r^2$. District officers who were 'izbah owners, which correlate at $.748 = r^2$ with former M.P.'s, also correlate at $.290 = r^2$ with the percentage of owners of 50 feddan or more in each province, and at $.673 = r^2$ with the percentage of land in fruits and citrus. Thus we find that where there are more family-set members, more large landholdings and more highly capitalized agriculture, there will we find more 'izbah owners, and more elite 'izbah owners who are district officers and former M.P.'s. It is in these provinces where the political phenomenon of the second stratum has expressed itself most completely, despite the fact that traditional political influence is still manifested to a significant extent.

Ten

Summary Analysis of the Provincial Distribution of the Second Stratum

> In fact, all significant agrarian policy measures . . . have tended to shift the centre of politico-economic gravity away from the old landed aristocracy and in favour of this new privileged stratum of rich peasants. . . .
>
> Mahmoud Abdel-Fadil,
> *Development, Income Distribution and Social Change*

In breaking down our data on the Egyptian rural elite by province, we have had two purposes in mind. The first of these was to describe the distinctive characteristics of each of the provinces and, in so doing, to see whether the aggregate pattern was an accurate reflection of political and social realities or merely a summation of quite diverse patterns. The second purpose was to see if we could not account for the distribution of elements of the second stratum, insofar as they vary from province to province, by means of statistical correlations with other information available regarding the provinces. Of course we have found significant differences among the provinces, and especially between lower and upper Egypt. These differences coincide with differences in levels of development, degrees of urbanization, qualities of urbanism, types of agriculture, degrees of "agrarianness," and the occupational composition of the National Union. Apparently, different variables are influential in different provinces, and we have not yet found any obvious consistency of pattern which might suggest a simple and univocal explanation of the complex distribution of the second stratum. Agricultural wealth is the primary basis of influence; but that basis is modified by a number of influences among which are proximity to an urban center or to Cairo, familial prominence or even dominance in an agricultural village, continuity of political prominence over a number of generations, and rural family links with the bureaucracy, the military, and the free professions. The second stratum is more numerous in the delta and just south of Cairo, but it is of longer standing and of more concentrated influence in upper Egypt.

The basic hypothesis was that the second stratum was more numerous and powerful in the more developed agricultural provinces and wherever agriculture itself was more developed and profitable. With this preliminary hypothesis, based on the distribution of family-set members among the provinces, in mind, economic and social profiles of the provinces were worked out in chapter 8. In chapters 8 and 9 the data on the membership of the National Union and all of its influential segments were broken down by province. With these two sorts of provincial profile available, one constructed of aggregate statistics and the other of political data, the original hypothesis might be tested. Presumably, tests could be made, not only of the central hypothesis, but also of hypothesized relationships between various subcategories of the elite and various dimensions of development.

In this exercise, no pretense to statistical sophistication is made. The instruments employed are crude. The political data and the aggregate measures differ in at least one methodologically crucial respect. They differ in order of magnitude because most of the political data refer to dozens or, at best, hundreds of members of the National Union, whereas the aggregate data refer at times to the entire work force. A further methodological stricture is the small number of provinces, and, as we have learned, their quite persistent distinctive characteristics. Together small numbers and uniqueness militate powerfully against statistical randomization. The significant differences among the provinces, however, make it easy to distinguish among their characteristics. The fact that the second stratum is agriculturally rooted and that these provinces are overwhelmingly agricultural makes it not unreasonable to compare the social characteristics of the elite and of the provincial population as a whole. These comparisons having been made and certain differences having been explained with a degree of plausibility, it will be worthwhile to try to develop some composite perspective by aggregating our simpler comparisons into a single "big picture." The results of this effort at collation will be suggestive rather than theoretical. Although these results will be descriptive to an important degree, it is safer to use the word "suggestive" insofar as it implies the construction of more precise hypotheses for more rigorous testing by the rising generation of students of Egyptian political sociology, now that the countryside is once again open to social scientific research. Throughout these simple statistical procedures, our explanations will rely on the magnitude of the differences between the provinces and on the plausibility of our findings. A number of different indices were constructed, and with each test changes were made in order to examine problems obscured by the previous test. Because each test revealed something of interest, we will describe all three runs, even though the last seems to us to be sounder and more sophisticated than the previous two.

In the first set of tests, ten measures of the rural elite were used, drawn mainly from chapters 8 and 9 and each presumably referring to a somewhat different aspect or a segment of the second stratum. The ten indices are:

1. Size of the second stratum (percentage of family-set members of all National Union members, table 44)
2. Influence of second stratum (percentage of former M.P.'s in family sets, table 59)
3. Concentration of elite status (percentage of former M.P.'s who were both district officers and members of family sets, table 59)
4. Dominance of second stratum (percentage of district officers and former M.P.'s who were in family sets by index of concentration, table 59)
5. District officer influence by size of constituency (table 60)
6. District officer influence by family-set size, by type of office, and by constituency (table 61)
7. Scale of central influence (former M.P.'s who were not officers, table 64)
8. Scale of local influence (district officers who were not former M.P.'s, table 65)
9. Continuity and concentration of elite statuses (ratio of former M.P. descendants to 'umdah descendants, table 71)
10. Scale of local influence of district officer descendants

These ten indices deal with members of family sets, former M.P.'s, district officers, and descendants of prerevolutionary M.P.'s. As such, the indices overlap a great deal in terms of their empirical referents. To the extent that they do differ, such differences will be due to the variations in the distribution of these elite groups among the provinces and not so much because each index measures an entirely distinct segment. There are, however, some important distinctions to be made. The first six indices include reference to family sets but the last four do not. The third, fourth, ninth, and tenth indices are concerned with the concentration of political influence, whereas the first, seventh, and eighth are more nearly measures of dispersion. All of the indices that measure district officer influence are more likely to reflect provincial contextual influences than are the others.

Given this degree of overlap, we would expect to find strong correlations among most of these indices, and we do. If we examine a nine
by nine correlation matrix, excluding the first index of percentage in
family sets, we find that of 72 possible meaningful correlations, fully
52 are above the .35 level and 25 are above the .50 level. Indices 3
and 4 correlate at .83 as might be expected since 4 is based on 3 and
merely takes account of the total number of former M.P.'s and officers.
Indices 2 and 4 are also correlated at .77, that is, former M.P.'s in
family sets are closely correlated with former M.P.'s who were district
officers also, controlling for the total of actual persons (rather than
incumbencies) in each province. Similarly, indices 5 and 6 are correlated at .91 since 5 is based on 6, but takes into account, in addition
to the size of the constituency of each district officer, his office and
family-set size. These additional factors do not seem to add any interesting information. Indices 7 and 8, measuring central and local
influence, do not measure family-set membership, nor are they mere
reciprocals. Hence these two are the least strongly correlated with the
remaining seven indices. They are, however, correlated with one another at .745, since wherever former M.P.'s are not district officers,
there will officers not be former M.P.'s, even if they may be members
of family sets. Indices 9 and 10, which are both measures of the influence of descendants, are not more closely correlated than .45, since
these two measure somewhat different things. Index 9 measures the
influence of what must be considered a national elite which has had
parliamentary status over several generations against rural notable families which have only local political influence. Index 10 reverses matters
by comparing the number of district officers who are not former M.P.'s
but who happen to be descendants of prerevolutionary M.P.'s with the
number of former M.P. descendants and thus measures the remaining
local influence of a declining group. Indices 7 and 8 are negatively
correlated with 2, 3, and 4 since 7 excludes family-set membership and
8 excludes former M.P.'s. Index 4, which measures the dominance of
the second stratum (a combination of M.P., officer, and family set—
controlling for total persons) correlates at .634 with index 5 and at
.651 with index 6 (both of which measure district officer influence in
terms of the number of members of the National Union in each province). Indices 5 and 6 are correlated at .91, but their strong correlation
with index 4 suggests a pattern of concentrated elite influence including
high district office, large family-set size, and multiple incumbencies, in
certain provinces. This conclusion is the more interesting because of the
high correlations between index 9 and indices 5 and 6 (.618 and .658,
respectively). Index 9 measures former M.P.'s against 'umad among

descendants of the prerevolutionary parliaments. These relationships are illustrated in figure 17.

Our various indices measure somewhat different dimensions of the rural political elite of Egypt, but it is clear that, in most cases, we are concerned with the same social phenomenon. Having thus established several statistical measures of this phenomenon, we may move beyond giving a profile of the individual provinces and try to see if we cannot find some correlates of these political indices drawn from other sources of information about the provinces of Egypt.

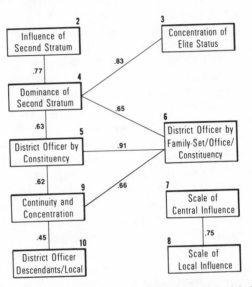

Fig. 17   Indices of Political Influence

In order to seek explanations of the distribution of the rural elite, three types of independent variables were utilized. The first group was discussed in describing the characteristics of the provinces in chapter 8. This group includes measures of illiteracy, of industrialization, of motor vehicles per capita, per capita municipal budgets, percentage of the labor force engaged in agriculture, and percentage of agricultural product in vegetables. These are all more or less measures of economic development. The second group of independent variables is the distribution of three sizes of landholding, 10–20 feddan, 20–50 feddan, and 50–100 feddan, among the provinces. The third group is the distribution of certain occupations (lawyers, civil servants, teachers, farmers) among members of the National Union. We have already explored in detail the relations between this third group and both the aggregate statistics for each province and the rural political elite, so it is possible to think of this group as intervening variables or as supplements in constructing plausible configurations.

We have already seen that intercorrelation of the first group (with the exception of percentage vegetables) has shown that illiteracy, per capita budgets, and percentage in agriculture are likely to be the most useful independent variables. Bearing in mind how closely correlated are our indices of the distribution of the political elite, we should note that the index of per capita municipal budgets correlates at −.30 or "higher" with eight of the nine indices discussed. The ninth is number 4 (dominance) which is correlated at −.25. The others correlate at this level with no more than three of the dependent variables.

The indices of industrialization, per capita motor vehicles, and per capita budgets, all measuring development, correlate negatively in 23 out of the 27 relevant cases. The indices of illiteracy and percentage engaged in agriculture correlate positively in 15 of 18 cases. In general, indices of the concentration of second stratum influence correlate negatively with indices of development, even though there are indications that family-set membership correlates positively with measures of agricultural development (percentage in vegetables, land rents, percentage of 'izbah owners). The three indices that are most strongly "influenced" by these aggregate variables are 5, 6, and 9. The first two are themselves closely correlated (.91) and refer to district level concentrations of influence. The third measures both the concentration of influence and continuity with prerevolutionary parliamentary elites. Hence provinces in which there are both greater concentrations of power among district officers and M.P. descendants have higher levels of illiteracy, lower levels of industrialization, fewer motor vehicles, and lower per capita budgets.

Taking indices 2, 3, 4, 6, 8, and 10, in turn as the dependent variable, each was regressed against four independent variables: illiteracy, industrialization, per capita motor vehicles, and per capita budgets. Of the six multiple regressions, five revealed per capita budgets as the strongest determinant, with the same independent variable listed as a close second in the sixth regression. In all cases, of course, per capita budgets correlates negatively with these indices. In five of six cases, per capita motor vehicles was the second most influential determinant, probably because it measures a somewhat different dimension of development than the others.

If there is any validity to these findings, they seem to confirm that the more rural or the less developed the province, the more will power be concentrated in the hands of a small segment of the second stratum. The weight of the evidence works in the same direction, regardless of which measure of power we take and regardless of how we construct the index.

Except for teachers, none of the occupations are strongly correlated with any of the sizes of landholding. All three sizes of landholding are closely correlated with one another, and teachers were correlated at −.485 (10–20 feddan), −.379 (20–50 feddan), and at −.609 (50–100 feddan). Teachers, in turn, are highly correlated with civil servants (.81) and both are strongly negatively correlated with the percentage of farmers in the National Union (−.576 for teachers and −.735 for civil servants). It doesn't seem to make much difference how much land a member of the second stratum has, as long as he has the minimum of 10 feddan. Alternatively, it may be suggested that since all three sizes of landholding are closely correlated, they will behave similarly statistically even though only one category has any causal influence. Were we to guess which category is most significant, we would select the largest landholdings because the 50–100 feddan group has the strongest negative correlation with the percentage of teachers and it has the strongest positive correlation with the percentage in family sets (.299).

Thus far we have left aside the percentage of family-set members in the National Union in each province because we know that it does not correlate so strongly with ruralism and underdevelopment. In the present context, however, strong correlations can be noted among political index 1 (percentage of family-set members), political index 2 (former M.P.'s in family sets), percentage in vegetables, and percentage of lawyers in the National Union (table 82). While these data do not refute our earlier findings, they do suggest that the determination of the power of the rural elite in Egypt is less a matter of general development or the lack thereof than it is due to the size of the second stratum which is directly proportional to development, while the power of each member of the second stratum appears to be inversely proportional to the size of the group as a whole in each province. The strong correlation with lawyers, with vegetable production, and with the largest landholdings may be no more than a description of certain characteristics of the second stratum (partial urbanization, access to higher education, mobility, strong agrarian base) rather than any sort of causal analysis, but since we are working with statistical correlations we are in any case unable to argue causality against description for any of our findings.

A further interesting, but not unexpected, relationship between certain occupations and family-set membership was found. We have seen

that teachers and civil servants are correlated with family-set membership at the relatively low levels of .13 and .19, respectively. They are,
however, more strongly correlated with vegetable production by province (.28 and .25, respectively) and vegetable production is correlated
with family-set membership at .46. It follows from this indirect linkage
that whenever teachers or civil servants who are members of the National Union committees are in provinces with a higher percentage of
agricultural product in vegetables, there are they more likely to be
members of family sets and hence more likely to be politically influential. Vegetable production, as we have seen, is an indicator of proximity to urban centers. Such proximity and the political access it affords
appear to be an alternative basis of influence to that of the more traditional segment of the elite which resides in the more rural areas.

Table 82   Correlation Matrix: Family-Set
                                     Members, Influence, and Develop-
                                     ment

	Political Index 1	Political Index 2	Vegetables	Lawyers
Political Index 1	--	.588	.461	.402
Political Index 2	.588	--	.301	.491
Vegetables	.461	.301	--	-.046
Lawyers	.402	.491	-.046	--

As suggested earlier, there does seem to be a segment of the elite
which has been mobilized via modernization and another segment which
has been relatively untouched by modernization. There is a segment
which has such influence that any government must work through them,
and another segment which is so numerous and competitive that nearly
any government can pick and choose among them. There is a segment
which has been influential for generations, and another segment which
has been struggling for recognition for a long while. There is a segment
which is not much differentiated in terms of occupations and which is
predominantly agrarian, and there is also a segment which is quite
varied occupationally. And then there are some provincial contingents
which are comprised of elements of both types.

Suspecting that we might not have been able to differentiate as much
as we should among these variables because of the way in which our
indices were constructed, we made another effort to correlate selected
variables after reconstructing our indices. Our indices were reconstructed
to reflect the comparison of the provinces with one another. This was
achieved by using indices based on the mean of all sixteen cases. Eleven

variables were chosen for this test. Three were political variables: percentage in family sets, former M.P.'s who were both in family sets and district officers, and the comparison of former M.P. and 'umdah descendants. These three are the same as political indices 1, 3, and 9. The three sizes of landholding were included as were five measures of development. The five measures of development included illiteracy, per capita budgets, percentage engaged in agriculture, percentage of farmers in the National Union, and percentage in vegetables. A series of stepwise multiple regressions was run taking each of the political indices as the dependent variable. Now let us turn to our findings.

The first political index, the percentage in family sets, is the most general measure of the second stratum, and, of course, the most undifferentiated measure thereof. It is notable that index 1 correlates strongly negatively with indices of agrarianness ($-.545$ with percentage engaged in agriculture and $-.484$ with farmers) but rather positively with the three groups of landholding and especially with the group of largest holdings, 50–100 (.406). Index 1 also correlates strongly with vegetable production (.462) but it is moderately negatively influenced by both illiteracy ($-.241$) and per capita budgets ($-.273$). In this test, as in others, our general picture of the second stratum remains that it is not primarily identified with ruralism but rather with a type of agriculture that requires capital, larger holdings and proximity to urban areas. Paradoxically, this most general political index is less strongly correlated with our index of the concentration of second stratum influence (index 3: $-.366$), and it is moderately negatively correlated with our index of the concentration of power in the hands of the descendants of prerevolutionary parliaments (index 9: $-.177$). These results would appear to coincide with our findings that the greatest concentration of traditional influence is in upper Egypt while the larger number of members of family sets is in the delta and near Cairo.

We are utilizing two measures of the concentration of political influence, one of which is based on multiple incumbencies and the other on continuity with prerevolutionary elites. This second measure of concentrated influence is also deliberately based on the small number of 'umad among descendants, though we know that 'umad are prominent among family-set members. Hence, we are quite clearly attempting to find characteristics which will differentiate among segments of the second stratum. Index 9, which measures both continuity (M.P.'s among descendants) and concentration (fewer 'umad) has nevertheless a strong rural dimension to it. This index is strongly positively correlated with illiteracy (.617), with percentage in agriculture (.526) and with percentage of farmers in the National Union (.710) and yet negatively with per capita budgets (−.538) and percentage in vegetables (−.125). It is apparent that where there are fewer 'umad, there are fewer villages, larger villages, and more farmers. Index 9, therefore, singles out the more traditional, less developed provinces of upper Egypt, while index 3 refers to characteristics common to many provinces in both the north and the south. The former M.P.'s who are also district officers and members of family sets are, of course, a very small group of the most influential of the rural middle class. Some members of this select group have been recruited from the more numerous group of local notables in northern Egypt as well as from the very small group of descendants of prerevolutionary influentials. Both groups tend to come from larger family sets, but their ecological bases are evidently quite different. The theoretical questions which arise out of this bimodal pattern are, first: Will increased development tend to increase the size of the rural middle class and hence increase political competition? Second, has increased political competition been the consequence of the size of the rural middle class or of the weakness of the traditional elite or of the power of the central government in bypassing the traditional elite in at least those areas near Cairo? Third, was the traditional rural elite powerful enough in some areas to prevent competition by preventing development?

When the three political indices are taken as dependent variables and the remaining, nonpolitical, indices taken as independent variables, some interesting results are achieved. A number of different combinations were tried in order to see whether indications of ruralism, urban influence, or size of landholding were most influential. The indicators of ruralism are illiteracy, percentage in agriculture, and percentage of farmers. The indicators of urban influence are vegetable production and per capita budgets, but, unlike the indicators of ruralism, these two are not closely intercorrelated in the Pearson correlations as they are in the Spearman.

The percentage in family sets, or index 1, the most comprehensive measure of the second stratum, is influenced by our dependent variables in the following order, first, percentage in agriculture; second, vegetable production; third, size of landholding; and fourth, per capita budgets. Percentage in family sets is, of course negatively correlated with percentage in agriculture, and it will be remembered that the variation in percentage in agriculture is not very great except for Aswan and Dumyat. Using the Spearman correlations, we get very nearly the same results, except that whenever percentage in agriculture is not used in the regression, illiteracy is the strongest influence. Size of landholding drops to a poor fourth. The examples of multiple regression summary tables 83, 84, and 85 illustrate these findings.

Table 83   The Second Stratum and Develop-
                                           ment: Test 1
                                           Dependent Variable: Percentage in
                                           Family Sets

Independent Variable	Multiple R (Pearson)	Multiple R (Spearman)
Percentage in agriculture	.546	.409
Per capita budgets	.643	.428
Illiteracy	.652	.452
20-50 feddan	.660	.475

Table 84   The Second Stratum and Develop-
                                           ment: Test 2
                                           Dependent Variable: Percentage in
                                           Family Sets

Independent Variable	Multiple R (Pearson)	Independent Variable	Multiple R (Spearman)
Farmers in NU	.484	Farmers in NU	.445
Per capita budgets	.768	50-100 feddan	.588
50-100 feddan	.835	Per capita budgets	.641
Illiteracy	.843	Illiteracy	(drops out)

Table 85   The Second Stratum and Develop-
                                           ment: Test 3
                                           Dependent Variable: Percentage in
                                           Family Sets

Independent Variable	Multiple R (Pearson)	Multiple R (Spearman)
Vegetable production	.462	.451
50-100 feddan	.758	.635
20-50 feddan	.764	.691
10-20 feddan	.768	.692

It is apparent that the independent variables which show the influence of urban proximity and large landholdings have substantial significance even after the very large negative influence of agrarianness is taken into account.

When we take index 3 (former M.P./district officer/family-set membership, or concentration of elite status) as our dependent variable we

have much weaker correlations. The strongest influence is the negative
effect of per capita budgets, followed by either percentage in agriculture or illiteracy, and then by vegetable production and size of landholding. The Spearman correlations are all but insignificant except for
the influence of size of landholding when all three sizes are regressed
at once. The examples in tables 86 and 87 illustrate these patterns of
influence.

Table 86   Elite Status and Development:
                                      Test 1
                                      Dependent Variable: Concentration
                                      of Elite Status (Index 3)

Independent Variable	Multiple R (Pearson)
Per capita budgets	.375
Illiteracy	.437
10-20 feddan	.465
Farmers in NU	.484

Table 87   Elite Status and Development:
                                      Test 2
                                      Dependent Variable: Concentration
                                      of Elite Status

Independent Variable	Multiple R (Spearman)	Simple R
50-100 feddan	.185	.185
10-20 feddan	.411	-.058
20-50 feddan	.458	.144
Vegetable production	.470	.135

It will be noted that the simple Spearman R is low in all four cases,
but the contrasting combination of the positive influence of the largest
landholdings and the negative influence of the smallest of the medium
landholdings gives us this surprisingly high multiple R. Index 3 is most
closely correlated with large landholdings and ruralism.

For index 9, continuity and concentration of influence (former M.P.
descendants as against 'umdah descendants), the correlations are much
higher, with either percentage of farmers or illiteracy usually accounting for over 80% of the multiple R. Per capita budgets, size of landholding and vegetable production bring up the rear. Summary table 88
illustrates this general conclusion.

When we drop percentage of farmers and illiteracy from the regression analysis, the results are ambiguous, as shown in table 89.

Common to both multiple regression analyses, however, is the relatively significant, negative influence of the middle- and larger-sized landholdings. We note further that, despite their close interconnection, the various sizes of landholding do not cancel one another out.

Table 88   Traditional Influentials and Development: Test 1
Dependent Variable: Continuity and Concentration of Influence

Independent Variable	Multiple R (Pearson)	Independent Variable	Multiple R (Spearman)
Percentage of farmers in NU	.710	Percentage of farmers in NU	.683
Per capita budgets	.741	Per capita budgets	.705
10-20 feddan	.787	Illiteracy	.708
Illiteracy	.789	50-100 feddan	.709

Table 89   Traditional Influentials and Development: Test 2
Dependent Variable: Continuity and Concentration

Independent Variable	Multiple R (Pearson)	Independent Variable	Multiple R (Spearman)
20-50 feddan	.242	Vegetable production	.290
50-100 feddan	.340	20-50 feddan	.304
Vegetable production	.380	50-100 feddan	.460
10-20 feddan	(drops out)	10-20 feddan	.462

These findings further strengthen our conclusions regarding the distinctions between two of three segments of the second stratum: the base of family-set members and those who have been influential at the parliamentary level for several generations. The family-set group has been shown to be more prevalent in lower Egypt and near Cairo, in the more developed regions of the country, nearer urban centers, where more highly capitalized agriculture prevails, where larger landholdings are more frequently found, where there is more literacy, where there are more professionals, more merchants, more civil servants, and more teachers. It is also apparent that these independent variables do, in fact, operate much more independently of one another in the case of index 1 than in the case of index 3 or index 9, both indices of the concentration of influence within the second stratum.

This second test has strengthened our ability to characterize two segments of the rural middle class, but it has obscured the special characteristics of the intervening strata. It was, therefore, decided to try yet a third test, expanding somewhat the number of dependent (political) variables to be examined. Emphasis, on this occasion, was to be placed on the middle strata of the rural middle class in terms of both dependent and independent variables. In this test all the original data were converted into Z scores ($Z = \dfrac{x - \bar{x}}{\sigma}$) rather than ratios to the mean. The consequence of this change was that data intervals below the mean were more accurately stated as negative numbers than as decimals. Again, both Pearson and Spearman correlations were used, but the Spearman results are more plausible and probably methodologically sounder, so we shall only report those.

The dependent variables employed were:

1. Percentage in family sets, equivalent to index 1 above
2. Percentage of 'izbah owners in family sets
3. Ratio of former M.P.'s to 'umad among descendants, equivalent to index 9 above
4. Political dominance of the second stratum, equivalent to index 4 above
5. Percentage of district officers who were descendants
6. Percentage of prerevolutionary seats held by ancestors of members of the National Union

This group of dependent variables retains both the base of the second stratum "pyramid" (family-set members) and at least the one element of its peak that we have analyzed (M.P.-'umdah descendants). To these we have added a number of intervening groups, two of which are more closely connected with family sets and two of which are more closely connected with descent from prerevolutionary parliamentarians.

The 'izbah owners who were members of family sets may well be generally more influential than those who are simply family-set members, but their distribution, as we have seen above, is fairly similar. Some 'izbah owners are very influential, but others are not, as in the case of family-set members. Political dominance refers to the group of family-set members who were also both former M.P.'s and district officers. This statistic was first stated as the percentage of incumbents who were both former M.P.'s and district officers multiplied by the percentage of incumbents who were family-set members. It is, thus, a statement of the combined probabilities for each province.

Of the two indices related to prerevolutionary parliamentarians, the first (percentage of district officers who were descendants) measures the influence of descendants, while the second measures the influence of parliamentary ancestors (percentage of prerevolutionary seats held by ancestors of members of the National Union). These two may be contrasted with the ratio of former M.P.'s to 'umad among descendants, which links both influential ancestors and influential descendants and which ignores or minimizes local, village-level influence.

The independent variables were also selected with a view toward focusing attention on factors which were neither wholly urban or developed nor wholly rural or undeveloped. These variables are also familiar from previous discussions: average rent per feddan, per capita municipal budgets, landholdings of 50–100 feddan, percentage of agricultural production in vegetables, percentage of farmers in the National Union, and number of members of agricultural cooperatives.

First, each set of variables was tested for the level of intercorrelation. The dependent variables were predictably divided between those linked to family sets and those linked to descendants, but the two sets were joined by the index of the dominance of the second stratum. Figure 18

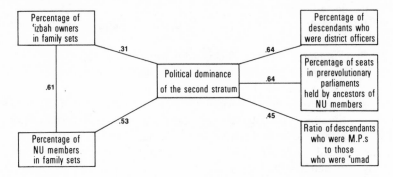

Fig. 18   Segments of the Second Stratum

illustrates the strongest, positive relationships among these variables. It is interesting to note that the percentage of 'izbah owners in family sets is farthest out of the picture on one side, as is the ratio of former M.P.'s to 'umad among descendants farthest out on the other side. There are, of course, solid links among all of these variables, indicating once again that we are dealing with a single phenomenon which has important variations. The two groups that seem to be joined by the politically dominant group of the second stratum are, evidently, a newly rising group of a'yan and a traditional notability of inherited influence. Yet it is likely that, in terms of the social mobility of the rural middle class the larger group to the left of political dominance is only a generation or two behind the group which is to the right of political dominance.

The organization of the independent variables is a little more complicated. Percentage of farmers and landholdings of 50–100 feddan are correlated at the modest level of .31, but they are both negatively correlated with all the rest. It is likely that percentage of farmers is a measure of rural underdevelopment, whereas holdings of 50–100 feddan is a measure of the presence of an affluent rural segment which may, in part, reside in less developed provinces. Thus, these two are in fact negatively intercorrelated, respectively, with two separate sets of independent variables, all of which refer to aspects of the middle levels of the second stratum. Percentage of farmers is negatively correlated with per capita budgets and with percentage of production in vegetables, both of which are linked to urban influence. Holdings of 50–100 feddan are negatively correlated with average rent and number of cooperative members, neither of which are strongly influenced by towns but are influenced by the productivity of land, its amenability to more highly capitalized agriculture, and the prevalence of farmers who are well enough off to be members of cooperatives. On the other hand, both groups of independent variables, one showing the urban basis of affluence and the other showing the rural basis of affluence are positively linked together and they are not mutually exclusive. This third test was able to sort things out a little better but not to isolate particular variables. Figure 19 illustrates the relationships among the independent variables. As we see there, it is the negative correlations which suggest the division of the four positively correlated variables into two groups.

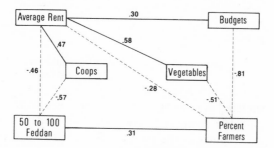

Fig. 19　　　　　　　　　　Indices of Developmental Characteristics of the Sixteen Agricultural Provinces

Six multiple regressions were run, taking each of the dependent variables in turn. We hoped to find one or more of the dependent variables closely correlated with one of the three indices of middle level agrarian affluence: average rents, coops, or vegetable production. It was assumed that the ratio of former M.P.'s to 'umad among descendants would still be closely associated with rural underdevelopment.

A schematic summary of the results of the six regressions is given in figure 20. In examining the summary it is well to remember that usually only the first two independent variables have any significant effect. Secondly, we should expect that when one of two closely intercorrelated independent variables emerges at the top of the list, its correlative independent variable will drop toward the bottom of the list. In figure 20 we will list the independent variables in the order of their importance but, at this stage, without giving the correlation values. Those that are

Dependent Variables ⟶

	Percentage of ʿizbah owners in family sets	Percentage in family sets	Political dominance	Percentage of district officers who were descendants	Percentage of prerevolutionary seats held by ancestors of NU members	Ratio of former M.P.'s to ʿumad among descendants
1.	Vegetables	Vegetables	Average rent	Coops	Average rent	Farmers
2.	Farmers	50-100 feddan	Farmers	Farmers	(Budgets)	Average rent
3.	(Budgets)	Average rent	50-100 feddan	Budgets	(50-100 feddan)	(Vegetables)
4.	Coops	Budgets	Vegetables	Vegetables	Vegetables	(Coops)
5.	50-100 feddan	(Farmers)	Coops	(50-100 feddan)	Farmers	(Budgets)
6.	--[a]	Coops	(Budgets)	Average rent	--[b]	(50-100 feddan)

(Independent Variables)

[a] Average rents dropped out.

[b] Coops dropped out.

Fig. 20   Schematic Summary of Correlations
                                         of Aggregate Data and Political Data

negatively correlated are in parentheses. A line is drawn between those correlated at a fairly significant level and those independent variables which fail to add much to the multiple R. As expected, percentage in family sets is highly correlated with indices of development, while the ratio of former M.P.'s to ʿumad among descendants is highly correlated with indices of underdevelopment. The remaining four, representing mixtures of second stratum segments, are correlated first with an index of rural affluence and second with an index of rural underdevelopment. It is also noteworthy that in all cases where we have one of each type of independent variable in first and second place, both are positively correlated with the dependent variable. In all cases except the ratio of former M.P.'s to ʿumad, the most important independent variable is one which is linked to middle level agrarian affluence.

Despite the small number of provinces we have to work with, it is amply demonstrated that the elite is determined by (*a*) rural social structure, and (*b*) one of two bases of agrarian affluence: ownership of highly productive land or accessibility of urban markets. These general conclusions may be modified for each of the dependent variables in the following manner.

Family-set members. This group is most influenced by the proximity of cities. It has been "mobilized" as a consequence of growing urban markets, the easier availability of education, and the consequent access to political decision makers in Cairo. Its agriculture tends to be more highly capitalized. We know from other data that family-set members correlate highly with those receiving loans from government agricultural credit programs. The summary table for this dependent variable is table 90.

Table 90   Intermediate Rural Strata: Test 1

Independent Variable	Multiple R	Simple R
Vegetables	.241	.491
50-100 feddan	.286	.148
Average rent	.409	.452
Budgets	.450	.032
Farmers	.493	-.101
Cooperatives	.505	.129

'Izbah owners in family sets. This group correlates positively with family-set members, but we know from other data that it correlates positively with higher fruit production. The variables used here do not seem to have explained enough about the prevalence of this group, although it is noteworthy that the independent variables vegetables and coops both precede holdings of 50–100 feddan. It follows that the establishment of 'izab is not the consequence of the existence of large holdings but the result of some other cultural or social influence.

Most 'izbah owners in family sets are to be found in al-Qalyubiyyah, Kafr al-Shaykh, al-Buhayrah, and al-Fayyum. These are agriculturally affluent areas. Two of these provinces are more rural than the average and three of them include areas very close to large cities. 'Izbah ownership is diffused in certain regions, as we have seen, but only among a fairly affluent agrarian elite. The spotty distribution of this group is illustrated by the lack of strong correlations and by the contradictory purport of the significant independent variables in table 90. Even though 'izbah owners in family sets are more closely correlated with family sets than any other dependent variable, it is clear that 'izbah ownership prevails relatively more in more rural and less developed areas than does the second stratum as a whole.

Ratio of M.P. to 'umdah descendants. The provinces where parliamentary power has been most continuous among a number of families are strongly rural. To some extent average rents are high where this group is found. Obviously this group is not strong in the areas influenced by large urban centers. The summary table for this dependent variable is table 92. Despite the relatively small correlation between average rents and M.P. descendants, this independent variable has a strong

Table 91   Intermediate Rural Strata: Test 2

Independent Variable	Multiple R	Simple R
Vegetables	.073	.270
Farmers	.261	.234
Budgets	.312	-.063
Coops	.343	.165
50-100 feddan	.399	.243

Table 92   Intermediate Rural Strata: Test 3

Independent Variable	Multiple R	Simple R
Farmers	.376	.613
Average rent	.556	.230
Vegetables	.635	-.326
Coops	.741	-.091
Budgets	.814	-.563
50-100 feddan	.835	-.117

effect in the multiple regression, and even though percentage of farmers and average rents are moderately negatively correlated, both are positively correlated with M.P. descendants. Hence, the continuity and concentration of influence of the parliamentary elite is greatest in the less developed provinces, and particularly in such provinces where agricultural land is more productive, i.e., al-Minia and al-Fayyum.

Political dominance of the second stratum. This dependent variable is surprisingly similar to the preceding, except that the two most significant independent variables are reversed. Political dominance is strongest in al-Sharqiyyah, al-Fayyum, and al-Minia, and these are not all the provinces with the highest rents, but al-Fayyum and al-Minia are among the highest. These most influential family-set members are found somewhat more in the regions of greater agricultural productivity than are the M.P. descendants. Thus political dominance overlaps with both family sets and the ratio of former M.P.'s to 'umad among descendants. The similarity is less apparent because of the small residual effect of the correlation between political dominance and the percentage of agricultural production in vegetables (see table 93).

Table 93   Intermediate Rural Strata: Test 4

Independent Variable	Multiple R	Simple R
Average rent	.342	.584
Farmers	.455	.155
50-100 feddan	.498	-.027
Vegetables	.518	.368
Coops	.525	.263
Budgets	.527	-.028

Percentage of ancestor seats. This dependent variable indicates the prevalence of members of the National Union who had influential ancestors. This group will include both those who were still influential after the 1952 revolution and those who were less so, yet not politically ostracized. The descendants of prerevolutionary M.P.'s are, not surprisingly, found in the areas of the greatest agricultural productivity and they are more strongly correlated with average rents than any other dependent variable. Otherwise, the percentage of ancestor seats shows the same sort of rural influences that we find for the three preceding dependent variables. It is, however, noteworthy that percentage of ancestor seats is strongly negatively correlated with landholdings of 50–100 feddan, unlike the percentage in family sets (see table 94).

Table 94   Intermediate Rural Strata: Test 5

Independent Variable	Multiple R	Simple R
Average rents	.456	.676
Budgets	.619	-.181
50-100 feddan	.691	-.574
Vegetables	.696	.309
Farmers	.704	.069

Officer-descendants. This dependent variable does not distinguish between those who are also M.P.'s and those who are only district officers. There is, nevertheless, a strong element of localism expressed here, because this group excludes M.P. descendants who are not district officers. We know that cooperatives, vegetables, and average rents are all closely correlated and are all relatively stronger in the more developed areas of the country; yet this is the only case in which membership in cooperatives has displaced average rents and vegetable production. This shift may well be due to the influence of al-Qalyubiyyah and al-Sharqiyyah and, above all, to the influence of the large number of cooperative members in Suhaj. At any rate, coop members are not wealthy landowners, but they tend to be members of the rural middle class. Nor are they usually absentee landowners. This group is more locally influential, of moderate income, and spread widely in both developed and more remote regions. It is noteworthy that the independent variable municipal budgets follows the percentage of farmers but influences the multiple R by a relatively large increment. The influence of these two independent variables attests to the wide geographical diffusion of officer-descendants, despite the fact that their correlational profile is most similar to that of members of family sets. It is worth emphasizing that this index includes nonfamily-set members, too, so that it identifies nonfamily-set influentials in the larger units with the family-set members in the smaller units (see table 95).

Table 95   Intermediate Rural Strata: Test 6

Independent Variable	Multiple R	Simple R
Cooperatives	.228	.477
Farmers	.306	.228
Budgets	.479	.022
Vegetables	.541	.134
50-100 feddan	.593	-.249
Average rent	.594	.434

Agrarian influence is characteristic of all six elite variables, but M.P. descendants are more clearly prevalent in rural underdeveloped regions while family-set members are more prevalent in the agriculturally developed regions. 'Izbah owners in family sets and officer-descendants are, like family-set members, closer to the base of the second stratum pyramid, but they are geographically more widely diffused. The most politically influential members of the second stratum (political dominance of family-set members) and those descended from influential (parliamentary) ancestors appear to be somewhat similar to the M.P. descendants. They are also from the more fertile of the less developed provinces. Though less widely diffused, they are no less beneficiaries of an important base of agrarian influence. While there are significant differences among various segments of the second stratum, both geographical and stratificational, it is also apparent that there is significant continuity among all of these elite segments.

In this chapter we have attempted to test three models of the second stratum. The three models are linked to the three types of influence structure analyzed in earlier chapters. These influence structures are (*a*) prevalence or the relative size of the second stratum, (*b*) concentration of authority or the degree to which local, district, and provincial (parliamentary) offices were held by the same individuals, and (*c*) continuity or the proportion of contemporary influentials who are descended from prerevolutionary parliamentary elites. Preliminary examination of the data indicated that these structures of influence were not entirely complementary and that they might be differentiated geographically. The geographic differentiation of influence structures presented an opportunity to test these structures against the distinctive social and economic characteristics of each province. Three explanatory models were hypothesized in the statistical exercises described in this chapter. The first hypothesis was that modernization or development, generally, might account for the differences in influence structure. We found that modernization accounted for prevalence but was less strong as an indicator of concentration and even less strong as a negative indicator of continuity. The second model hypothesized a sharp divergence between (at least) two segments of the second stratum, the first comprised of middle peasants from the high prevalence delta areas and the second traditionally influential rich peasants from upper Egypt. The second test did differentiate more sharply between these two segments, but it was clear that both showed a substantial number of influentials who held "concentrated authority." The third model hypothesized that there might be a stratum of well-to-do peasant landowners, with important links to the urban areas, who resided in the more fertile regions and who had succeeded in achieving at least modest accumulations of capital. The third test emphasized a number of measures of such middle peasant status and strongly sustained the assumption that the second stratum is nearly everywhere characterized by the presence of a segment of affluent peasants. These analyses indicate that the second stratum is comprised of several relatively distinct segments. Among these segments, prevalence and continuity come closest to characterizing relatively nonintersecting sets, while concentration and middling affluence appear to be diffusely present or comprise sets which intersect with the other two. The last test has greatly emphasized the common element in the second stratum. In the next chapter some of the distinguishing characteristics will be emphasized.

Eleven

The Geographical Distribution of the Rural Elite

> The traveller passing through the country is struck by the monotony of the landscape, and is hardly conscious of any difference between the region just south of Alexandria and that immediately north of Aswan.
>
> Charles Issawi, *Egypt in Revolution*

In chapter 8, it was established that the prevalence of the second stratum varies from province to province. In chapter 9, it was found that even where the second stratum was more prevalent, it was not always and not in the same manner more politically influential (as measured by incumbency in district office and assembly seats). In fact it is possible to argue, somewhat paradoxically, that where the second stratum has fewer members, each member is relatively more influential than where the second stratum is more numerous. This paradoxical finding is really not very unreasonable, but it allows of more than a single explanation. The political influence of the second stratum might be due to the role its structural position permitted it to play and to the cultural congeniality of that role; in such a case the statistical configuration of the politically influential segment would be determined simply by the number of offices available. If, however, political influence is not the result of the political role attributed to the stratum but rather to some individual characteristics of the relevant persons, then the statistical configuration of second stratum political influence would reflect the distribution of a high status segment of the second stratum. In chapter 9, we found evidence of both kinds, suggesting that the structure of the second stratum in lower Egypt differed from that in upper Egypt. In chapter 9 our conclusions were drawn from comparisons of data ar-

248

ranged in contingency tables, and those findings were summarized in a number of indices. In chapter 10 these indices were tested against a number of aggregate measures of social, industrial, and agricultural development. The second stratum was itself measured in terms of the three dimensions of prevalence, concentration, and continuity. In chapter 10 it was found that the strongest determinant of the distribution of the second stratum was agrarian development. It was also found that, although the provinces with the highest prevalence and the greatest continuity were most unlike, the combined pattern of concentration and agrarian affluence was found throughout most of the provinces.

In this chapter, the findings of chapter 10 will be further tested in a more manifestly geographical sense. The rationale underlying the provincial level analysis, even though expressed in contingency tables, has been geographical. Since the hypothesized determinants of the empirical configuration of the second stratum are essentially geographical, it follows that the configuration of the second stratum should be apparent geographically as well as statistically. In particular we should expect to find distinctive, if overlapping, geographical patterns for the distribution of prevalence, concentration, and continuity. It is also to be expected that, insofar as the influence of the second stratum is a consequence of its political role as a social structural unit and insofar as that stratum has a material base and insofar as that material base may have ecological determinants, the second stratum will have a coherent geographical configuration in the form of regional clusters. Certainly, where the influence of the second stratum is more the consequence of a few personalities or families, the geographical configuration of concentration will be dispersed and isolative.

Thus far we have differentiated among the provinces more in terms of their economic and social characteristics and not so much in terms of their contributions to a national geographical pattern of economic and social arrangements. Moreover, we have not differentiated among the parts of provinces, as if entire provinces were quite homogeneous units. It is, furthermore, obvious that, for purposes of correlational analysis, the units which are the subjects of the attributes represented by the statistics employed should be as small as possible in order to minimize ecological distortions. For these reasons it is advisable, despite the lack of availability of the most desirable sorts of data, to use whatever information is at hand for an analysis at the subprovincial level. In this chapter, three analytical goals will be pursued: (1) to see whether there is not a national or regional pattern(s) to the distribution of the second stratum which is unaffected by provincial boundaries; (2) to discover where, within each province, the rural elite or second stratum is to be found; and (3) to determine the extent to which modernity of the second stratum coincides with either prevalence or the concentration of influence, and whether there is some overall, national, pattern in the distribution of these characteristics.

In pursuing these three goals, we will use a diagrammatic map of Egypt on which the districts are indicated. On this map we will present information on the distribution of the National Union members, district officers, former M.P.'s, descendants, and 'izbah owners. There are two kinds of information to be examined on the diagrammatic maps. The first concerns the occupational composition of the family-set members in each district. Essentially, we wish to find out where the second stratum is more modernized and urban or more traditional, agrarian, and rural. The second kind of information refers to elite concentration. First each statistic will be presented separately, and then, in an attempt at a summary statement, composite maps showing prevalence, modernity, mixed occupations, concentration, and continuity will be shown. In the analysis of these schematic maps, the thing to look for is the frequency with which certain districts are shaded and the extent to which frequently shaded districts make up a cluster.

Map 2 shows the greater prevalence of family-set members in the west and north central delta. This prevalence declines noticeably in the northeast part of the delta and quite substantially to the south of al-Jizah province. The districts which lie on the east and west banks of the Rosetta branch are those with the highest percentage in family sets.

A second measure of prevalence, but a less general one, is the presence of more than one family set in a village committee. Such a situation may be taken as an indicator of potentially greater than usual political competition. Map 3 shows those districts in which there were at least three multiple family-set committees. The coincidence with the districts of the highest percentage in family sets is striking. There are less than three multiple family-set committees in all districts with less than 19% in family sets except for 8 districts, 6 of which are in the delta. By contrast there are 25 districts with more than 19% in family sets with fewer than three multiple family-set committees. Twelve of these districts are south of Cairo.

Earlier, it was shown that the highest percentages of family-set members were found in those provinces with the highest percentages in family sets of five or more members. Map 4 shows the districts that have at least one family set of five or more. Again we see a close coincidence of the shaded districts with both the districts of high prevalence and high competition. There are only 15 districts which have one or more of the largest family sets which have fewer than 19% in family sets—out of 55 districts with the largest family sets. Ten of the former

Map 2   Percentage of Members in Family
                                  Sets by District

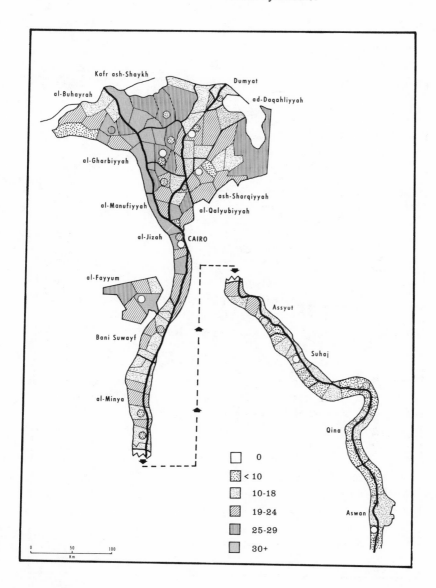

districts are in Bani Suwayf or in the provinces to the south of it, thus
illustrating the counter tendency of a few politically influential families
in upper Egypt to concentrate power even where the second stratum is
not so numerous.

Map 3

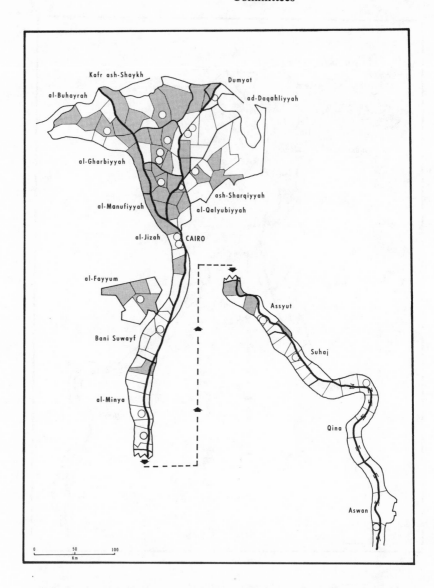

The size of family sets correlates with influence to some extent, but also with prevalence since there are larger family sets where there are more members of family sets. Map 5 shows where the proportion of the smallest family sets is lowest. In the shaded area family sets of two

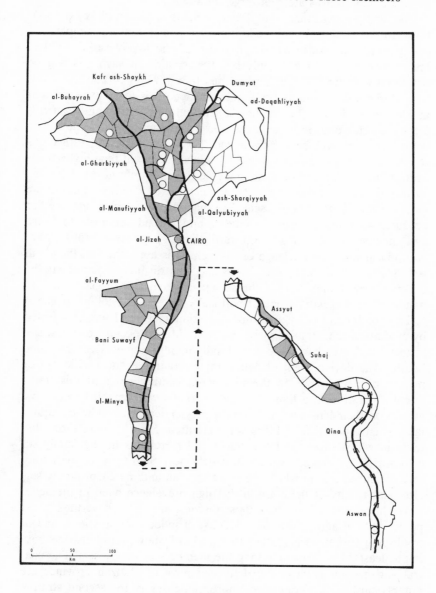

members comprise less than two-thirds of the total of family-set members. The largest family sets are again to be found where Kafr al-Shaykh, al-Gharbiyyah, and al-Buhayrah adjoin. It is noteworthy that the eastern and south central parts of the delta are not included in the shaded area. In upper Egypt, or rather central Egypt, al-Fayyum and al-Minia stand out as areas of larger family sets.

The next group of maps will illustrate the distribution of key occupations. In this section we will be looking for diversity in the occupational configuration of modernization. Because of the hypothesized political importance of the mixed family set, the location of such sets will be particularly relevant in explaining the concentration of political influence in the second stratum in certain districts. It is to be expected that in some areas the members of family sets will be predominantly agricultural in occupation; in other areas they will be mostly modern; and in yet others they will be mostly mixed. From our earlier investigations we expect that where they are mostly mixed there will be a higher concentration of influence—but this may be the case only in the delta.

Map 6 shows all those districts in which mixed family sets constitute more than 50% of all family sets. The shaded area is, again, the familiar broad band running from Alexandria and Rashid southeast to Cairo and then southward. The southward shading, however, stops rather abruptly at the southern edge of al-Jizah. It is apparent that the south is less modernized than the north, and this distinction shows in the occupational composition of the second stratum and probably also in its numbers, longevity, scope of political interests, and competitiveness.

The combination of agriculture and commerce need not be affected by modernization. Both of these can be traditional occupations. Usually farmers and merchants are not found among members of the same family. The development of commercial agriculture and the advent of private property rights in the nineteenth century changed this traditional separation to a limited extent. Farmers were enabled to borrow money on their land and merchant-moneylenders were able to acquire land when repayment of loans was defaulted. Map 7 shows those districts in which there are both 'umad and merchants in one family set or more. There are 23 districts in which more than 50% of the family sets are mixed and in which there are 'umdah and merchant family sets also, and twenty of these are in the high prevalence band in the delta.

We have now to see where those districts are which have the highest percentages of agricultural occupations, of modern occupations, and of traditional (urban-rural) occupations. Map 8 shows those districts having at least 35% farmers among the members of family sets. The central and eastern parts of the delta and most of al-Jizah province are notably unshaded. Farmers are more numerous in the second stratum on the periphery of the delta and from al-Fayyum all the way southward to Aswan.

The difference between high status agrarian and low status agrarian segments is brought out in map 9. This map shows those districts in

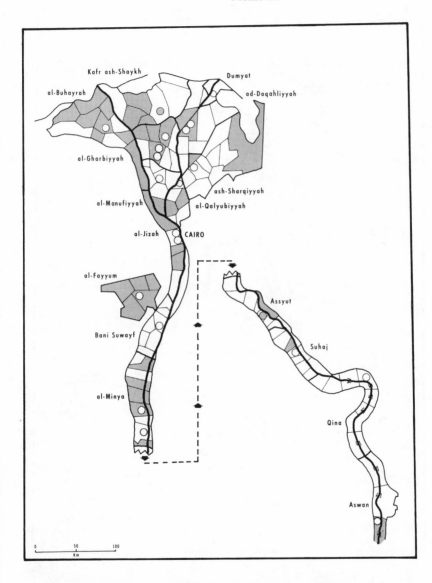

which more than 25% of the members of family sets are 'umad. It seems
that almost everywhere north of Assiut 'umdah families predominate
in the second stratum. 'Umdah families seem to be fewer in the immediate vicinity of Cairo, in the closest in districts of al-Sharqiyyah and

Map 6   Districts in Which 50% or More of
                                   Family Sets Are Mixed

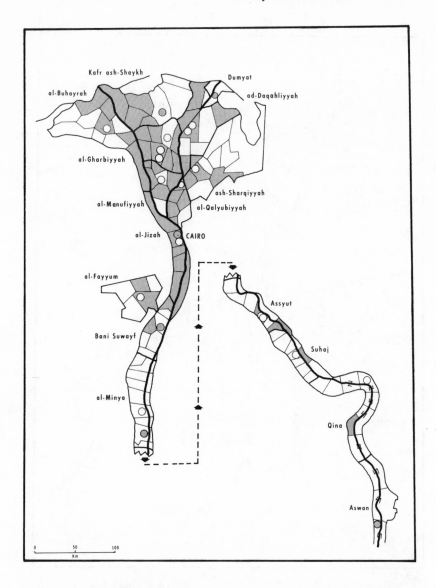

al-Daqahliyyah, and in Bani Suwayf. It is apparent that, in areas closer
to Cairo, modern occupations are more prevalent. Maps 8 and 9 show
how sharply different the distributions of high and low status occupations are among the second stratum. The small number of 'umad south
of Assiut is surprising and requires explanation.

Map 7   Districts in Which Both 'Umad and
                                            Merchants Are Found in the Same
                                            Family Sets

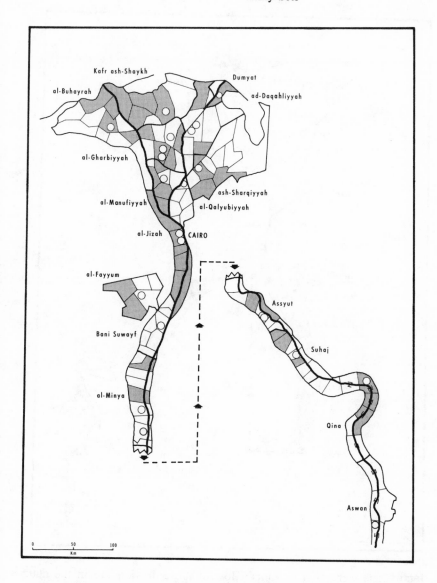

In order to measure the prevalence of modern occupations, the two
largest urban occupational groups, civil servants and teachers, were
used. Civil servants are of somewhat higher status than teachers. Map
10 shows those districts in which more than 10% of the members of

Map 8.   Districts in Which 35% or More of
                                  Family-Set Members Are Farmers

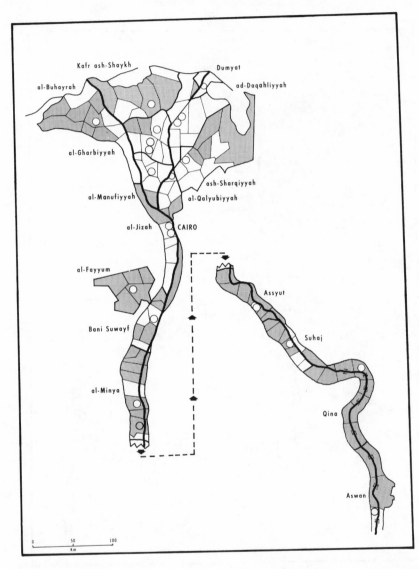

family sets were civil servants. Most of these districts are in the delta
and just north of Cairo in al-Qalyubiyyah, al-Manufiyyah, and nearby
districts. Surprisingly enough, in four of the eight districts of Bani
Suwayf there are more than 10% civil servants, but elsewhere in upper
Egypt there are significant numbers of civil servants only near the

Map 9   Districts in Which 25% or More of
                                      Family-Set Members Are 'Umad

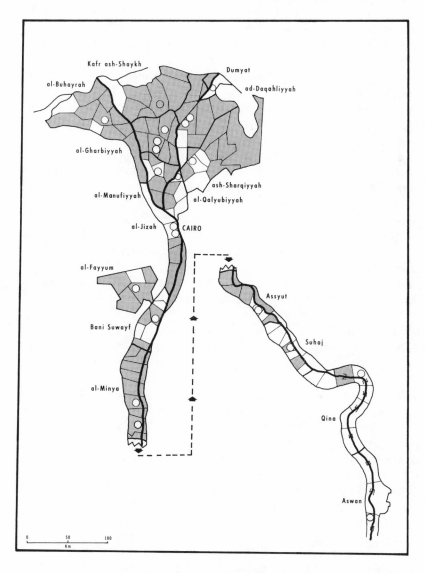

banadir of Assiut, Suhaj, and Aswan. Civil servants are where the
farmers are *not* (compare maps 8 and 10).

Map 11 shows where there were more than 10% teachers among the
members of family sets. The shaded areas of the map indicate that
teachers are also found in larger numbers in the south central delta

area, but not quite as close to Cairo as are civil servants. Maps 10 and 11 give us an interesting impression of the diffusion of social modernization from the capital city. The second stratum is clearly more modernized in al-Qalyubiyyah, al-Manufiyyah, and al-Jizah, and in those districts of al-Sharqiyyah and al-Daqahliyyah which are closest to Cairo. We note, also, that there are ten districts in upper Egypt, all of them south of bandar Assiut (where the number of 'umad in family sets declines) where there are more than 10% teachers in family sets. It is apparent that the status of teachers is higher the less developed the region and the more remote from Cairo. It is even more significant to note that even in these less developed districts, modern occupations are important aspects of the composition of the second stratum.

As measures of traditional nonagricultural occupations we will use merchants and 'ulama'. Often these groups are socially and economically interdependent. The 'ulama' often depend on both the landed proprietors and the merchant classes for economic support, and there is much intermarrying among these segments. The modern middle classes are less supportive of the 'ulama' and less sympathetic to traditional religious orientations. Map 12 shows where there were more than 5% merchants among the members of family sets. The shaded area suggests that merchants have a higher political status in the peripheral areas as well as in a cluster close to Cairo. There are fewer shaded districts in the arc of the central delta and in the middle Egypt region of al-Fayyum, Bani Suwayf, and al-Minia. It is generally not the case that where we find more merchants, we also find more merchant and 'umdah families.

Map 13 is perhaps the most fascinating and suggestive of all the occupational maps. It shows those districts in which there was at least one 'alim in a family set. Now a single 'alim is not many but the total number of 'ulama' was very small. For an 'alim to be in a family set, he must already have attained some kind of social, as well as religious, status. There must have been some intermarriage with other elements of the traditional elite or some connection with important institutions, some acquisition of land or income from awqaf, or the attainment of a modern education by some members of the family. The political attainments of the 'ulama' are an indication of the combination of traditional and modern status and interests which is parallel to the combination of agrarian and urban (bureaucratic, technical, professional) interests which we have already examined. The small number of 'ulama' casts some doubt on the validity of this measure, yet the shaded areas of map 13 appear to coincide with the districts in which there was the highest concentration of second stratum influence—with the exception of al-Jizah, al-Fayyum, and southern al-Minia.

Map 10

Districts in Which 10% or More of
Family-Set Members Are Civil
Servants

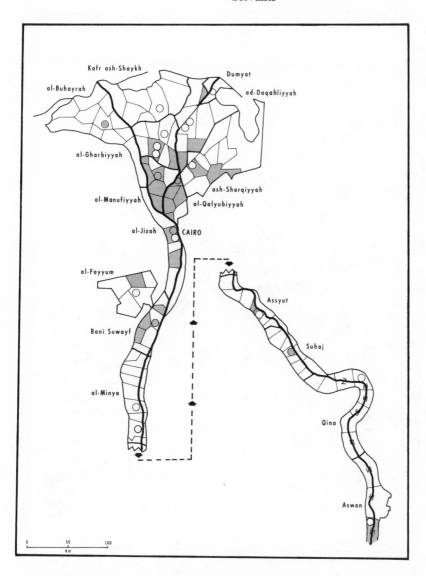

We turn now to the maps showing the various dimensions of concentration of influence. With few exceptions, most districts were represented
by two M.P.'s. An occasional district might have only one, and several
populous towns had more than two. Nevertheless, if two former M.P.'s

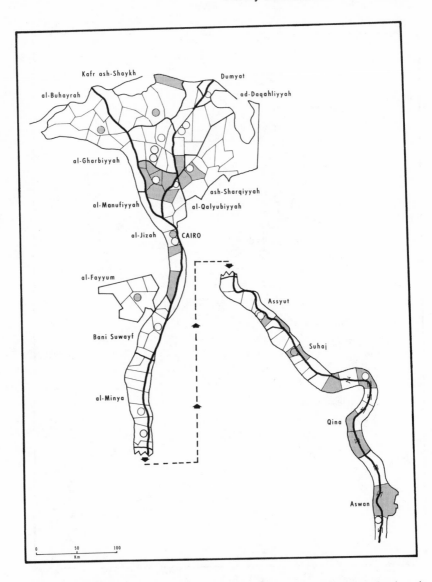

who were members of family sets were found in a single district, it
would indicate a high concentration of second stratum influence. On
map 14 the areas shaded indicate those districts in which one, two, or
three former M.P.'s were found to be members of family sets. There
are few blank areas in the central delta, but the most impressive clusters

Map 12   Districts in Which 5% or More of
                                        Family-Set Members Are Merchants

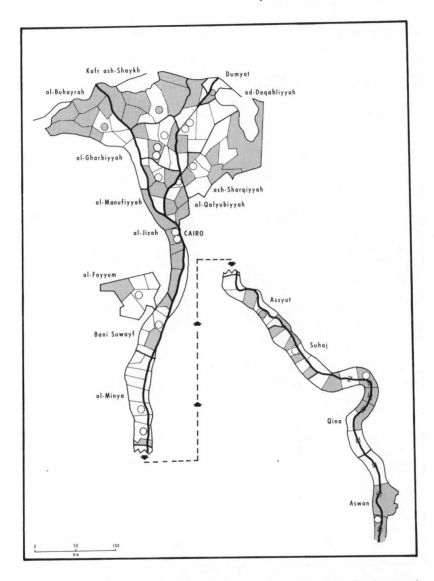

are to be found along the Rosetta branch from Bassiun district northward, in southwestern al-Sharqiyyah, in al-Fayyum, and in southern
al-Minia. It is easy to see that there are few former M.P.'s in family
sets in the banadir; but they are found almost everywhere else.

Map 15 shows different intensities of shading depending on whether

Map 13   Districts in Which 'Ulama' Are
                                        Members of Family Sets

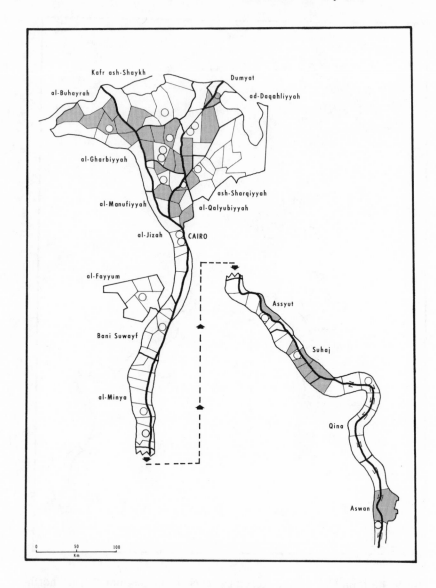

one, two, three, or four district officers were found to be members of
family sets. Once again, we find that officers were family-set members
in all parts of the country, thinning out a little only in Assiut and Qena.
The highest concentration is, however, found again along the Rosetta

Map 14   Districts in Which There Were 1, 2,
                                    or, 3 Former M.P.'s/Members of
                                    Family Sets

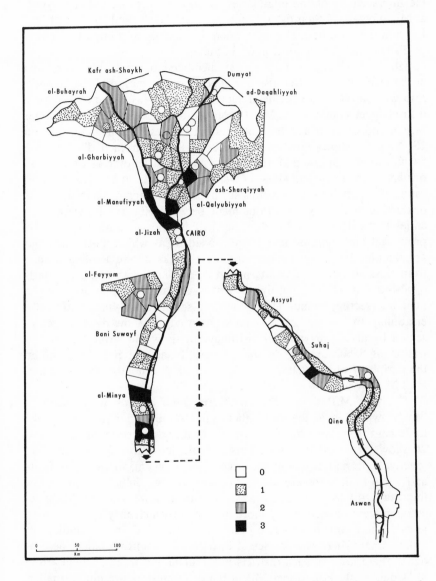

branch from Shibin al-Kom district northward, in southwestern al-
Sharqiyyah province, in southern al-Minia province, and in Suhaj.

Many of these officers were also former M.P.'s, and map 16 shows
where former M.P.'s who were district officers and also members of

family sets were found. The shaded areas on map 16 are more restricted to the northern part of the Rosetta branch, a large cluster at
the intersections of the boundaries of the provinces of al-Gharbiyyah,
al-Manufiyyah, al-Sharqiyyah, and al-Qalyubiyyah, and in al-Jizah, al-
Fayyum, and southern al-Minia. There is a persistently important group
of districts of high concentration in Suhaj.

'Izbah ownership and family-set membership are highly correlated
at the province level. Because our analysis of the data on 'izbah ownership was based on a provincial sample, there is insufficient data for a
district level comparison. Mr. Chesnin did collect data on all former
M.P.'s and officers; and this information is presented in maps 17 and
18. Map 17 shows how many former M.P.'s from each district were
'izbah owners, and map 18 shows how many district officers were 'izbah
owners in each district. There is a strong similarity in both maps, indicating that 'izbah ownership was strong in certain regions and that little
distinction in this regard is to be made between officers who were influential at the district level and former M.P.'s who were influential at the
provincial and national level. The shaded areas which most stand out
are familiar by now: the east and west banks of the Rosetta branch
from Bassiun north, the western part of al-Sharqiyyah and those parts
of al-Manufiyyah, al-Gharbiyyah, and al-Qalyubiyyah that are close to
their intersecting boundaries, al-Fayyum, southern al-Minia, and southern Suhaj. In fact the eastern and western edges of the delta, as represented by al-Sharqiyyah and al-Buhayrah, show the strongest concentration of 'izbah-owning district officers. 'Izbah ownership falls off in
the periphery of the delta, including al-Jizah and notably in the center,
in al-Manufiyyah.

If former M.P.'s and district officers differ slightly with regard to
'izbah ownership in the delta, they differ somewhat more with regard
to descent from prerevolutionary parliamentary ancestors. Maps 19 and
20 show former M.P. descendants and district officer descendants, respectively. In middle and upper Egypt, in al-Fayyum, southern al-Minia,
and Suhaj both maps are nearly the same. In the delta there are a few
important differences. There are, of course, fewer former M.P. descendants and, hence, many more districts in which they are not found
at all. There are, however, no districts south of Cairo (including al-
Jizah) where there is a former M.P. descendant and no officer descendant. There are five such districts in the delta and three of them are in
al-Daqahliyyah. For former M.P.'s the delta clusters are much smaller,
being restricted to five districts along the Rosetta branch and six or
seven from Kafr Saqr in al-Sharqiyyah to al-Quwaysina in al-Manufiyyah. For officer descendants the west delta cluster stretches south-

Map 15   Districts in Which There Were 1–4
                                    Officers/Members of Family Sets

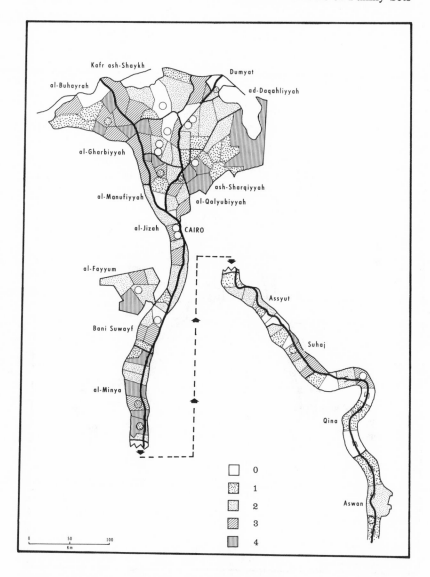

ward to Ashmun, al-Manuf, al-Shuhada', and Tala in al-Manufiyyah,
and, of course, further southward into al-Jizah. The inheritance of political influence is more widespread in middle and upper Egypt than is
the prevalence of the second stratum and, especially the more modern

Map 16   Districts in Which at Least One
                                        Officer is Both a Former M.P. and a
                                        Member of a Family Set

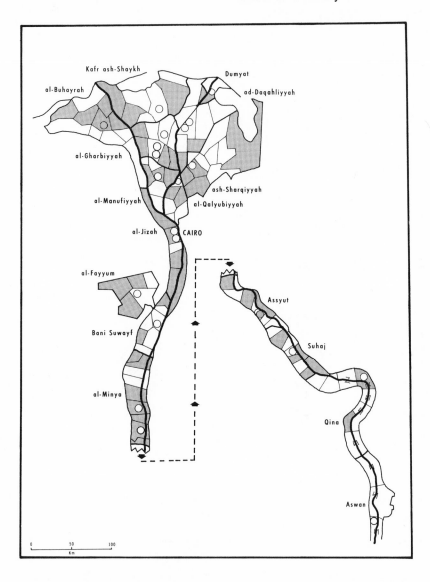

segment of the second stratum. In the delta, however, the pattern is less
consistent with concentration varying with prevalence in some districts
but not in others. Nevertheless, it remains clear that the second stratum
is most politically influential in a band of districts extending from

Map 17   Distribution of Former M.P.'s/
                                             'Izbah Owners by Markaz

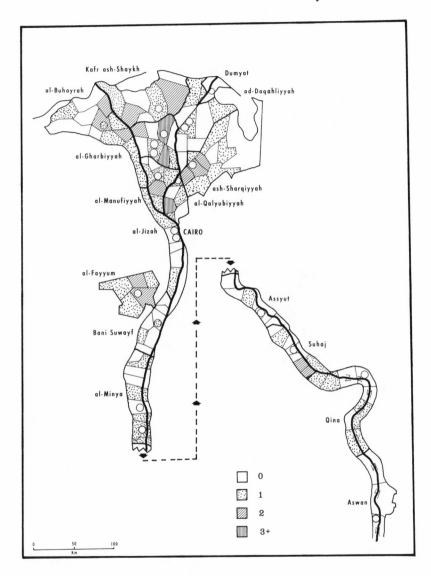

Qalyub to al-Zagazig in the southeast and to Fuwwah, to Bassiun, and
Kum Hamadah in the northwest, and, south of Cairo, in al-Fayyum,
southern al-Minia, and southern Suhaj.

Map 21 shows where the highest concentration of influence is to be
found. That map was constructed by assigning one point to each district

Map 18   Distribution of District Officer/
                                              'Izbah Owners by Markaz

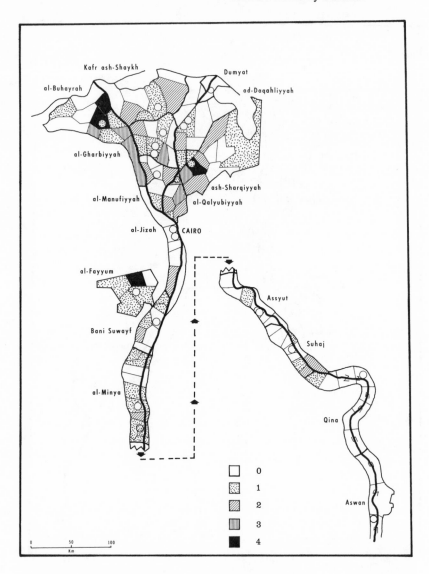

in which there was found an officer or former M.P. in a family set or
who owned an 'izbah or who was descended from a prerevolutionary
M.P. The shaded area represents all districts with a score of 8 or more.
The average for 130 districts (excluding Aswan and Dumyat) was 5.78
and the standard deviation was a high 4.27. In effect map 21 tells us

that, in the delta there are two concentrations, one in al-Buhayrah and neighboring districts in Kafr al-Shaykh and al-Gharbiyyah, and another in al-Sharqiyyah and neighboring districts in al-Qalyubiyyah and al-Manufiyyah. There are lesser groupings in al-Fayyum, al-Minia, and Suhaj.

Map 22 is a composite of maps 2–5 and it sums up the situation regarding the prevalence of the second stratum. It is apparent that the region of the greatest prevalence is in the central and northwestern part of the delta, al-Jizah, and al-Fayyum. The remaining areas of high concentration are areas of low prevalence. Most of al-Gharbiyyah, an area of high prevalence of the second stratum is also an area of lower concentration of political influence.

Map 23 is a composite of maps 6, 7, and 13. This map will serve to locate those districts where there seems to be a stronger representation of the traditional and modern occupational mix which we have attributed to the second stratum. The strongest mixed areas are in the group of districts running from Rashid and Fuwwah to Cairo and al-Zagazig. Neither the more heavily agricultural family sets as shown on map 8 nor the more strongly modern as shown on maps 10 and 11 have as much bearing on either prevalence or concentration.

Where we have both high prevalence and high concentration in the delta, we also find agricultural occupations more prevalent; and where we find low prevalence and high concentration in the delta, we will find more modern occupations. Al-Gharbiyyah province is the shatter zone, where we find high prevalence, high mixed family sets, two districts with many farmers, one with many civil servants, and two districts with high concentrations of influence.

The most important political region of the country seems to be that in which the mixed occupations of the second stratum are highest. Elsewhere, the pattern of elite strength seems less ambiguous, less open to change, and less influenced by events in the large urban centers. It is in the delta diagonal running from northeast of Cairo to the east of Alexandria that we find the prototypical second stratum families, and that is where we should expect to find them making their most vigorous demands for jobs, for educational opportunity, for inclusion in the local political process, and for legitimate participation in the national political process. The result of this sort of pressure ought to be the wider diffusion of both participation and access, and the reduced concentration of influence in well-established families.

It is clear that there are significant variations in the distribution of family-set members, mixed family sets, and influential family-set members within the provinces. Within the provinces, some districts have very high percentages of family-set members and some do not. Those

Map 19   Districts in Which There Were
                                              Former M.P./Descendants of
                                              Prerevolutionary M.P.'s

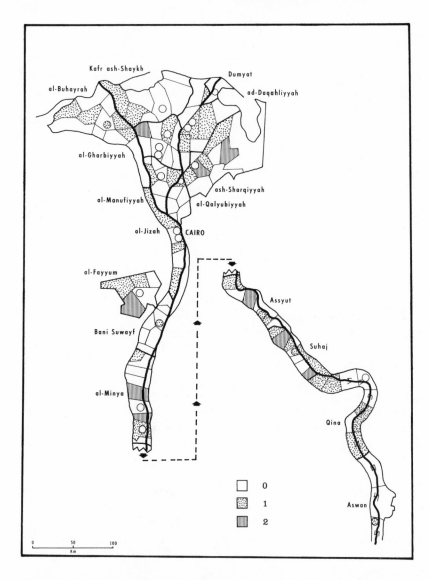

districts which have high percentages in family sets also have a high
percentage of mixed families, of large family sets, and, naturally, of
former M.P.'s, district officers, 'izbah owners, and descendants in family

Map 20   Districts in Which There Were
                                        District Officers/Descendants of
                                        Prerevolutionary M.P.'s

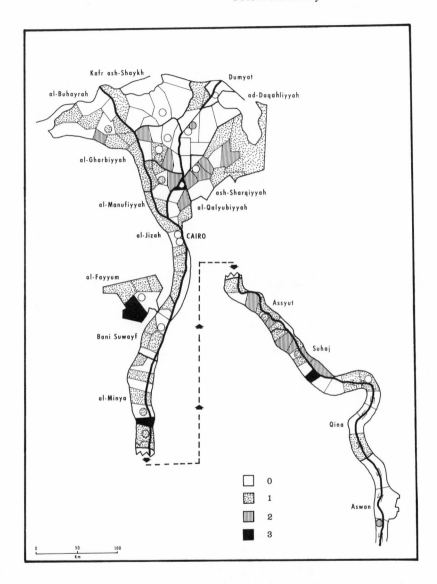

sets. In the south the percentages of family-set members are consistently
lower, the degree of difference of occupational composition of family
sets is smaller, but the concentration of former M.P.'s and officer sta-

Map 21   Concentration of Influence

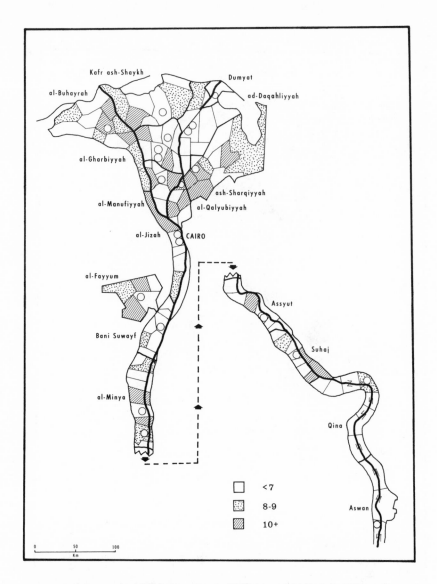

tuses is greater in a number of districts. The districts in which the second stratum is most prevalent (map 22) and most influential (map 21) are given in table 96.

Altogether there are nineteen of 144 districts where the prevalence of the second stratum is high and where there are many second stratum

Map 22   Prevalence of Second Stratum

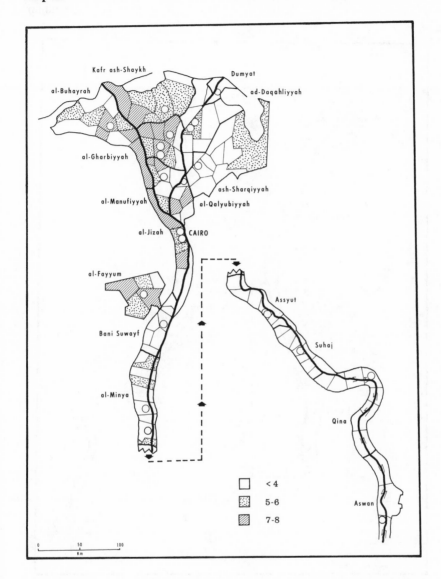

influentials. There are two contiguous clusters, of three districts and of
four districts, in which these complementary political characteristics
are found in the greatest degree. The first is the districts of Shibin al-
Qanatir, al-Qalyub, and Imbabah (in al-Qalyubiyyah and al-Jizah, near
Cairo), and the second is the districts of al-Dassuq, al-Bassiun, Hush

Map 23   Prevalence of Occupationally More
                                              Diverse Segment of Second Stratum

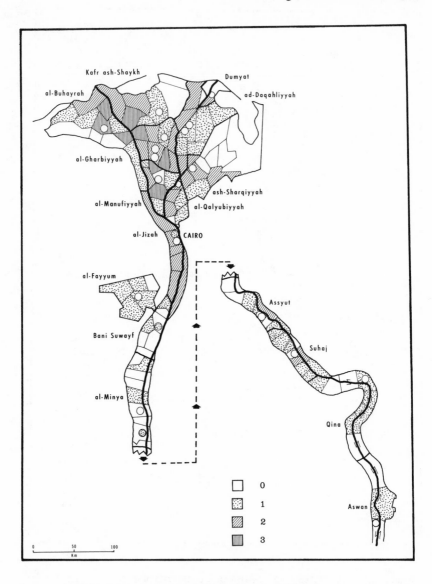

Isa, and al-Damanhur (in Kafr al-Shaykh, al-Gharbiyyah, and al-Buhayrah, on the Rosetta branch and near Alexandria). In all of these
districts, the occupational distribution of the second stratum is relatively
modern, taking into account the level of development of the province;

but these are not necessarily the districts in which the second stratum
has the highest percentage of modern occupations.

There are three other clusters of districts in which the second stratum
is influential, but where it is not as numerous. These clusters are in al-
Sharqiyyah, al-Qalyubiyyah, al-Minia, and Suhaj. The districts are listed

Table 96   Districts Where the Second Stratum
                                      Is Politically Influential and
                                      Prevalent

Province	District	Percentage in Family Sets	Percentage of Modern Occupations in Family Sets
al-Qalyubiyyah	al-Qalyub	31.9	50.9[a]
	Shibin al-Qanatir	29.0	59.3[a]
al-Sharqiyyah	al-Husayniyyah	26.6	25.2
Kafr al-Shaykh	al-Bila	25.3	29.9
	al-Dassuq	32.0	35.9[b]
	al-Fuwwah	33.2	38.2
al-Gharbiyyah	al-Bassiun	41.7	36.7[b]
	al-Santah	25.6	43.8
al-Manufiyyah	al-Shuhada'	30.3	57.1
al-Buhayrah	Shubra Khayt	26.4	30.1
	al-Damanhur	33.3	26.4[b]
	Hush Isa	33.7	38.9[b]
	Itay al-Barud	31.9	37.6
	Kum Hamadah	30.6	41.5
al-Jizah	Imbabah	32.4	47.8[a]
al-Fayyum	al-Sinuris	20.0	35.5
	al-Ibshaway	28.9	26.8
	al-Itsa	22.3	25.7
al-Minia	al-Maghaghah	18.8	25.8
Mean		29.2	37.5

[a-b]Geographical clusters.

in table 97. There are, altogether, 40 districts in which the second
stratum is most influential, or 28% of the districts. Of this number,
seven (4.9%) are districts of high prevalence and high concentration;
twelve (8.3%) are areas of moderately high prevalence and/or moderately high concentration of influence. Of the nine districts (6.3%)
with high concentration and lower prevalence, the first four (2.7%) resemble the high prevalence and high concentration group in terms of
percentage in family sets and percentage of family-set members in
modern occupations but not in other measures of prevalence. The sec-

ond stratum in al-Sharqiyyah does seem to be somewhat different in structure from that in the west delta, however, so it may be advisable to maintain the distinction between the two sections of each group. Similarly, it may be noted that the al-Fayyum group looks a bit like the al-Minia and Suhaj groups of districts.

Table 97   Districts Where the Second Stratum
                                                Is Politically Influential but Not
                                                Highly Prevalent

Province	District	Percentage in Family Sets	Percentage in Modern Occupations in Family Sets
al-Sharqiyyah	Bilbays	21.9	44.0
	Minia al-Qamh	22.3	47.6
	al-Zaqaziq	24.1	58.1
al-Qalyubiyyah	Banha	25.8	55.0
al-Minia	Samalut	19.6	21.3
	Abu Qurqas	14.2	22.2
Suhaj	Akhmim	16.1	36.3
	Awlad Tukh Sharq	13.0	11.3
	al-Balyana	9.0	24.9

The continuities between the two groups of districts are as suggestive as their differences. It is important to recognize that common influences are at work throughout Egypt, linking occupational diversification, modernization, traditional influence, and agrarian affluence. In each district, the mix is a bit different and, even though the resultant patterns are most interesting in 28% of the districts, and most striking in only 8.5% of the districts (seven high prevalence and high concentration districts and five low prevalence and high concentration districts), the same phenomena are found in nearly all the districts.

It is apparent that prevalence might be measured in more than one way. If we take family-set membership alone as a sufficient indicator of membership in the second stratum then certain anomalies arise with regard to the correlation of prevalence and concentration and the correlation of prevalence and modernity. It would seem that in some areas concentration correlates positively with the modernity of the second stratum and in other areas it correlates with the prevalence of large family sets. Modernity often coincides with a high percentage in family sets, regardless of size. But then there are also a few districts in which concentration appears to coincide with the presence of many descendants of prerevolutionary parliamentarians regardless of percentage in family sets or size of family sets. From our analysis however, it is apparent that these considerations of the dimensions of prevalence really refer to the possible stratification of the second stratum.

The summary maps are quite consistent with expectations derived from the statistical analysis in chapter 10. There are, in fact, three significant configurations. The summary map 22 showing the geographical configuration of prevalence is most unlike the two maps showing the configuration of continuity, maps 19 and 20. The maps diverge most for the upper Egyptian districts and for the eastern part of the delta. The configuration of concentration (map 21) shows a substantial overlap with both of the other patterns. Taken together, the evidence of these two types of analysis tend to confirm the proposition that the second stratum is perhaps better conceived of as a process rather than a structure. Its common structural elements have been documented. Insofar as regional differences may be attributed to ecological diversity and not to social or cultural patterns, to that extent can it be argued that the differences are likely to be influenced by development strategies and, in particular, by the balance of investment in social mobilization and agricultural technology. Theoretically, at any rate, the delta districts could become more like the districts of upper Egypt or vice versa —even though it is probable that the delta districts were, at one time, more like what the districts of upper Egypt are now.

Twelve

Regional Patterns of
Diffusion of Rural Elites

The whole structure of the village,
as well as that of the whole socio-
graphic region of G'afra, could be
likened to a centrifugal mechanism
spreading out and out in ever
widening circles.

H. Ammar, *Growing up in an
Egyptian Village*

The conclusions reached regarding geographical continuities at the district level will be further tested against data developed at the village
level in this chapter. This analysis will be informed by two problematical issues. The first of these is whether one or more comprehensive
regional patterns of the distribution of the second stratum can be discerned. The second issue is a more complicated one. Since we have
found significant differences in the relationships among prevalence of
the second stratum, occupational modernization, and concentration of
political elite statuses in various parts of the country, it follows that
there may be some tension between the integrative role of the second
stratum and either the differentiating influences of regional social structure in the less developed provinces, or the competitive aspects of the
local political process in the more developed provinces. It is likely that
the potentially integrative role of the second stratum will depend, in
part, upon how widely diffused it is. The political importance of the
second stratum will be accounted for by its prevalence and/or its concentration of elite statuses in any one province or district, but the wide
diffusion of the second stratum will account for its integrative capacity.
If this hypothesis is correct, the wide diffusion of the second stratum
will account for the minimization (at present) of interregional political
conflict in Egypt, despite significant disparities in levels of development.

280

It may, however, be expected, that even the effect of the wide diffusion of the second stratum can be offset by increasing disparities in prevalence and in levels of agricultural development.

To answer these questions a set of maps was drawn showing the exact location of each village, the size of the village committee, and whether there was a family set in that .committee. In order to render such information more easily intelligible, similarly scaled maps were prepared showing the district boundaries and names, the location of the district capital, and the percentage in family sets. A third group of maps was prepared with the aid of a computer, using village level NU data on "the percent engaged in agriculture" as the basis for determining which parts of the province were the more developed. It was hypothesized that, if development or modernization determined the location of the second stratum, these maps would confirm the findings of the provincial and district level analyses. It could further be argued that in pushing the analysis all the way to the local level the dangers of generalizing from data on large aggregate units would be diminished. Even though the mapping of this data was directed at this modernization hypothesis, the preparation of the maps was also genuinely exploratory and experimental, in the sense that surprises were expected. In fact, the only surprise was no surprise.

The most important finding of this analysis is that modernization and centrality of location determine the density or prevalence of the second stratum, but not its presence or absence. In fact, there is virtually no part of the country, with the possible exception of Aswan, from which the second stratum is absent—and this ubiquity of the second stratum, it must be remembered, is determined by reference to the precise geographical locations of the villages. There are, nevertheless, significant geographical differences in the distribution of the second stratum, some of which may be attributed to geographical variables and some to political and historical variables.

Rather than examine each of the detailed maps, a tedious exercise unwarranted by this first treatment of what may become an important subject of future research, a few summary generalizations will be offered which will, hopefully, yield some tentative hypotheses explaining the empirical variation. Only a few of the maps will be reproduced here as examples illustrating this discussion.

The agricultural provinces of Egypt present two general configurations, the compact "pie slice" of the delta and the elongated "vertebrate" of upper Egypt. The delta is bordered by the desert and the sea, but the development of irrigation has extended the agriculturally productive area into the desert, eastward in al-Sharqiyyah province and westward in al-Buhayrah province. Nevertheless, it is possible to distinguish between the core of the delta region—the interriverine zone—and the periphery, which includes areas farther to the east and west of the branches of the Nile, the areas along the saline seacoast and along Lake al-Manzalah, and the urbanized zones and vacant land near and in Cairo. The core area is all but uniformly densely inhabited, intensively cultivated, crossed by roads, railways, and irrigation canals, and dotted with important administrative and marketing centers. The social geographical uniformity of the delta core is somewhat modified by the influence of Cairo, by the pattern of roads and canals, and, of course, by the location of the branches of the Nile. The peripheral areas are less densely inhabited, have fewer urban centers, and are generally less developed; they are politically and economically more influenced by their provincial capitals than by the drawing power of Cairo, or by the polarized geographical field along the line from Cairo to Alexandria.

There is only one province which borders neither on the desert nor the sea and which is adjacent neither to Cairo nor to Alexandria. Al-Gharbiyyah province lies entirely between the branches of the Nile in the heart of the delta, and it is the geographical and agrarian core of lower Egypt. Al-Gharbiyyah is comprised of eight districts of roughly similar size, arranged in northern and southern tiers of four. If we similarly arrange the data on percentage in family sets and percentage engaged in modern occupations in geographical order, the data will look like a systematically ordered matrix in which the western and northernmost district ranks highest on prevalence and the eastern and southernmost ranks highest in development. The geographical intercept of social and occupational modernization and the political assertiveness and density of the rural middle class can be imputed to lie at a point in the center of al-Gharbiyyah province.

It is questionable whether a single nodal point can be determined as the location of the highest coincidence of prevalence and rural modernization, but if there is one, it appears to be located near the intersection of al-Gharbiyyah, Kafr al-Shaykh, al-Buhayrah, and al-Manufiyyah provinces. The falloff from this highest point is shallower to the east and south and steeper to the north and west. Hence, the second stratum is most prevalent and most modernized in those agricultural areas which are geographically most central, in which the agricultural land is least sandy, least saline, and most accessible to irrigation. Contiguous to this core are a number of clusters of towns and villages which are also high in prevalence and in rural modernization. These clusters are found in proximity to the provincial capitals of al-Sharqiyyah (al-Zagazig), al-Daqahliyyah (al-Mansurah), and al-Manufiyyah

(Shibin al-Kum). The shape of the clusters is influenced by the rail lines and the Nile branches.

The following maps will illustrate these contrasting patterns. The first, or core, pattern can be found in the maps for al-Gharbiyyah province, showing the district boundaries and percentage in family sets; showing the exact locations of the villages and towns; and the contour map showing the percentage engaged in traditional occupations. Map 24 is provided to help the reader locate the district capitals and to orient himself in terms of the administrative geography of the province. Map 25 illustrates the wide, relatively unbroken diffusion of family-set committees. Although the map does not readily show it, a close examination reveals that there are more towns and villages in the southeast sector, even though the percentage in family sets is higher in the northwest. This much can be attributed to the influence of the national capital. Map 26 does not conflict with the map showing village locations, but neither can it be said that the diffusion of family-set villages conforms in any obvious way to the diffusion of modern occupations. There are more family-set members in the larger units, and there is a slight tendency for those units to be closer to the district capital.

The second pattern, found in the delta periphery, is best illustrated by the family-set location maps for al-Buhayrah and al-Daqahliyyah. These provinces are on opposite sides of the delta, and both border on the desert, the sea, and on inland salt lakes (maps 27 and 29). Al-Buhayrah is, of course, an area in which the second stratum is very strong, but in al-Daqahliyyah the second stratum is surprisingly weak. The most striking similarity in these maps is the degree to which the diffusion of family-set villages conforms to the river bed, the major canals, and the railroads. Aside from important clusters near Damanhur and Kum Hamadah in al-Buhayrah, and another at al-Mansurah in al-Daqahliyyah, the family-set villages are generally strung out in long lines following the major ecological bases of agricultural development (maps 28 and 30).

Other delta provinces show intermediate patterns, with Kafr al-Shaykh looking more like the peripheral type and al-Sharqiyyah and al-Manufiyyah looking more like al-Gharbiyyah, except for the influence of the desert.

In upper Egypt, the diffusion of family-set villages conforms somewhat less to the contour lines of the diffusion of modern occupations than is the case in lower Egypt. The reason for this lack of conformity is that the diffusion of rural development is even less centralized in the south than it is in the north. The contour maps reveal two basic patterns of the diffusion of modern occupations. In all cases, the district

Map 24   Al-Gharbiyyah Province: Percentage
                                    in Family Sets

al-Gharbiyyah Province

PERCENT IN FAMILY SETS

31°00′

M. al-Mahallah al-Kubrā

27.2

M. Samanūd

24.5

M. Quṭūr

6.5

M. Basyūn

41.7   32.2

27.6

31.5   0.0   M. al-Sanṭah

B. Ṭanṭā

M. Kafr al-Zayyāt   6.7

30°45′

M. Ṭanṭā   25.6

22.7

M. Ziftā

DISTRICT BOUNDARY
PROVINCIAL BOUNDARY

0   5   10
MILES

31°00′

Map 25   Al-Gharbiyyah Province: Size and
Location of Family-Set Villages

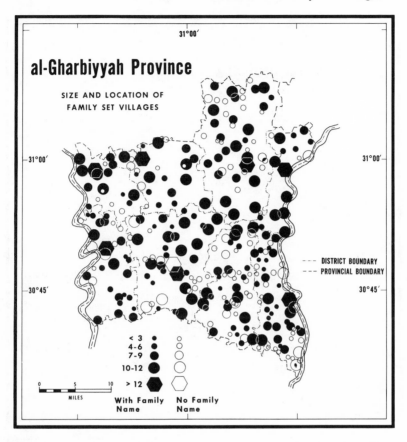

capitals and the provincial capitals are the nodal points of the diffusion
of modern occupations. Usually the patterns are quite symmetrical and
would look like series of concentric circles except for the fact that the
desert or some mountains impinge and occasionally two or more capitals may be so close that they influence the neighboring concentric
pattern. The contour maps differ, primarily, in terms of whether it is
possible to discern an interprovincial or provincial pattern as opposed
to a district level pattern only. Where the district has its own nucleus
and its occupational pattern is relatively unaffected by neighboring
districts, it may be said to be linked to other districts in a vertebrate
structure, or to look like a single cell in a DNA chain. Nucleated dis-

Map 26   Al-Gharbiyyah Province: Percentage
                                                  Engaged in Traditional Occupations

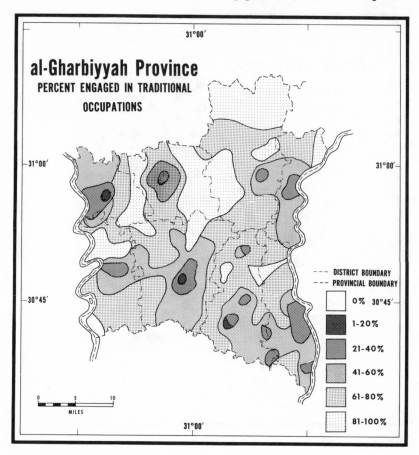

al-Gharbiyyah Province
PERCENT ENGAGED IN TRADITIONAL
OCCUPATIONS

DISTRICT BOUNDARY
PROVINCIAL BOUNDARY

0%
1-20%
21-40%
41-60%
61-80%
81-100%

tricts are generally found away from the delta core and especially in
the southern part of upper Egypt. It is more likely that the province
as a whole will show aspects of a concentric pattern where its component districts border on one another and where they cluster, to some
extent, around the provincial capital. Where, as in upper Egypt, some
districts border only on one district to the north and another to the
south, and both of these at the narrowest sides, it is unlikely that we
shall find a provincewide or an interprovincial pattern of diffusion of
modernization among the second stratum. Most of the delta provinces
show some characteristics of a provincial contour structure, as do al-
Jizah, al-Fayyum, and Bani Suwayf. Moreover, there are elements of a

Map 27   Al-Buhayrah Province: Percentage
                              in Family Sets

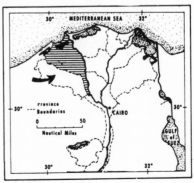

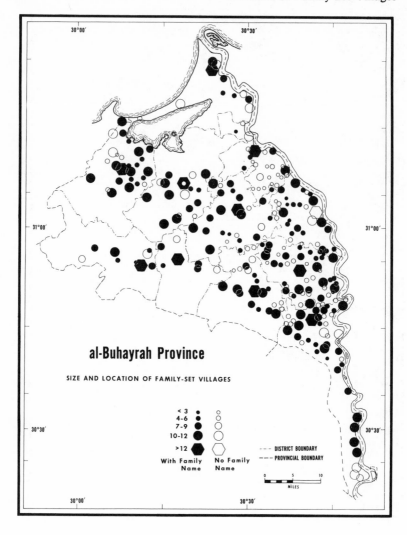

al-Buhayrah Province

SIZE AND LOCATION OF FAMILY-SET VILLAGES

	< 3	
---	4-6	---
	7-9	
	10-12	
	>12	
With Family Name		No Family Name

--- DISTRICT BOUNDARY
--- PROVINCIAL BOUNDARY

0   5   10
MILES

Map 29
Al-Daqahliyyah Province: Percentage in Family Sets

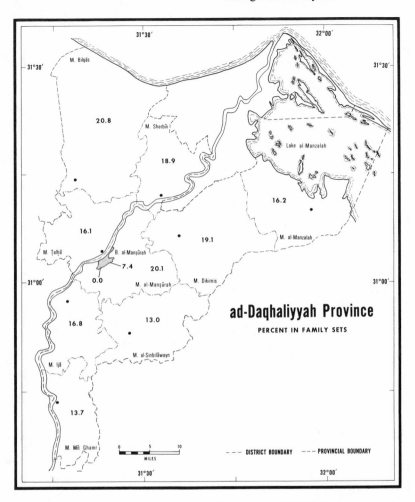

31°30′ 32°00′

31°30′ 31°30′

M. Bilqās

20.8

M. Sherbīn

18.9

Lake al-Manzalah

16.2

16.1

M. Talhā B. al-Manṣūrah

19.1

M. al-Manzalah

7.4 20.1

0.0

M. al-Manṣūrah M. Dikirnis

31°00′ 31°00′

ad-Daqhaliyyah Province

PERCENT IN FAMILY SETS

16.8 13.0

M. al-Sinbilāwayn

M. Ijā

13.7

M. Mīt Ghamr

0 5 10
MILES

– – – DISTRICT BOUNDARY   – – – PROVINCIAL BOUNDARY

31°30′ 32°00′

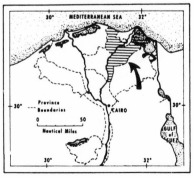

MEDITERRANEAN SEA

30° 32°

Province
Boundaries

CAIRO

0 50
Nautical Miles

GULF of SUEZ

30° 32°

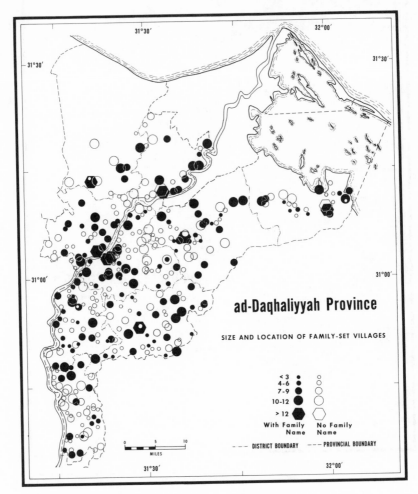

ad-Daqhaliyyah Province

SIZE AND LOCATION OF FAMILY-SET VILLAGES

regional contour pattern to be found in the central part of the delta as a whole. The farther south we go from Cairo, the less "modern" are the members of the second stratum and the less is there a provincial diffusion pattern and the more a decidedly district-nucleated pattern.

These points can be illustrated by maps of selected upper Egyptian provinces. Al-Fayyum is a good example of a province with a centralized pattern of diffusion (maps 31, 32, 33). Given the fact that there is such a high percentage in family sets, that there are so many large

Map 31   Al-Fayyum Province: Percentage in
                              Family Sets

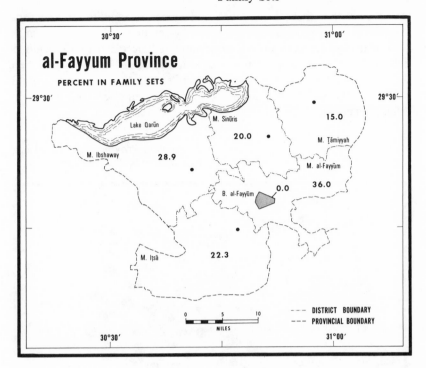

al-Fayyum Province

PERCENT IN FAMILY SETS

Lake Qarūn

M. Sinūris

M. Ibshaway

28.9

20.0

15.0

M. Ṭāmiyyah

M. al-Fayyūm

B. al-Fayyūm   0.0   36.0

M. Iṭsā   22.3

DISTRICT BOUNDARY
PROVINCIAL BOUNDARY

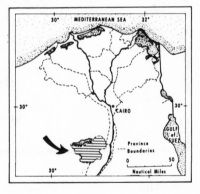

family sets, that there is so much concentration of elite statuses, and that there is no central cluster of family-set units, there is reason to believe that provincial politics are dominated by district level influentials. This pattern may be contrasted with that of al-Daqahliyyah, where there is a central cluster of family-set units near the provincial capital, but where the second stratum is both small in numbers and politically weaker than might be expected.

Map 32   Al-Fayyum Province: Size and Location of Family-Set Villages

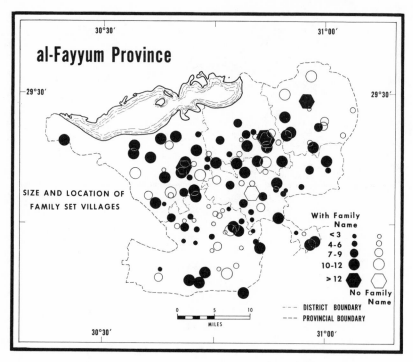

Al-Minia, Assiut, and Suhaj present three variations on the alternative nucleated pattern. All three are populous, rural provinces, relatively remote from Cairo, and are comprised of thin strips of cultivable alluvium lying mostly on the west side of the Nile. The contour maps for all three (maps 35, 37 and 39) show that the provincial capitals exercise only an attenuated regional influence compared with the counterinfluence of the district capitals. Frequently, in these provinces, there are no family sets in some of the larger towns and district or provincial capitals. The family-set units are diffused unevenly among the districts, but they show some tendency to cluster by district, especially in Suhaj (maps 34, 36 and 38). There is a substantial clustering in Mallawi district in al-Minia—the least uniform of the three provinces in terms of the district level diffusion of the second stratum.

The village committee maps show that family sets are located in every part of every province, with virtually no exception. The Egyptian

Map 33   Al-Fayyum Province: Percentage
                                       Engaged in Traditional Occupations

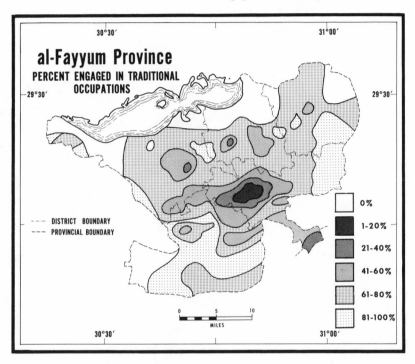

second stratum is not concentrated in a single region. The Egyptian case presents a sharp contrast to the situation of the rural elites in south Italy, the Sahel-based elites of Tunisia, the localized beneficiaries of the "green revolution" in India and Pakistan, the Hunanese in China, the Alawis in Syria, and the Takritis and other north central Tigris region Iraqis. In all of these cases and more, politically significant elements which are identified primarily in terms of geographical origin, have either achieved dominant positions or have challenged the estab-

Map 34

Al-Minia Province: Size and Location of Family-Set Villages

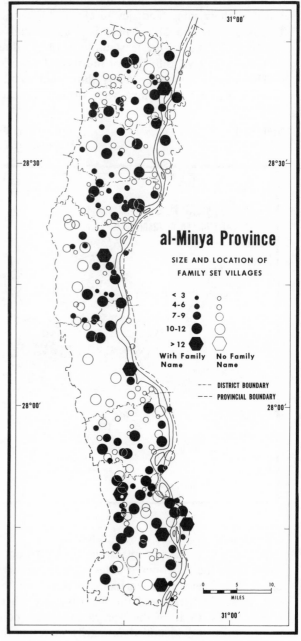

al-Minya Province

SIZE AND LOCATION OF
FAMILY SET VILLAGES

	With Family Name	No Family Name
< 3	●	○
4-6	●	○
7-9	●	○
10-12	●	○
> 12	⬡	⬡

- - - DISTRICT BOUNDARY
– – – PROVINCIAL BOUNDARY

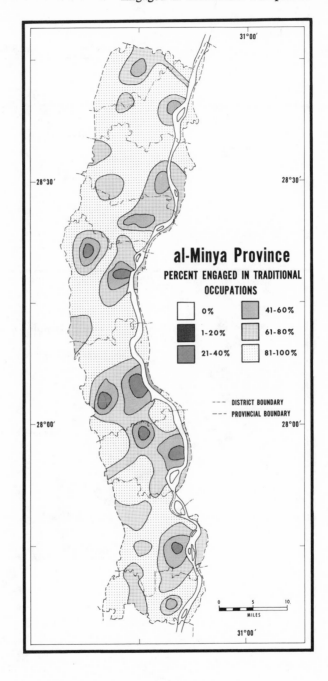

Map 36   Assiut Province: Size and Location
                               of Family-Set Villages

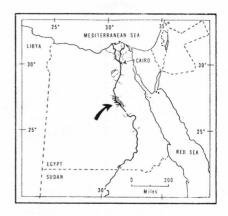

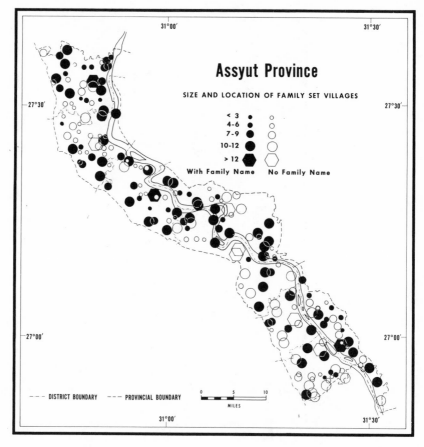

lished or traditional authority. In many developing countries such regionally based conflicts, especially when they are exacerbated by ethnic
and cultural differences, define the major issues of power and policy.
Egypt, however, has been twice blessed; first because it is virtually
without importantly differentiated geographically concentrated communities, and secondly, because of the general uniformity of the involvement of the rural middle class in the processes of modernization and
political participation.

Unfortunately, past blessings cannot be counted upon to prevent the
emergence of new problems. The phenomenon of the Egyptian second
stratum is an historical contingency and not a natural necessity, and it
may be expected to change. An examination of the geographic data on

Map 37   Assiut Province: Percentage En-
                                              gaged in Traditional Occupations

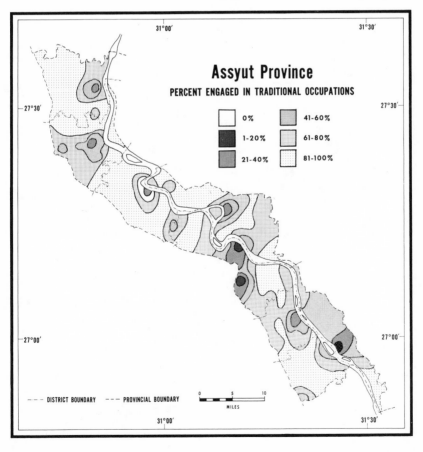

Map 38

Suhaj Province: Size and Location of
Family-Set Villages

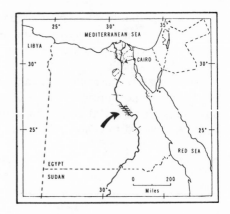

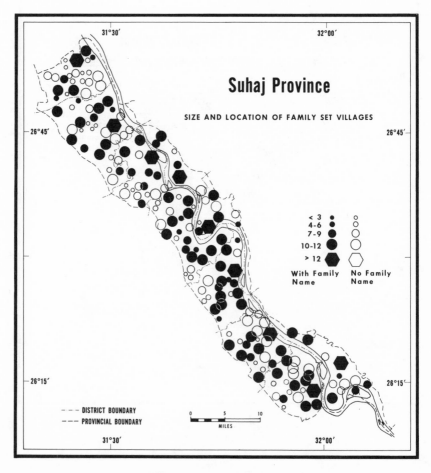

the diffusion of the second stratum suggests where potential problems may arise. If one remembers that the major reason why the second stratum plays a positive and integrative role is because its agricultural interests have not been damaged, it is to be expected that a major change in agricultural policy would stimulate efforts to alter the political role of the second stratum. Such policy changes could enhance the opportunities for large-scale, highly capitalized, private agricultural enterprise, or, contrarily, limit yet further private holdings and economic decision making. Politically, it is apparent that participation will be more meaningfully competitive than in the recent past. It is, therefore, likely, that the different regions of Egypt, will all react in terms of the possibility of the conscious political organization of the second stratum.

Map 39   Suhaj Province: Percentage Engaged
                                    in Traditional Occupations

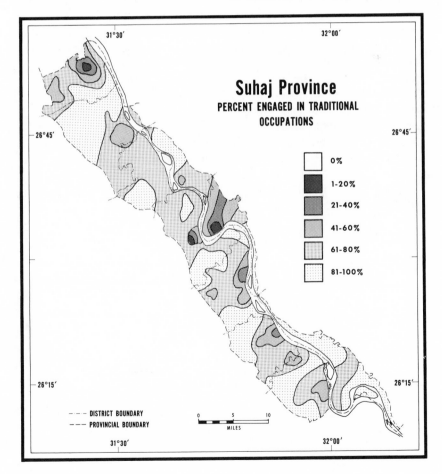

Such a transformation from a passive, atomized instrumentality into an active, self-aware collectivity is evidently far more likely to be the case in the delta core. Will the delta core then become a new Sahel or Sousse?

The prototypical social and economic conditions which have contributed to the emergence of the second stratum are illustrated by the characteristics of the delta core. The more developed rural areas produce more members of the second stratum. Rural development is structured in a pattern of diffusion from district capitals. The district administration appears to structure both economic and political activities except in two or three provinces. But in the delta core area, members of the second stratum appear to be participants in a set of economic, social, and political processes which are common to the region, whereas the parallel processes in al-Fayyum, al-Minia, Assiut, and Suhaj appear to be disjoined from one another and from the delta. Insofar as mediating elites are linked nationwide, it would appear that the creation of parliamentary and party institutions is partly responsible—as have been certain central economic institutions such as the banking system and the cotton market. Insofar as the second stratum is to be used for mobilization purposes, its ubiquity provides an enormous advantage over a more localized stratum. There are differences in the structure of the second stratum, especially among the delta core, the delta periphery, the secondary nodal concentrations in central Egypt, and the nucleated districts in the southernmost provinces. Under the Nasser regime, there was little evidence that these subgroups opposed one another or competed among themselves politically as groups—but that is not to say that such competition is unlikely in the future. This is an issue to which we shall return in the last chapter.

Part Three

The Arab Socialist Union
and the Second Stratum

Thirteen

The Founding of
the Arab Socialist Union

The experience of uniting Syria and
Egypt has shown that this unification cannot be achieved on a capitalist and anti-democratic basis.

Malumud Ata Alla, *Arab Struggle
for Economic Independence*

Although no precise date can ever be given for the occurrence of the
Marxist "moment of enthusiasm" for any country, the end of 1959
comes close to being the occasion of that moment in Egypt. At that
time, President Nasser had consolidated his regime. He had successfully
opted for a pan-Arabist foreign policy. The United Arab Republic had
been established, and all other Arab governments were on the defen-
sive. Domestically the National Union had been organized, elections
had been held, a parliament convened, and local "party" elections held
throughout the countryside. Nasser had emerged with firm control in
his own country and unchallenged as the dominant figure in regional
international relations. The president of Egypt, a son of the soil and a
speaker of the native tongue, appeared to be a remarkable, even a
charismatic, reflection of the spirit and values of the people he governed.

It is true that the Iraqi revolution, under Kassem and with the support of the Iraqi Communist Party, had refused Egyptian leadership and
had raised the question of social and economic reform. The Egyptian
revolution had attempted to avoid the class question and to put aside
the issue of whether a revolution required the adoption of socialist goals.
The elimination of class conflict is not quite the same thing as pursuing
the class struggle until victory is attained. Egyptian land reform did not
eliminate rural class differences nor even the political phenomenon of

landed wealth itself. The emerging tension between the Syrian Ba'th leaders and Nasser's government forbode controversies over both the nature of Nasser's Arabism and his notions of Arab socialism. If there were signs that American policy might shift toward the support of Egypt as the most viable exponent of the legitimate aspirations of Arab nationalism, there was also the beginning of Soviet political pressure on Egypt because of Nasser's attacks on Kassem of Iraq. Nor should we forget that in wresting power from Naguib, Nasser had decisively alienated both the Wafdist bourgeoisie and the Islamic fundamentalist Muslim Brethren. It would not be easy for Nasser to work with a right wing coalition.

Because of the unavailability of a truly bourgeois and religious alternative, Nasser's regime was not simply Bonapartist. The urban bourgeois support for Nasser was not negligible, but it was not simply enthusiastic either. These urban elements had specific economic and ideological demands. Nasser's rural support was, on the contrary, more enthusiastic than materially interested—although we must remember that their modest landed property was not yet threatened by the limited land reform which had taken place. Their support was nonideological in the sense that they neither proposed nor supported a doctrinaire program. It was sufficient that the regime be opened to them, that government and people be identified, not in any formal democratic sense, but in terms of culture, access to political positions, and the distribution of honors.

As we have noted, the National Union was not really an instrument of political mobilization. It was rather an instrument to preclude political mobilization by rival groups. It was a vehicle for the expression of enthusiastic support, and it is for this reason that the study of the structure of the National Union in 1959 is of particular importance. The National Union of 1959 reflects the geographical and class basis of political forces which have been largely left out of account in orthodox Marxist analyses of class conflict. Even when the rural notables are taken into account, it is generally assumed that they are automatically allied to the bourgeoisie by a Bonapartist leader. Nasser, instead, sought to resist the influence of the bourgeoisie without enhancing the influence of radical elements among the intelligentsia and the laboring classes. He relied on the sentiments of the rural middle class and of the abna' al-balad.[1]

Hans Kohn, in *The Idea of Nationalism*, identifies the clerks and the intelligentsia as the nationalist groups.[2] These social segments are not moved by class interests. They are prone to abstract ideological formulations and to arcane expressions of false consciousness. They are déclassé and their nationalist policies, when successful, fix regimes in arrangements that forestall the social processes predicted by Marx and Engels. There was, of course, no such nationalist segment in Egypt. The intelligentsia was certainly involved in the struggle against British imperialism and against royal autocracy. Some intellectuals, influenced by European models, did raise the question of the cultural identity of Egypt. Was it Muslim, pharaonic, European, or Arab? None of the proposed solutions seriously faced the fundamental question of how a relatively cosmopolitan elite could be linked to the rural and urban masses of Egypt. The strength of European nationalist movements lay in their ability to evoke enthusiastic responses from the masses, even if only for a moment. These moments, for Egypt, were in 1879, 1919, and perhaps in 1936—all revolutionary movements, and all directed against foreign imperialist influence. The 1936 demonstrations against British imperialism were essentially urban, but the 1879 revolt was led by rural notables and the 1919 revolt occurred for the most part in rural areas. The intelligentsia of Hans Kohn, although doubtlessly influential elsewhere in the Arab world, was not a significant political element in Egypt. This is indeed the message of Hourani, of Jamal Ahmed, of Safran, of Anwar 'Abd al-Malik, and of Charles Smith.[3] The intelligentsia and its varied attempts to formulate the content of Egyptian nationalism did not mediate the political coalition between Nasser and the rural notability, except insofar as they influenced the young Nasser.

The National Union itself was the means by which Nasser evoked the support of the rural notability, and it was by means of this instrumentality that Nasser could resist the pressures of both the urban right and the urban left while preventing either one of them from recruiting rural support. Or, we might say, that so long as the National Union could be maintained as a nonmobilizing structure for so long would Nasser be able to resist these pressures. If, on the other hand, the National Union was used either as a means of social transformation or as a vehicle for the expression of the policy preferences of its members, then the politics of enthusiasm would begin to be transformed into the politics of class interest. That process began in 1960 and its first important manifestation was in the passage of the July Socialist Laws of 1961.

Anwar 'Abd al-Malik and others have described the importance of the July Socialist Laws. He points out that their origin was in the announcement of a third five-year plan in 1959 and in the declaration by Nasser (against much expert advice) that national income would be doubled in ten years.[4] The pressure for this sort of rash policy determination came from the opposition of the intelligentsia, the criticism of the Ba'th, the propaganda war with Iraq, and the tension with the Soviet Union. Early in 1960, attempts were made to restrict the profits of Egyptian companies and to mobilize their capital for the third plan. Egyptian capitalists successfully resisted these efforts so an even more stringent program of capital mobilization was attempted in July 1961. These decrees, afterwards ratified by the assembly, did not in fact institute a socialist economy. The cotton trade was Egyptianized and brought under close government control. Corporations were compelled to distribute some profits to workers, taxes were raised, and maximum limits were set on the ownership of shares in joint-stock companies. A large number of corporations were nationalized wholly or in part against compensation. These laws were in fact a hodgepodge of regulations aimed at mobilizing capital, preventing the flight of capital, plugging loopholes in the regulations limiting corporate profits, preventing the shift of corporate profits to wealthy insiders, providing some managerial positions in industry for members of the ruling military-bureaucratic establishment, as well as answering critics of the regime on the left, in Baghdad, and in Moscow.

The July laws did not eliminate private property. Their major consequence was to create a larger and more powerful public sector which was now to become a labyrinth of bureaucratic power, in effect establishing a multiplicity of commercial, financial, and communications fiefdoms. By the summer of 1961 this move had long been anticipated in Egypt and was foreshadowed in Syria by new restrictions on the flight of capital. The repercussions in Egypt, where the commercial and industrial bourgeoisie were already submissive, were not very great. In Syria, however, the reaction to the July laws was decisive, not only for the breakup of the United Arab Republic, but for the demise of the National Union in Egypt and the gradual sharpening of the social issue in Egyptian politics.

At 9:00 A.M. on 28 September 1961 President Nasser addressed the Egyptian nation from the Cairo broadcasting station and announced that "A small group of army troops have moved from Katana camp seized the broadcasting station in Damascus, surrounded the Army Headquarters there, and broadcast a number of statements."[5] Later that night in another speech Nasser stated that he would not accept a bargained solution. Still comparing the Syrian coup with foreign, or anti-Arab, aggression, Nasser said, "This means that the rebellion was conducted only by a small force from the Katana barracks and that it has not been supported by the people."[6] On September 29, Nasser again spoke, revealing that he had first decided to send troops to Syria but then rescinded his order. He declared that the rebels had all along been separatists and that they had raised a few grievances of the military only to gain time and to mislead the people. The people were against the rebellion. "The people of Damascus came out to demonstrate. They were not afraid of the tanks or machine-guns. . . . What happened yesterday in Aleppo? The Aleppans demonstrated. . . . The Arab people were not deceived. . . . What was the reaction of the people in Deir El Zor, Latakia, Hama and Homs? The people rose to defend the union they had established."[7] But Nasser decided to avoid a battle in which the blood of the people would be shed by the mutineers, and he recalled his troops.

There is no need to expatiate on the extent and depth of the trauma of the Syrian separation. Indeed a restricted number of military officers with a variety of grievances and having important connections with the small Syrian bourgeoisie did succeed in less than two days in severing their links with the United Arab Republic and in dealing Nasser a political blow from which he never recovered. Many observers have pointed to the irony of the occurrence of Nasser's premature death nine years later on the anniversary of the separation.

In his 16 October 1961 speech, Nasser made a brief and pointed analysis of the coup, deriving two lessons therefrom. The first was that the reactionaries, the capitalists, and the feudalists had abused the good intentions of those who had urged the "possibilities of removing class distinctions peacefully within the framework of national unity."[8] The second was that the United Arab Republic had erred in establishing a deficient popular organization: "Consequently, reaction managed to infiltrate into the National Union . . . and to turn it into a mere organizational facade, unstirred by the forces of the masses. . . . some of those who are in the front ranks of the separatist reactionary movement in Syria, had been themselves in the front rank of the National Union organization. Hence the most important thing that faces us today is to reorganize so that the National Union may become a revolutionary instrument for the national masses. . . . The National Union should be for the workers, peasants, educated people, professionals and proprietors whose property is not based on exploitation, for officers and soldiers. . . ."[9] On 4 November 1961 Nasser announced a program for the reorganization of the National Union as the Arab Socialist Union.

Earlier we pointed out both the shortcomings and the probable political meaning of this second reorganization of the mass, single, party of Egypt. That analysis emphasized the symbolic significance of reaffirming the legitimacy of the regime through a ritual reorganization of the mass popular organization. The major purpose of the National Union was to prevent the continuation of prerevolutionary party activity and, evidently, not to mobilize. This perspective, and the substantial evidence for it, has been widely accepted; but we must also consider its anomalous aspects. There is no doubt that the Syrian secession was a grave political blow. Did that event evoke only a tactical and a "public relations" response, or did it cause some serious rethinking and at least a modicum of ideological change?

Nasser's speeches indicate that he believed that the National Union organization had failed to develop popular forces that could withstand counterrevolution, and that elements of the traditional landed elite and of the haute bourgeoisie had been able to exploit the legitimate standing which they had been given by the National Union. The indicated conclusion was that the same thing could happen in Egypt if the masses were not better organized and if the financial power of the old upper classes were not further restricted. These materialist-ideological conclusions were, however, beclouded by Nasser's reaffirmation of the legitimacy of "nonexploitative" private property, by his emphasis on the importance of indoctrination, and by his reference to the need to improve the efficiency of the administration. At the heart of the matter is the question of whether there are in fact or were for Egypt only two alternatives, a proletarian revolution or a repressive plutocracy. It is apparent that Nasser sought another alternative, so he stopped far short of turning the National Union into a revolutionary "cadre party"—to the dismay of the Egyptian left. Thus, as Nasser made clear in a long rambling speech at the opening session of the Preparatory Committee, there were two major tasks to be performed. The first was to purge or politically "isolate" the forces of reaction, and the second was to identify the popular forces. In point of fact, Nasser intended no more than a formal reorganization of the National Union, new parliamentary elections and further sequestrations of the property of the wealthiest families. The reorganization of the popular political organization was to be accomplished in four steps. First, a Preparatory Committee was to meet in November 1961. Second, the Congress of Popular Forces, the composition of which was determined by the Preparatory Committee, was to meet in the spring of 1962 and adopt a National Charter. Third, a new popular organization to be known as the Arab Socialist Union (ASU) was to be organized from the ground up. Fourth, a new National Assembly was to be elected.

The Preparatory Committee met from late November until the end of December, completing the regulations for the political disqualifications of the reactionaries and determining the representation of the popular forces. During January 1962 the fruit of the efforts of the Preparatory Committee were promulgated, and elections to the Congress of Popular Forces were held in factories, schools, professional syndicates and agricultural cooperatives during February. The Congress of Popular Forces met on 21 May 1962 and set about debating and then, after debate, adopting the National Charter of the Arab Socialist Union without change or amendment as presented by President Nasser. The Congress of Popular Forces also decided that at least 50% of the membership of every popular council and of the National Assembly would have to be either workers or peasants, and they went on to define what was meant by those terms. On 30 July 1962 the congress completed its deliberations.

On 2 July 1962 President Nasser presented the congress with the program for the organization of the Arab Socialist Union. In addition to provisions reserving 50% of the seats on all committees to workers and peasants, the new organization was to be comprised of a dual system of congresses and committees at the village or workplace level, at the district level, at the province level, and finally at the national level. The congresses would include all the committee members from the lower level units. Each congress would elect a committee to carry on the work of the ASU between congress meetings. Thus, the congress is supreme, but the committee is the more active and politically significant organization. The most powerful groups of all were, of course, the Central Committee of the ASU to be elected by the General Congress and the Higher Executive Committee to be elected by the Central Committee.

The details of the program of organization of the ASU were to be completed by October 1962, after which actual organization was to proceed. Furthermore, in accordance with Nasser's pronouncement of 4 November 1961, the General Congress of the ASU was to decide upon the timing and manner of the election of the National Assembly.

On 24 September 1962 President Nasser kicked off the organization of the ASU, announcing that the transitional period had come to an end and that the new era of nation building had begun. The president, himself, would supervise the process of organizing the ASU; and in order to free himself from other duties he proposed to establish a Presidential Council to share presidential responsibilities. It is not clear whether the new Presidential Council was a way of kicking certain people upstairs, or whether it was meant to solve political problems such as the relationship among some of the closest collaborators of Nasser. At any rate, a Presidential Council was created with 'Ali Sabri as its chairman. This council was to act as the temporary Higher Executive Committee of the ASU. One of the earliest acts of the Higher Executive Committee was to appoint a temporary Central Committee comprised of 40 members, including all twelve members of the previously appointed General Secretariat of the ASU.

In November the Higher Executive Committee formally issued the regulations for the organization of the ASU, stipulating that there were to be two types of basic unit. In addition to the residential unit or committee, there were also to be committees at the place of employment.[10]

The basic unit committees were to be reelected every two years, the district and province level committees were to serve for four years, and the Central Committee was to be reelected after six years. Altogether 6,889 basic units were set up, of which 2,442 were at places of employment and 4,447 were residential.

Unlike the National Union, no one was automatically a member of the ASU. The membership rolls were opened for application on 1 January 1963 and the first registration period closed on 20 January. Although, the intention was presumably to start selectively with a small militant group of members, the first registration numbered 4,885,932 candidate members. The Central Committee labored to purge the list of the politically disqualified, and the rest were accepted as active members. Under the supervision of the Central Committee candidates for membership of village committees of 20 were nominated from 6 April to 12 April 1963. Elections to these committees were held on 12 May 1963, and the following week the election committees of the Higher Executive Committee had to resolve some 5283 election appeals. The secretary and assistant secretary of these basic unit committees (except for the university committees, because of a conflict with the exam period) were then elected on 10 June 1963.[11] All those elected were supposed to be able to read and write. The one receiving the most votes was to be the secretary and the one receiving the second highest number of votes was to be assistant secretary.

The province congress was organized before the district level congress, for reasons unexplained. Each basic unit elected two delegates to the province congress and at least one of the two had to be a peasant or worker. This process was completed on 7 September 1963.[12] Nominations were then opened for election to the provincial committees (twenty members plus two from each district) but so many names were put in nomination (1800 in Cairo alone) that it was decided to postpone those elections until the provincial congressmen had had time to work together and to develop a leadership. In the meantime temporary provincial committees were appointed by the Higher Executive Committee and, early in 1964, those elected to the National Assembly in each province were added to the temporary provincial committee. These temporary provincial committees now presided over the formation of the district level committees. Presumably the members of the provincial congress hailing from each district comprised the district congress. The district congress elected the district (or bandar) committees on 18 January 1964; and on 1 February 1964 the district secretaries and assistant secretaries were elected. Before this aspect of the organization of the ASU was completed, applications for ordinary membership were once again accepted from 20 November to 26 November 1963. At the end of 1963 the Higher Executive Committee issued a regulation providing for the means by which "affiliated" (candidate) members could become active (militant) members.[13] Only active members could vote or hold office, and each of these was to be elevated from mere affiliation by the Higher Executive Committee itself on the basis of at least two semi-annual reports filed by the basic unit committee.

Following the organization of the ASU, preparations were made for elections to the National Assembly. The number of members of the assembly was fixed at 350, to be elected from 175 constituencies. At least one member from each constituency was to be a worker or peasant. The candidate's deposit was reduced from the usual LE150 to LE20—not a negligible sum. All candidates had to have been active members of the ASU for at least one year—although it is not clear how this was possible in 1964.[14] Nominations for the National Assembly were closed on 1 March 1964.

No fewer than 3,570 nomination papers had been requested by those who wished to contest 350 seats. Once again it was feared that confusion would result, and it was argued that perhaps the ASU ought to select a limited number of candidates. Ultimately, though, it was decided that there would be no restrictions on the candidacies for the National Assembly. In a way, therefore, the candidacies for the assembly were more open than those for any ASU office above the district level. Ultimately only 1,748 candidates actually entered the elections on 10 March 1964 and paid their deposits. Run-off elections were held on 19 March 1964 in 147 constituencies in which 482 candidates remained viable (down to two candidates per seat instead of five candidates).[15] The candidates were admonished not to attack or criticize one another since all represented the same ideology. Campaigning proceeded by personal contact, hanging posters, and by means of public meetings organized by the ASU at which all candidates were introduced to the voters. The government considered offering campaign loans to seventy peasants and may have done so. The Executive Committee of the Federation of Labor Unions decided in principle to offer such loans to as many as 600 labor candidates. The 107 candidates (30%) who won outright on 10 March received more than 50% of the vote in their constituencies. The remaining 243 winning candidates needed only the minimum of 20% of the vote but most received much more because of the small number of candidates. The newly elected National Assembly met on 26 March 1964 to begin debating the new draft constitution of the United Arab Republic, and on the same day President Nasser announced a new organization of the executive branch of the government. In place of the Presidential Council there would now be four vice-presidents (a first vice-president and three others) and a prime minister. 'Ali Sabri, who had been head of the Presidential Council, became the first prime minister under the new system.

The preceding chronological sketch of the reorganization of the political institutions of the United Arab Republic is meant to serve as context for our analysis of the relationship between the National Union elite and the ASU elite. In an earlier work I analyzed the social composition of the Preparatory Committee, the Congress of Popular Forces, and the assembly of 1964 and I drew the following conclusions.

> Thus the Preparatory Committee represents something approximating real power structure at the national level, the Congress of Popular Forces represents a rationalized ideal of a national cross section . . . and the Parliament represents at once the degree to which Egyptian society has not been penetrated by the revolution and also the measure of support which Egyptian society is willing to give the revolutionary regime. . . . Despite the wide representation of nearly all classes at the lowest levels of the mass party, the upward recruitment procedure has been selective enough to provide for the predominance of the most supportive element of all, the rural middle class and its urban offshoots.[16]

That confident conclusion asserted that there was little change in the class basis of the Egyptian regime from 1959 to 1964 despite the adoption of the charter and despite the trauma of the Syrian secession. That conclusion was also drawn on the basis of occupational categories rather than upon the continuity of the same individuals or families in positions of influence. In what follows we will extend the previous analysis by including some data on the ASU, we will try to indicate areas of change as well as continuity, and we will give some indication of regional differences.

As we have seen, the organization of the ASU was carefully prepared and was carried out in no less than fourteen months. Nevertheless, despite discussion about militant members, and despite the requirement that ordinary members take the initiative to enroll, the more than four million members were in fact indiscriminately enrolled. The party remained a mass party and not a cadre party. All members were automatically militants after the first enrollment. Only 1.5% of the January 1963 applicants were disqualified and only 7% of the November applicants were refused membership.

The representatives of the Higher Executive Committee presided over all committee elections, however, and might well have exercised decisive influence in many places. Instead of being organized from the bottom up, the ASU was organized from the top down to the province level, and then from the bottom up to the district level. There results a curious and potentially politically significant gap in the transmission belt of influence between the district and the province. Nevertheless, the candidates for the National Assembly were not handpicked by the Higher Executive Committee. Popular pressure caused 'Ali Sabri to relent on his decision to restrict the number of candidacies, and articles such as those of Muhammad Anis in *al-Ahram* helped persuade some officials to lend campaign funds to some of the poorer candidates.[17] The successful assembly candidates also became members of the provincial committees, thus linking up the lowest and the highest levels of the ASU and allowing us to compare the appointed and the elected members of the provincial committees. But perhaps the most important change from the NU to the ASU was the creation of nonresidential, workplace units in factories, government offices, and schools. Naturally, these units remained less numerous and less important in the largely agricultural provinces with which we have been concerned. Nevertheless, we must start by taking note of this new emphasis on nonagrarian representation in the ASU.

The total number of basic units organized was 6,888; of these 314 (4.6%) were urban units, 4,103 (59.5%) were rural, and 2,435 (35%) were from public and private establishments. All but 58 of the rural units were in the sixteen provinces we have studied. The totals for the sixteen agricultural provinces are 5,170 in all, of which 4,045 (78%) were rural, 168 (3.2%) were urban, and 963 (18.6%) were at places of employment. Nationwide, those who enrolled in January of 1963 comprised about 76% of all registered voters. For some reason Dumyat, al-Qalyubiyyah, and Kafr al-Shaykh fell far below this level (32%, 38%, and 48%, respectively) and al-Daqahliyyah and al-Buhayrah were way above (419%—probably a misprint—and 140%, respectively). The rest range from 69% to a high of 89%. Nationwide the percentage of workers and peasants among the ASU committees was 70%, and for the agricultural provinces it ranged from 58% in Dumyat to 79% in Qena. For all sixteen agricultural provinces there were 70% peasants and workers in the ASU basic unit committees.

Nationwide, 52% of the unit secretaries and assistant secretaries were peasants and workers, and in the agricultural provinces only 50% of the secretaries and assistant secretaries were peasants and workers.

The crucial question is how many of the National Union members continued to hold significant positions in the new Arab Socialist Union. As we have seen, only 1.5% of those who applied for membership were disqualified, but only 82 of 350 members of the 1964 National Assembly had been elected in 1959. While the almost anarchic profusion of assembly candidacies might explain the turnover in M.P.'s, elections at the village level were both more closely supervised and presumably more constrained by existing village social structure and status considerations. But any expected continuity of village level influence would be limited by the changes in the number and type of basic units. Table 98 compares the number of residential basic units in the NU with the number of residential basic units in the ASU. As we see, there were 12% fewer residential units in the sixteen agricultural provinces. We have already seen that 18.5% or so of all the basic units were workplace units. Hence only about 78% of the ASU residential units were also NU residential units, and the maximum expected continuity would be 78% also.

Table 98   Comparison of Basic Units of NU and ASU

Province	NU Basic Units	ASU Units in Which Elections Were Held	Work-place Units	ASU Residential Units	Decline in Residential Units
al-Qalyubiyyah	196	362	179	183	7.0%
al-Sharqiyyah	455	479	60	419	8.0
al-Daqahliyyah	430	478	93	385	10.5
Dumyat	62	75	20	55	11.3
Kafr al-Shaykh	205	213	31	182	11.2
al-Gharbiyyah	347	388	112	276	20.5
al-Manufiyyah	311	337	46	291	6.5
al-Buhayrah	385	475	53	422	(+9.5)
al-Jizah	177	268	152	116	34.5
al-Fayyum	169	170	22	148	12.5
Bani Suwayf	222	233	33	200	10.0
al-Minia	350	352	62	290	17.2
Assiut	247	259	63	196	20.6
Suhaj	276	273	28	245	11.3
Qena	210	202	28	174	17.2
Aswan	80	99	47	52	35.0
Total	4,122	4,663	1,029	3,634	12.0%

NU-ASU continuity was measured by comparing the names of the ASU secretaries and assistant secretaries with the names of the members of the NU basic unit committees. If the ASU officials were also members of the basic unit committee of the NU, we shall say that they have retained their political influence. The list of secretaries and assistant secretaries is derived from a list of basic units which is more extensive than that used for table 98, but this list also shows that there were about 13% more ASU units in the sixteen provinces than there were in the NU. Of the 9,186 names of secretaries and assistant secretaries, 5,527 or 60% were found to correspond with the same or very similar names in the NU committee list. Of the total, 3,629 names, or 39.5%, were identical with those of NU committee members, and 16.75% (1,538) of the secretaries and assistant secretaries were linked with NU family sets. Thus, about 28% of all the located secretaries and assistant secretaries were members of family sets, a much higher percentage than that of the NU committee members who were not officers. If one takes into account that about 13% of the basic units of the ASU were not found in the NU list and that most of these were not residential units but workplace units, it appears that there was little political turnover in the sixteen agricultural provinces at the "grass roots" level. If we take account of the units not on the NU list, then our level of continuity of village-level influence rises to 69%.

The same sort of conclusion can be drawn from a comparison of the occupational data on the secretaries and assistant secretaries on the one hand with the data on those NU members linked to the ASU secretaries on the other. Table 99 presents this data and, as we see, there is hardly any significant difference with the great bulk of both groups being either 'umad or farmers, with teachers, merchants, and civil servants being next most important. The only differences that seem worthy of note are between the secretaries and the assistant secretaries. These differences are not very surprising, and, in any case, they do not mitigate the major conclusion, which is that there were no great political or social (occupational) changes at the bottom level of ASU organization.

As we have seen, the Higher Executive Committee appointed the members of the provincial committees in two installments. The first group was simply appointed from the members of the provincial congress. The second group was composed of those elected to the National Assembly. Since National Assembly candidates had been nominated without much interference from the Higher Executive Committee, it appeared interesting to compare the first and the second installments of the provincial committee, and to compare them both with the

National Union equivalent. Unfortunately, we do not have the names of members of the National Union provincial committees, if there were any. Instead we have decided to compare the ASU provincial committee members with the NU district officers.

We found that 27% of the members of the provincial committees of the ASU had been district officers in the NU. Interestingly enough, only 24% of the appointed group had been district officers, while 33% of those elected to the National Assembly in 1964 had been district officers. Only 23% of the M.P.'s elected in 1964 had been M.P.'s in 1959. The continuity of district level influence was slightly higher at 27%.

Table 99   Distribution of Occupations of ASU
                                       Secretaries and Assistant Secretaries
                                       and Related NU Committee
                                       Members

Occupation	Secretaries	Assistant Secretaries	Secretaries and Assistant Secretaries	Related NU Committee Members
High government official				.03%
Cabinet minister				.03
Doctor	.9%	.5%	.7%	.8
Lawyer	3.0	2.3	2.8	3.1
Businessman	.6	.6	.6	.7
Teacher	7.6	12.6	9.6	8.7
Former M.P.	2.6	.6	1.8	1.6
Engineer	2.8	1.2	2.2	2.5
Student	.5	.7	.6	1.1
Merchant	4.9	6.6	5.6	5.4
Journalist	.05	.07	.06	.08
Ex-army or ex-police officer	.2	.07	.14	.3
Civil servant	5.6	7.2	6.3	6.6
Worker	.5	.8	.6	.7
Local council member	.9	1.2	1.0	1.2
ʿUlamaʾ	.9	1.9	1.3	1.1
ʿUmdah	37.7	23.6	32.1	29.4
Farmer	27.7	34.6	30.4	32.8
Unknown	3.3	5.3	4.1	3.9
Total	99.75	99.84	99.9	100.04

It appears that the class composition of the district/provincial elites did not change greatly from 1959 to 1964. A certain number of well-known family names are missing in 1964, but the rural notability is more influential in the aggregate than as individuals. Political purges seem to have had less effect on limiting district level influence continuity to 27% than the impact of Higher Executive Committee selection and the constraints of two member constituencies with roughly equal demographic bases. Thus the most important political conclusions to be drawn do not sustain the view that the ASU became radicalized, but rather that there was some tendency to tighten control over some levels of the party by the center. There is little evidence that local notables and their relatives were being passed over, but some indication that alternative members of the rural middle class were being selected at the provincial and parliamentary levels.

We have emphasized the fact that the M.P.'s were apparently elected with little central control. It is, therefore, significant that 23% of those originally appointed as members of the provincial committees were also subsequently elected as M.P.'s; and of this group, more than half had been district officers in 1959. Thus even in the centrally selected group there remained a great many with strong local support and long-standing influence. The distinction between the two groups is not great and should not be exaggerated. Nevertheless, five years is a short time as these things go, so that the personnel changes made between 1959 and 1964 may, in retrospect, turn out to be more important than they now seem.

If there were even slight indications of a trend to be discerned in the preferences of the central apparatus, these indications might reveal whether the Higher Executive Committee preferred those of greater or lesser traditional status. Our best measure of traditional status is descent from prerevolutionary M.P.'s. The total number of descendants among the members of the provincial committees was 69, or 15% of all members. About 58% of these descendants were appointed in the second installment of members of the provincial committees; and just under 50% of all descendants had been NU district officers. A little more than 40% of the descendants were 1964 M.P.'s and had also been district officers in 1959. The descendants certainly retained a good deal of influence.

Presumably, members of the National Assembly are more influential than those appointed to the provincial committees, but, as we have seen, some M.P.'s were appointed to the provincial committees only after their election to the assembly. Furthermore, we have noted that only 82 of the 1959 assembly members were reelected in 1964. We have not taken this as indicating a wholesale change in the social basis of the regime, but simply as an indication of the broad stratum of those eligible for service in the assembly. It is, therefore, interesting to note that for the sixteen provinces 68 former M.P.'s were reelected in 1964 or just a little above the 23% for the whole country. But this number was unevenly distributed over the provinces, as we see in table 100. The provinces in which the largest percentage of former M.P.'s were reelected were al-Sharqiyyah, al-Jizah, al-Fayyum, and al-Minia, all provinces in which the traditional large family set, rural middle class was strong. We are not surprised to find the lowest reelection percentages in al-Daqahliyya, Bani Suwayf, and Aswan.

Table 100   Provincial Distribution of Percentage of Members of National Assembly of 1964 Who Had Been Members of the National Assembly of 1959

Province	Percentage of Total 1964 Members
al-Qalyubiyyah	21.4
al-Sharqiyyah	33.3
al-Daqahliyyah	11.5
Dumyat	16.7
Kafr al-Shaykh	16.7
al-Gharbiyyah	23.8
al-Manufiyyah	20.0
al-Buhayrah	18.0
al-Jizah	35.3
al-Fayyum	41.7
Bani Suwayf	8.3
al-Minia	59.1
Assiut	27.8
Suhaj	18.2
Qena	20.0
Aswan	--
All 16 provinces	24.8

Turning now to the provincial distribution of the secretaries and assistant secretaries of the basic units of the ASU, we find much less variation. Table 101 presents four distributions: first, the percentage of ASU units corresponding to units of the NU; second, the percentage of ASU secretary names corresponding to similar NU committee member names; third, the percentage of ASU secretary names corresponding to NU family-set names; and fourth, the percentage of ASU secretary names corresponding to names which are exactly the same in the NU register.

It will be noted that there is a considerable discrepancy between the data on located units presented here and the data on the number of agricultural units in the ASU presented in table 98. Table 98 is based on official aggregated statistics, whereas table 101 is based upon our checking of listed basic units. The listing from which our data was compiled was also dated later than the official statistics. It is, therefore, likely that our own data (table 101) are more correct.

In table 102 we provide an index of the continuity of NU personnel in the ASU, controlling for the percentage of identical basic units. That

Table 101   Provincial Distribution of ASU
                                           Secretaries and Assistant Secretaries

Province	Units Located	Corresponding to NU Names	Corresponding to NU Family-Set Names	Names Exactly Same as NU Names
al-Qalyubiyyah	60.22%	58.37%	19.60%	38.76%
al-Sharqiyyah	89.55	57.06	16.89	40.27
al-Daqahliyyah	87.62	54.28	13.38	40.57
Dumyat	94.94	49.33	9.33	36.66
Kafr al-Shaykh	94.02	61.44	20.18	40.58
al-Gharbiyyah	89.57	59.29	25.53	39.57
al-Manufiyyah	84.98	62.70	19.93	47.42
al-Buhayyah	87.67	56.18	21.25	37.09
al-Jizah	79.35	47.84	16.86	32.35
al-Fayyum	95.19	52.24	18.82	37.35
Bani Suwayf	98.45	61.61	13.38	45.47
al-Minia	87.05	63.34	16.99	45.92
Assiut	82.81	68.65	14.28	47.81
Suhaj	97.37	51.68	8.61	37.75
Qena	97.84	51.10	11.72	34.73
Aswan	89.52	44.14	5.85	27.47
All 16 provinces	87.04%	60.16%	16.74%	39.50%

table shows us that the continuity (for the agricultural and residential units, of course) was highest in al-Qalyubiyyah and Assiut, and lowest in Dumyat, Qena, and Aswan. The figure for al-Qalyubiyyah is artificially inflated because of the larger number of workplace units established by the ASU. Actually the level of continuity in the agricultural units of al-Qalyubiyyah is the same as elsewhere.

The family-set members maintained roughly the same relative position province by province as they had in the NU, except that al-Gharbiyyah appears to be a little higher and al-Jizah a little lower than expected. Table 103 presents the percentages of family-set members in the NU and the percentage of family-set members among the ASU secretaries. As we see in the third column of table 103, the percentage of family-set members among the ASU secretaries was about 42% higher than was to be expected. The higher than expected percentage of family-set members was fairly uniform throughout the country, with the greatest discrepancy being no more than −2.5% in Kafr al-Shaykh.

Table 102   Index of Continuity of NU Per-
                                       sonnel in ASU by Province

Province	Index
al-Qalyubiyyah	.97
al-Sharqiyyah	.64
al-Daqahliyyah	.62
Dumyat	.52
Kafr al-Shaykh	.65
al-Gharbiyyah	.66
al-Manufiyyah	.74
al-Buhayrah	.64
al-Jizah	.60
al-Fayyum	.55
Bani Suwayf	.63
al-Minia	.73
Assiut	.83
Suhaj	.53
Qena	.52
Aswan	.49
All 16 provinces	.69
Standard deviation	.1217
Mean	.645

Table 103   Percentage in Family Sets Compar-
                                       ing NU and ASU

Province	NU	ASU	Expected ASU Percentage	142% of Expected Percentage
al-Qalyubiyyah	24.5	19.6	14.3	20.3
al-Sharqiyyah	19.5	16.9	11.1	15.7
al-Daqahliyyah	16.7	13.4	9.1	12.9
Dumyat	12.6	9.3	6.2	8.8
Kafr al-Shaykh	26.1	20.2	16.0	22.7
al-Gharbiyyah	27.4	25.5	16.2	23.0
al-Manufiyyah	22.4	19.9	14.0	19.9
al-Buhayrah	25.9	21.3	14.5	20.6
al-Jizah	27.1	16.9	13.0	18.5
al-Fayyum	25.5	18.8	13.3	18.9
Bani Suwayf	13.4	13.4	8.3	11.8
al-Minia	16.9	17.0	10.7	15.2
Assiut	15.3	14.3	9.8	13.9
Suhaj	11.4	8.6	4.4	6.2
Qena	9.5	?	4.9	6.9
Aswan	3.8	?	1.7	2.4
All 16 provinces	19.5	16.7	11.7	16.6

These statistics are strong testimony to the continued influence of the rural middle class, but we must bear in mind that the ASU secretaries had a somewhat higher political status than did committee members of the NU basic units, and thus we would expect the percentage of family-set members to be higher unless the basis of political influence were substantially changed in the agricultural areas.

The occupational distribution for the ASU secretaries is presented in table 104. As anticipated, there are few surprises in this table. Usually from 50% to 60% of the secretaries were either 'umad or farmers. Teachers are prominent, but civil servants are fewer than expected. Merchants and professionals (doctors, lawyers, engineers) are about as numerous as expected. We note a few exceptions, however, such as the large percentage of 'umad in al-Gharbiyyah and al-Minia, always an indication of traditional rural middle class dominance. Al-Buhayrah and al-Qalyubiyyah have about the same percentage 'umad, but 35% is high for al-Qalyubiyyah and low for al-Buhayrah. As expected, there are more 'umad than farmers in lower Egypt, and fewer 'umad in upper Egypt, but note the exception of al-Minia. The very high combined percentage of 'umad and farmers in al-Minia is a further indication of agrarian dominance. The weakness of the rural middle class in Qena is evidenced by the low percentage of 'umad.

There may be some signs of incipient change embedded in this occupational data, but they are difficult to discern. If anything, the requirement that workers and peasants constitute 50% of all ASU structures had a decidedly ruralizing effect upon the composition of the secretaries. Despite some early loose talk about barring 'umad from holding office, it is apparent that few poor peasants were elected as unit secretaries, and that the 'umad (and the village cooperative boards) were back in charge of local affairs.

At the province level there are, however, some interesting differences in elite continuities. Table 105 presents data on those members of the temporary (appointed) provincial committees who had held important positions in the NU. Our purpose in presenting all of this material in one table is to demonstrate the consistency with which a segment of the traditional elite appears to maintain its position in certain provinces. Al-Minia and Suhaj show the greatest carry-over of the 1959 influentials and the greatest concentration of influence. Al-Fayyum and al-Buhayrah show more traditional influence from prerevolutionary times. Al-Qalyubiyyah also demonstrates a considerable degree of both continuity and concentration of influence, as does al-Sharqiyyah. This pattern suggests that the greatest turnover of political personnel occurred in those provinces which had the largest and least stratified rural middle

Table 104

Distribution of Occupations of ASU
Secretaries and Assistant Secretaries

Province	ʿUmdah	Farmer	Teacher	Civil Servant	Merchant	Professional	Clergy	Former M.P.	Armed Forces
al-Qalyubiyyah	35.8%	15.9%	18.2%	7.4%	5.1%	7.4%	1.1%	2.3%	0.0%
al-Sharqiyyah	30.9	26.1	8.4	7.4	7.1	9.0	.8	2.1	.5
al-Daqahliyyah	32.7	28.5	7.7	7.1	5.8	6.1	1.1	1.1	.3
Dumyat	23.6	14.5	14.5	9.1	21.8	7.2	1.8	1.8	0.0
Kafr al-Shaykh	33.9	31.6	2.8	4.5	6.8	6.8	.6	2.8	0.0
al-Gharbiyyah	41.5	22.0	9.6	6.4	3.2	5.8	2.9	1.3	0.0
al-Manufiyyah	30.2	23.4	20.7	9.5	5.8	5.4	.3	1.0	.3
al-Buhayrah	35.4	33.3	7.0	3.8	5.0	6.7	.3	.9	0.0
al-Jizah	24.8	31.5	9.0	7.9	9.7	6.4	2.3	4.2	.6
al-Fayyum	26.3	30.1	10.5	7.5	7.5	5.3	0.0	3.0	0.0
Bani Suwayf	31.6	35.9	9.1	10.0	3.5	3.9	.8	.9	0.0
al-Minia	40.1	37.0	5.2	3.1	1.8	3.6	.4	1.2	0.0
Assiut	33.2	38.2	7.9	3.7	5.4	4.1	0.0	2.1	0.0
Suhaj	23.9	39.4	10.1	3.2	5.9	2.7	.4	2.7	0.0
Qena	14.6	45.2	12.7	2.5	5.7	5.1	6.4	3.2	0.0
Aswan	31.1	32.8	1.6	11.5	4.9	1.6	1.3	0.0	0.0
All 16 provinces	32.1%	30.4%	9.6%	6.3%	5.6%	5.7%	3.3	1.8%	.14%

class, that is, al-Gharbiyyah, al-Manufiyyah, Kafr al-Shaykh, and al-Jizah.

We have no data for district level committees of the ASU, but by tracing the 1959 district officers in the provincial committees it was possible to construct a map showing those districts in which 1959 officers were appointed to the temporary provincial committees of 1964. Map 40 illustrates this distribution. We note that although there were four officers for each district, no more than three were appointed to the provincial committees in any district.

Table 105   Provincial Elite Continuities between
                                         the NU and the ASU

Province	ASU Provincial Committee Members Who Had Been, in 1959:				
	NU Officers	NU Officers, also M.P.'s in 1964	Descendants	Descendants, Officers and Were M.P.'s in 1964	ʿIzbah-owning Officers
al-Qalyubiyyah	29.6%	42.8%	14.8%	75.0%	50.0%
al-Sharqiyyah	32.4	37.5	14.7	60.0	19.0
al-Daqahliyyah	24.4	23.0	14.6	16.7	13.0
Dumyat	15.8	33.3	5.2	0	0
Kafr al-Shaykh	18.8	16.7	12.5	0	0
al-Gharbiyyah	27.3	38.1	18.2	0	12.0
al-Manufiyyah	27.6	20.0	13.8	25.0	11.0
al-Buhayrah	33.3	40.9	20.0	66.7	24.0
al-Jizah	17.8	29.4	8.9	25.0	0
al-Fayyum	30.0	33.3	20.0	50.0	28.0
Bani Suwayf	15.4	16.7	7.7	50.0	31.0
al-Minia	55.2	63.6	20.7	62.5	45.0
Assiut	18.2	27.8	11.1	33.3	0
Suhaj	43.8	40.9	21.9	57.1	50.0
Qena	22.6	25.0	19.4	16.7	0
Aswan	22.6	50.0	5.6	(100.0)	0
All 16 provinces	27.6%	34.0%	15.1%	40.1%	24.0%

The officers were not concentrated in any one area, and the phenomenon of middle elite continuity was not regional. There are large blank areas in Kafr al-Shaykh, Bani Suwayf, and Assiut. Only for Kafr al-Shaykh does this seem surprising. The darker shading is concentrated in al-Qalyubiyyah and generally east of the Damietta branch of the Nile, and in al-Minia and Suhaj. We might have expected a greater continuity of district level influence in the region where al-Buhayrah, al-Gharbiyyah, and Kafr al-Shaykh meet, but that group of districts is clearly outweighed by the districts at the southeast part of the delta.

Map 40   Number of NU District Officers
                                                  Returned to Provincial Committees
                                                  of the ASU, 1963–64

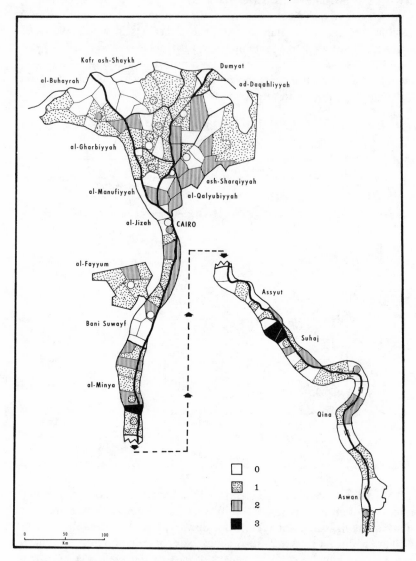

Here, indeed, may be some further evidence of a substructural trend
favoring the more traditional and highly stratified segment of the rural
middle class despite the employment of increasingly emphatic leftist
rhetoric. This trend may be explained as the result of the openness of

the assembly elections, which may have been but a temporary defeat of those ASU leaders who desired to strengthen the central apparatus at the expense of local influence structures. These issues of central as against local influence and of converting the ASU into an instrument of political control dominated the next phase of political organizational development in Egypt.

Fourteen

The Cadre Party and the Elections of 1968

> But the Vanguard of the Socialists did not fill the political vacuum that caused Gamal 'Abd al-Nasser sleepless nights.
>
> Ahmad Hamrush, *Mujtama'a Jamal 'Abd al-Nasir*

The reorganization of the national political organization in the guise of the Arab Socialist Union was part of the response of the Nasser government to the secession of Syria from the United Arab Republic. At certain times, during the period between the end of 1961 and mid-1964, the highest political authorities were intensely, if briefly, involved in this reorganization process. But, it should not be thought that the concern with the Arab Socialist Union was of the highest priority throughout the period. In point of fact, interest waned considerably as opportunities for international political maneuvers presented themselves and as economic problems mounted. The combination of these opportunities and pressures returned attention to the ASU for a time in 1965 and 1966; and in the aftermath of the defeat in the June War of 1967, the ASU was itself reorganized in 1968. In this chapter we will examine the events leading up to the 1968 reorganization, and we will see how far new political and ideological developments produced changes and compensatory reactions in the composition of the mass party.

During this period, an attempt, the seriousness of which is in question, was made to create within the ASU a militant cadre of socialist revolutionaries. This organization has been variously referred to as a political vanguard, a socialist party (as opposed to a Socialist Union), a political leadership, the vanguard of the socialists, and a political apparatus. Sometimes, it was called a militant-socialist-revolutionary-avant-garde-political apparatus, in the rather infelicitous Arabic rhetorical style of contemporary armchair intellectual leftists. It is clear, regardless of the terminology employed, that the creation of a militant ideological cadre would radically transform the Egyptian system and the political role of the ASU. The moment of enthusiasm would have been transformed into the political routinization of coordinated administrative and party apparatuses; and the bases of power would shift more completely from traditional social structures to bureaucratized party, government, and military structures.

It is safe to say that this experiment did not succeed, although we cannot conclude that it had no long run effects that may not surface at some time in the future. The traditional structure of relationships and attitudes prevailing in the rural provinces was not smashed, even if strained and, in a few villages, broken. Agriculture has not been harnessed to the wagon of development, and the smallholder member of the village cooperative society is still the mainstay of rural society. This failure is not astonishing, simply because a militant cadre is not likely to be successfully built on a nationwide scale in a year or two. It is further not surprising because a militant cadre is not likely to be installed in agricultural villages without a large number of violent incidents, as affluent peasants tenaciously resist forces they know will deprive them of their influence, their wealth, and the traditional marks of honor. What is surprising is that the experiment should have been tried at all, and, of course, once it was tried, that it was so abruptly abandoned. Before attempting to measure the impact of the cadre party experiment, we shall examine the events that moved Nasser toward acquiescing in the tightening of the mass political organization.

The Syrian secession was a great blow to the political influence and prestige of the Nasser regime, and its first response was to tighten political control on the home front. Virtually simultaneously, Egypt launched an attack on the "separatist regime" in Syria, accusing its leaders of being traitors to the cause of Arab unity, of being stooges of imperialism, and of being reactionary exploiters of the people.

The Syrian separatist regime was a shaky and narrow coalition, and it was brought down by a combination of internal and external pressures. In March 1963, approximately 18 months after the secession and about one month after the Kassem government in Iraq was overthrown by a coalition including important Ba'thi elements, the separatists were replaced by a coalition dominated by the Syrian Ba'th. The Ba'thi elements in power in Syria and in Iraq insisted on their commitment to Arab unity and felt in need of the popular legitimacy which

correct if not friendly relations with Egypt would bring. The question
of some new form of political unification was raised, and a series of
discussions, some might say debates, were held in Cairo throughout the
spring of 1963 in which political recriminations and ideological differences were aired in an extremely strained atmosphere. These discussions, the "tripartite talks," were surreptitiously recorded and afterwards
published in Egypt when they failed to produce any results.[1] It appears
that Nasser was willing to accept a verbal formula providing for a
paper political unification, in spite of his harsh criticism of the Syrian
Ba'th and in spite of his attempts to humiliate their leaders. But neither
the Syrian nor the Iraqi governments were strong enough to withstand
their own internal pressures. In the event, the radical wing of the Syrian
Ba'th increased its power while non-Ba'thi elements came to the fore in
Iraq. By the end of May it was clear that no common ground existed
and the agreement to work toward the unification of the three countries
was left unsigned. Nasser's apparent willingness to adhere to a mere
declaration of unificational aspirations is some indication of Egyptian
perceptions of the harm done by the separation. It further appears that
Nasser was stung by criticisms of the lack of ideological consistency in
Egyptian policy. In particular Nasser was made to feel the challenge
of the Ba'thi left by the manner in which the project was dropped.

During the same period Egypt became militarily involved in the
Yemen civil war. At the end of 1962 the Imam was overthrown by a
military coup aided by coastal, commercially interested elements. The
Shi'ite mountaineer tribesmen remained loyal to the Imam's son even
after a democratic Arab republic was declared. Nasser first threw his
political support behind the military, while Saudi Arabia, apprehensive
of an Egyptian threat to its oil wealth and its domination of the still
conservative Arabian peninsula, supported the "monarchists." Feeling
the need to recoup lost prestige and to regain the political initiative in
Arab affairs, Nasser began to commit troops to Yemen. Saudi Arabia
had no troops to send, but they did supply the monarchists with weapons and ammunition. On occasion Egyptian planes bombed Saudi towns
bordering on the monarchist-held areas of Yemen. Despite the superior
training and equipment of the regular Egyptian forces, they were unable to decide the issue, though they gained some initial successes. In
fact, Egypt became bogged down in Yemen, increasing its expeditionary
force to 25,000 in 1965 and to 40,000 in 1967, at enormous economic
cost and without substantial political or military gain.

The United States became concerned about the situation, fearing for
the security of the Saudi oil fields and worrying about the increasing

Egyptian dependence upon the Soviet Union for military support. The United States went so far as to recognize the Egyptian-backed government of al-Salal on the understanding that Egypt and Saudi Arabia would both agree to refrain from interfering in Yemeni affairs. The two Arab states did not trust one another and could not come to any agreement, and so the American policy of limited support for Nasserism (but not for the expansion of Egyptian political control) was changed. Under President Johnson considerable economic pressure was brought to bear on Egypt, first, to withdraw from Yemen and, second, to cease criticism of American policy in Viet Nam.

In 1964 Egypt was overcommitted in Yemen, pressed by Syria and other Arab states to take a more militant stand against the Israeli Jordan River project, and at an impasse in its relations with the United States. Influenced, in part, by Ben Bella and Sukarno, and encouraged by Khruschev, Nasser turned toward the Soviet Union for economic assistance and military support. Under Khruschev, Soviet policy toward neutralism and third world nationalism had virtually abandoned all ideological caution. Ben Bella's Algeria and Nasser's Egypt were declared to be on the noncapitalist road to development, and on the way to becoming socialist states. Both leaders were referred to as comrades and they were personally praised. Algeria was considered to be more genuinely revolutionary, however, and many Soviet leaders had grave doubts about the wisdom of a policy of unconditional support of what was essentially a bourgeois nationalist regime in Egypt. This tension was revealed during Khruschev's visit to Egypt in mid-1964 when he chided his hosts for being more committed to Arab nationalism than to proletarian revolution. Of course, Khruschev, himself, was responding to criticism of his own policies at home; and it is generally believed that among the reasons for his removal from office shortly after his visit to Egypt, was a severe skepticism regarding the revolutionary potential of Nasser's regime and others like it.

Despite the fact that there had been some tension between Nasser and Khruschev, Nasser certainly felt more comfortable with Khruschev than with his successors. It was not until mid-1965, at least, that a new understanding was worked out with the Soviet Union when, even though a considerably cooler relationship ensued, Soviet political and military support was secured. It is not clear what price Egypt had to pay for this support. Certainly relations with the United States remained bad, but that was due to differences between Egypt and the United States and not to Soviet influence. Indeed it was these differences that influenced Soviet policy rather than the expectation of close Soviet-

Egyptian cooperation. But there was at least one issue which had troubled Khruschev considerably and which was important to Khruschev's critics, and that issue was the status of Egyptian communists.

In the late 1950s and early 1960s many Egyptian communists were held in prisons and detention camps. There was continuous Soviet pressure to get the Egyptian government to relent as a condition of Egyptian-Soviet cooperation, but Egypt resisted. Matters came to a head in 1959, when Soviet support for the then communist-leaning Kassem regime in Iraq angered Nasser.[2] The Egyptian leader criticized the Soviet Union for interference in the internal affairs of Egypt, and he refused to release the communists from jail.

Nevertheless, as expectations of cooperation with the Kennedy administration were disappointed and with the demise of the Kassem regime, Nasser began to release some of the Egyptian communists. At the end of 1964, after Khruschev's removal from office, Nasser declared an amnesty for the great majority of the communists. A number of these communists were politically rehabilitated, and plans were made to issue a new monthly magazine to be edited by a group of communists, to be published by Muhammad Hasanain Haykal's *al-Ahram* Institute and to be called *al-Tali'ah* (The Vanguard). The first issue of *al-Tali'ah* came out in January 1965. In March and April of 1965, the Egyptian communists, or at least the Haditu faction, discussed the developmental stage through which Egypt was then passing and then resolved to disband the Egyptian Communist Party and to join the Arab Socialist Union as individuals. They declared the ASU, under Nasser's leadership, to have a genuine socialist and revolutionary potential and to be the best political vehicle for furthering their own revolutionary goals.

The term "al-tali'ah" and the vanguard concept were quite familiar and widely used in contemporary Arab political discourse. The Ba'th party, for example, considered itself to be a vanguard party and its publishing house was called Dar al-Tali'ah. The Leninist implications of the term were well known to many intellectuals and leftists. The concept also appears in the National Charter of the Arab Socialist Union—but, as various writers in *al-Tali'ah* pointed out, there is some ambiguity in the use of the concept in that document, and in the organic law of the ASU.

There are three relevant passages in the charter: one refers to the army acting as the vanguard of the nation in the 1952 revolution, another refers to Egypt as the vanguard of the Arab nation as a whole, and the third, which is of most interest here, states that "there is a dire need to create a new political organization within the framework of the

Arab Socialist Union, recruiting elements fit for leadership. . . ."[3] The
original Arabic makes the sense of this passage unequivocal. The term
for political organization is jihaz siyasi, or political apparatus, and
the phrase for "within the framework" leaves no doubt that the jihaz
referred to is not identical with the entire ASU.[4] It is this jihaz siyasi
or political apparatus which the Egyptian left insisted was to be the
political vanguard. But even they admitted that a passage in the pre-
amble to the organic law of the ASU has a contrary meaning.[5] There
the ASU itself is described as "the Socialist vanguard, which will lead
the masses, express its will, and direct national work . . . and the ASU
will conjoin—as a popular political organization [tandhim, not jihaz]—
the working forces of the people and will represent those forces in an
alliance within the framework of national unity."

It might be possible to reconcile these two passages by referring to
the distinction between candidate members and working members (who
would be the vanguard) of the ASU, but, as we have seen, the provisions regarding working members were not implemented for the purpose
of the ASU elections of 1963. Furthermore, while the charter allows
for an interpretation which provides for the formation of a Leninist
party of militant socialist revolutionaries, the organic law of the ASU
reemphasizes the elements of national unity, interclass alliance, and the
social heterogeneity of the working forces of the people. Those working
forces include workers, peasants, intellectuals, soldiers, and national
capital. Since the Egyptian leftists asserted that the role of the–militant
vanguard was to advance the interests of the workers and peasants and
to resolve contradictions (i.e., class antagonisms) within the alliance
in the same spirit, it follows from their point of view, that the description of the ASU as a whole as the vanguard contradicts the text of the
charter.

It must, nevertheless, be remembered that the idea of a vanguard or
a militant cadre was included in the original draft of the charter in May
1962, and was not an invention of the communists. The politics of the
integration of the communists into the ASU were described by Shamir
as follows: "the April 1965 proclamation [of self-dissolution] . . . reflected the intention to bring about a revolution much more radical
than that desired by the regime . . . the agreement was valid only during the transitional period. . . . even during that period Marxists within
this alignment would uphold the principles that set them apart."[6] Shamir
later wrote that the Egyptian Marxists repeatedly pressed the regime
to fulfill its "commitment to form a vanguard party to be established
exclusively on cadres which would represent the interests of the working class."[7] But these demands were voiced, or at least echoed, else-

where. The goal had already been adumbrated in official theses, and the differences between the published position of the Marxists and that of the ruling authorities were not obvious. Shamir's view is that the implementation of the cadre party provisions of the charter by Nasser was an attempt to "neutralize" communist influence. He wrote: "while the Marxist cadres were being accepted into the ASU, Nasser simultaneously initiated the formation of another, much more powerful cadre-system in that body."[8]

Shamir's description of the cadre formations created by 'Ali Sabri as "powerful" is based in part on the revelations and accusations made in 1971, after Sadat had 'Ali Sabri, Sha'rawi Goma'a, and others arrested for plotting against him. Presumably, the 'Ali Sabri group intended to take power from Sadat by means of some official action of the Central Committee or the Higher Executive Committee of the ASU, after the manner in which Khruschev was ousted in 1964. Sabri, Goma'a, Sharaf, and the rest were accused of having erected a "secret apparatus" or a "special apparatus," responsive to themselves, within the ASU.[9] This apparatus functioned as a sort of intelligence and security service, especially in urban institutions where its members harassed and intimidated a number of people. Shamir concludes that there were two "systems" or structures within the ASU: the first, a group of Marxists linked to Muhammad Hasanain Haykal and connected with the journal al-Tali'ah, which advocated the creation of a cadre party of committed socialist revolutionaries, and the second, a secret apparatus set up within the ASU by 'Ali Sabri.

Although the ex-communists continued to hold high positions and despite the fact that they were able to pressure the regime on ideological and organizational matters, it does not appear that there was any overt organization of excommunists. Their only structural character was dependent upon their membership in the editorial "family" of al-Tali'ah, or their alliances with either Haykal or Sabri, or possibly even with other powerful patrons. The emphasis on secrecy and on the personal loyalty to 'Ali Sabri of the jihaz al-khass (special apparatus) appears to be somewhat exaggerated as a result of the distorted hindsight of the politically encouraged reaction against 'Ali Sabri and company after May 15, 1971.

According to Ahmad Hamrush, the cadre organization, which he refers to as "the Vanguard of the Socialists" (tali'at al-ishtirakiyyun), was founded by Nasser himself in mid-1963, shortly after the breakdown of the unity talks with Syria and Iraq.[10] Nasser summoned 'Ali Sabri, Haykal, and Ahmad Fu'ad. Sami Sharaf, afterwards notorious for his direction of a secret police apparatus within the vanguard organization, was also present in his capacity as chief presidential aide. The idea was to establish a political apparatus within the ASU similar to the League of Communists within the Yugoslav Socialist Union. Among the founders, only Ahmad Fu'ad had been a member of the Haditu branch of the communists in Egypt. Each of the founding members was to nominate trusted friends and co-workers to become members of vanguard cells. The cells were to be limited to ten members. Each candidate was to be approved by Nasser himself, presumably after being checked out by the secret police (or by Sami Sharaf?). The existence of the organization and its membership, despite the provision for a vanguard in the charter, were to remain secret. Officially, at any rate, its existence was a secret until August 1966, when Nasser stated that it had come into being two years before (that is in mid-1964 rather than in mid-1963).

Hamrush is critical of the vanguard organization, arguing that it was not an effective instrument for a socialist transformation, nor could it be, since those who did the recruiting could not overcome their own class interests and perceptions. For the most part, the leading officials who were made members of the vanguard recruited their chief administrative subordinates. Hamrush gives us virtually no dates after the founding, but it appears that for the first year and a half or more the Vanguard of the Socialists was organized in branches. Each branch was probably comprised of the cells derivative of the original cells formed by the founding group, but additional branches may have been set up. Hence one branch was organized by Ahmad Fu'ad and it was composed almost entirely of "leftist and progressive" elements. This branch had as many as 250 members at an early stage when the membership of the other branches lagged considerably.

It is evident that the rapid organization of so large a group of leftists caused some concern. Hamrush feigns uncertainty regarding Nasser's decision to include 'Abd al-Hakim 'Amr, chief of the general staff, in the secretariat of the leftist branch of the vanguard and to require that all business be transacted through him. 'Amr would not engage in ideological discussions with the leftist leadership in the vanguard and he did make some effort to keep them under surveillance.

The status and organization of the leftist branch was substantially changed in 1965. Through 1963, but especially after Khruschev's visit in 1964, the government had been releasing communists from prison. At the end of 1964 virtually all the communists were freed and a general amnesty declared. Late in 1964 or early in 1965 Ahmad Fu'ad was commissioned to bring the communists into the Arab Socialist Union. Ultimately only the Haditu group agreed to dissolve their own party and to become members of the Socialist Union. This self-dissolution was declared in March or April 1965 and the group which signed the agreement was admitted *as a group* to the Vanguard of the Socialists. Thereafter each former communist would have to apply and be admitted individually.

It is not clear from the Hamrush account whether the vanguard was still organized in ideological and factionally oriented branches, but sometime during 1965 the organization of the vanguard was changed. These changes probably were begun under the direction of Husain al-Shafi'i and then continued under 'Ali Sabri after he became the director of the Arab Socialist Union. The new organization patterned the vanguard after the Arab Socialist Union in that the primary basis of organization was either residential or institutional rather than ideological. The communist members were now dispersed among noncommunist and not so progressive members, most of whom were drawn from the bureaucracy.

Hamrush's description of the Vanguard of the Socialists is full of ambivalence. He would like to make several points in the same piece and still maintain an apparent simplicity of style and attitude. At the core of his presentation of the "events" is the question whether the communists should have dissolved their party. His answer is negative. Did they have a reasonable expectation that they would forward the prospect for revolution in Egypt? Affirmative. He more or less excuses the self-dissolution of Haditu as based on his belief that Nasser was gradually and genuinely moving toward Marxism, but Nasser, unlike Fidel Castro, did not make a coalition with the Communist Party. Hence, the communists were not so much mistaken in supporting Nasser and joining the Arab Socialist Union as was Nasser mistaken in failing to take advantage of an historic opportunity to transform Egyptian society decisively. Nasser did not go far enough because he did not wish to antagonize 'Abd al-Hakim 'Amr and because he relied upon 'Ali Sabri and other exponents of the interests of what the communists now call the bureaucratic bourgeoisie.

There is little doubt that the Egyptian communists now are inclined to lay heavy blame on 'Abd al-Hakim 'Amr for their lack of "progress" during the mid-sixties. They have also taken the posture of being, then and now, pro-Nasser and hence opposed to the de-Nasserization efforts of Anwar al-Sadat. 'Ali Sabri is recognized as having been open to Marxist influence, but Hamrush hardly conceals his criticism and contempt for 'Ali Sabri's policies of bureaucratizing the vanguard, diverting it to the goals of political control and antisubversion surveillance, and constructing a center of power within the cadre organization.

When 'Ali Sabri took over the leadership of the Arab Socialist Union he also gained control of the Vanguard of the Socialists. He then proceeded to implement a key proposal of the Marxists, which was to "free" ranking members of the political cadre from other bureaucratic, professional, or economic activities so they could devote full time to political work—to exploring the needs of the people, articulating those needs, and organizing the masses so they could satisfy those needs. The Marxists also recommended, and 'Ali Sabri agreed, that executive bureaus, composed of such specialized cadres, be put in charge of party activity in each province.

Instead of selecting devoted activist Marxists, 'Ali Sabri selected "personal followers who were far from any supervision or connections with Gamal 'Abd al-Nasser . . . and 'Ali Sabri came to have effective influence in the Socialist Union . . . an influence which was not popular because his introverted and quiet personality was incompatible with that . . . but rather a personal influence among those elements that were attached to his orderly thinking."[11] 'Ali Sabri is credited with invigorating the political activity within the Arab Socialist Union, and Hamrush emphasizes the achievements of the Youth Organization and the Socialist Institutes.

Hamrush appears to suggest (by the context) that Nasser became more concerned about the vanguard because of the growing influence of the Marxists so he added to the General Secretariat of the vanguard several officers who were close to him. "The secretariat came to be composed of seven officers, five of whom had worked in counterintelligence, and four civilians."[12] Even though Hamrush says that this change "expressed a more leftist and progressive tendency" because of the ideological inclination of these officers, he goes on to complain that the real Marxists were hamstrung for two reasons. The first was that the political apparatus (the vanguard) of the ASU could issue no directives without Nasser's approval. The second was that "the writing of reports on the tendencies of popular opinion almost became the most important activity of the members, and that was the natural consequence of former counterintelligence officers bearing this new political responsibility and inhibiting the left from any real participation in political work."[13]

Hamrush concludes that the leftist tendency within the ASU and the vanguard continued to increase, but the Vanguard of the Socialists failed to fulfill its original purpose and the historic opportunity was lost. The communists made a strategic error, but much of the blame falls on 'Abd al-Hakim 'Amr, on Gamal 'Abd al-Nasser, and on 'Ali Sabri, Sha'rawi Goma'a, and Sami Sharaf. The communists failed because they were prevented from organizing the vanguard within the armed forces, because they could not control appointments to the executive bureaus of the political apparatus, and because the vanguard had no executive power.

Al-Tali'ah began publication in January 1965 and at the time the issue of the formation of a cadre party within the ASU was already being widely discussed. In December 1964, after the national congress had been postponed, Husayn al-Shafi'i, one of the more conservative of the original group of revolutionary officers, was appointed secretary general of the ASU and he proceeded to set up a secretariat comprised of twenty sections. His first task was to create an organizational apparatus.

Sometime in January 1965, Nasser met with the Higher Executive Committee of the ASU and with the twenty members of the secretariat. The purpose of the meeting was to hear a progress report from Husayn al-Shafi'i, and the statements made at the meeting were reported in full in *al-Tali'ah* of March 1965 (pp. 9–24). Nasser rather rudely interrupted al-Shafi'i's reading of a vaguely formulated program, insisting that the most important issues were those of organization and the selection of cadres. The outline of the formal organization of the ASU was but an empty promise. Nasser flatly demanded the creation of a jihaz siyasi.

The discussion then turned to the method of selecting cadres, particularly whether they were to be drawn from those persons elected to the committees at various levels or whether the militants were to be selected by some other, presumably Leninist, method. Nasser's own position appears to be somewhat inconsistent. He repeated his oft quoted theme that there exists a counterrevolutionary opposition within the ASU which must be combatted by militant socialists. Although there is some suggestion here that Nasser recognized the importance of personality characteristics and indoctrination for the role of a political vanguard, he came down on the side of popular elections as the means of selecting cadres. Nasser went so far as to reject the idea that the ASU would formally nominate trade union leaders as in the USSR, and he rejected a proposal that individual candidates standing for election should campaign on the basis of alternative programs rather than on the basis of their personal qualifications and their personal commitment to socialism. In all of this Nasser seemed to be rejecting recommendations of the left.

More specifically, at the same meeting it was decided that when, in April 1965, the term of the basic unit committees would be completed, new elections would not be held. Instead, new elections would be post-

poned until after the national congress was held, and the congress
would be best held after the organization of a party cadre which might
determine the composition of the congress.

Thus, the January 1965 meeting simply allowed for the dissolution
of the basic units of the ASU and turned attention to the creation of an
organizational apparatus. Nasser insisted that the leaders of the provincial organizational sections be elected even though the mu'awinin (deputies) in charge of the ASU departments would be selected by Husayn
al-Shafi'i. The provincial party secretariats would be made up of full-
time employees, essentially civil servants, who were to be freed of their
regular administrative duties. These civil servant-apparatchikis would
continue to receive their salaries from the government ministries but
they would have only "political" duties. These decisions and Nasser's
statements are all consistent with the interpretation that holds that the
purpose of the vanguard was to control the leftists and prevent their
gaining political influence.

It is obvious that this was not the image of the militant cadre held
by the editors of al-Tali'ah. Writer after writer defined a party as representative of the interests of a class. The ASU, it was pointed out, was
not a party but a coalition of classes. The task of the cadre was to
represent the interests of the peasants and workers and to peacefully
resolve the contradictions between the various classes in the coalition
by assuring the ultimate victory of the interests of the proletariat. The
intellectuals are not necessarily bound by class interests, and so the
militant cadres should be drawn both from those classes who have
been benefited by the revolution and from those who are intellectually
and emotionally committed socialist revolutionaries. The model of revolutionary action was drawn from the experiences of Russia and China,
and so there was a problem of adapting these concepts to a situation
where the government was, presumably, already in the hands of socialist
revolutionaries. This problem was, in part, overcome by reference to
Nasser's statement that there were two parties in the ASU. Hence for
the Marxists of al-Tali'ah, building the avant garde cadre was equivalent to building a true socialist party.[14]

Lutfi al-Kholi, the editor of al-Tali'ah and among the most politically
active of all of the ex-communists, wrote a number of articles in 1965
calling for the creation of a vanguard and criticizing the ASU for its
bureaucratic ways, its lack of effective coordination, and its reliance on
the government administration for carrying out its functions.[15] In the
August 1965 issue, al-Kholi called for the devotion of the fourteenth
year of the revolution to the creation of the jihaz siyasi. Al-Kholi
emphasized that the promised cadre party or political apparatus had

not been built. This was two years after the founding of the Vanguard of the Socialists, and one year before Nasser announced its existence. Al-Kholi had been a member of the vanguard since 1964.

Nasser, for his part, made two important statements on the matter in March and May 1965. On 15 March 1965, Nasser accepted his nomination for a further term as president of the United Arab Republic. Nasser had discussed the possibility of devoting full time to the ASU, and, even if the idea was not taken seriously, it indicates the desire to emphasize the importance of the mass political organization. In his speech Nasser talked of making way for the next generation. The first task of his administration would be to prepare the next generation to take over leadership of the revolution, a task to be achieved by means of creating political cadres. Nasser's theme of the transitional character of his own presidency was to be picked up and commented on by al-Kholi at a much later date, when 'Ali Sabri had been chosen to replace Husayn al-Shafi'i as secretary general of the ASU (al-Tali'ah, November 1965, pp. 6–8).

A second statement, also frequently used as a text to justify Marxist demands that a truly militant cadre be erected, was Nasser's speech to the parliamentary party of the ASU on 16 May 1965. That was the speech in which Nasser said that there were actually two parties in Egypt, the socialists and the reactionaries. The reactionaries had already infiltrated the ASU, said Nasser, so it was necessary to mobilize militant revolutionary elements even while constantly seeking to purge the ASU of counterrevolutionary elements (ibid., June 1965, p. 106).

After Nasser's visit to Moscow in August 1965, a Muslim Brethren plot to assassinate Nasser at the airport upon his return was uncovered, and as part of the general reaction to this threat, the ASU was called upon to mobilize public opinion against the Brethren and in support of Nasser. In October, 'Ali Sabri was appointed secretary general of the ASU, Zakaria Muhi al-Din was appointed prime minister, and Husayn al-Shafi'i was moved to the office of comptroller of accounts. These changes suggest that Nasser sought more vigorous efforts to mobilize support through the ASU, that he sought to mollify right wing opinion by appointing a prime minister who was identified with a pro-American policy, and that he was exasperated with Husayn al-Shafi'i. Noting these changes, Lutfi al-Kholi pointed out that 'Ali Sabri, though he was a vice-president, did not hold a cabinet post. Al-Kholi welcomed the possibility that Sabri might now seriously try to create a specialized political apparatus that would not be part of the bureaucracy (ibid., November 1965, p. 8).

On 18 November 1965, Nasser talked to a large group of young people assembled at an indoctrination camp. He said, "for the past year our major task has been to build a political vanguard. We did not announce this because we were testing the membership of the ASU, but now we can say that we have accomplished much of this task" (ibid., December 1965, p. 111). 'Ali Sabri, in a speech opening the second cycle at the Cairo Institute of Socialist Studies stated that the biggest task facing the ASU was the completion of the building of a full-time political apparatus. He also announced that he had already succeeded in appointing new provincial secretaries general and that executive bureaus composed of full-time cadres had been appointed for each province (ibid., p. 112). In January 1966, Nasser and 'Ali Sabri met in Cairo with 170 members of the provincial executive bureaus and Nasser gave them a "pep-talk." He said that everyone complained that the ASU did nothing, but that was because it lacked leadership. Now the members of the executive bureau would change all that. They would win the confidence of the people and stay in touch with the masses.

As the shape of the apparatus 'Ali Sabri had in mind became clearer, various writers in *al-Tali'ah* attempted to influence his policies by their usual combination of supporting comment and theoretical didacticism. Dr. Muhammad al-Khafif acknowledged that a militant vanguard could not be elected since theirs was a leadership and not a representative function, but how were they to be chosen? They were to be chosen "in part" by the leadership of the revolution ('Ali Sabri) but also by "acclaim of the masses," as was Nasser in 1952 (ibid., p. 39). Michel Kamil wrote that care should be taken so that the ASU apparatus would not become just another administrative organization as in government or industry, and he argued that there were contradictions between the government and political organizations even under socialism and even when the political organization was the highest authority (ibid., pp. 48–52). Muhammad Sayyid Ahmad seemed to be somewhat doubtful of the universal validity of the Leninist party model, citing the Chinese experience in drawing cadres from among the poor peasants (ibid., pp. 56–57).

These and other articles published in *al-Tali'ah* during the first half of 1966 suggest the dismay of the Marxists at the manner in which the vanguard was being selected. The references to the role of the masses in selecting the cadres gradually became clearer references to elections as opposed to selection by 'Ali Sabri and his close collaborators. It is also clear that the Marxists did not believe that the Sabri appointees were devoted revolutionaries nor committed socialists nor militant agitators. They saw this political apparatus as another bureaucracy and an extension of the stifling government and economic bureaucracy. From this time until late in 1967, after the defeat, *al-Tali'ah* devoted little attention to the question of the vanguard party.

The Egyptian left had very little influence on the building of the political apparatus of the ASU. In March 1966, after the provincial and district level executive bureaus were set up, 'Ali Sabri pressed the organization of "leadership groups" in each village and in each basic unit. These groups were also appointed, they were of varying size, evidently included many civil servants, and, wherever available included some who had taken courses at the institutes of socialist studies. In the village which he studied, Iliya Harik reports that the leadership group numbered almost 40; and part of the group, the membership of which was secret, constituted the "special apparatus" or the "secret apparatus" referred to by Shamir.[16] Harik's assessment of the political significance of the building of this apparatus is much more positive than is the assessment of Shamir or of the editorial family of *al-Tali'ah*. Harik credits the establishment of the leadership group in place of the ASU committee of twenty with transforming the political structure of the village and allowing for increased political awareness and participation at the village level. He does not credit the leadership groups with the radicalization of village politics, but with the partial democratization of village politics and the weakening of the influence of the well-to-do peasant.[17] Harik concludes that the appointment of these cadres from outside, but with reference to various village economic structures, resulted in a degree of political development in the non-Marxist sense of the term.[18] The editors, commentators, and correspondents writing in *al-Tali'ah*, however, tend to disagree, not with the specific report on the single village studied by Harik, but with the notion that the power structure in the villages was substantially changed.

It is safe to say that *al-Tali'ah* subordinated the issue of the vanguard in early 1966 and began to stress criticism of the weakness of the trade unions and the continued domination of village politics by the rich and the middle peasants. It may even be the case that this criticism is what led to sharp attacks on *al-Tali'ah* by various writers in *al-Katib* and *al-'Amal*, which Shamir refers to as a conflict between Haykal and 'Ali Sabri.[19] Since *al-Tali'ah* was not so sharply critical of 'Ali Sabri's apparatus, and since that apparatus had not yet much of a chance to function in the villages, it would appear likely that official impatience with the editorial family of *al-Tali'ah* had more to do with the realization that they were exacerbating social conflict than that they were criticizing 'Ali Sabri.

The Kamshish affair broke in May 1966, but as early as September 1965 *al-Tali'ah* carried material critical of the ASU in the villages. In a letter to the editor, a reader stated, "it may be observed that in most of the villages the committees of twenty are formed on the basis of a coalition of a few families or by the formation of a bloc among several large families, sometimes these are the families that monopolized the administrative posts in the village . . . these families divide the offices . . . they are only interested in material benefits for their own family members, hence the committees of twenty are completely paralyzed, never meet, and members of the committees do not even remember one another" (*al-Tali'ah*, September 1965, p. 150). Similar letters and complaints of inactivity of the basic unit committees appeared in later issues (ibid., October 1965, p. 137; November 1965, pp. 143–45; December 1965, pp. 133–36). The articles by Michel Kamil (ibid., December 1965, p. 49) and by Muhammad Sayyid Ahmad (ibid., pp. 56–67) link the issue of cadre formation to responsiveness to the masses and especially the peasants. In March 1966, Muhammad Kamal Bayumi Shanim wrote that elections in the villages were based upon an elaborate system of social courtesies. The committees of twenty, he wrote, always include the 'umdah, one or two shuyukh, and other reactionaries. The leadership and the employees of the village cooperatives always exploit the peasants, so that the peasant has to appeal to the governmental bureaucracy, outside of the framework of the ASU. Sometimes villagers try to hold meetings apart from those of the committee of twenty, but the reactionaries oppose such efforts (ibid., March 1966, p. 92).

On 1 May 1966, in the village of Kamshish, Salah al-Din Muhammad Husain of the Muqallid family was killed by agents of the head of the Fiqqi family. Al-Fiqqi was by far the largest landowner in the village and he had completely dominated village life under the monarchy. The Muqallid family had been the second most important in the village. The Muqallid family was established in the village by an immigrant teacher of religion. The Muqallids challenged the Fiqqis and they lost much of their land in losing the political struggle. Husain al-Muqallid responded eagerly to the promises of the revolution of 1952 and he became active in the various political organizations established thereafter. At first al-Fiqqi managed to get around the land reform laws and he used his political influence to bar al-Muqallid from political activity as a communist or, alternatively, as a member of the Muslim Brethren. After 1961, the land reform was applied to the Fiqqi family and al-Muqallid succeeded in winning political rehabilitation. Al-Muqallid then influenced the committee of twenty to write to ASU headquarters accusing al-Fiqqi of attempting to organize a reactionary political meeting under the guise of a funeral ceremony. The letter called for the expropriation of the Fiqqi mansion and for its use to house health and cultural services for the village. At the time, al-Fiqqi had been pretty much forced out of the village, but he was trying to convert his holdings to capitalize a food processing enterprise. Husain al-Muqallid made it clear that he wished to reduce al-Fiqqi to the status of a landless agricultural laborer, and al-Fiqqi dispatched two of his clients to kill al-Muqallid (ibid., June 1966, pp. 10–16).

In addition to the universal appeal of the lurid aspects of this story, there were obvious political morals to be drawn. The government and the leadership of the ASU were seriously embarrassed, not because of the failure of the efforts of 'Ali Sabri, but because of the revelation of how little had been accomplished in the countryside since 1952. Nasser's statement about the persistence of the counterrevolutionaries and the need for action by devoted socialists was more than borne out. The apparent slowness of the reaction of the higher ASU authorities prior to May 1966 was a central part of the story. The astonishing publicity given the affair suggests that it was an element in a political struggle. The martyred hero was presented as the prototype of the many militant socialist revolutionaries dispersed among the peasantry waiting to be called to serve in the vanguard of the ASU. The concepts of political struggle and revolutionary activity were given concrete referents by the story.

It may well be that one of the consequences of the Kamshish affair was that the task of appointing the leadership groups in the villages was speeded up, or that greater care was paid to excluding the largest remaining landholders. The most salient official reaction was the creation of the Committee to Liquidate Feudalism, under the chairmanship of 'Abd al-Hakim 'Amr, with full executive powers to take action on any case that came before it. This committee received complaints regarding the political activities of landowners and took a variety of actions. By January 1967, that is, six months later, following a directive from Nasser, the Committee to Liquidate Feudalism turned its attention to the problem of corruption in the public sector. The goal of its activities was now to increase production and to meet the plan targets (ibid., February 1967, p. 72).

It is difficult to avoid the conclusion that the government was not very interested in pressing for changes at the village level. Rather than exploit the Kamshish affair to create substantial political awareness at the base, the government was still far more concerned with keeping the lid on and with increasing production. No one has suggested that

the Committee to Liquidate Feudalism accomplished anything of en-
during political significance. The creation of the committee was a diver-
sionary gesture, but it is noteworthy that the task assigned to it was not
given to the ASU and to 'Ali Sabri.

Under 'Abd al-Hakim 'Amr, the Committee to Liquidate Feudalism
stepped into the most explosively political agrarian issue since the land
reform of 1952, and it effectively prevented that issue from being exploited by the Egyptian left. While this task was being accomplished,
'Ali Sabri was either wittingly or unwittingly the instrument of a vigorous effort of at least a segment of the Egyptian left to achieve the
political penetration of the armed forces by the ASU and its vanguard.
It may well have been that the demand that the army be politicized
was a mere reaction to 'Amr's taking over the Kamshish affair and thus
intruding into Sabri's political territory. Nevertheless, the persistent
references of Egyptian leftists to 'Amr as their chief opponent during
this period suggests that 'Amr was called upon consistently by Nasser
to control and inhibit the activities of the leftists. Hamrush and other
leftists have, however, sought to exonerate Nasser of the blame for
'Amr's reactionary political role and for his military failures as well.
They explain Nasser's support for 'Amr as motivated by the apprehension that 'Amr's dismissal might have brought vigorous protests, at
least from many of the officers among whom 'Amr was extremely
popular.

The Kamshish affair was thoroughly discussed in *al-Tali'ah*, and it
served as an ideal vehicle for concretizing the abstract didactic, and
abstruse theorizing of the editorial family. The articles on rural power
structure and on the rural economy became more straightforward, included some empirical data, and they were more clearly, even if less
emphatically related to the question of the role and consequences of a
militant political cadre.

Lutfi al-Kholi set the central themes of the *Tali'ah* interpretation of
the Kamshish affair and of the problem of rural power structure in
Egypt. After relating the factual background, al-Kholi drew five conclusions:

1. The call for a struggle against feudalism or against the traditional
   large landowners is misleading and quixotic. The real opponents
   of the revolution are the middle and rich peasants, whose lands,
   though legally divided among family members, were farmed as a
   unit. These rich peasants have tried to acquire the power of the
   former absentee feudalists through the instrumentalities of the new
   regime. These rich peasants are now employing capitalist methods
   of agricultural enterprise, but they are to be considered "para-

sitic capitalists" and not national capitalists (i.e., one of the five coalition classes) because of their political role in the villages.

2. "Parasitic capital" has succeeded to substantial political power as evidenced by the fact that Salah Husain al-Muqallid was declared to be both a communist and a Muslim Brother by an acquiescent basic unit committee of the ASU.

3. There are village residents capable of serving as political cadre.

4. The local administration should be in the hands of the revolutionary cadre rather than be comprised of petty bureaucrats who are responsive to the agrarian capitalists.

5. It is possible to exploit traditional rural disputes to advance the cause of socialist transformation in the villages.

The argument about the development of a new rural capitalism is the most interesting and the most important. Hasan Riad had already pointed out that the number of owners of 5–20 feddan had not declined over the last several decades in spite of the Islamic inheritance laws which require the equal division of the estate among all the sons and a half share to daughters. But the *Tali'ah* authors pointed out that this rural middle class of village notables was actually growing in economic and political strength. Dr. Abbas Kasibah wrote that 3.2% of all landowners, owning 10–100 feddan, owned 35.2% of all land in 1964 (ibid., June 1966, p. 60). Michel Kamil cited statistics showing that the income of owners of 30–50 feddan had increased by 24% since the revolution of 1952 (ibid., September 1966, p. 60). Adil Shanim wrote that the number of owners of 30–50 feddan had increased from 22,000 to 29,000 from 1952 to 1964, and they had increased their share of cultivated land from 10.9% to 13.3% (ibid., p. 67). He further pointed out that capital intensive farming had increased in that the number of feddan in vegetable gardens and fruit groves had nearly doubled between 1952 and 1964, and that 82% of all tractors were owned by members of the private agricultural sector (ibid., pp. 67–68). Writing in 1967, Dr. Kasibah stated that 27% of the cultivated area was farmed by the sharecropping method and another 50% was rented, often to landless peasants. This land was owned by the less than 100,000 persons who owned 5–100 feddan (ibid., May 1967, pp. 16–18).

The political consequences of the transformation of the notables into agrarian capitalists were important, as well. Various articles in *al-Tali'ah* argued that the cooperative boards were still dominated by the larger owners even though a 1964 law required that four-fifths of the board members own 5 feddan or less. The reason for this was that the smaller owners were relatives of the larger owners or that the votes of the smaller owners could be purchased for a pittance. Sharecroppers and renters do not have accounts with the cooperatives, and so the land-owners kept their accounts, charged higher prices for seed and fertilizer, misrepresented the quantities delivered, or charged for services which the coop was supposed to supply free. Michel Kamil wrote, "In all the evidence that has come in, except for the land reform villages, the fam-ilies [i.e. influential families] gained economic mastery over all the po-litical and democratic institutions and occupied all of the offices . . . beginning with the committees of the ASU and the village council or city council and the 'amudiyyah and the shaykhat of the town and the headship of the village police and the cooperative society and the syndi-cate of agricultural laborers" (ibid., September 1966, p. 62).

But the major structural defects in the rural political situation were the lack of coordination among a multiplicity of political, administra-tive, and economic organizations and the prevailing bureaucratic mode of dealing with all issues. These problems could be resolved, according to the *Tali'ah* authors by means of the proper utilization of political cadres. A militant cadre would substitute political methods for bureau-cratic methods, and would achieve coordination by controlling key positions in all the village organizations (see esp. ibid., June 1966, pp. 25, 35). Amin 'Izz al-Din wrote that there are two ways in which the vanguard and the mass might be related: organically or through coop-eration. An organic link required that members of the vanguard hold key positions in all mass line organizations, but Nasser had decided against the organic link and in favor of the method of external cooper-tion among diversely interested leaderships of mass line organizations (ibid., p. 45). In a similarly critical vein, Dr. Kasibah drew the con-clusion that the charter, in denying the need for the public ownership of land, rendered the problem of agricultural production dependent upon the cooperative system. That system had failed, however, and it was now necessary to replace the bureaucratically oriented cooperative administrators with politically oriented cadres (ibid., pp. 63–64). Writ-ing almost a year later, when the new leadership groups were already ubiquitous in the villages, Dr. Kasibah was even more explicitly critical. He then held the view that the village agricultural cooperative was the only suitable arena for a political confrontation between the small peasants and the notables. There, their interests would be clearly diver-gent and the small peasants would be able to act with political con-sciousness. He denied that the intellectuals, even if drawn from the village itself, could substitute for leadership from the peasants them-selves. He also flatly asserted that there was still no trained cadre available for the ASU in the villages and that the governmental apparatus lacked real revolutionary consciousness, in what was almost a frank criticism of 'Ali Sabri's policy of installing appointed bureaucratic cadres in the village leadership groups (ibid., May 1967, pp. 21–22). Even after the defeat in the June War, but before the dissolution of the leadership groups, the *Tali'ah* authors had little good to say for the structural reforms of 'Ali Sabri and for his version of the vanguard party (ibid., February 1968, pp. 28–29, 31, 70, 76–77).

The most comprehensive critique was that of Adil Shanim. Writing "On the Problem of the New Class in Egypt," he pointed out that the phenomenon of the new class (i.e., as developed in the writing of Milovan Djilas) was particularly sinister in a transitional situation because under such circumstances a bureaucracy could use its position to transform itself into a capitalist elite. Egypt was particularly vulnerable to such a development because its revolution had occurred without a revolutionary party and it had proceeded without destroying the existing administration, which had been a reactionary and backward agrarian administration. And, of particular relevance to our investigation, he went on with reference to the agricultural areas:

> As a consequence of their greater economic social and political weight in the villages, the rural bourgeoisie was able to push its members into the political and administrative leadership positions in the councils of the village, the district and the province, not to speak of the committees of the ASU and the cooperatives; and thus was the new class brought into being in the villages, its main supports being the administrative and political cadres drawn from the rich peasants. [Ibid., p. 85]

While bearing in mind the considerable possibility of biased reporting in *al-Tali'ah* (although most observers agree with these reports),[20] we cannot avoid drawing certain tentative conclusions from the juxtaposition of this information with that of Shamir and Harik. Our problem is to establish whether or not the official cadre party policies resulted in important changes at the village level. Such changes would be the consequence of either the creation of a secret, security-oriented party apparatus in the villages or the unleashing of new political forces through the setting up of leadership groups drawn from more modest social groups in the village. The material from *al-Tali'ah* argues against either conclusion without asserting that nothing at all had changed in the villages.

In the criticisms of the ASU which followed the defeat in 1967 the two most repeated complaints referred to the bureaucratic attitudes of the ASU leadership and the creation of centers of power. President

Nasser himself called for an end to government by the secret police in a speech made in November 1967. Nevertheless, at this time no one appears to have complained that the ASU was engaged in political surveillance. Rather, it is the case that the ASU was exploited for purposes of factional competition at all political levels, including the village, and one of the devices employed, as in the Kamshish case, was to impugn the political loyalty of the opposing faction. Lutfi al-Kholi recognized the revolutionary potential of village level factional strife, and Harik also noted that under favorable circumstances factional strife could invigorate an electorally competitive system. If anything, Harik demonstrates the looseness rather than the tightness of the political linkage between the village and the higher levels of the ASU, and even if there was a secret apparatus within the leadership group, it does not appear to have had a significant political role, nor to have provided an efficient transmission belt for the ASU leadership. Harik's description of the politics of his village makes it difficult to believe that the sort of structures Shamir discusses as existing in urban institutions existed in the villages. Harik himself tells us that the leadership group and the secret apparatus in his village were simply abolished after the defeat in the June War, and there is no evidence that their earlier existence had any residual effect in the reorganization of the ASU by electoral means in 1968.[21]

Obviously, there was great variation in political and social structure from village to village. The important difference between land reform and non-land reform villages is generally acknowledged. In the former there were lower class elements, mobilized by the land reform and cooperative bureaucracy who could challenge the traditional rural notability. There were villages that had been dominated by a single absentee landowner with strong connections to the crown. There were villages that had been dominated by several large peasant families allied with the 'umdah. There were villages that were rent by factional strife among a few well-to-do peasant notables. There were villages with few owners of 2–5 feddan and many landless laborers, and there were villages, especially land reform villages, with many owners of 2–5 feddan. The possibilities for the appointment of leadership groups and the political consequences of their appointment for village factional struggles would vary according to these structural elements, and they might be influenced by the presence of personalities like Salah Husain al-Muqallid. But such reciprocal responsiveness and political adaptiveness is neither new nor necessarily irreversible in Egyptian or other villages. We discover nothing new when we discover politics at the village level. What would be new would be the crystallization of village level politics in a process that might have consequences beyond the village itself and thus significantly increase the political self-determination of the peasant.

One useful measure of the long-term effects of the experiment in the building of a cadre party will be found in the results of the elections to the ASU and to the National Assembly after the 1967 defeat. In the aftermath of that disastrous military failure, the ASU came in for the same merciless criticism that was directed against all Egyptian institutions. The editorial family of *al-Tali'ah*, writing at a time when Egypt was heavily dependent upon Soviet military assistance and diplomatic support, blamed the defeat on the reactionaries and those who wished to freeze the revolution. These counterrevolutionary and nonrevolutionary elements had been successful because of the absence of a militant vanguard, they argued. The members of the provincial executive bureaus were the personal choices of 'Ali Sabri. Some Marxists had been deprived of their political rights. Charter provisions had been disregarded. The most aggressive suggestions of the Marxists were for arming the masses and for drawing the military leadership from those indoctrinated with a socialist and revolutionary ideology. The demand for the election rather than the appointment of the ASU leadership was easier to accede to.

Marxist criticism of the regime and of the ASU was strongest up to January 1968. 'Ali Sabri made some attempt to justify his stewardship, claiming that the Cairo ASU played an important role in the popular demonstrations of 9 and 10 June 1967, whereby Nasser was persuaded not to resign the presidency. Sabri did not, however, assert that he had built an effective cadre. He made no reference to any secret apparatus. Nasser himself had placed much of the blame on the military leadership and he showed some disdain for the ASU and 'Ali Sabri. Matters changed, however, after the trials of the offending military officers and the announcement of relatively light penalties. University students in Cairo and Alexandria demonstrated in February 1968 against the leniency of the sentences, and they compelled the retrial of the officers. This sort of responsiveness to mass demonstrations was unusual and it illustrated the regime's weakness. It is unlikely that the student demonstrators were drawn from a single ideological group, but observers have tended to identify them with either political liberalism or Islamic fundamentalism or both. At any rate, one of the central demands to emerge from the demonstrations was a demand for the political liberalization of the regime. Hence Nasser was neatly caught between the leftists demanding the creation of a tightly organized cadre party which would press the class conflict which had been in abeyance under the ASU alliance and the liberals and right wing religionists pressing for competitive elections, freedom of the press, and freedom from political surveillance. At the same time Nasser was concerned about the loyalty of his officer corps and about the depressed economic position of the country.

President Nasser presented his solution to the Egyptian people in the (Bayan) declaration of 30 March 1968. The Bayan was aimed at the political mobilization of the Egyptian population as part of the continuing struggle with Israel. In particular it was meant to reduce domestic political pressures until such time as some military riposte or diplomatic gain could be made. It was believed to be necessary to convince the politically active portion of the Egyptian people that significant changes were to be made in all phases of Egyptian life including the administrative, the political, and the military. Nevertheless, the major emphasis of the Bayan was upon change in the ASU. The tone of the declaration was relatively optimistic and conciliatory. Some progress had been made and so it was possible to look to the future now, and to make plans. The country was able to defend itself and was no longer open to the attack of the enemy at whim. The economic situation had been brought under control with some outside assistance. The mistakes and the corruption of the past were brought into the open in a series of trials. The international diplomatic position of Egypt was being improved. And interestingly enough, the third area of achievement upon which Nasser remarked in the opening section of the Bayan was the liquidation of centers of power or political cliques and factions, at least some of which were located in the ASU and were the product of the system of cooptation instituted by 'Ali Sabri. Nasser was not harsh with those who had set up centers of power. He said, "It was in the nature of things and the nature of people that they [centers of power] should appear at various stages in our struggle—political work is not done by angels but by human beings." But these "centers of power stopped short in the midst of the corrective operation, afraid of losing their influence and of the revelation of their surreptitious activities."[22] If this situation were not corrected, it would have deleterious effects on the morale of the people, and so these centers had to be broken up.

The same conciliatory tone was taken in Nasser's speech at Mansurah on 18 April 1968. There he said the ASU exists and functions, but "whatever works makes mistakes, whoever does not work and sits at home, how can he make a mistake? . . . but there are many people among the leaders of the ASU today who have carried out their roles faithfully and constructively—but conditions are now different from what they were when the leadership of the ASU was appointed. . . ."[23]

In the Bayan, Nasser explicitly denied that the most important part of the change was a change of personnel. "The desired change must be a change in conditions and in the climate, and if not, then any new individuals under the same conditions and in the same climate, will go along the same way as the others who preceded them. The desired change must be clearer thought, stronger mobilization, a more precise plan. . . ."[24] In calling for a complete reorganization of the ASU, Nasser reaffirmed its dual character: an alliance of five classes with a political organization set up "in its midst comprised of a vanguard capable of leading the political interaction toward the goal of closing the gaps between the classes."[25] The trouble with the ASU was not in the original idea but in the way it was carried out and especially because the ASU was not built up by free elections from the "base to the summit." Nasser admitted that on the previous 23 July 1967, when he announced his intention of convening a new Central Committee of the ASU, he had intended that it be constituted by appointment. Now he decided that "appointment was not the best of methods, and in the end it will get us nothing but those who are singled out by the centers of power."[26]

Taken together, these statements do not constitute a severe criticism of 'Ali Sabri's ASU and his cadres. The ASU was not given credit for the popular movement of 9 and 10 June 1967—this was attributed to the spirit of the masses themselves. The criticisms of the ASU as an organizational anomaly were ignored, and Nasser maintained the ambiguous formula of an interclass alliance and a vanguard. Some changes of personnel were projected, since the ASU would be entirely reconstructed by elections, but the previous leadership was not explicitly excluded from returning. The executive bureaus at the provincial and district levels, the leadership groups at the village level, the institutes of socialist studies, and the youth organization and camps were all abolished, and they appear to have left very little trace behind them. How are we to understand such a far-reaching political reorganization without an accompanying political purge?

It is apparent that Nasser was not responding to problems arising out of the action or inaction of the ASU. The possibility that some of the leaders of the ASU might have been using their positions to build centers of power did not disturb him much. Indeed it *was* natural that they should do so, since under the system of full-time ASU service, they could not rely upon their links to other administrative structures in feathering their own political nests. It was also natural, with the transformation of the ASU top echelon into a political fiefdom which paralleled the ministries, the nationalized industries, and the special institutes, that there might be friction between the ASU leaders and other political fief-holders. Nasser was not disturbed by such conflicts so long as they did not involve foreign powers. It is noteworthy that the increased dependence of Egypt upon the Soviet Union that was the immediate consequence of the 1967 war coincided with an increased stridency in the leftist demands for a reorganized cadre party. This leftist pressure declined relatively suddenly after the disturbances of February 1968. It was not only the leftist journalists and political functionaries who were silenced, but as the major symbol of Soviet-Egyptian cooperation, 'Ali Sabri himself was increasingly frustrated and humiliated as the Soviets failed to agree to Nasser's demands for military and political support in 1969.

As we have seen, one of the major alternate demands to emerge out of those demonstrations was for political liberalization and for freedom of political expression. This demand was seen as ambiguous, in that it might simply be a device whereby the so-called counterrevolutionary forces, that is, the Muslim Brethren and the capitalists, could use the instrumentalities of liberal democracy to overthrow the socialist, or the "socializing," regime.[27] The Bayan of 30 March, therefore, announced that the new National Assembly would proceed promptly to draw up the permanent constitution of the country, after the reorganization of the ASU, the election of a Central Committee and a Higher Executive Committee, and the holding of parliamentary elections early in 1969. The major provisions of the new constitution would include a statement "on the firm connection between social freedom and political freedom, and would grant full guarantees of personal freedom and security to all citizens . . . and would grant full guarantees of freedom of thought, expression, publication, opinion, of scientific research, and of the press."[28] In addition the constitution would provide for a clear delimitation of the powers and functions of various high elected officials, for the limitation of the term of office for all elected incumbents, for the political neutrality and immunity of the judiciary, and for a supreme constitutional court.

If these provisions were carried out in spirit as well as in the letter, along with the elections from the "base to the summit" within the ASU, the regime would have been considerably liberalized. But the ASU was still to have a monopoly of all political action and expression, and there would be no purge even if the cadre structures of 1965–66 were to be dropped. In fact, what was new was the return to the structures and methods of 1962–64. The danger of excessive political liberalization would be controlled by maintaining the ASU political monopoly; and the marginal risk that the ASU might be turned into an instrument of significant political power was also avoided. In a not entirely unexpected manner, the demands for political liberalization became intertwined with the factional infighting among the ASU executive, the members of the cabinet, the vice-presidents, the heads of the nationalized enterprises, and the heads of various institutions including, most importantly, Haykal of *al-Ahram*. The more that the ASU came under the control of a single faction, the more did opposing groups, and especially Haykal and the *Tali'ah* editorial family, demand a further liberalization or provision for political competition and the more did they criticize the ASU's performance in the years 1965 to 1968.

Nasser did not clearly take sides in this conflict. It is true that Nasser announced, on 30 March, that the ASU executive and administrative apparatus would be dissolved and that a new committee of fifty would be appointed to organize the ASU elections. Nevertheless, Sha'rawi Goma'a, the only member of the ASU executive who had held a government post, was again made the link with the government, and designated as the executive of the committee of fifty. Goma'a and 'Ali Sabri were part of the same faction.

The conflict surfaced most importantly in the election of the executive committee of the ASU by the Central Committee in November 1968, and (in the aftermath of the student rioting in Mansurah and Alexandria on 24 and 25 November) in the preparations for the election of the National Assembly. The reorganization had proceeded as planned and without important hitch through the election of the Central Committee. The Bayan was put to a referendum, and after a number of mass meetings at which the Bayan was explained, it was approved overwhelmingly on 2 May. Thereafter election committees were established. New definitions of peasants and workers, who were to have 50% of all seats, were adopted. 'Umad and mashayikh were prevented from holding party office unless they gave up their administrative posts. Relations to the fourth degree were prohibited from being members of the same basic unit or district level committee. The basic unit committee could have only 10 members, and the voter could vote for as few as 5 candidates. And many, many more regulations were passed by the committee of 50. On 25 June elections were held in the basic units. On 4 July the district congresses were elected, and on 8 July the provincial congresses were elected. Finally on 23 July, on the sixteenth anniversary of the revolution, the National Congress met. The speed with which all this was achieved is reminiscent of the previous organizational efforts of the ASU and the National Union. It is unlikely that national and central influences would have had much effect on local elections held under these circumstances, and neither our data nor reports of Harik suggest that there was much outside influence. *Al-Tali'ah* (July 1968, p. 97) reported that there was some tension between the urban and rural delegates within some of the provincial congresses. It was, of course, more likely that elements of the Vanguard of Socialists, including its Marxist members, would have more influence on urban elections, while the second stratum would still dominate rural elections. The chastened but still leftist *al-Tali'ah* was suggesting that a conflict along these ideological lines had emerged. Other observers claim that 'Ali Sabri and Sha'rawi Goma'a attempted to continue their control over the ASU by electing their allies, members of their "centers of power" in the vanguard. Still other observers believe that the leftists and the centers of power were cooperating against the right wing, despite the differences between Haykal and 'Ali Sabri. The rural delegates, it was said, feared that the delegates from Cairo and Alexandria, together with the delegates from nonresidential constituencies might dominate the National Congress. The same sources noted that influential families had not lost their political strength in Assiut and al-Minia and that many of those who had formerly been elected at the provincial level were reelected unopposed on this occasion (ibid., p. 96).

The National Congress met formally on 23 July, elected a steering committee of one hundred, and then adjourned until 14 September 1968.[29] The National Congress proceeded to the constitution of a Central Committee comprised of 125 "elected" members, 25 appointed members, and 50 alternates. Actually, the 125 elected members were selected from among 250 candidates nominated by the ASU Provincial Councils, as were the 50 alternates.[30] The selection was made by Nasser and his close associates from a variety of factions. On October 19, the Central Committee elected the Higher Executive Committee, and President Nasser excluded himself from direct involvement in the process, but Dekmejian suggests that candidates might have been screened by Sha'rawi Goma'a.[31] Candidates could be elected only if they received a majority of the 150 Central Committee votes. Ten members and four alternates were to be elected, but only eight received the required majority. Surprisingly, the balloting was stopped at this point by Nasser, who recommended that the remaining seats be filled at a later time. Judging by subsequent events it appears that the eight elected members rather too neatly divided into two factions, or at least into supporters of 'Ali Sabri, Sha'rawi Goma'a and the ASU central secretariat, and their opponents. The four opponents, or non-ASU factionalists, were Husayn al-Shafi'i, Anwar al-Sadat, Mahmud Fawzi, and Kamal Ramzi Stinu. At the time, this group appeared to be politically weak, of mixed and uncertain political ideological orientation, and loosely, if at all, allied with one another. Their election could only have represented the opposition to the Sabri-Goma'a group built into the Central Committee

by themselves, the support of Nasser, and the vague hopes on the part
of a loose coalition of liberals, intellectuals, religionists, Christians, and
the bourgeoisie that their views might somehow be represented.

The ASU central executive elected 'Ali Sabri, Diya' al-Din Da'ud,
'Abd al-Muhsin Abu al-Nur, and Labib Shuqayr. All four were on the
losing side in the May 1971 conflict between 'Ali Sabri and Anwar
al-Sadat. Seven of the twenty candidates for the executive committee
were tried after May 1971; one (Khalid Muhi al-Din) was let off for
insufficient evidence, one was acquitted ('Ali al-Sayyid 'Ali), one received a suspended sentence (Labib Shuqayr), and the remaining four
received sentences ranging from a few months (Kamal al-Din al-Hin-
nawi) to life ('Ali Sabri). 'Ali Sabri received more votes than any other
candidate, but the remaining five candidates (excluding Khalid Muhi
al-Din, who is unlikely to have been a faction member) were grouped
in sixth to tenth place. The lowest number of votes received by any of
the six candidates was 62.

Another possible measure of the cohesiveness and political effectiveness of the 'Ali Sabri faction might be the loyalty of the provincial
party secretaries, twenty-one of whom were elected to the Central
Committee. Only one of these secretaries, Farid 'Abd al-Karim, party
secretary for al-Jizah province, was tried, convicted, and given a death
sentence, later commuted to life imprisonment.

These small bits of evidence confirm the view that there may, indeed,
have been a politically powerful faction connected with the ASU headquarters in Cairo (and al-Jizah), but that it did not extend deep into the
ASU, and it was not based upon a disciplined and organized cadre nor,
even more certainly, upon a group having a common ideological orientation. The 'Ali Sabri group did not put up a full slate for the executive
committee election. They may have been able to count on a minimum
of 62 of 150 Central Committee members for support, but they could
not prevent many of these from voting for the four anti-ASU faction
candidates, all of whom polled at least 112 votes. Unfortunately, none
of our sources gives any account of why only 87% of the possible total
of 1500 votes were cast. What is clear, however, is that 37% of the
votes cast went to the four "conservatives," and at least 123 of the 150
members voted for them. Furthermore, there may have been only 130
members who cast ballots.

Since the ninth- and tenth-ranked candidates were both closer to 'Ali
Sabri than to the conservatives, it would appear that Nasser's decision
was meant to block the political advance of the 'Ali Sabri group. Con-
tradictorily, however, Nasser acquiesced in the formation of a joint
committee to supervise the day-to-day work of the ASU secretariat.[32]

This committee was comprised of the heads of five functional committees and Sha'rawi Goma'a, who continued as minister of the interior. Altogether, this meant that the supervisory committee was made up of five members of the 'Ali Sabri group ('Ali Sabri, Sha'rawi Goma'a, Abu al-Nur, Da'ud, and Shuqayr) plus Anwar al-Sadat. It is, of course, possible that Nasser did not look upon these people as members of a closed faction.

It is evident that Nasser was seeking some sort of balance among diverse views, but he may also have felt that it was important to maintain a close link between the ASU and the security services under the ministry of the interior. It appears that such a connection was first established in 1963 or 1964 after the communists were admitted into the ASU, and it is in the nature of such administrative linkages that Parkinson's law is particularly applicable.[33] After Nasser's death, it was the Higher Executive Committee that designated Anwar al-Sadat as the new president of Egypt; but it was the supervisory committee that was most active in trying to oust Sadat and set up 'Ali Sabri as the new leader.

The conflict between 'Ali Sabri and Hasanain Haykal was much more obvious and more tied to issues than the Sadat-Sabri standoff. Sabri and Haykal each used their press vehicles and their Marxist communicators in their struggle, the former to urge both a more monolithic control of the ASU and a more univocal political strategic expression in the media. Haykal found himself backing the intellectuals, calling for greater freedom of expression, for political debate among the five allied classes, and for some decentralization of the ASU. Actually, Haykal appeared to be more interested in attacking the ASU as the power base of his opponents than in either capturing control of it or changing it along the lines preferred by the *Tali'ah* editorial family. Dekmejian documented the activity of Haykal, through his weekly editorials in *al-Ahram*, criticizing over-eager security personnel, adumbrating the concept of an open society, calling for open debate and mutual checks and balances among the social, political, and economic institutions and agencies, and defending the student demonstrators in some measure.[34] In all of this, it is clear that Haykal was not challenging Nasser himself, but neither was he acting as spokesman for Nasser. The president allowed this debate between *Akhbar al-Yom* representing the 'Ali Sabri faction and Haykal's various publications. As we have seen, several formal statements of intent to liberalize the regime were issued during 1968, but, in fact, Haykal and the liberals achieved no great successes. In December 1968 Haykal was hard pressed in a struggle to prevent the ASU executive from gaining effective control over the press through a Supreme Press Council.[35] On 13 December 1968, Haykal wrote, "The error into which the ASU has fallen on a number of occasions is that it always started from the position that it was the sole expression [of the views or will] of all of the masses of the people, and also their undisputed leader; and that is something that no organization in the world has ever attained, nor has anyone claimed to have done so. . . . Therefore it [the ASU] has fallen into an error no less dangerous than the error of the 'divine right' claimed by the kings." Haykal succeeded in preserving a measure of autonomy for the press, but he did not build a political faction. The opponents of 'Ali Sabri in the ASU executive did not come out openly in favor of liberalization, and they certainly did not identify with the independent and proud Haykal. Haykal and Sadat cooperated with one another only during and after the crisis of 1971 until Haykal was forced out of *al-Ahram* by Sadat in 1974.

The "liberals" made one more effort to weaken the ASU executive, by arguing against the formal ASU endorsement of candidates for the National Assembly, which was elected in January 1969.[36] The liberals preferred that, as in the past, aspiring candidates who met the qualifications merely present themselves, so long as they were members of the ASU. Once again a compromise formula was worked out which, as usual, appeared to respond to liberal demands but which, in effect, allowed the ASU leadership and the government to maintain close control. The ASU would endorse two candidates in each of the 175 two-member constituencies, but other ASU members could also stand for election.[37] Only 23 of 350 seats were won by the ASU independents while 93% of the seats were won by ASU-endorsed candidates. This was the kind of control which Nasser expected of the ministry of the interior, and he refused to dismantle the apparatus which produced it. He certainly refused to dismantle it by means that would allow wider participation in policy debate and policy decision making. Moreover, the ex-communists were now thoroughly weakened as a political force and they required no delicate institutional arrangements to keep them out of serious affairs. If the Vanguard of the Socialists played a significant role in the elections of 1968, and the evidence is simply unavailable yet, then its successes are to be counted as the successes of Sha'rawi Goma'a and not those of the Egyptian left. The Egyptian left held on to a dwindling position in the vanguard and in the parent organization, even while criticizing its shortcomings from time to time and in restrained language.

In the countryside, things reverted back to a reasonable facsimile of the way they were in 1964. Certainly, efforts were made to respond to the criticisms of the 1963 elections. The new definition of peasants (for purposes of carrying out the regulation requiring that 50% of all elected bodies be comprised of peasants and workers) now stipulated that to be counted politically as a peasant one could own no more than 10 feddan, be mainly employed in agriculture, derive one's major income from agriculture, and live in a rural area. Furthermore, as we have seen, 'umad and mashayikh had to resign their administrative posts if they wished to be candidates for ASU office, and close relatives could not be elected to the same committees. These rules limited the number of influentials who could retain ASU office, and the former incumbents also found opposition from those who had emerged to prominence in the leadership groups, in the agricultural labor unions, and in the cooperatives (under the rules requiring that four-fifths of the coop councils be drawn from those owning 5 feddan or less).

We should expect considerable change in the composition of the 1968 ASU at the lowest levels. Yet the seriousness of the intent of the government to change village power structure may be questioned. These rules all have the effect of barring certain individuals from office, but they do not affirmatively designate alternatives. In fact, they tend to bring to the fore "lesser" members of the large and influential families, but they do not alter the distribution of voting power, and they do not create new structures as did the leadership groups and the secret committees in at least some cases. Furthermore restricting the number of members of the basic unit committee to ten would also tend to favor the larger and better-known families.

We do not have data on the village level elections to the basic units, but it may be useful to remind ourselves of the outcome in the village studied by Harik. Naturally, it is absolutely misleading to suggest that the events in one village are in any way typical of what happened throughout Egypt. Our data comparing the diverse provinces, districts, and even intradistrict regions should have clearly established the fact that conditions vary considerably from village to village. Furthermore we have the repeated statements of many observers that new political forces have emerged in the land reform villages, especially among the new smallholders and among the government-appointed officials. But Harik's report is particularly interesting because in the village he studied there were some smallholders who had benefited from the land reform, and there was also some evidence that new political forces had been mobilized under the leadership group and cadre party experiment. Of course, Harik had deliberately sought out a village with some political heterogeneity, and he reminds us of the variety of rural conditions in discussing both his choice of a research site and the diverse fates of the secretaries of the leadership groups in different villages.[38] We cannot and need not review the richly detailed and insightful analysis of the 1968 ASU election in "Shubra al-Gedida," which Harik has given us. We need only point to his interesting conclusion: Harik writes, "The 1968 elections thus illustrate . . . conditions of free political choice at the local level and limited freedom nationally."[39] Before the revolution and up to 1961, the political life of Shubra had been dominated by a family which Harik called Samad—large landowners who had been well connected with the Wafd party. The central government "undermined the economic basis of the Samads' power . . . [and thereby] contributed to their political decline and exclusion by official measures."

> Not all the economically privileged, however, were subject to official opposition. Many, such as the Kuras, were actually encouraged by the national government to assume leadership in order to contain and defeat the older and more threatening oligarchy that had been associated with the older regime. At the same time villagers from the lower social stratum such as agrarian reform peasants were encouraged to participate in village politics through the official party. . . . In short, the effects of the national government on local politics have been to make local leadership roles insecure.[40]

Despite this conclusion, Harik tells us that the Kuras, who had emerged in the political leadership of the village in 1961, only to be replaced by the leadership group in 1965, made a comeback in 1968. Harik argues that the Kuras did not recover their former strength, and that politics in Shubra is now more fluid and pluralistic than it was prior to 1965. Nevertheless, "the Kuras received the lion's share of the delegation to the Markaz Committee."[41]

In a sense, Harik presents us with the "worm's eye view," but an examination of whatever data is available on the ASU and parliamentary elections of 1968 and 1969 confirms the conclusions he draws for Shubra al-Gedida in a general way. The creation and the demise of the leadership groups left a residue of a few activist peasants, but did not leave behind any organizational or factional structure. The basis of political competition at the village level is still primarily related to village society and village problems rather than national issues and national ideology. Governmental involvement does seem to prevent the rigidification of power structure, but most of what the government wants done in the land reform villages is done by land reform officials, and in villages without land reform the government relies upon the influential, peasant owners of moderate to large holdings. The cooperatives, the agricultural labor unions, the youth groups, and the ASU "mass line" groups did not prove to be very effective except in a limited number of cases of which Shubra al-Gedida may have been one. It is apparent that the government was not that interested in revolutionizing relationships in the countryside—although that goal was not totally out of reach in the delta, at least. But neither was the government committed to supporting particular factions that had become established in particular villages. The result was a half-hearted policy of issuing administrative and political regulations which might be used by highly motivated and relatively educated village elements to enhance their influence in the village. For the most part, where competitive politics arose, new families attained political recognition but they were usually of the rural middle class (e.g., the second largest landholder in the village) or they might be clients of the middle peasants. The requirement that ten seats be filled in the basic unit committee and the prohibition on members of the same family holding seats on the same committee, according to the 1968 rules, increased the average number of committee positions by about 40% above the NU average of 1959 and reduced the number of seats controlled by family sets by 50% (i.e., to 10% of the 1959 seats). Naturally, many new families, clients, and incipient factions would be expected to turn up on the rolls of the ASU committees. What continues to surprise, however, is the size of the group which has maintained its influence and its interest in holding ASU office at the village level.

We do not have extensive data on elections to the basic unit committees. One series of publications was issued giving partial listings of some of those who won in some districts. The list also included a large number of obvious errors such as listing the same name twice or giving an incomplete name or running several committees into one another. Nevertheless, it was possible to put together a fairly complete and fairly accurate list for the province of al-Gharbiyyah.[42] Once again, a warning is in order: al-Gharbiyyah is not all of Egypt and not even all of the delta. We have already examined the differences among the provinces, so that we have a kind of political profile of the province. At least we know enough to say that, despite its unrepresentative character, if we had to choose one province for purposes of this analysis, it would be al-Gharbiyyah.

Excluding the most highly urbanized areas of Bandar al-Mahallah al-Kubra and the two districts of Tanta city, there are 319 residential (not institutional or occupational) basic units in al-Gharbiyyah province. The total membership of these units was 3,190, but we did not have a full listing for each unit. Comparing those elected in 1968 with the list of secretaries and assistant secretaries of the basic units (committees of twenty) elected in 1963, we find that at least one of the two officers was reelected in 1968 in 48% (n = 156) of the units. The number of reelected secretaries and assistants was 179 or 28% of the hypothetically possible number (two officials per unit). The degree of turnover appears to be rather usual, but the fact that the same influentials were returned in such a large number of basic units confirms Harik's view that while new elements have been encouraged to participate, the veteran political leadership has not been excluded. Checking the members elected in 1968 with those elected to the National Union village committees, we find that at least one NU member was returned in 60% (n = 192) of the ASU units. A total of 292 individuals, former members of the NU were reelected in 1968, making up only 9% of the 3,190 total elected in al-Gharbiyyah at the lowest level. Although the total does not appear to be impressive, the fact that these members are so widely spread (in only one case were there four members reelected to the same unit, usually there was no more than one) sustains the argument that the early postrevolutionary elite is still quite influential. New elements may have been admitted to participation, but in each case we should examine whether they have been admitted as clients or as independent political forces. It may be noted that of the 292 reelected NU members, 76 or 26% were members of family sets in the 1959 register. Of those elected in both 1968 and 1963, 37% (n = 66) had been elected in 1959, and of this group of persistent winners, 44% (n = 29) were members of family sets in 1959. In other words, 29 out of the 76 family-set members (38%) did not lose any of the three elections while only 27 of 216 (17%) nonfamily-set members were persistent winners. Moreover, since the NU winners came back in 36 more villages than did the 1963 ASU winners, in some ways the 1959 elections may offer a more accurate picture of the distribution of political strength in the countryside.

Moving now to the district level, we have the list of names of those who were elected to the district (markaz and qism) committees of the ASU in 1968.[43] Since this is an extensive list, and since the task of comparing district and village lists is time consuming, it was decided to base our comparison of the 1968 district winners with the register of the National Union on a 10% sample. Starting randomly, every tenth name on the list was selected, following the evidently random listing of the provinces and the districts within the provinces in our source. The total selected was 241, but they were divided very unevenly among the provinces. It is obvious that the list is not complete and not accurate, but we do not know what margin of error to allow for. We have no data for Aswan, most of al-Minia is omitted, and some districts in other provinces were left out. Our results are not useful for examining differences between provinces, but they can give us a good general idea of the situation for the country as a whole and for the differences between lower and upper Egypt. Table 106 presents the results of our count of those elected in 1968 at the markaz level who were also elected to the National Union basic unit committees in 1959. The provincial

Table 106   Sample of Members of District
                                        Committees Whose Names Were
                                        Found in the NU Register

Province	Certain	Probable	Total	Percentage Certain	Percentage Certain and Probable
al-Qalyubiyyah	2	3	14		
al-Sharqiyyah	12	-	22		
al-Daqahliyyah	8	1	20		
Dumyat	1	2	8		
Kafr al-Shaykh	5	-	15		
al-Gharbiyyah	8	-	22		
al-Manufiyyah	10	1	17		
al-Buhayrah	12	2	24		
al-Jizah	4	-	8		
al-Fayyum	2	3	12		
Bani Suwayf	3	2	14		
al-Minia	3	-	4		
Assiut	7	3	22		
Suhaj	2	5	21		
Qena	2	1	18		
Aswan	-	-	-		
Total Lower Egypt	58	9	142	40.8	47.2
without Banadir	54	9	121	44.6	52.0
Total Upper Egypt	23	14	99	23.0	37.0
without Banadir	23	14	85	27.0	43.0
Total	81	23	241	33.6	43.2
without Banadir	77	23	206	37.4	48.5

data is given but is not very helpful. In all, 81 of the sample of 241 were positively identified and 23 more names were identified as probable. Our uncertainty stems from the facts that the full name was not given in the 1968 list, the spelling was often garbled, and, in some cases, the shortened name was so common that one could not be certain that one had found the same individual. In addition to differentiating between upper and lower Egypt and between the certain and the probable identifications, the results were also differentiated by taking the totals without including the data on the most highly urbanized districts of the provincial capitals.

If we take the certain and the probable identifications together, and if we leave out the large urban centers, we find that as many as 48.5% of our sample of 1968 district committee members were also elected in 1959 to the National Union basic unit committees. The figure is even higher for the delta region but lower in the south. The probables also make up a higher proportion of the sample from the south because of the less frequent use of "family names." The lower degree of continuity in the south need not be construed as evidence of the decline of the families who were influential in 1959, because we know that there was less competition, or fewer influential families in the south to begin with. In any case, there are clear indications from this sampling that there was substantial continuity of influence for the National Union elite. It is also worth noting that the data for al-Gharbiyyah province indicates that it is very close to the average for all 15 agricultural provinces at 36%. It also appears that the National Union winners did somewhat better at the district level than at the village level if the data on al-Gharbiyyah is used as a measure, for the highest estimate of village level continuity in that province is about 17% (taking account of the increase in committee seats and the restrictions on family-set members and on 'umad).

Early in July 1968, elections were held to choose the eight delegates from each district who would participate in the provincial and the national congresses. The names of those elected in the 142 districts with which we have been concerned were published except for 19 districts, including all 8 in al-Jizah, 4 in Kafr al-Shaykh, and 3 in al-Manu-fiyyah. In three cases districts were split up into two, where there was an urban center for which a new administrative status was declared. Altogether 1,005 names of those elected to the provincial congresses in the sixteen provinces were traced, and 236 were located in the register of the National Union. The result of just under 24% is consistent with our findings thus far, showing a substantial continuity of elite status; but by no means do we find a monopoly of political influence on the part of a small group of families. It is, of course, more than likely that the actual continuity of family influence is understated in these figures because we recorded only identical names and not those of persons apparently closely related to the district level delegate. At any rate, understated or not, the 24% figure would work out to about an average of two delegates per district. There were only 22 districts (16%) which had no delegates that had been in the National Union and four of those districts were in Aswan. Table 107 gives the percentages for the 16 provinces and the most striking thing about the distribution of traced delegates is how evenly they are distributed in all the provinces.

Table 107

Provincial and National Congress Delegates Elected in 1968 Who Were Traced to NU Membership Roll of 1959

Province	Percentage of Delegates
al-Qalyubiyyah	22.8
al-Sharqiyyah	28.4
al-Daqahliyyah	21.5
Dumyat	9.3
Kafr al-Shaykh	15.6
al-Gharbiyyah	30.7
al-Manufiyyah	22.5
al-Buhayrah	28.4
al-Jizah	?
al-Fayyum	16.6
Bani Suwayf	34.9
al-Minia	19.3
Assiut	23.7
Suhaj	23.7
Qena	22.2
Aswan	7.5
Lower Egypt	24.75
Upper Egypt	22.22
All Egypt	23.6

The National Congress met on 23 July 1968, as mentioned above, and its meeting, even though largely ceremonial, capped the process of reorganizing the mass political organization. This reorganization was preliminary to the elaboration of a number of equally ceremonial policy positions at the September meetings of the congress, and, in a politically more serious vein, was preliminary to the surprisingly sharp conflict over the manner in which the parliamentary elections were to be carried out. We have already, briefly, described this controversy, which was discussed in the press as the problem of the relationship between the ASU and the parliament. In this controversy, Haykal and "his" Marxists took the bourgeois democratic position of arguing for the political and constitutional autonomy of the parliament, while the 'Ali Sabri group of ASU apparatchiki evidently wished to subordinate the parliament to the ASU. This conflict foreshadows the conflict between

'Ali Sabri and Anwar al-Sadat of 1971, and it strongly suggests that the ASU secretariat was thought of as a center of power in 1968.

The controversy over the parliamentary elections surfaced in the press in November 1968, but despite the possibility that we may be using too much hindsight, there is some ambiguous evidence suggesting that preparations were being made to control those elections as early as August. I do not think that the anticipated control was to be directed at the creation of a real "machine" so much as to render the candidates beholden to the ASU secretariat and to facilitate implementation of a rule whereby membership in parliament was to be made dependent upon maintaining party discipline. Party discipline was, presumably, not to be determined by the parliamentary party, but by the ASU executive.

On 8 August, in a rather surprising announcement, al-Ahram carried a report from the ASU headquarters listing the district secretaries and assistant secretaries who had been elected the day before. On 7 August 1968, each district elected one secretary and two assistant secretaries, "thus completing the organization of the base of the ASU." This announcement was surprising because the election took place after the National Congress had formally met, and after all the stages of reorganization set out by the committee of fifty had been completed. It would appear that the stage of electing district level officers should have been completed when the district delegations were elected, unless the election of these officers was a matter of concern to the ASU secretariat and not to the committee of fifty which had to produce a National Congress, a Central Committee, an executive, and then a parliament. The connection with the elections is in the fact that most parliamentary constituencies coincide with the boundaries of administrative districts.

It is of some interest, therefore, to examine the relationship between those elected at the district level in 1968 and those who served earlier in the National Union and the Arab Socialist Union. Presumably, if there are many new names and faces, we have some circumstantial evidence for the view that these elections represent an attempt on the part of the ASU secretariat to extend their control down to the district level rather than to permit the influence of village level leadership to percolate upward to that level. It is not that the ASU secretariat might have selected members of another social segment and not members of the second stratum. It is rather that the second stratum is broad enough so that competition is possible within that stratum and that such competition was encouraged as a more or less inadvertent consequence of a power struggle over the influence of the central ASU secretariat. This competition was encouraged in much the same way that Sidqi Pasha

brought new rural middle class elements into political participation in
the early 1930s.

The district officers of 1968 are by no means an entirely new group.
Moreover, those officers who had held political positions in the past
were, characteristically broadly distributed throughout the country.
Nevertheless, it is interesting to note that few of the district officers or
none had been elected to the National Congress in July and that few
or none had been elected as district officers in 1959 in the National
Union. Nevertheless, in the announcement issued in *al-Ahram*, there
was included the further straightforward comment that many of these
district secretaries were reelected and that many ran unopposed. It was
further noted that the members of the district committees worked matters out by mutual agreement in a great many cases so that there were
no competitive elections. Unfortunately we do not have the list of district officers for 1963 so we could not compare the two lists. Instead,
the list of secretaries of the basic units of 1963 was used and the register of the National Union was also used to determine how many of
these district officers might be new political faces. Table 108 shows the

Table 108   District Secretaries of 1968 Traced
                                           in the List of Basic Unit Secretaries,
                                           1963

Province	Number Traced	Total Secretaries	Percentage
al-Qalyubiyyah	10	27	37.0
al-Sharqiyyah	9	33	27.3
al-Daqahliyyah	7	30	23.3
Dumyat	1	12	8.3
Kafr al-Shaykh	5	24	20.8
al-Gharbiyyah	3	33	9.0
al-Manufiyyah	7	27	25.9
al-Buhayrah	6	36	16.7
al-Jizah	3	24	12.5
al-Fayyum	2	18	11.1
Bani Suwayf	5	24	20.8
al-Minia	-	-	-
Assiut	5	24	20.8
Suhaj	-	-	-
Qena	1	24	4.2
Aswan	2	15	13.3
Lower Egypt	48	222	21.6
Upper Egypt	18	129	14.0
All 16 provinces	66	351	18.8

number and percentage of the names of the district officers also found in the list of basic unit secretaries for 1963. As can be seen, our source omitted the information for the provinces of al-Minia and Assiut.

In lower Egypt more than 20% of the district secretaries can be traced back to positions of influence in 1963, but in upper Egypt the percentage drops appreciably. There were many districts in which none of the three could be traced back to 1963, but there were also very few where more than one member of the troika was traced. In only a few more than 50 of the 117 districts surveyed were the incumbents traceable.

A small sample of 19 districts (16% of the total available) was selected for tracing these district secretaries back to those who were elected to the basic unit committees of the National Union in 1959. Only 18 of a possible 57 names were found, or nearly 32%. In only 4 districts, or about 21% of the total, were no names traced. In other words, if the sample is any indication of the situation in all of the districts, a substantial segment, widely distributed throughout the country, of the district officers were still drawn from the old National Union reservoir.

If the evidence is somewhat ambiguous for these district secretaries, it is unambiguous for those actually elected to parliament. The members elected from the 16 agricultural provinces were for the most part drawn from National Union members. Of course, there was quite a turnover in parliamentary membership, but the socioeconomic pool from which the members were drawn was identified in 1959. Tables 109, 110, and 111 present the detailed information for the country and for each province. In all, 262 members were elected from the agricultural provinces in 1969. All constituencies were two-member constituencies, and one of those elected had to be a worker or a peasant. In each constituency there were two candidates officially backed by the ASU and others, members of the ASU, who decided to run on their own. Nationwide there were 350 official candidates and 643 independent candidates.[44] Only 23 of the independents won and of these only 15 were from the 16 provinces. As we see in table 110, the profile of the independents is much like that of the ASU-supported candidates except that the elected independents had somewhat higher status in 1959 and might be considered to have more traditional standing.

If we include both those whose names were found in the NU register and those related to those in the NU register, we find that more than 60% of the M.P.'s elected in the agricultural provinces were members of the National Union. Of this group of 159, there were 51 or 32% members of family sets, 12.2% elected to the parliament of 1959, 7.3%

descendants of prerevolutionary M.P.'s, and 4.2% 'izbah owners. More important yet is the fact that more than 30% of the total (262) had been elected to parliament in 1964 and of this group of 84 M.P.'s, 30 had also been elected in 1959. (See table 111.) Dekmejian tells us that

Table 109   Parliament of January 1969, Part 1

| Province | Number of M.P.'s | Found in NU Register | | | Members of Family Sets | M.P. in 1959 |
		Same Name	Similar Name	Percentage Same and Similar		
al-Qalyubiyyah	14	8		57.1	6	1
al-Sharqiyyah	22	7	4	50.0	5	5
al-Daqahliyyah	26	10	4	53.8	4	2
Dumyat	6	2	3	83.3	1	
Kafr al-Shaykh	12	2	3	41.6	3	1
al-Gharbiyyah	22	13	4	77.2	3	2
al-Manufiyyah	20	5	5	50.0	3	1
al-Buhayrah	22	9	4	59.0	3	2
al-Jizah	16	2	6	50.0	6	3
al-Fayyum	12	5	3	66.7	2	1
Bani Suwayf	12	9	1	83.3	3	
al-Minia	22	6	10	72.0	3	4
Assiut	14	7	2	64.3	2	
Suhaj	22	10	4	63.6	5	4
Qena	14	5	4	64.3	2	6
Aswan	6	2		33.3		
Total	262	102	57		51[a]	32
Percent	100%	38.9%	21.8%		19.5%	12.2%

[a] 32% of total of those in NU register.

only 117 former M.P.'s were candidates in 1969 but 92 of these were elected.[45] Of the 92 former M.P.'s, 84 were elected in the 16 agricultural provinces.

Although more than 60% of the 1969 M.P.'s were also members of the National Union, many were at best members of the lowest level committees and they showed little evidence of being traditionally established notables rather than merely members of the rural middle class. Once again we find evidence of a considerable turnover in personnel of a sort that indicates some social distinction but no great political difference.

If the central secretariat faction did try to manage the elections of the district secretaries with a view to controlling the parliamentary elections, and if the Vanguard of the Socialists was in any way the instrumentality of this effort, they must have failed because this parliament voted for Sadat and against 'Ali Sabri in 1971. Their apparent failure may be traced to the fact that the executive committee member who was charged with political affairs and hence most responsible for screening the proposed candidates was Anwar al-Sadat.

Table 110   Unofficial Candidates Elected to
                                       Parliament of January 1969

Province	Total Elected	M.P. in 1959 or 1964	Member Provincial Committee 1964	District Officer 1959	Member of Family Set	NU Member	Descendant	'Izbah Owner
al-Qalyubiyyah	2		1			1		
al-Sharqiyyah	2	1		1	1	1		
al-Daqahliyyah	2		1			2		
Dumyat								
Kafr al-Shaykh								
al-Gharbiyyah								
al-Manufiyyah								
al-Buhayrah	5	4	2			4	1	1
al-Jizah								
al-Fayyum	1	1		1	1	1	1	1
Bani Suwayf								
al-Minia	2					1		
Assiut								
Suhaj								
Qena	1	1				1		
Aswan								
Total	15	7	4	2	2	11	2	2
Percent	100%	46%	27%	13%	13%	73%	13%	13%

It seems fairly clear that President Nasser did intend to create a stalemate among the various contending factions by stopping the elections to the executive committee before they were completed. It was also no accident that Anwar al-Sadat was made supervisor of the political subcommittee rather than 'Ali Sabri. Nor can we neglect entirely the alternative explanation that, despite some petty political disputes, there was really no intention to make important social changes in the composition of the ASU and the parliament and that, whatever else may have happened, our data simply reflect the essential stability of the regime and the passivity of the ASU apparatus.

The founding of the Vanguard of the Socialists and the admission of the Haditu communists to that organization afforded segments of the Egyptian left an opportunity to influence the course of political events (political development, s.v.p.). Nasser desired both to control and to exploit the left and 'Ali Sabri was selected to do the job. 'Ali Sabri was willing and not unsuccessful in this duplicitous operation, but his political skills and ambition led him into nasty conflicts with powerful opponents in the army, in the media, and in the bureaucracy. In these

Table 111   Parliament of January 1969, Part 2

Province	Number of Members	Former M.P.'s	1964 Provincial Committee Members	District Officers 1959	Descendants	ʿIzbah Owners
al-Qalyubiyyah	14	5	6	5	1	3
al-Sharqiyyah	22	8	6	3	1	
al-Daqahliyyah	26	7	7	3	2	
Dumyat	6	3	3		1	
Kafr al-Shaykh	12	3	3	1		
al-Gharbiyyah	22	7	8	2	2	
al-Manufiyyah	20	5	3		1	
al-Buhayrah	22	9	7	4	3	3
al-Jizah	16	5	5	2	1	
al-Fayyum	12	1		1	1	1
Bani Suwayf	12		1	1		
al-Minia	22	8	8	5	4	3
Assiut	14	6	5		1	
Suhaj	22	12	10	4		1
Qena	14	7	3	1	1	
Aswan	6	1	2			
Total	262	86	77	32	19	11
Percent	100%	32.8%	29.4%	12.2%	7.3%	4.2%

conflicts, 'Ali Sabri and the leftists became allied by the force of circumstances. The degree of cooperation that prevailed was determined by considerations of expedience, with some leftists exceeding from time to time the limits within which they could count on 'Ali Sabri's support. For their part, the leftists maintained constant pressure on Sabri to practice the socialism he continuously preached.

It is probably safe to say that Nasser was not greatly concerned about the possibility of a political challenge by 'Ali Sabri—especially since Sabri was decisively estranged from the army. Nasser demonstrated that he was able to step in and obstruct leftist tactical operations whenever 'Ali Sabri was tempted to cooperate too closely with the former communists. This uneasy but not untypically Nasserist balancing arrangement did not test the limits of the regime's capacities, manipulative and psychological, until the defeat in 1967. The claim that the

Vanguard of the Socialists sided with Nasser against elements of the
armed forces on 9 and 10 June 1967 and the increased dependence on
the Soviet Union at the very time when the forces Nasser had employed
against the leftists were gravely weakened led Nasser to attempt political structural changes of a strategic magnitude.

In fact, Nasser's reaction was slow and indecisive until after the demonstrations of February 1968. Nasser did not abolish the Vanguard of
the Socialists because that organization was the context in which the
communists were observed and controlled. The counterintelligence function of the vanguard was stepped up, instead. Nasser did abolish the
socialist institutes, the indoctrination camps for youth, and the leadership groups. The most important action taken by Nasser was, however,
to call for the reorganization of the Arab Socialist Union "from the
base to the summit" by means of elections rather than appointment.
The operation was to be dominated by Sha'rawi Goma'a as the chief
domestic security authority. The major political structural goal of this
reorganization was to prevent the communists from developing any
important influence, linkage, or administrative leverage over the masses
of workers and peasants by means of their position in the Vanguard of
the Socialists. The demonstrations of 9 and 10 June 1967 and those
of February 1968 were understood as forebodings of the possible course
of domestic politics, recalling the political anarchy of the 1946–52
period before the revolution. To prevent any attempt to manipulate
mass enthusiasm or mass alienation against the regime, the Vanguard
of the Socialists was isolated from the people and its bureaucratic structure and domestic spying functions emphasized.

One of the secondary consequences of this strategy was the weakening of the political influence of 'Ali Sabri. Sabri's influence declined
because of the narrower role of the Vanguard of the Socialists and not
because he failed to have his supporters elected at many levels of the
Arab Socialist Union. In fact, his men, it appears, were notably successful in the district bureaus and in the Central Committee if not in the
same measure in the National Assembly. Factional loyalty was, however, essentially opportunistic and responsive to the perquisites which
each leader might have available for distribution. The only reliable
solidarities were those of kinship, of bureaucratic organization, and of
the ideologically committed communists.

It is in this light that Nasser's curiously ineffective attacks on the
"centers of power" might be examined. Presumably the most notorious
centers of power were those established by 'Ali Sabri together with
Sha'rawi Goma'a and Sami Sharaf. It is not at all clear that these three
were weakened as a group even if 'Ali Sabri himself lost influence. But

the center of power that was most clearly restricted, though again not abolished, was that of the leftists within the Vanguard of the Socialists.

The ultimate consequence of Nasser's restructuring strategy was to be revealed in May 1971, when, in desperation, Sabri, Goma'a, and Sharaf attempted to employ the vanguard as an effective political instrument to save themselves. It was then apparent that the Vanguard of the Socialists had been almost completely absorbed into the bureaucratic organism which rests as heavily as the pyramids on the Egyptian soil. It was also apparent, after but a brief interlude punctuated by the martial excesses of 'Abd al-Hakim 'Amr in "liquidating feudalism," that the regime had once again repaired to its cautious reliance on the second stratum.

Fifteen

Political Change in Egypt

The Arab Socialist Union will not
perform any political function. . . .
The Arab Socialist Union will have
nothing to do with politics at all.

Anwar al-Sadat, *al-Ahram*

We have identified at least two geographically and politically differentiated segments of the second stratum. The first was located primarily in the west delta and Cairo region and the second in upper Egypt. The first segment is found in the more developed rural districts, close to major towns, and in areas of high yield, high capital agriculture. The second is found in the less urbanized districts of the less developed provinces. The first segment is more educated, more modern occupationally, and more numerous. The first segment is more often associated with medium-sized villages. The first segment appears to be more influential in the aggregate, or at least we may say that the regime seems to have been more responsive to the needs of this first segment, even though party office is more diffused among its members.

Party office and political influence are more concentrated among the members of the smaller and more closely related second segment. That second segment appears to be a more truly provincial elite, rather than a village elite. It is more traditional in the sense that its component families have been influential for several generations, as well as in the sense that fewer members of these families have modern occupations and advanced academic degrees.

The two segments are not neatly separated, and there are not only elements of both types to be found in nearly all the provinces, but there is substantial evidence of some kinship connections among members of the parliamentary stratum of both segments. In particular, we find over-lapping patterns in al-Minia and al-Buhayrah, al-Fayyum and al-Shar-qiyyah, and in Kafr al-Shaykh and various districts in upper Egypt. The overlapping patterns suggest that there is no sharp dichotomy of rural political-social structure in Egypt, but that given the same devel-opmental conditions, it is likely that many upper Egyptian districts will come to resemble lower Egyptian districts with a large, modernized, and politically competitive second stratum. Of course, it is not likely that the conditions which will obtain in the future will recapitulate the developmental experience of the more advanced districts of lower Egypt. Nor is it likely that the lower Egyptian districts will stand still while various upper Egyptian areas "catch up." Indeed, serious predic-tion is impossible because we do not control all the variables, because we have cautiously built plausible explanations rather than causal anal-yses on the foundation of our descriptive statistics, and because there are important uncertainties of ideology and of international politics that will impinge on policy choices.

It may be doubted that policy choices will be based on the expected consequences for the political system of any change in rural socio-political structure. Nevertheless, it may be expected that even the crudest sort of allocative or redistributive policies will have functional consequences (i.e., largely unintended) for the structure of the second stratum and hence for the range of political process alternatives avail-able to the Egyptian political leadership. The influence of formal ideo-logical or doctrinal commitments is not to be discounted, but, assuming the existing range of ideological alternatives (Nasserism, Sadat's liber-alism, Islamic neotraditionalism, etc.), one can expect that any sub-stantial change in the structure and distribution of the second stratum will impose constraints on the possibilities of attaining any preferred institutional and process changes. More particularly, it may be expected that political reforms directed primarily at urban population groups and at economic structures which are urban-centered will probably have only unintended consequences for rural structures, as was the case in Egypt during various periods between 1924 and 1954. We shall attempt to explore what some of these consequences might be in the light of the structural configurations we have uncovered and in the light of the political issues which have been discussed in the last two chap-ters.

The relevant problems may be stated as questions:

1. Under what circumstances is it likely that the character of the second stratum in upper Egypt will become more like that in lower Egypt?

2. Under what conditions is it likely that the traditional influentials in the south will hold their political positions?

3. Under what conditions is it likely that the second stratum in lower Egypt will change so that it becomes (a) more hierarchical and less competitive or (b) more individualistic and urban oriented?

4. What are likely to be the consequences of policies (a) which favor the urban bourgeoisie, (b) which encourage more highly capitalized agriculture, (c) which encourage the formation of ideologically oriented political parties, or (d) which encourage foreign investment?

5. Is it likely that members of the second stratum will evolve toward a more specific definition of their own interests and that they will create specialized political structures to compete more vigorously with other social segments that are now being encouraged to enter the political arena?

6. If the second stratum responds to possible opportunities for interest-oriented participation, will Egyptian political processes shift toward the pragmatic or the ideological, or will competing political groups continue to vie over who best represents the interests of the whole nation?

7. If the second stratum becomes fragmented, weakened, or otherwise changed, is it reasonable to expect that there will be a sequence of class-interested moments of enthusiasm or is the rural middle class really the only segment that could play the integrative role?

8. Is there a situational (if not a necessary theoretical) link between authoritarian government of the party, army, bureaucracy, or all three, and the enhancement of the political status of the rural notables in the smallest villages?

Before we can proceed to speculate on the answers to these questions, it may be useful to provide a groundwork of two elements: first, a general characterization of the way in which the Nasserist system worked and how that working was related to the political availability of the second stratum, and second, an accounting of the modifications in the Nasserist system which have been occasioned by Sadat's succession. Some of these changes have been the result of ideological differences, but others are probably no more than the result of Sadat's limited range of options in responding to both domestic and foreign political challenges.

The Nasserist regime was in many ways revolutionary, but, as we have seen, it was far less discontinuous in substructural terms than it claimed to be. The continuity of the political significance of the rural

middle class was the important link between the pre-1952 regime and
the Nasserist system, but the role of the rural middle class was not the
same during both periods. The political evolution of the rural middle
class can be fixed, if somewhat arbitrarily, in terms of the dates of
important parliamentary changes and of important political upheavals.
As we have seen, the Egyptian parliament has always been characterized by strong rural representation, but in 1881 and again in the period
1924–29 there was some decline of agrarian representation. Both 1881
and 1924 were periods of strong nationalist agitation and challenge to
the authoritarian head of state. By contrast, 1870 and 1931 were periods of acquiescence in authoritarian leadership and they coincide with
the virtual dominance of the rural middle class in parliament. Yet
Egyptian historians tell us that in 1879 and 1919 the Egyptian countryside supported the national movement against the British and against
the Muhammad 'Ali dynasty. Granting that there was such a rural rising
in 1919, that it was led by the rural middle class or at least its urban
offshoots, and that it was countrywide, it is similarly apparent that this
enthusiastic rural response was episodic and that it subsided quite as
suddenly and decisively as it erupted.

It is more relevant to note that the period from 1931 to 1952 saw a
steady increase in the representation of the rural middle class, an increasing corruption of parliament as a credible spokesman for the
national cause, and a continuing subordination of parliament to the
king despite occasional conflict and much friction. It is apparent that,
during the period just before the revolution, the rural middle class
allied itself with the large landowners, the cotton financiers, and the
industrialists in order to hold their declining position in the countryside.
The haute bourgeoisie compromised with the rural middle class in order
to prevent them from joining forces with the king, as had happened in
1931. Increasing pressure was brought to bear by students and by the
Ikhwan, who in the late 1940s represented urban guild, craft, lower
middle class, and intellectual groups.

The new regime slowly and hesitantly worked out its policy toward
both sets of urban political protagonists. The coalition of the modernized haute bourgeoisie and the largest landowners, which was represented by the Wafd, was the source of the greatest challenge. But the
Revolutionary Command Council also had to deal with political pressures from students, from factory labor, from the professional classes,
and from the religious zealots. Eschewing the formation of political
alliances and rejecting the option of allowing a measure of political
competition, the Revolutionary Command Council, under Nasser's leadership, moved to subdue or neutralize their urban rivals. As it succeeded

in reestablishing political order in the cities, the revolutionary regime also came to rely upon the rural middle class for a variety of political purposes.

In its concern to establish its legitimacy and to provide a functional equivalent of a political organization, the revolutionary regime did not attempt merely to exploit the traditional influence of the village notables. The Nasserist regime attempted, rather, to transfer the spirit of village Egypt to the seat of power in Cairo.[1] Large landowners, finance capitalists, the educated minorities, industrialists, urban professionals, merchants, industrial labor, and even students were all repressed in the name of a regime devoted to the welfare of the peasant and the worker, to mass democracy, and, above all, to reestablishing national dignity.

The Nasserist regime presented itself as continuing and completing the national movement begun in the nineteenth century. That movement had been built on student anti-imperialism, labor unrest, rural middle class antagonism toward the accumulation of large estates and toward absenteeism, Ikhwan xenophobia and religious revivalism, neoromanticism in literature, and the failure or irrelevance of liberalism in influencing the rural middle class. The revolutionary regime, and Nasser personally, decided quite consciously to lead and not to follow these so-called revolutionary elements; but in depriving the urban groups of political power, it also ran the risk of depriving itself of political support. The regime might have simply relied upon the army, but it is not at all clear that the army was then capable of detaching itself from Egyptian society. Moreover, the army had split during the controversy between Naguib and Nasser.

In the ensuing years the Nasser regime groped its way to a political structure which not only used the village to sustain its claim to wide popular support and to being concerned with the problems of the peasantry, but which also ruled through the urbanized and educated kin of the rural middle class. Even before the revolution, the relatives of the rural middle class had begun to move into the civil service and the professions, but they were not dominant in numbers and certainly not dominant in influence. Their numbers and influence had gradually grown, but they have always been controlled and used by the military oligarchy. It has been easy for this group to identify its interests with those of the ruling group because they were not affected by land reform nor by the socialist laws.

The ruling group is not, however, primarily concerned with maintaining the position and interests of the rural middle class. The rural middle class is congenial in spirit, loyal, and cooperative with the ruling group which shares with the rural middle class many values.[2] The rural middle class, especially insofar as increasing numbers of that segment have acquired education and professional or technical qualifications, are the instruments by which the rule of the military oligarchy can be carried out. The professional, technical, and functionary classes have been subjected to an economic squeeze, but the rural middle class segments of these groups have thereby been more widely admitted to professional, technical, and functionary leadership positions, to compete with the older professional, technical, and functionary groups—but all the while, the average compensation of these groups and their influence has been declining. There are several reasons why the rural middle class does not object: because it has certain cultural affinities with the rulers, because their agricultural interests remain intact, and because within the general framework of anti-intellectualism and antagonism toward the middle class intelligentsia, the urban kin of the rural middle class have been beneficiaries of the political processes which have developed as a means of realizing the goals of the regime. Within what appears to be the framework of popular, socialist democracy and nationalism, with a neutralist and self-interested foreign policy, various processes permitted the ruling clique to use selectively elements of the professionals, the technicians and the bureaucracy, and even the intellectuals as their second stratum, but without ruling on behalf of that stratum and without being directly responsive or responsible to it. There were several processes whereby the regime could realize such control and stability.

Cooptation. The rulers selected from among the pool of professionals, technicians, functionaries, and intellectuals those who could be trusted on cultural and sociological grounds.

Infeudation. This is another of Mosca's terms used here to describe the way in which virtual proprietary rights over certain administrative, economic, or educational activities have been attributed to managers, editors, deans, and bureaucrats.

Symbolic mobilization. The rulers repeatedly reorganized the mass national movement or party to symbolize cleansing of the political machine, reaffirmation of values, reinvigoration of militants, and political unity against all opposition. As we have seen, the rural middle class continued to have a most prominent position in the Arab Socialist Union and in the parliaments which were elected after such reorganization, even when efforts were made to reflect the support and unity of administrative and bureaucratic structures.

Syndicalization. This is the process of organizing all interest groups or functional groups and labor groups so as to tie them to the mass party, to prevent opposition or dysfunctional lobbying, and to symbolize the attachment of all modern differentiated structures to the regime.

It was thought by some to be possible to dispense with this sort of practice after the organization of the ASU in institutional as well as residential units and with the insistence that half the members of all ASU committees be either workers or peasants. Despite this organizational policy, the students, bureaucrats, intellectuals, and others have preferred the interest group pattern as more representative of the real state of political affairs and of their interests than the more symbolic ASU. Appointment to leadership of the syndicates is another kind of cooptation and of infeudation.

Redress of grievance. Redress was primarily offered to members of the lower classes, and in any case it was only operative in individual cases and not for larger collectivities. This process operated through the ASU and through the syndicates and less frequently through the bureaucracy and hardly ever through the press. The consequence was that redress hardly ever challenged the position and privileges of the rural middle class established in the ASU while permitting the upwardly mobile members of the syndicates from the rural middle class to press the leadership of the syndicates if that leadership was not congenial to the regime.

Administrative rationalization. This form of rationalization entailed not only centralization of control and intelligence in the presidency and related establishments, but also concentration of power in fewer and fewer structures as well as experimental restructuring aimed at increasing efficiency and reducing corruption but having the effect also of purging, intimidating, or keeping under surveillance. The presidency has become less and less dependent on other structures for administration and policy control. A number of structures have emerged almost autonomously from ministries although linked to the presidency. The greatest weakness remains control over the army, which does not fit exactly with any of these processes.

System maintenance (a). This form of system maintenance utilized symbol manipulation by communications, information, and propaganda specialists in a variety of media for domestic and foreign consumption with heavy emphasis on the foreign policy aspects and with special utilization of Nasser himself as a symbol. Reference was also made to the values of populism, Egyptianism, Islam, Arabism, socialism, democracy, anti-imperialism, and nonalignment.

Control and coordination of intellectual activity. This was achieved mainly through control of the communications media and the universities and institutes of research and publication houses. Fees, salaries, and royalties were offered for writing books, articles, pamphlets, radio shows, and other propaganda materials. Another important basis of control is by special communications aimed at intellectuals, telling them what the regime wants, will stand for, and the like; most especially important here were Haykal's editorials.

System maintenance (b). Intelligence and secret police organizations were widely and more or less effectively used to maintain the regime, and not only as a last resort.

Bearing in mind the loose linkage between the military elite and the second stratum, and considering the ambivalence regarding the Arab Socialist Union, the Nasserist regime was remarkably well integrated and relatively secure. The economic and military performance of the government left much to be desired, but its political opponents on both the right and the left succeeded in no more than fruitless and inept conspiracy. This regime weathered not only the 1956 military reversal, but the political disaster of the Syrian secession, the military failure in Yemen, the catastrophe of 1967, and the military conspiracy of 'Abd al-Hakim 'Amr. Despite the evident strength of the regime, there were important contradictory tendencies that might have resulted in significant political change even had Nasser's death not intervened. Anwar al-Sadat had not only to cope with the vicissitudes of a succession crisis, but also to deal with the incipient dysfunction of the processes that had characterized Nasser's last years. While it is obvious that much of the strength of the regime was drawn from Nasser's own personality, it is also apparent that the effectiveness of some of Nasser's political solutions was declining. Consequently, just as we can say that Sadat faced problems that Nasser did not have to confront, so can we say that there were other problems which Nasser himself would have had to face, had he lived, which Sadat merely inherited. These emergent tendencies had not yet succeeded in changing the Nasserist system, but it was also not clear that Nasser would be able to cope with those challenges without adaptive acquiescence in the development of new political processes.

The emergent dysfunctional processes may be summarized as follows:

1. Increased involvement and more systematic consultation of the military in policy making, or, at least, increasingly outspoken military criticism of policy and more vigorous attempts to protect individual officers from punishment, transfer, or retirement

2. Increased alienative behavior of neglected urban elements who had no rural middle class connections (it might be expected that

urban dissatisfaction would increase unless decreasing material prospects could be compensated for by means of international political or military victories or symbolic rewards)

3. Affirmative emphasis on traditional, and especially on Islamic symbols after June 1967, thus strengthening Ikhwan and allied elements

4. Continued urbanization of the educated elements of the second stratum and the relative decline in the weight of their rural agrarian interests

5. Application of rationalizing principles in the reorganization of the Arab Socialist Union—especially in developing militant and ideologically indoctrinated cadres within an inner party apparatus

6. Expansion of foreign influence as the price of foreign assistance

7. Continued decline in Nasser's "charisma" as a consequence of defeat, political frustration, compromise on the Egyptian-Israeli front, and the opposition of other Arab states

8. Decline in the rate of economic development as a result of the Yemen conflict, the 1967 war, the evacuation of the Canal Zone cities, and the cost of the war of attrition

9. Increasing emphasis upon exclusively Egyptian political cultural symbols to the detriment of the employment of pan-Arab and Palestine-centered symbols

If these were the major change-producing processes to which Nasser was responding in the years between the defeat of 1967 and his death, these same processes together with the still effective structure built by Nasser constituted the political context within which Sadat was thrust to leadership in the fall of 1970. Less than eight months after becoming president, Sadat was faced with a crisis, the resolution of which had enormous implications for both the domestic and foreign policies of Egypt. In the resolution of that crisis, the structure of the Arab Socialist Union and the relationship between its administrative apparatus and its officeholding members were crucial. Moreover, the resolution of that crisis reaffirmed some of the "Nasserist processes" but also intensified the impact of some of the dysfunctional or change processes that emerged during Nasser's last years.

As we have seen, perspectives on foreign policy, if not the realities of foreign policy, were significantly integrated with interpretations of the domestic political situation. The notion prevailed that Egypt was compelled to respond to a global political environment in which the most powerful forces were those of capitalism and communism. It was further assumed that there existed, within Egyptian society, natural class and ideological allies of each of these forces. From this perspective, there was no essential difference between domestic and foreign politics, and, thus, the devices which were utilized to limit the influence of the extreme left and the extreme right within Egypt were also the major props of a foreign policy aimed at maintaining national independence. Most importantly, by basing the domestic political processes upon the structure, capacities, and orientations of the second stratum, Nasser minimized the influence of those social segments that might be considered political allies of the great powers. But Egypt's foreign policy was not and could not have been that of isolating itself nor of opposing all great power initiatives. Nasser recognized that important benefits could be gained by cooperating alternately with one or another great power. The greatest danger was, of course, to succumb to some form of neoimperialism. It might be slightly less bad to be dominated by means of an arrangement among the powers. The greatest material cost would result, however, from being ignored by both powers.

Nasser developed a number of ways of dealing with the powers which had both symbolic and possibly prophylactic effect. One of these devices, as we have seen, involved the treatment of members of the Egyptian Communist Party. Another had to do with participation in, or lending prominence to, religious ceremonies. The most important device was the alternation in high office of certain close political associates of Nasser who were generally identified as leftist and pro-Soviet or as rightist and pro-American. 'Ali Sabri was the best-known symbol of a pro-Soviet foreign political orientation, while Zakaria Muhi al-Din came to be known as the pro-American symbol. Since 'Ali Sabri was first thought to be pro-American, and since neither of the two were strongly ideologically committed, it was fairly obvious that the installation of either in important office represented neither a complete nor an irrevocable alignment with either great power.

Moreover, the appointment of either or both simultaneously could be used in combination with ambiguously contradictory policies of expanding the socialist sector of the economy or tightening surveillance on ex-communists in the media industries. Perhaps the lowest level of commitment was expressed in simply sending either Muhi al-Din or Sabri off on missions to talk to the Americans or Russians and to persuade them of something, as when Muhi al-Din was sent to Washington on the eve of the June War of 1967 and when 'Ali Sabri was sent to Moscow on the eve of the War of Attrition in 1969. When both served as vice-presidents, they were reduced to mere symbols, but when Zakaria Muhi al-Din was made prime minister and 'Ali Sabri made head of the Arab Socialist Union, symbolic balancing was complemented by at least a measure of pragmatic competition.

It appears that 'Ali Sabri was far more the happy political warrior than Zakaria Muhi al-Din. In any case Muhi al-Din was soon overshadowed in the conflict with 'Ali Sabri by Muhammad Hasanain Haykal of *al-Ahram*. Furthermore, Muhi al-Din was all but completely out of the picture after he had been named by Nasser as his successor on 9 June 1967. 'Ali Sabri was also named as a possible successor, and he was gradually discredited as having been an incompetent leader of the ASU. Zakaria Muhi al-Din virtually faded away politically in 1968 and 1969, but 'Ali Sabri hung on tenaciously, exploiting his personal connections with various ASU officials as well as his identification with the Soviet Union—during a period of great dependence upon the Soviets, obviously. 'Ali Sabri was able to give substance to the notion that he was the Soviet political connection in Egypt, whereas Muhi al-Din either failed to do likewise or was simply not interested in that game, or was doomed to political failure by the further deterioration in American-Egyptian relations which followed the June War. 'Ali Sabri did not demonstrate great political skills, but he nevertheless persevered; so that even when he was disgraced in September 1969 upon his return from Moscow, he was allowed to retain his membership in the Higher Executive Committee of the Arab Socialist Union.

A most significant dimension of the political process we are describing is that Nasser carefully avoided any serious discussion of the problem of political succession. Except for the extreme case of his speech on 9 June 1967, he did not single out any of his associates as potential successors. Moreover, in appointing five vice-presidents at once, and then abolishing the office altogether, Nasser certainly added to the uncertainty surrounding the question. The constitution of 1964 provided that the president of the republic would be succeeded by the first vice-president, a provision which had made 'Ali Sabri the heir apparent. But in 1969 when the single office of vice-president was reestablished, Anwar al-Sadat was appointed to this post.

Anwar al-Sadat had emerged in 1968 as the most important political, as opposed to media, counterweight to 'Ali Sabri. While Haykal and his clients did battle with 'Ali Sabri's writers, Anwar al-Sadat was every bit as much a political competitor as Sabri, but he was considered, incorrectly as it turns out, to have been even more of an intellectual lightweight than Sabri.

The kind of political process we are discussing, involving the linkage of foreign policy with a certain amount of domestic squabbling or jockeying for position, was not of central importance during Nasser's lifetime. His sudden death transformed the significance of this process.

Quite unexpectedly, the two major symbols of this dialectical process became two concrete individuals competing for the highest political office. Furthermore, in this competition, it was inevitable that they should use the political resources that accrued to them as the result of their identification with certain kinds of policy. The succession struggle became also, and perhaps inevitably even if unintentionally, a struggle over the foreign policy orientation of Egypt. Thus, a structure of symbolic competition which had been created to minimize external influence in Egyptian politics became the very device whereby succession to the most powerful office was rendered dependent upon the question of which great power Egypt would cooperate with. While domestic policy was loosely linked with foreign policy on ideological grounds, it would be misleading to say that domestic policy shifts were simply derivative of this competitive struggle.

The competition between Anwar al-Sadat and 'Ali Sabri, symbolic and personal, culminated in Sadat's successful purge of the Sabri group in May 1971, but the story begins much earlier. After the June War of 1967, there was substantial open criticism of the ASU and, by implication, of 'Ali Sabri. In the reorganization of the ASU, the special cadre organizations, at least at the basic unit level, were dropped in favor of the old committee system. Sabri was replaced as chief administrative officer of the ASU and his group was carefully balanced by Sadat and others in the Higher Executive Committee. The parliamentary elections of 1969 were a standoff between the two factions—a situation which evidently coincided with Nasser's preference. By early 1969, the reorganization of the ASU and the election of the parliament were completed, and in March 1969 Nasser ordered the beginning of the War of Attrition against the Israeli forces on the Suez front.

The War of Attrition was begun by means of heavy artillery attacks on fixed Israeli emplacements, and it was backed by small-scale commando raids into Sinai. The Israeli response, after taking losses sufficient to establish the effectiveness of the Egyptian tactic, was to use their superior air power against the Egyptian artillery, to make daring commando raids against Egyptian military bases, and to extend bombing raids against strategic targets deep into Egyptian territory. Israeli strategists hoped to discourage the continuation of the War of Attrition, to reverse its effects, to demonstrate the incompetence of the Egyptian army, and to break the political morale of the Egyptian people. The relative success of the Israeli counterattack led Nasser to demand more military and political support from the Soviet Union, and it is apparent that the Soviet response was dissatisfying in the summer of 1969.

We do not know exactly what Nasser demanded of Moscow nor what their unacceptable terms were, but a number of events of significance surfaced in 1969. Egyptian military frustrations peaked after the bold, successful Israeli raid on the western shore of the Gulf of Suez on 9 September. On 18 September it was reported that 'Ali Sabri had been removed from his post in the ASU. On 19 September it was reported that both the army chief of staff and the head of the navy had been dismissed. On 21 September it was reported that 30 journalists working for *al-Akhbar*, the pro-Sabri, anti-Haykal newspaper, had been either fired or sent on "indefinite vacations." The newspaper *al-Akhbar* and the journalists were loosely described as leftist.

While these events fell together, Haykal attempted to convince his readers that they were quite separate. The military dismissals were obviously related to the failure to control the Israeli counterattacks and to prevent Israel from taking the initiative. The downgrading of Sabri was linked to his trip to Moscow in July 1969, but was described as nonpolitical. Some members of his entourage had imported luxury items from the Soviet Union and had not paid customs duties on them. Sabri was thus humiliated as a petty smuggler and voluptuary by implication, but he did not lose his membership in the Higher Executive Committee. More significantly he gave up his position as chairman of the ASU committee on organization.

Among the possible linkages between the military and political aspects of these changes of September 1969 are (*a*) that 'Ali Sabri opposed dismissing the army and navy chiefs, (*b*) that Nasser desired to put pressure on the Soviets to increase their military support by giving him better equipment (more effective antiaircraft missiles and/or surface-to-surface missiles capable of hitting strategic and civilian targets in Israel), or, (*c*) that Nasser was responding negatively to quite specific Soviet demands that there be improved party-to-party relations as promised in 1965.

Although the Soviets increased shipments of some categories of weapons during the fall of 1969, the military situation continued to decline. Nasser moved more desperately in December at the Rabat Summit of the Arab League, threatening to break up the meeting unless all aspects of the conflict with Israel were recognized as subordinate to the battle on the Egyptian front. On 20 December 1969, Nasser reestablished the office of vice-president and he appointed Anwar al-Sadat as the sole vice-president and constitutional successor to the presidency. In January 1970, Nasser travelled to Moscow, and this time succeeded in convincing the Soviets that they had to come to his aid if political disaster for both were to be avoided.

Little came of Egypt's attempts to gain additional financial support
from the Arab League, but by early spring of 1970 it was clear that
the Soviet Union was not only supplying and directing the use of the
latest and best antiaircraft missile systems available, it was also using
Soviet pilots and aircraft to defend the Egyptian heartland. The Israeli
air force was assigned the task of wiping out the air defenses set up
within 20 miles of the west bank of the canal in order to prevent artillery attacks or the staging of a crossing onto Israeli-held territory. The
costs to the Israeli air force were great, but they persevered. The Soviets, in turn, maintained their support of Egypt and even expanded
the air defense network. The United States now agreed to replace lost
Israeli aircraft, and the possibility of a dangerous confrontation grew.
The weakest element in the crisis was, of course, the direct involvement
of Soviet personnel and equipment. It was this difficulty, as well as the
unwillingness of any of the combatants to accept a setback, that led to
the compromise cease-fire of 7 August 1970. The cease-fire was the
result of an American initiative, but it conformed to Soviet preferences,
as well, since the Soviet Union did not wish to risk a direct confrontation with the United States and did not wish to enter into an unlimited
commitment to the military success of a state which was not communist,
which would not allow the Communist Party to function, and which
would not even allow an effective pro-Soviet faction to develop.

The cease-fire of 1970 has been interpreted as an American success
and in retrospect it can be seen as a turning point in Egyptian-Ameri-
can relations. Evidently, Nasser resisted Soviet urgings that he accept
the cease-fire. During his prolonged 18-day visit to Moscow in July,
Nasser was also treated for illness, but there were some difficult political discussions which confirmed the suspicions on both sides. Nasser's
reluctant acceptance of the cease-fire has been interpreted as a decision
to try the alternative of cooperating with the United States since the
Soviet option had been pressed as far as it could go without incurring
unacceptable domestic political costs.

Nasser died on September 28, while engaged in putting the final
touches to a solution of the Black September crisis. At that point it
was too early to know whether a decisive shift had occurred in Egyptian policy. As vice-president, Anwar al-Sadat succeeded Nasser as
acting president, and though there was some speculation that 'Ali Sabri
might be elected by the National Assembly, on 6 October the ASU
Higher Executive Committee nominated Sadat unanimously, the National Assembly confirmed him on 8 October, and he was elected by
plebiscite with 90% of the vote on 15 October. 'Ali Sabri was appointed
vice-president along with Husayn al-Shafi'i. Sha'rawi Goma'a remained

minister of the interior. Sabri's ally, 'Abd al-Muhsin Abu al-Nur, became secretary general of the Arab Socialist Union. Dr. Mahmud Fawzi
became prime minister.

The profile of the new government did not appear to be rightist, nor
did it exclude 'Ali Sabri and his supporters or allies. There is in fact
little evidence of serious conflict between Sadat and Sabri until Sadat's
policies of developing the American option and strengthening the middle
classes became evident. Nevertheless, there is some contrast in the emphasis of the Soviet-Egyptian communiqué marking the end of 'Ali
Sabri's trip to Moscow on 20 December 1970 and in the speeches of
President Podgorny at the ceremonies dedicating the Aswan dam on
14 January 1971, and Sadat's note to the United States on the opening
of the canal and his decree returning illegally sequestrated property to
its original owners in December 1970. The Soviet Union was now
promising substantial economic support and attempting to divert attention from the military issues to social issues and the problems of development. Sadat, however, set out to win the confidence of the United
States and to revive the diplomacy of the Rogers plan as a means of
bringing American pressure to bear on Israel. Sadat's plan involved a
multifaceted program of encouraging an interim arrangement for the
opening of the canal, encouraging foreign investment, blocking or coun-
tering Soviet and communist influence in other Arab countries, mobilizing the support of the conservative Arab regimes, offering the prospect
of an end of belligerency with Israel, and yet threatening renewed
fighting and renewed reliance on the Soviet Union if his overtures were
not accepted. Sadat was virtually assured of a measure of success when
he boldly announced acceptance of the Jarring proposal, which urged
that peace with and recognition of Israel be exchanged for the return
of occupied territories, and when the Meir government flatly rejected
that proposal. That there were many cloudy aspects of both responses
is less important to our analysis than the fact that Sadat's increasing
pursuit of the American option had obviously paid off in that he was
gaining American support without having to deliver any concrete con-
cessions to Israel—thanks to Israel's less than skillful responses.

It would now appear that 'Ali Sabri and his supporters became disturbed about the possibility that they would either lose political influence or that Sabri's chances for succeeding to the presidency (with
Soviet support?) in the foreseeable future were rapidly diminishing.
Sabri cast about for an issue on which to confront Sadat and he found
a bad one. He also sought a political process by which he might be able
to exploit that issue, and it turned out to be inappropriate. The issue

was the proposed union of Egypt, Libya, and Syria, and the political means entailed the use of the Arab Socialist Union.

We cannot be certain why Sabri chose the proposed union with Libya and Syria as the occasion to challenge Sadat; but it is possible to speculate that he felt that increasingly Sadat was acting independently, that he sought to forestall the rapprochement with the United States indirectly rather than directly, and that the occasion was more important than the issue. The challenge came in April 1971. On 18 March Sadat had met with Qaddafi at Tobruk. On 24 March President Asad of Syria announced that the Tripoli Charter States (Syria, Egypt, and Libya) would soon propose a federation uniting all three. On 27 March Sadat met with Numayri at Khartoum. Numayri, it will be remembered, had become involved in a political conflict with the Sudan Communist Party. At about the same time, the pro-Sabri newspaper *al-Jumhuriyyah*, the semiofficial organ of the ASU, bitterly attacked Haykal and his editorials (of 5 and 18 March) supporting the pro-American turn in Sadat's policy. Secretary of State Rogers was to arrive in Cairo early in May. On 13 April the presidents of all four states met at Cairo to work out details of the federation. Finally on 17 April 1971, the Benghazi Declaration, announcing the intention of the three countries—Syria, Egypt, and Libya—to form a federation, was issued.

In tracing the events that followed, we are constrained to rely on the official interpretation because the accused were not allowed to present their version publicly. Nevertheless, with slight adjustment for exaggeration, it seems to me that the story rings true. In what follows, we present our interpretation of the events as reported in the press.

At Benghazi, 'Ali Sabri accused Sadat of exceeding his authority in proposing to sign a declaration of intent to join a federation without first obtaining the approval of the Arab Socialist Union and the National Assembly. Evidently, Sadat deferred to Sabri and the Benghazi Declaration included the proviso that the declaration would not be valid unless approved by the ASU and the assembly before being submitted to a popular referendum in September. Sadat later reported that Sabri openly disagreed with him, and the issue was referred for discussion by the Higher Executive Committee of the ASU. On 20 April there was a strategy meeting of some opponents of Sadat at the office of 'Abd al-Muhsin Abu al-Nur, then secretary general of the ASU. On 21 April the Higher Executive Committee met. This was the same committee elected in November 1968 except that Kamal Ramzi Stinu had been replaced by Labib Shuqayr, the speaker of the assembly. Sabri attacked Sadat at the meeting and the vote went against Sadat by 5 to 3. With

Sadat were Husayn al-Shafi'i and the premier, Mahmud Fawzi. Against him were the four members of the Sabri group and Shuqayr. A very disturbed Sadat then called for discussions of the matter by the 150-member Central Committee—and he asked that the members of the Higher Executive Committee refrain from addressing the Central Committee.

In the meantime, on the night of the fateful executive committee meeting, Sadat summoned his military leaders to his office and he sought to determine how far he might rely on their support. It is reported that defense minister General Fawzi was reticent but chief of staff Lt. General Muhammad Sadiq offered his support and swung the remaining high officers behind him. It appears that this meeting was decisive, as might be expected. According to the official prosecutor's reconstruction of the plot, General Fawzi was to have ordered some troop movements during the period between the expected two meetings of the Central Committee. The plan was that Sadat would be challenged at the Central Committee meeting, but that Sabri would take a moderate stand calling for a postponement of the issue while leaving the strongest attacks to others. In the event, Sabri was warned in advance of the first Central Committee meeting that he was to be dismissed as vice-president; and General Fawzi was intimidated and prevented from moving any units of the armed forces during the crucial last week in April, although later he did put some units on alert and he tried to call meetings of various military committees.

Sabri's group may have attempted to influence the members of the Central Committee in advance, but it appears that the most persuasive effort was a vitriolic four-hour attack on Sadat by Sabri in contravention of the alleged agreement to remain silent at the meeting. There are two reports on the results of this meeting of the Central Committee. Sadat is quoted as saying that all but three members of the Central Committee opposed him. But it is not clear that an actual vote was taken because another report states that the meeting became disorderly and that completion of the discussion and voting were delayed until a subcommittee could bring in a compromise recommendation providing that all decisions by the executive of the proposed federation (i.e., the three heads of state) be made by unanimous vote.

On 29 April the Central Committee met again. Some say the meeting was "stormy," but it is likely that some observers have confused the first and second meetings. At any rate, the Central Committee endorsed the amended federation proposal; and it was ratified on the same day by a unanimous vote of the National Assembly. On May 1 Sadat made a vigorous May Day speech condemning those who wished to usurp the people's power, and on 2 May he dismissed 'Ali Sabri from his position as vice-president.

Sadat seemed to have the upper hand but the matter did not rest there. 'Ali Sabri pressed Sha'rawi Goma'a and the leadership of the ASU to take action. According to the prosecutor, a complex plot was developed including efforts to hold protest meetings within the ASU, the youth groups, and probably the trade unions or factories; to instigate popular demonstrations; to make various announcements and to play patriotic anthems on Radio Cairo in order to alert the masses and to bring them into the streets; to disrupt traffic in Cairo and generally to create chaotic conditions so that General Fawzi might order the army to intervene to restore order. During the period 3 May to 13 May it would appear that efforts were made to carry out some parts of the plot, but activities seem to have been sporadic and limited, for the most part, to Cairo, al-Jizah, and environs. There are reports of some anti-Sadat activities in al-Manufiyyah and Dumyat. There was also a report of a meeting of the parliamentary party on 10 May.

These reports of widespread agitation are, however, all rather late and the result of lengthy investigation. The earlier reports put great emphasis on the intelligence side of the drama. According to this alternative perspective, Sadat did not know what was going on because his own chief of intelligence, who was reporting to Sami Sharaf, minister of state for presidential affairs, knew that Sharaf himself was involved in the conspiracy. Ahmad Kamil, chief of the intelligence agency, had, in fact, taped many of the conversations of the conspirators. But so had Sharaf done some taping of his own, and Sha'rawi Goma'a's ministry of the interior had their listening apparatus as well. Presumably, the break came on the night of 11 May, when an army officer brought Sadat some tape recordings of the conspirators' conversations implicating Sha'rawi Goma'a and revealing the intention of utilizing ASU cadres to create public disorder. It is not clear to what extent these revelations implicated Sami Sharaf and General Fawzi.

Whichever story one accepts, it is clear that not much was accomplished by the conspirators during the ten days prior to 13 May. It is, moreover, possible to doubt that the conspirators intended to do anything without military support. In any case, by 12 May Sadat had decided to reorganize the ASU in order to remove this instrument from the hands of his enemies, and on 13 May he decided to dismiss Sha'rawi Goma'a from his post as minister of the interior and, as such, the person most responsible for domestic security.

It was at this point that the members of the Sabri faction became desperate and decided to implement their program at once. There is reason to believe that almost nothing was done before 13 May and that most of what was done, except for conversations with General Fawzi, would fall into the category of what we might consider the quite legitimate activities of the ASU leadership and their selected cadre apparati. On 13 May General Fawzi called a meeting of the Supreme Council of the Armed Forces but Lt. General Sadiq prevented the meeting from taking place and dismissed Fawzi, Goma'a, and Sharaf from the general headquarters. Agents bent on inciting demonstrations were hurriedly dispatched to some of the major mosques in the popular districts such as those of al-Sharkass, al-Kikhia, Abdin, al-Manshawi, and Bahjat al-Salam, but these efforts did not succeed. The most important move that the conspirators made was to resign en masse in an expression of solidarity with Sabri and Goma'a—again, hardly an illegal act. Their intention, however, was to create disorder, it was alleged, because they arranged for Radio Cairo to announce the resignations at the very moment they were presented to Sadat. Radio Cairo was also supposed to have broadcast some misleadingly spliced tapes of some of Sadat's old speeches and to have followed this with some martial music in the expectation that the masses would rush out into the streets as they had on 9 June 1967 and at Nasser's funeral. Radio Cairo did not broadcast this sort of stuff, traffic was not blocked in Cairo, the faithful in the mosques were not incited, the army did not move, the "thousands" of members of the vanguard organization did not mobilize the members of the ASU, and the conspiracy—if there was one—collapsed. Officials of the ASU ordered that files of secret documents and tapes of telephone conversations be taken out of town to Sakkarah and there burned on the instructions of Sha'rawi Goma'a or Sami Sharaf or both. On Friday, 14 May the conspiracy was broken, and on Saturday Sadat made a speech revealing that a plot had been hatched within the ASU and the internal security apparatus and that it had been broken. Sadat's speech was followed by supportive popular demonstrations.

This ambiguous, if lurid, story has been presented in some detail because it relates to the first and only test of the political role of the ASU. The conspiracy has been described as having emerged from the organizational leadership of the ASU whose principal instruments included units variously called "the vanguard apparatus," "the special apparatus," "the secret apparatus," and "the Nasserist vanguard." The problems are: (1) Did these groups come into being after 1968 or were they merely new names for vestiges of the Vanguard of the Socialists? (2) What was the composition of these groups? (3) How do we account for the virtually total failure of these groups to accomplish anything in 1971? (4) How was Sadat's attitude toward the role and composition of the ASU affected by the political challenge from its organizational leadership?

As we have seen, one of the precipitating actions leading to the "conspirators" revealing themselves in a mass resignation was Sadat's statement that he intended to reorganize the ASU. The Sabri group had shown their effectiveness in influencing members of the Central Committee, and, through Labib Shuqayr, they tried to influence the parliamentary party. But Sabri's supporters were not able to move the masses. If they did control some kind of special party apparatus or if they attempted to use the Vanguard of the Socialists, it follows that these cadres were not in touch with the people and they were not able to mobilize even the elected members of the basic unit committees in Cairo and its vicinity; or, of course, it is possible that they were falsely accused of attempting to overthrow the established authority by merely calling meetings at which Sadat was criticized, but at which no further action was called for.

At first, an impression was created that a procommunist or crypto-communist group within the ASU had attempted a coup. Later Sadat and Haykal made it clear that they were referring to a cadre group called al-jihaz al-sirri, or the "secret apparatus." Haykal wrote that the conspirators had begun planning to take power almost immediately after Nasser's death. They planned to use the ASU as the instrument of gaining power. Yet in Haykal's first statement on the issue he wrote that the secret apparatus was to be used to lead the masses in public demonstrations protesting the resignations of the Sabri group—that is, only at the last moment was there a plan to mobilize "thousands of members of the secret apparatus." It was also alleged that it was the secret apparatus which burned incriminatory documents and tapes at Sakkarah on the night of 13 May. Even the confession of the leader of the ASU youth organization that he was involved in preparing demonstrations in Cairo and al-Jizah refers to Friday, 14 May as the target date, as did the newspaper articles naming members of the National Assembly who were also members of the secret apparatus whose task it was to incite those at the mosques in their own districts after the Friday prayers.

In the prosecutor's reconstruction of the chronology of the conspiracy, the first attempts to stir up popular opposition began on 3 May, and from 5 May to 8 May many meetings were held at various levels. On 12 May the general secretariat of the vanguard organization (al-tandhim al-tali'i), the term used in the official regulations of the ASU for the originally proposed cadre group, met at its Cairo headquarters. This general secretariat included most of the top conspirators. They discussed the moves that Sadat planned against them, and allegedly planned the illegal countermeasures which were implemented on 13 and 14 May. But in December 1971, at the time of the sentencing of those found guilty, the summary of charges noted that "during the first week of May, hundreds of meetings were held, reaching to the basic units in villages and factories—even military factories, including military factory 82 and military factory 71."[3]

All in all, these accusations do not amount to very much. The government sought to create the impression that there was a closely organized, possibly ideologically influenced, secret apparatus within the ASU. This group engaged in conspiratorial activity aimed at taking over power by subversive means, and it employed three devices toward this end, all of which were quite unpopular with the educated classes. The first was a privileged group of ASU insiders, the second was a domestic intelligence apparatus of its own, and the third was the internal propaganda apparatus of Radio Cairo. Sadat took advantage of the fact that the minister of the interior was among the conspirators to identify all domestic surveillance with the conspiracy. He held a public ceremony to burn tape recordings of telephone conversations and of pillow talk from bugged bedrooms.

The reaction to the vanguard organization was ambiguous. In the first place, the organic law of the ASU called for such a structure and the *Tali'ah* group had been continuously agitating for the creation of a real cadre. We are consequently astonished to discover that one capable of attempting to carry out a conspiracy already existed—and I suppose that not a few sophisticated Egyptians were, also. Much was made of the fact that this was a secret apparatus, and there was some editorializing about the need to have an "open" or "public" cadre system. In somewhat contradictory fashion, however, it was alleged that the blame for the conspiracy rested not so much upon the vanguard organization itself, but upon secret groups within the vanguard organization. It was reported, for example, early in June 1971, that investigations had revealed that Sha'rawi Goma'a established secret groups within the vanguard organization after the death of Nasser and that it was the members of these groups that carried out the condemned actions.[4] Despite these confusing statements, the creation of secret apparatuses within the vanguard organization did not become part of the extensive list of crimes of which the defendants were accused in the conspiracy trial. Later in August, in an article in *al-Ahram*, Muhammad Sayyid Ahmad, of *al-Tali'ah*, simply discussed the drawbacks flowing from the secret character of the vanguard organization itself, as had Haykal in his early editorial on 28 May.[5] Nothing has ever been revealed about the structure of the secret or the special apparatus.

It is possible that some sort of intelligence apparatus was established within the Vanguard of the Socialists with the express purpose of reporting on statements made at ASU meetings and carrying out electronic and telephone bugging. This organization may have been called the secret or special apparatus. For the most part, the vanguard organization ceased to exist in the villages and remoter parts of the country after the abolition of the leadership groups in 1968. Nevertheless, there was no decree abolishing them, so that it was possible that many ASU members in the countryside still considered themselves to be members of the vanguard organization. In and near Cairo, however, many administrative posts in the vanguard organization simply coincided with parallel posts in the larger ASU. There was no important group of ASU officials who were not in the vanguard organization who, for example, openly sided with Sadat or opposed the conspiratorial leadership. In fact the list of the 91 accused abounds in the names of high ASU officials who were full-time ASU bureaucrats and/or members of the National Assembly and/or trade union, youth, or professional syndicate leaders and/or heads of nationalized companies. It appears that all of the accused were chiefs and that there were very few indians altogether. After all, it was the members of the National Assembly themselves who went to the mosques on Friday, 14 May.

In 1971 the vanguard organization was little more than an intelligence apparatus, possibly also a communications system among high officials, and a list of titles added to the public titles of the ASU bureaucracy, some ministers, and other members of the elite. An examination of the list of those accused and their positions will bear out this interpretation. Only 23 of the 91 accused were listed as members of the vanguard organization, and 2 of these were recorded as officials of the Nasserist vanguards, evidently a youth section of the main organization. Of the 21 accused officials of the vanguard organization, 6 were cabinet ministers, 4 were members of the National Assembly, 2 were high level bureaucrats, 2 were high level employees in government-controlled enterprises, 2 were party apparatchikis, 2 were leading media officials, and one was chief of the intelligence agency. None of the remaining 68 were listed as members of the vanguard organization, although they may have been rank and file members. Of this group, 22 were high officials, top apparat members, or members of the National Assembly. The remainder were district level officials of the ASU or even lower echelon members. Most of the lower and middle level party officials—about 20 or so—were responsible for youth activities in local branches of the ASU in the Cairo vicinity. None of the accused, nor any of those identified as members of the vanguard organization were identified as members of organizational branches outside of the Cairo–al-Jizah area.

There is no substantial evidence that the Soviet Union was directly involved in the conspiracy. It is clear, however, that foreign policy considerations were never far removed during this crisis. Secretary of State Rogers arrived in Cairo on the day after 'Ali Sabri's dismissal to discuss a possible separation of forces agreement which might allow a reopening of the Suez Canal. The evident progress made in those talks in combination with the arrest of 'Ali Sabri and his supporters was more than the Soviets could take with equanimity. On 25 May President Podgorny arrived in Cairo, and on 27 May Sadat and Podgorny signed a fifteen-year treaty of friendship and cooperation—including a clause calling for party-to-party cooperation. As a result of Soviet apprehension, Sadat was compelled to proceed more slowly in improving relations with the United States, and, of course, he had to give some attention to the reorganization of the ASU.

The reorganization of the ASU, a process with which we are now quite familiar, was carried out in the usual manner. The campaign was kicked off on 10 June 1971. Elections were to take place "from the base to the top" between 1 July and 23 July. On 23 July the National Congress would meet and the policy for the next phase would be set down, after which the National Assembly would be elected. There was the usual profusion of rules, regulations, provisos, definitions, exclusions, and such. The elections proceeded without a hitch. This time candidates did not have to prove that they were out of debt. Villages, factories or schools with fewer than 200 members could not have basic unit committees of their own. Two youth and one women's representative had to be elected in each unit. The restriction on two members of the same family being elected to the same committee was relaxed a bit. Members of basic unit, district, or provincial committees could not be members of two or more committees regardless of level. It was reported that many of those who stood for the youth and women's positions were elected unopposed because there were not enough candidates for these posts. In 609 of the 5,400 units the number of candidates was less than half of the number of seats available. It was also reported, somewhat surprisingly, that 95% of the secretaries and assistant secretaries of the basic units were elected unopposed because the committee members simply caucused and agreed on their leaders. Only about two-thirds of those eligible to vote actually did so.

The elections do not seem to have generated much enthusiasm nor does it appear that a great deal was done to purge the party of pro-Sabri elements. There were reports that nearly 75% of the basic unit secretaries of 1968 were reelected in all provinces except al-Jizah. With this exception, Sadat's concern to prevent the creation of new "centers of power" in the ASU and to carry out the policy of "rectification" was evidenced at other levels. Sadat himself selected the members of the Central Committee. He laid down restrictive rules regarding the number of full-time party workers and the level of their compensation. He appointed the provincial and district secretaries of the ASU. He abolished the office of secretary general of the ASU and in its place proposed the election of two secretaries to the Central Committee. His long-time close associate, Dr. Muhammad 'Abd al-Salam al-Zayyat, was elected as first secretary to the Central Committee and then appointed as director of the bureau of political and foreign affairs. Eight other bureau directors were appointed as well, in order to diffuse power widely. The vanguard organization, which had been dissolved in May by a presidential decree, would be reconstituted, but it would not be controlled by a single anonymous leader at the top. It is not clear, however, that the vanguard was actually reestablished.

In the elections for the National Assembly, Sadat moved further toward the diffusion of power and the encouragement of competition among members of the second stratum. There would be no official ASU candidates. No one could be a member of both an ASU local council and the National Assembly. Any elected official of the ASU who stood for an assembly seat and lost would also be deprived of his ASU post. As a consequence of these pressures 50% of those elected to the National Assembly held no post in the ASU higher than a member of the basic unit committee and almost 30% held no post at all. The National Assembly was elected in November 1971. In January 1972, Sadat restored political rights to 12,000 persons who had been deprived of the right to participate politically because they had been considered enemies of the regime or because their land or economic enterprise had been nationalized.

Since the end of 1971, and especially after the October War of 1973, Sadat's domestic policies have become ever clearer. He has moved toward the right, restoring some political influence to members of the urban middle and upper classes. He has opened Egypt to foreign private investment, especially encouraging the influx of Arab capital. He has restricted the influence of doctrinaire leftists, and he has tolerated some assertiveness on the part of traditionally religious groups. Students and workers have been carefully watched, but not yet suppressed in a consistent manner. Some land has been restored to its original owners after having been illegally sequestrated under the land reform decree. There is no doubt, therefore, that important changes are taking place, but it is not clear that these changes have gone so far, or will ever go so far, as to destroy the link between the rural middle class and the regime which has been the basis of the system for the last twenty-five years. It is not yet clear that Sadat has committed himself to policies which so benefit the urban bourgeoisie and so neglect the urban off-shoots of the rural middle class as well as the students and workers that critical political change will be induced. There seems to be little doubt, now, about Sadat's own political predilections, but he has proven himself to be a skillful tactician rather than an ideologue. His first test was to build a personal constituency by means of a distinctive policy rather than merely seeking the dubious and undifferentiated legitimacy of simply inheriting the Nasser mantle. In seeking a more secure base of social support, Sadat was limited by both the achievements of the Nasser regime and by Soviet anxieties. Sadat did not and was not able to go to extremes, with the result that his policies have essentially encouraged political pluralism.

Thus far, Sadat's equivocal and even reluctant maintenance of the ASU has been pivotal to his policy of encouraging pluralism without committing himself to an irreversibly liberal bourgeois position. After the October War Sadat announced a new policy of liberalism and free-dom of expression. The possibility of a multiparty, competitive system was openly discussed. In the interim, however, the virtues of interclass coalition were preferred. In March 1976 scope was provided for or-ganized expression of diverse political preferences by means of the innovative device of allowing a multiplicity of "platforms" representing diverse political tendencies. In October 1976, after the elections to the parliament, the three platforms became political parties, even though the ASU was allowed to persist. The liberal bourgeoisie, for the most part ex-Wafdists, seem even more anxious for the return to a competi-tive party system than are the extreme leftists—so it is not anticommu-nism that led Sadat to think again before abolishing the ASU. The enhancement of pluralism within the ASU and especially within the media has been useful in weakening Sadat's enemies, but to proceed further might create formidable centers of power on the right.

To sum up then, Sadat's policies have brought Egypt to a political crossroads. We shall first review those policies and then examine the alternative paths along which Sadat's Egypt might move.

In the area of political organization, Sadat has continued the process of reorganizing the party, he has restored political participatory rights to formerly excluded groups, he has prevented the formation of militant cadres, he has encouraged competition for office, he has encouraged the geographical diffusion of influence, and he has sponsored a "hundred flowers" type of proliferation of ideological views.

In the media Sadat has repeatedly pressured leftist journalists, he has brought back and restored the influence of old right wing editors and he has eliminated the unofficial post of presidential spokesman once held by Muhammad Hasanain Haykal.

The bureaucracy has been deprived of some of its choicest perquisites through the denationalization of some enterprises and through the encouragement of the more vigorous self-assertion of professional associations. But Sadat also continues the policy of maintaining a large cabinet including many technicians and many former military officers.

Economically, Sadat has put his hopes on both politically induced foreign investment and the role that Egypt can play as broker between Europe and the Persian Gulf. A liberalized domestic economy is an important component of this policy and it is also justified by widespread disappointment with the results of Nasserist socialist policies. The domestic aspect of Sadat's economic policy is aimed primarily at the urban bourgeoisie, but the well-to-do members of the rural middle class have also found opportunities to increase their holdings, to shift to more profitable types of agriculture, to increase the capitalization of agricultural enterprise with the aid of government loans, and to become more independent of the village cooperative society.

Thus far Sadat has succeeded in recruiting political support from right wing and religious groups without alienating the rural middle class. The left has grown increasingly hostile, but the left was gravely weakened by Nasser, and all but committed political suicide by joining the ASU in 1965. The position of the left is made all the more difficult because of the assumption that a domestic shift to the left would be accompanied by a high degree of cooperation with the Soviet Union. Haykal, alone, seems to be advocating a pro-Soviet foreign policy without any leftward shift domestically. Sadat has weathered attacks from the students, from leftist-oriented media specialists, and even large-scale demonstrations by workers. Neither the army nor elements of the rural middle class have supported leftist protest.

For the moment Sadat appears quite capable of maintaining his situation, but the inherent stability of that situation may be doubted. Once before, the Egyptian bourgeoisie made an effort to win political dominance. In the mid-thirties and after, the Wafd sought to limit the power of the king and to establish a liberal constitutional system. In that struggle, the Wafd was willing at first to use the deprived and alienated urban lower classes and petite bourgeoisie. The logical conclusion of that struggle was, perhaps, the burning of Cairo in January 1952. The Wafd had, to a large extent, created its own monster in the shape of the urban mob, and it succumbed to that monster after succeeding in destroying the legitimacy of the throne. In allowing the mob to run free and in refraining from using the army, the king tried to destroy the Wafd. The eventual resolution of this suicidal struggle might be called Bonapartist, but in this case the regime turned against the bourgeoisie and based itself upon the twin supports of the rural middle class and the alienated urban classes. Nasser in part adopted and in part contributed to the new model of the mobilizing, excolonial regime.

Sadat has modified this model. His regime is no longer mobilizing— it is pluralizing. Nevertheless, Sadat has retained, during a critical transitional period, the key structure of the Arab Socialist Union and its rural middle class support. He is probably losing control over the urban alienated elements that challenged the king in 1936, that destroyed the hopes of the Wafd in 1952, and that Nasser ultimately came to control through the National Union. This loss of control may not constitute so much of a threat to Sadat's government if he can keep the support of the urban bourgeoisie, the urban branches of the rural middle class, the majority of the rural middle class itself, and, of course, the army. Sadat's policies are, not unwisely, directed at maintaining the support of these groups, but the very means by which their support is sought can initiate significant changes in the structure of such groups and can lead segments of each group to redefine their interests. Sadat's policies will inevitably encourage a steeper stratification of both urban and rural classes while further differentiating them and encouraging them toward political competition. Hence, a policy of merely straddling is unlikely to work out in the long run. If he has the chance, Sadat will have to make a deliberate choice.

Obviously, it is impossible to canvass all the alternatives that may arise as historical events unfold in the coming months and years—nor would such a procedure suit our present purposes. To speculate responsibly and economically regarding the political future of Egypt it will be sufficient to consider only three major ideological configurations that present themselves and that are in large measure existentially compelling.

The first alternative emerges out of some of the policies already being pursued by Sadat and is more fully developed by those who see these beginnings as ideologically motivated and therefore but the first steps in a well developed program to "de-Nasserize" Egypt, to turn history back to 1952, and to do a proper job of establishing a bourgeois state. In order to accomplish this program, the ASU must be dismantled, a multiparty system instituted, freedom of expression must be guaranteed to those who can pay for it—at least, corporativism is to be diminished, the public sector of the economy is to be denationalized, and agriculture is to become more highly capitalized and less labor-intensive. The class basis of such a regime would require a coalition of the urban bourgeoisie and elements of the rural middle class, so policies would have to be devised to create among the rural middle class an agrarian segment which might identify its interests with those of the liberal bourgeoisie. In this manner might the defects of the capitalist and multiparty development of the 1930s be corrected and the distortions of Nasserist Bonapartism be overcome. To this end, it would be necessary to combat the "new class" of bureaucratic feudalists and apparatchikis, to separate the new class from the armed forces, and to press policies of stimulating economic development, the redistribution of land by means of market mechanisms, and bringing about a "green revolution." Internationally, such a policy orientation would expect and probably receive support from the United States, from the conservative regimes of the Persian Gulf, and from some European states. Although this alternative proposes a liberal capitalist orientation, it is most often presented by Marxist critics of Sadat's policies and may be called the Marxist alternative because it is so strongly oriented to class struggle. Since the policies described will result in enhancing stratification in both urban and rural settings, it is also possible to refer to the dominant processes of this first alternative as differentiating.

The second alternative puts far less emphasis on class structure and much more on the development of representative institutions. Rather than intensifying the class struggle or advancing the historical dialectic beyond the transitional phase of the Nasserist interlude, this policy would strengthen political democracy and political participation as a means of overcoming the alienative consequences of the existing social, economic, and cultural gaps among Egyptians. To achieve this sort of goal it would probably be necessary to legalize a multiparty system, to restore legislative power to the parliament, to guarantee the independence of the judiciary, and to end press censorship. It would also be necessary to decentralize the administration of economic matters and to diffuse development in regions more distant from Cairo and Alexandria. But these policies concentrate on the creation of formal structures and on bureaucratic reforms which are unlikely to result in a significant change in the political process unless groups interested in the diffusion of liberal, pluralist, competitive democracy can be located and strengthened. Recent historical events suggest that such groups are un-

likely to be found either among the urban haute bourgeoisie or the
classes of students, petty functionaries, and abna' al-balad or among
the poorer peasantry. We have, however, located within the second
stratum, in some regions, groups that appear to be politicized, participant, and competitive and that respond to opportunities for both educational advancement and agricultural development. It would appear
to be the case that, for a policy of political liberalization to succeed,
the political influence and organization of the second stratum in those
provinces in which it is highly prevalent and competitive would have
to be strengthened—and in those provinces in which the second stratum
is more highly stratified and culturally more traditional, its transformation would have to be encouraged. If all political power is concentrated
in Cairo, and if the political contest remains essentially an urban confrontation, liberal democracy will not have enough support to become
viable in Egypt. The dominant processes of this second alternative are
participatory, but it must be remembered, as for the established western
democracies, that such participation is limited and differentiated in its
efficacy along the lines of class, culture, and other parameters. Experience has not yet demonstrated that liberal democracy will thrive under
conditions of universally effective and equal participation. Representation is the device whch can legitimize structured and limited participation, if the representatives can be identified with the nation. In the
Egyptian situation, this second alternative requires moving from merely
exploiting the legitimating effect of second stratum representation to
the devolution of political power to the second stratum in such a manner as to encourage the competitive political involvement of more
members of this stratum in more parts of the country. It goes without
saying that agricultural policies related to finance, marketing, and the
diffusion of technology, that is, the green revolution, would have to be
coordinated with institutional reform. There is little likelihood of strong
foreign support for a policy of this sort.

   The third alternative is the already familiar Nasserist formula which
is primarily mobilizational. This is a variation on the third world, integrative model. Its goals are modernization and development, with
particular emphasis placed upon enhancing the capacity of the state
administrative and military organizations. The devices are those of increasing the size of the public sector, integrating economic and bureaucratic structures, controlling political activity through a national rally
or union, maintaining a government monopoly over the media, and
organizing the occupations and professions in corporativist structures.
The key to the successes of this system—such as they were—has been
the identitive and integrative role of the second stratum, the rural mid-

dle class and its urban branches. The mobilizational character of the system was limited by ideological ambivalence, the need to keep the support of the second stratum, and by the Bonapartist tendencies of the Nasserist regime. Selection of this alternative by Sadat or, more likely, his successors, would not bring much change unless the mobilizational policies were pressed to the point where the two segments of the second stratum were divided, with the urban segment becoming integrated into the "new class" and the rural segment being subjected to a more radical land reform program. Internationally, this policy would receive support from the Soviet Union, from the more radical of the third world countries, and, in particular, from the radical Arab states. This reinvigorated Nasserism, which is not advocated by the communists so much as by the 'Ali Sabri wing of the ASU and, paradoxically, by Muhammad Hasanain Haykal, might also entail a renewal of the policy of seeking to establish a regional political hegemony and to strengthen inter-Arab or pan-Arab integrative mechanisms.

In presenting these three alternatives, it has not been our purpose to relativize the significance of the empirical data on the second stratum. Instead, we have argued for the empirical validity of the structural description of this stratum regardless of the ideological perspective selected. It is probably the case that no Egyptian government will, in the foreseeable future, pursue one of these virtually ideal typical alternatives in "pure" form. But the choice of policy will be influenced by, and will be judged according to, these or similar ideological configurations. The ideological frame of reference is not a mere alternative; it is rather largely determinative of the shape of the political process itself. Nevertheless, each alternative ideological structure includes implicit or explicit contradictions: the alternative of differentiation entails the Marxist contradiction of advanced capitalism, the alternative of participation entails the egalitarian contradiction of the hypothesized functionality of limited nonparticipation, and the alternative of mobilization entails the contradiction of the necessary integrative role of mediating elites. Empirical realities, and especially the empirical reality of the structure of the second stratum, are likely to intrude into and disrupt political change processes which are oriented to one or another of these ideological configurations. From this perspective, concentration upon the political potentiality of the second stratum reunites the branching alternatives into a single complex process which can be monitored, though not easily, by means of empirical investigation into key areas of acknowledged political significance.

If these reflections concerning the current Egyptian situation can be generalized, we reach the following conclusions:

1. Development and modernization or westernization does proceed first in the urban centers, or at least those urban centers which are accessible to foreign influence. It is similarly the case that the processes of modernization are cumulative and politically nondisruptive for some period, but when a sufficient accumulation of nonelite members of modern sector groups occurs, some political conflicts may emerge. There is, consequently, some sort of threshold of urbanization, the spread of literacy, industrialization, and the like, which must be passed before the processes we have been discussing become relevant.

2. The political dialectic which may proceed in the major cities is not directly paralleled in the rural areas. Modernization is diffused from key urban centers, but not necessarily in uniform, centrifugal patterns. The persistence of rural elites must be taken into account, and the possibility of centripetal tendencies must be considered. Furthermore, agricultural patterns, ecological structure, and demographic features, in addition to rural social structure must be taken into account. In any case, class and ideological conflict as emergent in the urban areas is not usually relevant in rural settings, so that the diffusion of political modernization will often follow administrative, familial, economic, or cultural linkages. The cultural linkages are the least bound by structural factors, thus lending particular importance to the distinction between countries of homogeneous and heterogeneous cultural identities. The invocation of indigenous, traditional, cultural affinities in urban-rural political alliances tends to restrict rather than diffuse the orientations of urban political conflict.

3. The urban and rural political processes are separated and they are differentiated in terms of their relation to the state bureaucracy. Rural areas are not apolitical, nor without their own forms of social conflict. Even when nationalist ideologies are exported to the countryside, or when the oppression of the peasantry is adopted as a political slogan by the bourgeoisie, the two political arenas are not yet united. In the countryside politics remain essentially local and, as a consequence, far more subject to the influence of those bureaucratic functionaries who are assigned responsibility over an administrative region or district. In the urban areas, the bureaucracy forms a class with its own interests and its own political techniques, in addition to whatever role it may play in structuring other arenas of politics. The central ruling authority may find it expedient to insulate local rural politics from the conflicts of the urban areas without attempting to change rural patterns. If, however, localized rural elites are eliminated politically, it is relatively easy to substitute a rural bureaucratic authority.

Under such circumstances, it may be difficult to maintain the separation between the urban and rural arenas.

4. The central ruling authority may not be primarily nor even consciously concerned with the political fate of rural elites, but it is likely that whichever political strategy is chosen, it will have some impact on those elites. The three models we have suggested, emphasizing differentiation, participation, and mobilization, would not likely be adopted out of primary concern for their impact on rural elites. Nevertheless, we have seen how it is possible that each of these as policy orientations, would have a profound influence on the structure and role of the rural elites.

5. Some might hold the view that it is reasonable to select political strategies on the basis of the urban situation, since that is where the dialectic of modern class conflict will work itself out. From this perspective, attempts to link urban and rural political arenas are essentially retrogressive attempts to slow down political development and to strengthen either the urban bourgeoisie or a Bonapartist regime which has only limited military support. It is possible to interpret the *Eighteenth Brumaire* in this manner.

6. Moore has argued otherwise, insisting on the indispensability of a rural policy. From his point of view, political alliances between urban and rural elites are not likely to be merely temporary interruptions of the dialectic of development. They are far more likely to be determinative of the resultant form of the modern polity which will emerge from the political crises of development. The suppression of rural elites (all of them? everywhere?) is only one alternative. Its consequences or those of merely transforming rural elites depend upon how one sets about doing it, upon who it is that does it, and upon the social, cultural, and geographical characteristics of the rural elites. Those consequences include such important matters as the equality of income distribution and the extent to which democratic processes may be institutionalized.

7. Having thus formulated the problem, it does not seem compelling to conclude that either the urban process alone or the urban and rural link is absolutely crucial. It seems sensible to argue that what is most important will vary with the circumstances. If different outcomes are possible, it follows that in some cases rural elites and masses may resist the conclusion that urban political outcomes ought to be accepted as legitimately constitutive. Inquiring into the circumstances under which rural elites are likely to accept the urban process as constitutive, and, hence to identify with certain of the urban elites, we can contrast three historical cases. The first is the case of prepartition India, in which

rural elites of each community tended to identify with the interests of their urban coreligionists even though there might be profound class differences among them. The second case is interwar Egypt, where rural elites were, for the most part, alienated from the urban political struggle. In the Indian case, because it was a communal struggle, pressure was brought to bear on the rural elites of the opposition minority community after partition and not on all rural elites. In Egypt, those rural elements clearly identified with the Wafd were penalized to some extent, but it was recognized that rural elites (not the absentee owners of the largest estates) had been relatively uninvolved in the urban political arena and that there was no need to alienate large segments of those elites because of their tentative and superficial identification with certain of the major urban political protagonists. Neither in India nor in Egypt were the victorious urban elites ideologically committed to transform the rural society and productive order. In the third case, Viet Nam, the success of the revolution depended upon convincing rural elites of the legitimacy of an essentially urban formulation of the problem and its solution. The presence of foreign military and administrative forces enhanced the possibility of legitimating the urban political struggle in the rural areas.

8. Egypt is the prototype of the situation in which there was a significant hiatus between the urban and rural political arenas. Under such conditions, the social linkages between urban and rural segments become more important than the relatively weak connections between the two political processes. In the Egyptian case, the most important link is that between the rural middle class and members of the officer corps, although the importance of the number of civil servants, teachers, and "free" professionals from rural elite backgrounds is also significant.

9. It follows that the linkages between rural and urban political classes must also be understood in terms of the structure of rural elites. That is to say that the various segments of the urban branches of rural elite families must be related back to the stratificational, cultural, geographical, and economic discontinuities among the rural elites. In Egypt we found that these discontinuities were probably of much less importance than might be expected elsewhere.

10. Since rural elites contribute differentially to the formation of urban social segments, and since there may be significant discontinuities among rural elites, it follows that some rural-urban linkages will mitigate class conflict in urban arenas, while alternative patterns may exacerbate urban political conflict.

11. Where a rurally based, urban elite segment is drawn from one geographical area, and from one ethnic or religious group, and where

it has acquired differentiated economic interests, there will we find the greatest political tension. In such cases it is likely that the urban-rural political gap will be minimized. Lebanon is an example of this case.

12. Where, on the contrary, the rurally based, urban elite segments are drawn from a stratum which is ubiquitous, which is culturally, ethnically, and religiously homogeneous and undifferentiated from the great majority, and where its economic interests are widespread, there we should expect the least exacerbation of the urban political struggle. Egypt comes close to exemplifying this case.

13. For the class of cases in which urban-rural linkages are thought to be of central political significance, and where those linkages are more of the Lebanese variety, it could be argued that the participatory alternative is to be preferred. Mobilization is likely to result in more severe fighting in Lebanon, as rural groups would attempt to preserve their autonomy and identity. Differentiation in both urban and rural settings by means of the diffusion of virtually unregulated capitalist enterprise and the unparalleled import of unproductive capital has already shown itself to be dangerous. The moderately redistributive policies of President Shihab worked for a while, but the enhanced economic differentiation of recent years fueled the informal processes which nullified Shihabism. The coincidence of confessionalism and a steeper stratification system—under rather special conditions, it is true —led to the uneasy government by a coalition of militias which preceded the civil war.

14. For Egypt, the participatory solution is not as necessary even if many would prefer it. A limited form of mobilization was attempted and, as we have seen, there has been some reversal of those policies. Part of the reversal has been occasioned by Sadat's decision both to enhance the pluralism of the political process and to create new constituencies for himself. Thus far, he has concentrated on the urban arena, leaving the relatively placid rural elites alone, and in some cases even returning expropriated land to its previous owners. In the longer run, though, it will be necessary to gain the approval of the rural elites for whatever may be the urban political outcomes. Mobilization which presses them too hard may be resisted or differentiation which does not include the creation of a large enough class of agrarian capitalists may create alienation. For the moment, the rural middle class is not organized to defend its interests nor are those interests expressed in doctrinal terms. If the wrong choices are made, and if urban-rural linkages remain as important as they have been, we can confidently expect some reaction. That reaction is most likely to come as a demand for a more participatory solution, such as true multipartism, or the

intervention of a military group to restore a Nasserist type of mobilizational regime.

President Sadat has, however, shown himself to be extremely resourceful, and he is not likely to allow events to overtake him. So much depends on just how much time one thinks one has, or on intuitions concerning the rhythm of social change. The intuitions of distant academic observers are bound to differ from those immediately engaged. Still, it may be acknowledged that the personality, skill, and value orientation of the head of state will matter quite a lot. Nevertheless, in the longer run, the thing to watch for will be whether any ideologically oriented governmental formula is pushed so far that it destroys the instrument without which the rulers cannot rule.

Notes

Chapter One

1. S. Shamir, "The Marxists in Egypt: The Licensed Infiltration Doctrine in Practice," in M. Confino and S. Shamir, eds., *The USSR and the Middle East* (Jerusalem: Israel Universities Press, 1973), p. 315.

2. P. J. Vatikiotis, *The Egyptian Army in Politics* (Bloomington: Indiana University Press, 1961), p. 235 and passim.

3. N. Safran, *Egypt in Search of Political Community* (Cambridge: Harvard University Press, 1961), p. 256. But see the quite different interpretation of Anouar Abdel-Malek, *Idéologie et renaissance nationale: L'Egypte moderne* (Paris: Editions Anthropos, 1969), p. 405.

4. M. Halpern, *The Politics of Social Change in the Middle East and North Africa* (Princeton: Princeton University Press, 1963).

5. R. Dekmejian, *Egypt under Nasser* (Albany: State University of New York Press, 1971), pp. 262–63.

6. Anouar Abdel-Malek, *Egypt: Military Society* (New York: Random House, 1968), pp. 288 ff.

7. Shamir, "The Marxists in Egypt," p. 315.

8. H. Riad, *L'Egypte nassérienne* (Paris: Les Editions de Minuit, 1964), pp. 72 ff.

9. Mahmoud Hussein, *Class Conflict in Egypt, 1945–1970* (New York: Monthly Review Press, 1973), p. 356.

10. Tawfiq al-Hakim, *'Awdat al-Wa'iy*, 2d ed. (Beirut: Dar al-Shuruq, 1975); Sami Jawhar, *al-Samitun Yatakalamun: 'Abd al-Nasir wa-madhbahah al-Ikhwan* (Alexandria and Cairo: al-Maktab al-Misri al-Hadith, 1975); Fathi 'Abd al-Fattah, *Shuyu'iyyun wa-Nasiriyyun* (Cairo: Rose al-Yusuf, 1975).

11. Ahmad Hamrush, *Qissat Thawrat 23 Yuliu*, vol. 2, *Mujtama'a Jamal 'Abd al-Nasser* (Beirut: al-Mu'assasah al-'Arabiyyah lil-Dirasat w'al-Nashr, 1975), pp. 211 ff.

12. E.g., Hassanain Karum, *al-Samitun Yakdhabun* (Cairo: Dar Ma'mun, 1976).

13. I. Belyaev and E. Primakov, *Misr fi 'Ahd 'Abd al-Nasir* [Egypt during the Nasser period] (Beirut: Dar al-Tali'ah, 1975), chap. 1.

14. S. Akhavi, "Egypt: Neo-Patrimonial Elite," in F. Tachau, ed., *Political Elites and Political Development in the Middle East* (Cambridge: Schenkman, 1975), p. 78.

15. Ibid.

16. Ibid., p. 99.

17. *Al-Ittihad* (Haifa), 17, 21, and 24 October 1975.

18. E. Shils, "Primordial, Personal, Sacred and Civil Ties," *British Journal of Sociology* 8 (1957): 130–45.

19. M. Weber, *The Theory of Social and Economic Organization* (Glencoe: Free Press, 1947), p. 117, and T. Parsons, *The Structure of Social Action* (Glencoe: Free Press, 1949), p. 650.

20. "Functional requisites" is the term used in T. Parsons's later work. See T. Parsons, R. F. Bales, and E. Shils, *Working Papers in the Theory of Action* (Glencoe: Free Press, 1953), pp. 63 ff.

21. But see L. I. Rudolph and S. H. Rudolph, *The Modernity of Tradition* (Chicago: University of Chicago Press, 1967).

22. See, for example, B. K. Johnpoll, *The Politics of Futility* (Ithaca: Cornell University Press, 1967).

23. H. Kohn, *The Idea of Nationalism* (New York: Macmillan Co., 1961), and C. Geertz, "Ideology as a Cultural System," in D. Apter, ed., *Ideology and Discontent* (Glencoe: Free Press, 1964).

24. M. Halpern, *Middle Eastern Armies as the Vanguard and Chief Political Instrument of the New Middle Class* (Santa Monica: Rand Corporation, 1959). Also cited in Vatikiotis, *The Egyptian Army in Politics*, p. 219.

25. C. H. Moore, "Authoritarian Politics in Unincorporated Society: The Case of Nasser's Egypt" (Paper prepared for the Annual Meeting of the American Political Science Association, 1972).

26. *Religion and Politics in Pakistan* (Berkeley: University of California Press, 1961); *Iran: Political Development in a Changing Society* (Berkeley: University of California Press, 1962).

27. *The Ideological Revolution in the Middle East* (New York: John Wiley and Sons, 1964); "Egypt: The Integrative Revolution," in L. Pye and S. Verba, eds., *Political Culture and Political Development* (Princeton: Princeton University Press, 1965); and "Political Recruitment and Participation in Egypt" in J. LaPalombara and M. Weiner, eds., *Political Parties and Political Development* (Princeton: Princeton University Press, 1966).

28. "National Integration and Political Development," *American Political Science Review* 58 (1964): 622–31.

29. *Writings of the Young Marx on Philosophy and Society*, ed. and trans. L. D. Easton and K. H. Guddat (New York: Doubleday and Co., 1967), pp. 469–70.

30. J. H. Meisel, *The Myth of the Ruling Class: Gaetano Mosca and the Elite* (Ann Arbor: University of Michigan Press, 1962). Subsequent quotations are taken from this source.

31. A. Gramsci, *The Modern Prince and Other Writings* (New York: International Publishers, 1957).

32. K. Marx, "The Critique of Hegel's Philosophy of Law," in *Karl Marx, Early Writings*, trans. and ed. T. B. Bottomore (New York: McGraw-Hill, 1964), pp. 55–57.

33. K. Marx, *The Eighteenth Brumaire of Louis Bonaparte* (New York: International Publishers, 1969), p. 123.

34. Ibid., p. 125.

35. Ibid., p. 131.

36. B. Moore, Jr., *The Social Origins of Dictatorship and Democracy: Lord and Peasant in the Making of the Modern World* (Boston: Beacon Press, 1966), pp. 70–71.

37. G. Baer, *A History of Landownership in Modern Egypt, 1800–1950* (London: Oxford University Press, 1962).

38. *L'Egypte nassérienne*, pp. 27–28.

39. K. Deutsch, *Nationalism and Social Communication* (New York: Technology Press and John Wiley and Sons, 1953), p. 100.

40. D. Apter, *The Politics of Modernization* (Chicago: University of Chicago Press, 1965), pp. 36, 361.

41. S. Huntington, *Political Order in Changing Societies* (New Haven: Yale University Press, 1968) and S. Huntington and J. M. Nelson, *No Easy Choice* (Cambridge: Harvard University Press, 1976), p. 168, n. 4.

42. M. Weiner, "Political Participation: Crises of the Political Process," in Binder et al., *Crises and Sequences in Political Development* (Princeton: Princeton University Press, 1971).

43. M. Rodinson, "The Political System," in P. J. Vatikiotis, ed., *Egypt since the Revolution* (New York: Frederick A. Praeger, 1968), p. 100.

44. G. A. Almond and S. Verba, *The Civic Culture* (Boston: Little, Brown & Co., 1965), pp. 16–18.

45. J.-P. Sartre, *Search for a Method* (New York: Random House, 1968), p. 173.

46. Ibid., p. 103 and passim.

Chapter Two

1. Al-Mustaqbal, *al-Sajil al-Dhahabi li'l-Ittihad al-Qawmi* [The Golden Register of the National Union] (Cairo: Madkur and Sons, n.d.).

2. Vatikiotis, *The Egyptian Army in Politics*, p. 105.

3. Ibid., p. 112.

4. Ibid.

5. Anouar Abdel-Malek, *Egypt: Military Society*, p. 117.

6. Ibid., p. 367.

7. U.A.R. Presidency of the Republic, Statistical Department, *Statistical Pocket Yearbook, 1958* (Cairo: Government Printing Office, 1959). Lajnat al-Tahtit al-Qawmi, al-Lajnah al-Markaziyyah li'l-Ihsa', *Majmu'a al-Baya-*

nat al-Ihsa'iyyah al-Asasiyyah (Iqlim Misr) January 1960; al-Jumhuriyyah al-'Arabiyyah al-Mutahidah, Maslahat al-Ihsa' wal-ta'addad, *al-Ihsa' al-Sanawi al-'Am, 1957–1958* (Cairo: al-Hayah al-'Amah li-Shu'un al-Matba'a al-Amiriyyah, 1960); and *al-Ihsa' al-Sanawi al-'Am, 1962* (1963).

8. Mahmoud Hussein, *Class Conflict in Egypt*, p. 45.

9. Belyaev and Primakov, *Misr fi 'Ahd 'Abd al-Nasir*, pp. 43 f.

10. Mahmoud Abdel-Fadil, *Development, Income Distribution and Social Change in Rural Egypt (1952–1970)* University of Cambridge Department of Applied Economics Occasional Paper 45 (Cambridge: Cambridge University Press, 1975), p. 56.

11. Ibid., pp. 42, 43, 49, 60; see also chap. 4 below.

Chapter Three

1. J. Berque, *Histoire sociale d'un village égyptien au XXème Siècle* (Paris: Mouton, 1957), p. 66.

2. M. Duverger, *Political Parties* (New York: John Wiley and Sons, 1955).

3. J. M. Landau, *Parliaments and Parties in Egypt* (Tel Aviv: Israel Oriental Society, 1953), p. 29.

4. The Earl of Cromer, *Modern Egypt*, 2 (New York: Macmillan Co., 1909): 186.

5. G. Baer, *Studies in the Social History of Modern Egypt* (Chicago: University of Chicago Press, 1969), pp. 17–18, 49.

6. *Histoire social d'un village égyptien*, p. 59.

7. *Studies in the Social History of Modern Egypt*, p. 60.

8. *Histoire sociale d'un village égyptien*, pp. 49–50.

9. Mahmud 'Awda, *al-Qariyah al-Masriyyah baina al-Tarikh wa'l-Ilm al-Ijtima'* (Cairo: Sa'id Rafat, 1972), p. 155.

10. *Studies in the Social History of Modern Egypt*, p. 53.

11. *Histoire sociale d'un village égyptien*, p. 67.

12. Hamed Ammar, *Growing up in an Egyptian Village* (London: Routledge and Kegan Paul, 1954), pp. 79–80.

13. Luwis Kamil Malikah, *al-Jama'at wa'l-Qiyadat fi Qariyah 'Arabiyyah* (Sirs al-Layanah: Markaz al-Mujtama'a fi al-Alam al-'Arabi, 1963), p. 17.

14. Ibid., pp. 17, 22, 86.

15. Ibid., p. 87.

16. Ibid., p. 22.

17. Ibid., p. 24.

18. Ibid.

19. Ibid., p. 75.

20. Iliya Harik, *The Political Mobilization of Peasants: A Study of an Egyptian Community* (Bloomington, Indiana University Press, 1974), pp. 49, 186–87 and passim.

21. Ibid., pp. 110, 214.

22. Ibid., p. 116.

23. Ibid., pp. 73, 75, 76.

24. Ibid., p. 215.

25. Ibid., p. 217.

26. Ibid., p. 39.

27. Ibid., p. 75.

28. *L'Egypte nassérienne*, p. 19. See also Mahmoud Abdel-Fadil, *Development, Income Distribution and Social Change*, p. 56, n. 19.

29. *L'Egypte nassérienne*, p. 16.

30. Ibrahim 'Amr, *al-Ardh wa'l-Fallah, al-Mas'ilah al-Zira'iyyah fi Misr* (Cairo: al-Dar al-Misriyyah li'l-Taba'ah wa'l-Nashr wa'l-Tawzi'ah, 1958), p. 116.

31. Ibid., p. 117.

32. Riad, *L'Egypte nassérienne*, p. 21.

33. Ibid., p. 24.

34. Ibid., p. 25.

35. 'Amr, *al-Ardh wa'l-Fallah, al-Mas'ilah al-Zira'iyyah fi Misr*, pp. 117–19.

36. Ibid., pp. 121–22.

37. Baer, *A History of Landownership*, p. 78.

38. Riad, *L'Egypte nassérienne*, pp. 25–26.

39. Baer, *A History of Landownership*, pp. 54–55.

40. Ibid., pp. 53–54.

41. Ibid., p. 55.

42. Berque, *Histoire sociale d'un village égyptien*, p. 11.

43. Ibid., p. 47.

Chapter Four

1. Baer, *A History of Landownership*, pp. 50–51.

2. Ibid., p. 51.

3. Ibid., p. 54.

4. S. Chesnin, "A Subclass of Egyptian Rural Elites" (M.A. thesis, University of Chicago, 1974).

5. Ibid., pp. 2-1 and 2-2.

6. Ibid., p. 1-6.

Chapter Five

1. Baer, *Studies in the Social History of Modern Egypt*, pp. 244–45.

2. Ibid., p. 232.

3. Baer, *A History of Landownership*, p. 143.

4. Abdel-Malek, *Idéologie et renaissance*, p. 86.

5. Ibid., p. 87.

6. Ibid., p. 88.

7. Ibid., p. 87.

8. *Parliaments and Parties in Egypt*, p. 9.

9. *L'Egypte nassérienne*, p. 24.

Chapter Six

1. See L. J. Cantori, "Political Mobilization in Pre-Revolutionary Egypt: The Wafd Party 1918–1924" (Ph.D. diss., University of Chicago, 1966).

See also Zaheer Masoud Quraishi, *Liberal Nationalism in Egypt: The Rise and Fall of the Wafd Party* (Delhi: Alwaz Publishing, 1967), esp. pp. 49 f.; M. Deeb, "The 1919 Uprising: A Genesis of Egyptian Nationalism," *Canadian Review of Studies in Nationalism* 1 (1973): 106–7; and Hafiz Mahmoud, "Thawrat Tashih Lithawrat 1919," *al-Ahram*, 8 March 1976, p. 5. The literature on this subject is very extensive, indeed.

2. Baer, *Studies in the Social History of Modern Egypt*, pp. 93 f.; J. Berque, *Egypt: Imperialism and Revolution* (London: Faber and Faber, 1972), pp. 130, 235.

3. *Parliaments and Parties in Egypt*, p. 39.

4. 'Abd al-Rahman al-Rafi'i Bek, *Fi A'qab al-Thawrah al-Misriyyah* (Cairo: Maktabah al-Nahdhah al-Misriyyah, 1949), 2:109.

5. Ibid., p. 143.

6. Asim al-Dasuqi, *Kubar Mulak al-Aradhi al-Zira'iyyah wa-Dawrihum fi al-Mujtama'a (1914–1952)* (Cairo: Dar al-Thaqafah al-Jadidah, 1975), pp. 212–13.

7. Ibid., p. 214.

8. John Anderson, "Representative Systems and Ruralizing Elections" (M.A. thesis, University of Chicago, 1976), p. 123.

9. Ibid., p. 128.

10. Ibid., p. 116.

Chapter Thirteen

1. This term, employed by al-Jabarti, among others, has been explicated by Sawsan al-Missiri (M.A. paper, American University, Cairo). It refers to indigenous Egyptians, of urban origin and urban residence, who differentiated themselves from the peasants and the ruling classes of Mamluks, Ottomans, and other non-Egyptians.

2. Kohn, *The Idea of Nationalism*, pp. 329–34, 457.

3. A. Hourani, *Arabic Thought in the Liberal Age, 1798–1939* (London: Oxford University Press, 1962); Jamal Ahmed, *The Intellectual Origins of Egyptian Nationalism* (London: Oxford University Press, 1960); N. Safran, *Egypt in Search of Political Community*; Anouar Abdel-Malek, *Idéologie et renaissance*; Charles Smith, "The Crisis of Orientation: The Shift of Egyptian Intellectuals to Islamic Subjects in the 1930's," *International Journal of Middle East Studies* 4 (1973): 382–410.

4. Abdel-Malek, *Egypt: Military Society*, p. 131.

5. *President Nasser's Speeches, January–December 1961* (Cairo: Information Department, n.d.), p. 243.

6. Ibid., p. 256.

7. Ibid., p. 259.

8. Ibid., p. 312.

9. Ibid., pp. 313–14.

10. Al-Ittihad al-Ishtiraki al-'Arabi, *al-Kitab al-Sanawi, 1964* (Cairo: Dar wa-Mataba'a al-Sha'b, n.d.), pp. 20, 21.

11. Ibid., pp. 24, 25.

12. Ibid., p. 26.

13. Ibid., pp. 28, 147.

14. Ibid., p. 70. According to *al-Ahram*, 9 November 1963, all ASU members were declared to be "active" members by means of a special law passed by the National Assembly.

15. In 96 constituencies two seats were at stake, and in 51 only one seat was at stake.

16. In LaPalombara and Weiner, eds., *Political Parties and Political Development*, pp. 239–40. See also Abdel Malek, *Egypt: Military Society*.

17. Muhammad Anis, "What Guarantees Are There for the Application of the Charter in the Coming National Assembly Elections?" *al-Ahram*, 30 December 1963; "Is There Ground for Concern about the Laborers and Fellaheen in the Coming Elections of the National Assembly?" *al-Ahram*, 2 January 1964.

Chapter Fourteen

1. *Mahadir Jalsat Mubahathat al-Wahda* (Cairo: National Printing and Publishing House, 1963). See also M. Kerr, *The Arab Cold War, 1958–1964: A Study of Ideology in Politics* (London: Oxford University Press, 1965), p. 63.

2. Abdel-Malek, *Egypt: Military Society*, p. 127.

3. *The Charter*, 21 May 1962 [Draft] (Cairo: Information Department, n.d.), p. 47.

4. *Al-Mithaq wa-Qanun al-Ittihad al-Ishtiraki al-'Arabi* (ASU, Guidance and Socialist Propaganda, n.d.), p. 46.

5. Ibid., p. 111.

6. Confino and Shamir, eds., *The USSR and the Middle East*, p. 297.

7. Ibid., p. 302.

8. Ibid., p. 309.

9. Ibid., p. 310.

10. *Qissat Thawrat 23 Yuliu*, 2:9–10.

11. Ibid., p. 257.

12. Ibid., p. 258.

13. Ibid., p. 259.

14. E.g., Husain Sha'lan, "Political Organization after 23 July 1952," *al-Tali'ah*, July 1965, pp. 104–5.

15. "The State and the Political Apparatus in Egyptian Experience," *al-Tali'ah*, July 1965, p. 110.

16. Harik, *The Political Mobilization of Peasants*, p. 87.

17. Ibid., pp. 99, 126.

18. Ibid., pp. 260–61.

19. Lutfi al-Kholi, "Observations on the Intellectual Conflict in Our Society," *al-Tali'ah*, December 1966, pp. 5–26. Confino and Shamir, eds., *The USSR and the Middle East*, p. 311.

20. Abdel-Fadil, *Development, Income Distribution and Social Change*, offers some evidence in support of the criticisms of *al-Tali'ah*; see esp. pp. 43, 49, 60, 123.

21. Harik, *The Political Mobilization of Peasants*, pp. 233, 240.

22. *Bayan 30 Maris, iladhi alqah al-ra'is Jamal 'Abd al-Nasir fi 30 Maris 1968* (Cairo: Wazarat al-Irshad al-Qawmi, al-Hay'ah al-'Amah li'l-Ista'alamat, 1968), p. 4.

23. *Khatab al-Ra'is Jamal 'Abd al-Nasir fi al-Mu'atamar al-Sha'bi al-Kabir bi'l-Mansurah* (Cairo: Wazarat al-Irshad al-Qawmi, al-Hay'ah al-'Amah li'l-Ista'alamat, 1968), p. 23.

24. *Bayan*, p. 7.

25. Ibid., p. 9.

26. Ibid.

27. This is the usual understanding of the book by Muhammad Jalal Kishk, *Ma Dha Yuridh al-Talabah al-Masriyyun?* (Beirut, 1968).

28. *Bayan*, p. 13.

29. The composition of the committee, the proceedings of the congress, and many other details of the reorganization process are discussed in R. Dekmejian, *Egypt under Nasser*, pp. 272–73 and passim.

30. Ibid., p. 276.

31. Ibid., p. 279.

32. Ibid., pp. 281–82.

33. Hamrush, *Qissat Thawrat 23 Yuliu*, 2:240–42.

34. Dekmejian, *Egypt under Nasser*, pp. 262–64.

35. Ibid., p. 283.

36. Dr. Jamal al-Utaifi, "Observations on the Elections to the National Assembly," *al-Ahram*, 15, 16 November 1968.

37. *Al-Ahram*, 13 December 1968.

38. *The Political Mobilization of Peasants*, pp. 7, 233.

39. Ibid., p. 225.

40. Ibid., pp. 238–39.

41. Ibid., p. 234.

42. Professor Iliya Harik was kind enough to lend me this document.

43. *Al-'Umal*, no. 35, supplement, 18 July 1968.

44. *Egypt under Nasser*, p. 285.

45. Ibid.

Chapter Fifteen

1. See, for example, Binder, *The Ideological Revolution in the Middle East*, pp. 221–22.

2. "The officers who came to power knew the conditions of the Egyptian village. Many of their relatives were peasants" (Belyaev and Primakov, *Misr fi 'Ahd 'Abd al-Nasir*, p. 56).

3. *Al-Ahram*, 10 December 1971, p. 11.

4. Ibid., 3 June 1971, p. 1.

5. Ibid., 4 August 1971, p. 5, and 28 May 1971, p. 3.

Selected Bibliography

'Abd al-Fattah. *Shuyu'iyyun wa-Nasiriyyun.* Cairo: Rose al-Yusuf, 1975.

'Abd al-Rahman al-Rafi'i Bek. *Fi A'qab al-Thawrah al-Misriyyah.* Vol. 2. Cairo: Maktabah al-Nahdhah al-Misriyyah, 1949.

Abdel-Fadil, Mahmoud. *Development, Income Distribution and Social Change in Rural Egypt (1952–1970).* University of Cambridge Department of Applied Economics Occasional Paper 45. Cambridge: Cambridge University Press, 1975.

Abdel-Malek, Anouar. *Egypt: Military Society.* New York: Random House, 1968.

———. *Idéologie et renaissance nationale: L'Egypte Moderne.* Paris: Editions Anthropos, 1969.

Ahmed, Jamal. *The Intellectual Origins of Egyptian Nationalism.* London: Oxford University Press, 1960.

Akhavi, Shahrough. "Egypt: Neo-Patrimonial Elite." In *Political Elites and Political Development in the Middle East,* edited by F. Tachau, pp. 69–113. Cambridge: Schenkman, 1975.

Ammar, Hamed. *Growing Up in an Egyptian Village.* London: Routledge and Kegan Paul, 1954.

'Amr, Ibrahim. *al-Ardh wa'l-Fallah: al-Mas'ilah al-Zira'iyyah fi Misr.* Cairo: al-Dar al-Misriyyah li'l-Taba'ah wa'l-Nashr wa'l-Tawzi'ah, 1958.

Anderson, John. "Representative Systems and Ruralizing Elections." M.A. thesis, University of Chicago, 1976.

415

Anis, Muhammad. "What Guarantees Are There for the Application of the Charter in the Coming National Assembly Elections?" *al-Ahram*, 30 December 1963.

———. "Is There Ground for Concern about the Laborers and Fellaheen in the Coming Elections of the National Assembly?" *al-Ahram*, 2 January 1964.

'Awda, Mahmud. *al-Qariyah al-Misriyyah baina al-Tarikh wa'Ilm al-Ijtima'*. Cairo: Sa'id Rafat, 1972.

Ayrout, Henry Habib. *The Egyptian Peasant*. Boston: Beacon Press, 1963.

Baer, Gabriel. *A History of Landownership in Modern Egypt, 1800–1950*. London: Oxford University Press, 1962.

———. *Studies in the Social History of Modern Egypt*. Chicago: University of Chicago Press, 1969.

Bayan 30 Maris, iladhi alqah al-ra'is Jamal 'Abd al-Nasir fi 30- Maris 1968. Wazarat al-Irshad al-Qawmi, al-Hay'ah al-'Amah li'l-Ista'alamat, n.d.

Belyaev, I., and Primakov, E. *al-Misr fi 'ahd 'Abd al-Nasir*. Beirut: Dar al-Tali'ah, 1975.

Berque, Jacques. *Egypt: Imperialism and Revolution*. London: Faber & Faber, 1972.

———. *Histoire sociale d'un village égyptien au XXème siècle*. Paris: Mouton, 1957.

Binder, Leonard. *The Ideological Revolution in the Middle East*. New York: Wiley, 1964.

———. *Iran, Political Development in a Changing Society*. Berkeley: University of California Press, 1962.

———. *Religion and Politics in Pakistan*. Berkeley: University of California Press, 1961.

———. "Egypt: The Integrative Revolution." In *Political Culture and Political Development*, edited by L. Pye and S. Verba, pp. 396–449. Princeton: Princeton University Press, 1965.

———. "National Integration and Political Development." *American Political Science Review* 58 (1964): 622–31.

———. "Political Recruitment and Participation in Egypt." In *Political Parties and Political Development*, edited by J. La Palombara and M. Weiner, pp. 217–40. Princeton: Princeton University Press, 1966.

Cantori, Louis J. "Political Mobilization in Pre-Revolutionary Egypt: The Wafd Party 1918–1924." Ph.D. dissertation, University of Chicago, 1966.

Chesnin, Sidney B. "A Subclass of Egyptian Rural Elites." M.A. paper, University of Chicago, 1974..

The Earl of Cromer. *Modern Egypt*. 2 vols. New York: Macmillan Co., 1909.

Al-Dasuqi, 'Asim. *Kubar Mulak al-Aradhi al-Zira'iyyah wa-Dawrihum fi al-Mujtam'a (1914–1952)*. Cairo: Dar al-Thaqafah al-Jadidah, 1975.

Deeb, Marius. "The 1919 Uprising: A Genesis of Egyptian Nationalism." *Canadian Review of Studies in Nationalism* 1, Fall (1973): 106–19.

Dekmejian, Richard. *Egypt under Nasser*. Albany: State University of New York Press, 1971.

Durrell, Lawrence. *The Alexandria Quartet*. London: Faber & Faber, 1969.

Fisher, W. B. *The Middle East: A Physical, Social and Regional Geography*. London: Methuen & Co., 1952.

Al-Hakim, Tawfiq. *'Awdat al-Wa'iy*. 2d ed. Beirut: Dar al-Shuruq, 1975.

Halpern, Manfred. *Middle Eastern Armies as the Vanguard and Chief Political Instrument of the New Middle Class*. Santa Monica: Rand Corp., 1959.

———. *The Politics of Social Change in the Middle East and North Africa*. Princeton: Princeton University Press, 1963.

Hamdan, Jamal. *Shakhsiyyat Misr, Dirasah fi 'Abqariyyat al-Makan*. Cairo: Dar al-Hilal, 1967.

Hamrush, Ahmad. *Qissat Thawrat 23 Yuliu*. Vol. 2, *Mujtama'a Jamal 'Abd al-Nasir*. Beirut: al-Mu'assasah al-'Arabiyyah li'l-Dirasat wa'l-Nashr, 1975.

Harik, Iliya. *The Political Mobilization of Peasants: A Study of an Egyptian Community*. Bloomington: Indiana University Press, 1974.

Hourani, Albert. *Arabic Thought in the Liberal Age, 1798–1939*. London: Oxford University Press, 1962.

Hussein, Mahmoud. *Class Conflict in Egypt: 1945–1970*. New York: Monthly Review Press, 1973.

Issawi, Charles. *Egypt in Revolution: An Economic Analysis*. London: Oxford University Press, 1963.

Al-Ittihad al-Ishtiraki al-'Arabi. *al-Kitab al-Sanawi*. Cairo: Dar Wa-Mataba'ah al-Sha'b, 1964.

———. *al-Nashrah al-Idariyyah* 1, no. 7 (5 October 1963), "Contents of this issue: Names of the secretaries and assistant secretaries of the committees of the Arab Socialist Union for the basic units."

Jawhar, Sami. *al-Samitun Yatakalamun: 'Abd al-Nasir wa-madhbahah al-Ikhwan*. Alexandria and Cairo: al-Maktab al-Misri al-Hadith, 1975.

Al-Jumhuriyyah al-'Arabiyyah al-Mutahidah, Maslahat al-Ihsa wal-ta'addad, *al-Ihsa al-Sanawi al-'Am, 1957–1958*. Cairo: al-Hayah al-'Amah li-Shu'un al-Matba'a al-Amiriyya, 1960.

————. *al-Qawanin al-Ishtirakiyyah*. Cairo: Maslahat al-Isti'alamat, n.d.

Karum, Hassanain. *al-Samitun Yakdhabun*. Cairo: Dar Ma'mun, 1976.

Kerr, Malcolm. *The Arab Cold War, 1958–1964: A Study of Ideology in Politics*. London: Oxford University Press, 1965.

Khatab al-Ra'is Jamal 'Abd al-Nasir fi al-Mu'atamar al-Sha'bi al-Kabir bi'l-Mansurah. Wazarat al-Irshad al-Qawmi, al-Hay'ah al-'Amah li'l-Ista'alamat 18 April 1968.

Al-Kholi, Lutfi. "Observations on the Intellectual Conflict in Our Society." *al-Tali'ah,* December 1966, pp. 5–26.

Kishk, Jalal. *Ma Dha Yuridh al-Talabah al-Misriyyun?* Beirut, 1968.

Lajnat al-Tahtit al-Qawmi, al-Lajnah al-Markaziyyah li'l-Ihsa'. *Majmu'a al-Bayanat al-Ihsa'iyyah al-Asasiyyah: Iqlim Misr*. N.p., January 1960.

Landau, Jacob M. *Parliaments and Parties in Egypt*. Tel Aviv: Israel Oriental Society, 1953.

Lutfi al-Sayyid, Afaf. *Egypt and Cromer: A Study in Anglo-Egyptian Relations*. London: John Murray, 1968.

Mahadir Jalsat Mubahathat al-Wahdah. Cairo: National Printing and Publishing House, 1963.

Mamoud, Hafiz. "Thawrat Tashih Lithawrat 1919." *al-Ahram,* 8 March 1976.

Malikah, Luwis Kamil. *al-Jama'at wa'l-Qiyadat fi Qariyah 'Arabiyyah*. Sirs al-Layanah: Markaz al-Mujtama'a fi al-Alam al-'Arabi, 1963.

"Manifesto of the Egyptian Communist Party." *al-Ittihad* (Haifa), 17, 21, 24 October 1975.

Marx, Karl. "The Critique of Hegel's Philosophy of Law." In *Karl Marx, Early Writings*. Translated and edited by T. B. Bottomore. New York: McGraw-Hill, 1964.

Meisel, James H. *The Myth of the Ruling Class: Gaetano Mosca and the Elite*. Ann Arbor: University of Michigan Press, 1962.

Al-Mithaq wa-Qanun al-Ittihad al-Ishtiraki al-'Arabi. ASU, Guidance and Socialist Propaganda, n.d.

Moore, Barrington, Jr. *The Social Origins of Dictatorship and Democracy: Lord and Peasant in the Making of the Modern World*. Boston: Beacon Press, 1966.

Moore, Clement Henry. "Authoritarian Politics in Unincorporated Society: The Case of Nasser's Egypt." Paper prepared for the Annual Meeting of the American Political Science Association, 1972.

Al-Mustaqbal. *al-Sajil al-Dhahabi li'l-Ittihad al-Qawmi*. Cairo: Madkur, n.d.

President Nasser's Speeches, January–December 1961. Cairo: Information Department.

Quraishi, Zaheer Masoud. *Liberal Nationalism in Egypt: The Rise and Fall of the Wafd Party*. Delhi: Alwaz Publishing, 1967.

Riad, Hasan. *L'Egypte nassérienne*. Paris: Les Editions de Minuit, 1964.

Rodinson, Maxime. "The Political System." In *Egypt since the Revolution*, edited by P. J. Vatikiotis, pp. 87–113. New York: Praeger, 1968.

Safran, Nadav. *Egypt in Search of Political Community*. Cambridge, Mass.: Harvard University Press, 1961.

Sha'lan, Husain. "Political Organization after 23 July 1952." *al-Tali'ah*, July 1965, pp. 104 ff.

Shamir, Shimon. "The Marxists in Egypt: The Licensed Infiltration Doctrine in Practice." In *The USSR and the Middle East*, edited by M. Confino and S. Shamir. Jerusalem: Israel Universities Press, 1973.

Smith, Charles. "The Crisis of Orientation: The Shift of Egyptian Intellectuals to Islamic Subjects in the 1930's." *International Journal of Middle East Studies* 4 (1973): 382–410.

U.A.R. Presidency of the Republic, Statistical Department. *Statistical Pocket Yearbook, 1958*. Cairo: Government Printing Office, 1959.

Al-'Umal, no. 35, 18 July 1968 Supplement.

Al-'Utaifi, Jamal. "Observations on the Elections to the National Assembly." *al-Ahram*, 15, 16 November 1968.

Vatikiotis, Panayotis J., ed. *Egypt since the Revolution*. New York: Frederick A. Praeger, 1968.

———. *The Egyptian Army in Politics*. Bloomington: Indiana University Press, 1961.

Index

Abaza family, 116–17
Abbas I, 113
Abna' al-balad, 304, 400
Absenteeism, 72, 122, 376
Accountants, 162, 164–66
Administration, 5, 47, 53, 89, 308, 338, 344, 346, 378; aspects of, 40–41, 79–80, 87, 117, 337, 341, 349, 355, 357, 402
Administrative system, 73, 171
Administrators, 3, 345
Agrarian: affluence, 241–43, 249; development, 177; influence, 246, 321; structures, 154, 167, 174, 192, 254
"Agrarianness," 226, 234, 236
Agricultural: areas, 186, 188, 244, 281–82, 319, 321, 346; development, 23, 182, 184, 231, 249, 254, 281, 283, 400; enterprise, 4, 22, 25, 44, 72, 110, 137, 149, 183, 225–26, 238, 240–41, 243, 299, 309, 344, 372, 374, 397, 399; policy, 299, 400; production,

24–26, 71, 110, 182, 187, 232, 234, 243–45, 345; provinces, 31, 47–48, 55–57, 75–78, 93, 95, 104, 130, 140, 151, 173, 182, 193, 205, 227, 281, 313–15, 362–63, 366
Agriculture, 37, 112, 160, 167, 180, 189, 194, 284, 327, 357; percentage engaged in, 231, 234–35, 237, 281; transformation of, 24–26, 279
Agriculturist, 49, 51–52, 59
Ahmad, Jamal, 305
Ahmad, Muhammad Sayyid, 339, 341, 392
al-Ahram, 153, 156, 313, 330, 352, 355–56, 364–65, 382, 392
Akhavi, S., 6–7
al-Akhbar, 384, 387
Akhbar al-Yom, 355
Aleppo, 307
Alexandria, 55, 73, 114, 148, 152, 173–75, 178, 180, 182, 213, 254, 271, 276, 282, 348, 352–53, 399
Algeria, 1, 329

421